For Bill Danly
intrepid cyclist

Also by Robert Downes:

Planet Backpacker
Biking Northern Michigan
I Promised You Adventure
Windigo Moon: A Novel of Native America
Bicycle Hobo
Sandy Bottom
The Wolf and The Willow

CONTENTS

Praise for *The Wolf and The Willow*:

"a quest of Homeric dimensions... ... a riveting reading experience. Downes captures a saga of both everyday travails and the larger sweep of history in an accessible, compelling, and colorful page-turner." - *Marquette Monthly*

Praise for *Windigo Moon*:
The Sequel to *The Wolf and The Willow*

"A simply brilliant work of historical fiction"
Midwest Book Review

First Prize: Cascade Writers Group, 2014 Grand Rapids ArtPrize Competition for the first chapter, "The Raid"

Gold Medal, "Best Regional Fiction, Great Lakes Region"
Independent Publisher Magazine

Honorable Mention, "Best Historical Fiction"
Foreword Reviews   INDY Books of the Year

"We truly enjoyed this beautiful historical novel about the Ojibwa Indians. Essentially a love story, the characters are welldrawn and the landscape lives and breathes. Don't miss this one!"
W. Michael Gear and Kathleen O'Neal Gear, *New York Times* bestselling authors of *Moon Hunt*.

"Robert Downes's *Windigo Moon* is one of the best novels I've read in a long time."   Tyler Tichelaar, *Marquette Monthly*

"Intricately researched, tightly woven, and vividly imagined, *Windigo Moon* should be on any must-read list."
Glen Young, *Petoskey NewsReview*

RAW DEAL

THE INDIANS OF THE MIDWEST AND THE THEFT OF NATIVE LANDS

ROBERT DOWNES

The Wandering

PRESS

TRAVERSE CITY, MI

Published by
The Wandering Press
Traverse City, Michigan

Library of Congress Control Number: Pending

ISBN 979-8-9898136-0-5
Raw Deal is available at a discount
when purchased in bulk for educational or fundraising use,
or by organizations.

www.robertdownes.com

The Wandering

PRESS

Cover: A bridge in Ojibwe/Odawa country, east of Sault Ste. Marie, Canada
photo by Robert Downes
Back cover: Detail from the 1807 Treaty of Detroit

BOOK FOUR • WAR IN THE FOREST

BOOK FIVE • THE DEVIL'S BARGAIN

My Thanks

Bibliography

Index

Before the White Man

OJIBWE

Approximate location of Native peoples in 1600. The Indians were highly fluid in their movements and their tribes often relocated hundreds of miles due to warfare and other disruptions. Some of these locations, such as that of the Potawatomi and Dakota Sioux, are based on speculation by historians or Native oral legends. By 1650 this map will be completely reshuffled. By 1700, reshuffled again...

MISSISAUGA

NIPISSING

AMIKWA   ODAWA

ODAWA

POTAWATOMI?

HURON

TIONONTATI

MASCOUTEN

SAUK   NEUTRALS

MIAMI   IROQUOIS >

ERIE

A FEW WORDS

The recording of Indian tribal names by writers of European descent suffered from misunderstanding, language barriers, and often the repetition of disparaging names uttered by hostile neighboring tribes met early on. This resulted in misspellings, wildly inaccurate names, and the foibles of various dialects that are argued over to this day by Native speakers.

For the purposes of this book, the following tribes are described as follows. Interchangeable terms (ie. Odawa/Ottawa) are quoted from historical records.

The Anishinaabek (or Anishinaabeg) refers to the "Three Fires," a loose alliance of the Ojibwe, Odawa and Potawatomi, but also inclusive of a number of related, smaller tribes such as the Nipissing and Mississauga.

Algonquians: a broad range of many tribes throughout the eastern United States and Canada, related by linguistics.

Delaware: also known as the Leni Lenape

Fox: also known as the Mesquakie

Miami: also known as the Myaamia

Ojibwe: also known as the Ojibwa and Chippewa

Odawa: also known as the Ottawa

Potawatomi: also known as the Botawatomi

Hurons: originally known as the Wendat, later known as the Wyandot

Iroquois: also known as the Haudenosaunee

Tionontati: the "Tobacco People," also known as the Petun Huron

Ho-Chunk: later known as the Winnebago Sioux

Illinois: also known as the Illini

Sauk: also known as the Sac

PREFACE
ECHOES OF THE PAST

Stop by a farm on a quiet summer day and you can hear the rustle of the corn growing as their stalks reach for the sun and rain. As a child living on my grandfather's farm near Rockford, Michigan in the 1950s, I often thought that this eerie rustle was the whispering of Indians, long gone, yet still speaking from the earth.

In a sense that was true.

My father, Joseph Edwin Downes, was a farmer until the age of thirty, working the fields of his own father, James, as had been the way of things among our Irish ancestors for thousands of years. Beyond the issue of my brother, sister and me, Dad's legacy included unearthing traces of the Indians that were thousands of years old.

Throughout the 1940s and '50s my father found scores of spear points, arrowheads and other Native artifacts while plowing the fields of the Downes farm. Each spring, the newly-plowed soil would be washed by rain, revealing more treasures in stone; and as is the custom, Dad would write the month and year in pencil on each one that he found. There was also a mysterious mound in the forest to the east beyond the cornfield that had an unnatural rise, given the flatness of the surrounding terrain. Our family thought it might be an old Indian mound, created hundreds of years ago.

As a child, I was deeply impressed with my father's collection of arrowheads. Like most Americans, I'd been brought up to believe that there were relatively few Indians scattered here and there in the forests across the country prior to the arrival of white pioneers. Yet here in my own hands was proof that there had been countless Indians passing right where I stood. Even as a child I reasoned that if all of these arrowheads had been found in a mere one-hundred-acre field, how many thousands might there be packed within a square mile of our farm?

In time I learned that bands of the Odawa Indians had migrated up western Michigan's Grand River Valley in the 1700s. Members of an Odawa band called the Blackskins had established villages throughout the region.

Dad said that once, there had been an Indian trail leading through the farm, running ten miles to the Grand River. The Odawa would likely have stored their canoes on the riverbank under a mash of wet leaves to keep them supple; transporting their trade goods of furs, baskets, berries and quill-work downriver to a rough trading post at Grand Rapids and on to Lake Michigan.

Yet that didn't explain the mystery of my father's arrowheads, because by the 1750s the Odawa owned smooth-bore trade muskets and their arrows, if they used them at all, would have been tipped with iron points. In time I learned that my father's collection far preceded the Odawa; an archeologist from Michigan State University told me that many were 5,000-7,000 years old, dating back to what was called the Archaic Period of the Indians. Most, in fact, were dart points, propelled by spear-chuckers called atladls, since the Indians of North America didn't acquire the bow and arrow until around 500 A.D.

Yet all that was left of the Odawa and the ancient Indians who came before them had been reduced to whispers. The land around Rockford had been taken from the Odawa in the one-sided Treaty of Washington in 1836, in which they and the Ojibwe of the Upper Peninsula ceded 21,621 square miles totalling 37 percent of present-day Michigan to the federal government for settlement by white farmers, loggers, miners and speculators. The treaty left the Odawa and Ojibwe in a state of limbo, terrified by the threat that they would soon be forcibly removed to reservations west of the Mississippi, as had been the fate of scores of other tribes.

Like many Americans who have the skeletons of slavery and genocide buried in family memory, I assumed that all of the above had nothing to do with me. Yet, while reading a family history compiled by a relative with an interest in genealogy, I came upon an ugly truth. I learned that one of my great-great-great-grandfathers, Michael "Boss" Farrell, had profited from the sale of land in the region around my grandfather's farm that had once belonged to the Odawa.

A civil engineer who emigrated to America from Ireland in 1830, Boss Farrell had helped to engineer the Erie Canal and the Michigan Central railroad. He was instrumental in bringing the first train engine to Michigan, and served as its first engineer on the route from Detroit to Ypsilanti.

In 1842, he obtained warrants for acreage at forty cents on the dollar for lands in the Grand River Valley that had been ceded by the Odawa in the Treaty of 1836. He acquired several thousand acres vacated by the Indians and also borrowed 4,000 half-dollar coins, which he lent to settlers so that they might buy land and erect their cabins. These were sold for the most part to Irish immigrants who were delighted to find a land even richer than the country they had left behind, free of the plague of landlords. The

Odawa's farms, orchards and villages were quickly gobbled up by the newcomers.

I had always assumed that my family had nothing to do with what had befallen the Indians, since my paternal great-great-grandfather, Michael Downes, didn't emigrate from Ireland to America until 1850. It never occurred to me to consider the role of my grandmother's side of the family, the Farrells, who had profited from the Odawa's loss.

Growing up, I had enjoyed reading about the Indians and famous personages, including Black Hawk, Pontiac, Tecumseh, Sitting Bull, Crazy Horse, Red Cloud, Geronimo, Cochise and Black Elk. All had one thing in common: their struggle against the strangling web of the white man. These books were uniformly about great battles and heroes, seldom mentioning the role of Native women or the dismal treaties that came after their defeat and captivity.

Yet it wasn't until I reached my early forties that I heard any mention of the Treaty of 1836 and its crushing blow to Michigan's Indians. This was from a social activist in our town who was prone to preaching about the abuses of 1836 to anyone who would listen. Few did. To me the Treaty of 1836 was dusty old stuff that only a lone eccentric in our town seemed to know or care about.

Who knew? We never learned anything about the fate of the Indians in school. At best, I recall a few segments on Michigan's history in the fourth and fifth grades in which we were informed that once there had been some mighty big glaciers here and that long ago a few widely-scattered Indians lived in our state, traveling in birch bark canoes and dwelling - rather unlikely, we thought - in bark wigwams. Other than a mention of Pontiac's siege of Detroit in 1763 there was seldom a word taught of what befell the Indians of the Upper Great Lakes who had lived here for up to thirteen thousand years. For all we knew, they had simply disappeared.

Perhaps my teachers were as ill-informed as me because the history books of the day often spared only a few pages for Native peoples, barely mentioning them at all. In his bestselling book, *Michigan: A History*, historian Bruce Catton offered this breezy summation of swindling the Indians of the entirety of the state:

"Arranging the treaties by which these huge parcels were acquired was not really very difficult. The Indians had got used to the white man by now and were more or less adjusted to the fact that he was there to stay..."

Adjusted? Catton failed to mention that Michigan's Indians lived in terror of being forced to march to reservations beyond the Mississippi at the point of bayonets wielded by white soldiers. That, in fact, is exactly what happened during the Potawatomi Trail of Death in 1838.

Then there is this gem from 1954's *Michigan in Four Centuries*, another bestseller from University of Michigan history professor F. Clever Bald:

"Although the Indian was a savage, he developed skills and inventions which the white man found useful, and it is only fair to acknowledge the debt we owe to the first people of Michigan."

Of course, it might also be fair to acknowledge the 1.5 billion acres taken from indigenous peoples over the course of 367 treaties ratified by 1871, often made in bad faith with little or no return. What little payment or reservation land that the Indians did receive was often spirited away by traders, swindlers and tax collectors, who tended to have the weight of the law on their side.

Of note, whenever the Indians sold their lands, the vast inequity in the sale price *paid for their annuities and the cost of their removal*. This is because land obtained by the government for pennies per acre (or less) was resold at an astronomically higher rate to settlers, enriching the federal treasury. There was no federal largesse involved in land purchases: If the Indians could have sold their land outright to settlers prior to being settled on reservations they would have come out far ahead.

It wasn't until I discovered the handprints of my great-great-great grandfather on the fate of the Indians that the impact of the Treaty of 1836 began to sink in along with a desire to know more, and thus, this book.

What we've come to know as "history" is often just tales of men behaving badly. We'll cover that ground, but also wander down some avenues which may seem unrelated to the fate of the Indians of the Midwest and Great Lakes, yet invariably had consequences. The Spanish conquistadors, for instance, decimated Native civilizations of the South, the refugees of which gave rise to the much-diminished remnant tribes that impacted or allied with the Indians far to the north. The same is true regarding the battlegrounds of the French and Indian War, the hunting grounds of Kentucky, and the tribal homelands in Ohio, which rallied many warriors from the Great Lakes region in the cause of protecting their turf. I have also included a chapter on the Irish and European immigrants, not as an apologia for their actions, but in an attempt to show why so many pioneers were callous, if not merciless, in their treatment of the Indians.

Today, we walk in the footsteps of a Native people who are only a few generations removed. Our cities are built on the sites of what were once Indian villages; our highways travel along their ancient trails; and when we walk down the street we are likely treading on artifacts that are thousands of years old, buried not only in the earth, but also in memory.

Book One
Sandy Lake

CHAPTER 1

THE WISCONSIN
DEATH MARCH

In the summer of 1851, boaters on Sandy Lake in northern Minnesota saw what looked like clumps of snow scattered along the western slope of the lake.

But what appeared to be snowdrifts were actually graves. According to stories passed down by Ojibwe elders, these were among the bodies of four hundred men, women and children who died of hunger, disease and exposure in the winter of 1850-'51 after the U.S. government broke its promise to provide food and treaty payments to Indians living in Wisconsin and Michigan's Upper Peninsula. Unable to dig graves in the frozen ground, the starving survivors had wrapped the bodies of those who died at Sandy Lake in birch bark and left them scattered along the shore.

For many years thereafter, the Ojibwe considered Sandy Lake to be a haunted graveyard.

Imagine the situation of an Ojibwe father who has canoed more than three hundred miles down a tangle of winding rivers from Michigan's Upper Peninsula to Sandy Lake with his eldest son in October of 1850. He has come to collect the cash and goods promised to his people in a treaty signed eight years before in 1842.

In the past, he had collected his annual treaty payment and supplies at a government substation on Madeline Island at the western end of Lake Superior - a place that was easy to get to. But the location of the payment has been moved to Sandy Lake 150 miles to the west for reasons he can't understand, and now, he and his son have waited for weeks as the winter deepens with none of the promised food, blankets, tools and cash to show for it. Expecting to make a speedy return home to Michigan, they had left their heavy fur cloaks at home. But as the winter deepens they are lightly dressed and starving with no way to send word home to their loved-ones. At night they sleep beneath their overturned canoe, knowing it will be useless on the frozen rivers and will have to be left behind; its loss will be devastating. Camped with five thousand others in the marshy land outside the substation, they witness people all around them dying of disease, hunger and freezing cold. By December, the father's son is stricken with measles. Soon, he too will lie beneath a shroud of birch by the shore.

The Sandy Lake Tragedy is unknown to most Americans, even those of us who live in the Upper Midwest. I stumbled upon it while camping at the Sandy Lake Dam Campground in the fall of 2017 while on a book tour of northern Minnesota. There by the lakeside amid the golden aspens and shimmering maples stands a memorial that was erected in 2000 by members of Minnesota's Mille Lac Band of Ojibwe. One hundred and fifty years had passed with barely a mention of the disaster.

Despair gripped those who lingered by the shore of Sandy Lake as the winter of 1850 set in. They had little or no food, no warm clothing and no shelter. An icy darkness settled over the land by five o'clock every afternoon, with the safety of home lying hundreds of miles away beyond icebound rivers and trails deep with snow.

Over the course of six weeks that winter, 167 Ojibwe died of exposure, dysentery, measles and hunger on the shores of Sandy Lake. Another 230 died making the long trek home in the depths of January. Many made journeys of 220-460 miles home in a disaster that became known as the Wisconsin Death March, or the Chippewa Trail of Tears.

Recast as a drama, the events of 1850 have a Shakespearean array of twists and players, including evil politicians, their unscrupulous toadies, heartless traders, warring tribes, conflicting presidents, an outraged nation, a beleaguered people, valiant chieftains and the "richest man on earth." All this, and an unexpected final act featuring a hero in his nineties.

According to their own traditions, the Ojibwe were relative newcomers to the Upper Great Lakes. They were among the Anishinaabek, the "true people," who included the Odawa and Potawatomi. According to stories told over the fires of many generations, the Anishinaabek had migrated west from the Atlantic seaboard over the course of hundreds of years, eventually settling in Michigan and as far west as Minnesota.

Typically, the Ojibwe lived in small bands of up to two hundred souls, guided by a chieftain along with a council of elders. Within their villages would be the members of various clans. This is a simplification, but basically, a clan was a sort of extended family defined by an animal totem, often with a specialty, such as leadership, warfare or healing.

By 1850, there were an estimated nine thousand Ojibwe living along the shores of Lake Superior within the boundaries of the United States. By then, the Ojibwe were no longer hunter-gatherers, relying on bows & arrows, clothing from animal skins, game drives and foraging to get by. They had benefited from the French and English trade goods of muskets, iron axes, knives, brass kettles, needles, fish hooks and manufactured clothing for more than two hundred years and while some still lived in wigwams of elm and birch bark, others lived in log cabins, similar to those of their white neighbors. Yet many spoke little or no English beyond the rudiments required for trading, Dependence on white trade goods, language barriers, and a radically different orientation toward the earth and its resources put them in a vise that was easily squeezed.

Initially, the Indians traded beaver pelts and other furs for European goods that made their lives so much easier, but by the mid-1800s, the fur-bearing animals of North America had been hunted and trapped almost to extinction and the whims of fashion moved on to embrace other materials such as silk. As a consequence, the Indians ranging from Lake Superior to Florida had little to trade but their land. Added to this was the constant threat of forced removal under the guns and sabers of the U.S. Army.

Thus, in a series of coercive treaties in which they had no other option than forced removal, the tribes of the Midwest ceded their homelands and hunting grounds in exchange for annual allotments of food, cash and services. Typically, an area held in common was "reserved" for those who signed the treaties, from which the term reservation is derived. The goal of the U.S. government was to turn "savages" into tax-paying Christian farmers who would, in time, be assimilated into white society.

Yet even without furs for trade, the Indians living at the western end of Lake Superior had prospered through fishing, logging and mining operations, working with white newcomers while maintaining their traditional way of life. Little did they know in 1850 that they were the targets of a malicious scheme to rip them from their homeland.

The Sandy Lake Tragedy and the subsequent Death March were the outcome of a scheme hatched by the administration of Zachary Taylor to force the Ojibwe of Upper Michigan and Wisconsin to move west to reservations beyond the Mississippi River in the newly-created Minnesota Territory. The end-game was to bolster the territory's economy. Treaty payments made to the Ojibwe would be spent in Minnesota, boosting the fortunes of local businesses, politicians and bureaucrats in the process.

The Minnesota Territory had been created only the year before in 1849, extending all the way to the Missouri and White Earth rivers, far beyond the state's current boundaries. This was nineteen years after President Andrew Jackson had signed the Indian Removal Act of 1830, which resulted in the forced removal of up to 100,000 Indians from the eastern United States to bleak reservations west of the Mississippi. Thousands had died on the Cherokee Trail of Tears, and then on the reservations of Kansas and Oklahoma in what was called "Indian Country."

America's reservations became the model for British concentration camps in the Boer War, in which close to 50,000 Afrikaner and black indigenous prisoners were systematically starved to death (including 22,000 children). The reservation system also inspired Adolph Hitler, who, according to historian John Toland, "often praised to his inner circle the efficiency of America's extermination - by starvation and uneven combat - of the red savages who could not be tamed by captivity."

Treaties were used to facilitate the removal of the Indians to west of the Mississippi. In his best-selling book, *Michigan - A History of the Wolverine State*, historian Willis F. Dunbar offered this bleak assessment of the treaty's value as a weapon:

"What the pioneers wanted was the Indian's land; what became of the Indians was of no concern to them. To the land-hungry pioneers who poured into Michigan during the early 19th century, the Indian was not a romantic figure. He was a nuisance. Bullets, rum, and treaties, hardly worth the paper their terms were written on, were used without compunction to rid Michigan of its Indians and open the land to the farmer, the road maker, and the lumberman. Of all these methods the treaty was the most effective."

Multiple treaties designed to acquire Indian land led up to the Sandy Lake Tragedy:

• In 1826, a treaty required the Ojibwe to establish a boundary with the neighboring Winnebago and Menominee of Wisconsin. Article 3 of the treaty granted the United States "the right to search for, and carry away, any metals or minerals from any part of their country."

• In 1837, the Ojibwe signed the so-called "Pine Treaty," which ceded eleven million acres of central Wisconsin and Minnesota. The treaty cleared the way for large-scale lumbering operations.

• But it was the Copper Treaty of 1842 that spiraled into the events leading to the Sandy Lake Tragedy eight years later.

The Ojibwe living at the western end of Lake Superior might have remained undisturbed forever were it not for the mineral riches beneath their feet. While surveying the coast of Lake Superior in the early 1840s, geologist Douglas Houghton confirmed that the region held some of the richest copper deposits on earth. Acquiring the region became a top priority for the War Department, which oversaw the Bureau of Indian Affairs.

The Indians of Lake Superior had been digging for copper in thousands of pit mines as far back as 1800 B.C. Long before the Ojibwe arrived, Indian miners had stabbed at the earth with wooden implements, fashioning copper jewelry, spear-points, bracelets, earrings and such. These were traded to the so-called Mound Builders living far to the south in hundreds of towns scattered down the Mississippi and its arteries, all the way to the Gulf of Mexico.

To the Mound Builders, copper was as rare and valuable as gold and diamonds are to us today. The rarity of copper imbued it with supernatural powers. Copper ornaments were used in religious ceremonies and as signs of prestige. For the most part, copper was worn only by the elites and notable warriors of Mound Builder societies.

Copper mining by the Indians fell off around 1600 even before they gained access to the white man's superior iron goods. Having little knowledge of the worth of the copper beneath their feet, the Ojibwe were easily convinced to trade it away when ceding their land.

In 1841, foundry owner and Democratic New York Congressman Gouverneur Kemble proposed hiring Ojibwe men to work in the new copper mines, paying them a percentage of the profits, instead of purchasing their land. This idea was quickly dismissed by the War Department, cutting the Ojibwe out of any ownership or profits from mining operations. As had been the case with dozens of other treaties across the country, the U.S. government resolved to purchase the Ojibwe's land outright, netting its timber and minerals.

Today, there's a common misconception that the U.S. government simply seized Indian lands through conquest, but in fact, Indian tribes were considered sovereign nations with diplomatic rights and standing. Federal policy required the purchase of Indian lands and by 1880, $275 million would be paid for the domain of hundreds of tribes. Yet the government paid just pennies per acre, far less than what Native lands were worth, and such was the case in the Treaty of 1842.

Forty-one Ojibwe leaders gathered at Madeline Island at the western end of Lake Superior in early October, 1842 to consider the Treaty of La Pointe, also known as the Copper Treaty. The chieftains were asked to cede twelve million acres to the U.S. government. This included the western half of Michigan's Upper Peninsula and an even bigger slice of northern Wisconsin. They were assured that they would be able to continue living on the land - the whites simply wanted their copper.

Madeline Island is the largest of the Apostle Islands in Wisconsin's Chequamegon Bay. During the 1660s the island had been settled by many Odawa, Tionontati and Huron refugees, fleeing Iroquois war parties during the so-called Beaver Wars of the period. To the Indians, the island was known as Shaguamikon, meaning something gnawed on all sides, owing to a sandy promontory that jutted into Lake Superior. The French had established a trading post on the western end of the island in 1692 and called their settlement La Pointe for the same reason.

Today, the Ojibwe call the island Mooningwanekaaning - Home of the Golden Breasted Woodpecker - and it's a popular tourist destination reached five miles across the water from the mainland by ferry.

La Pointe served as the commercial hub, spiritual center and council grounds of the Lake Superior Ojibwe. It was also where they received payments and provisions from the Pine Treaty of 1837.

By 1842, La Pointe was a bustling outpost of civilization in the northern wilderness, serving the trade in furs, minerals and timber. Across the water, the cities of Superior, Wisconsin and Duluth, Minnesota were as yet unknown and would not be founded until the 1850s.

Here, over three days in the fall of 1842, the Ojibwe were offered a like-it-or-lump-it deal for the purchase of their land by U.S. negotiator Robert Stuart, the acting superintendent of Indian Affairs. In a glaring conflict of interest, Stuart was a former agent of the defunct American Fur Company, which stood to receive the lion's share of the Indians' cash to resolve old debts. John Jacob Astor, the "richest man in the world," had appointed Stuart the manager of his company's Northern Department at Mackinac Island in 1819. Stuart had decades of experience trading with the Indians and certainly knew how to pull their strings in finessing a deal.

Robert Stuart & the Oregon Trail

Robert Stuart's involvement in the Copper Treaty of 1842 doesn't even rate a mention in his Wikipedia bio. That's because he was best known for his discovery of the Oregon Trail.

Born in Scotland in 1785, Stuart emigrated to Canada in 1807 to work in the fur trade. At the age of twenty-five he set sail on John Jacob Astor's ship, the *Tonquin*, to establish a trading post for the Pacific Fur Company at the outlet of the Columbia River at present-day Astoria, Oregon.

The journey was a step beyond sheer terror. The *Tonquin* had to round Cape Horn at the tip of South America, where mariners reported waves up to two hundred feet high with troughs a mile wide between the rollers. One story goes that Stuart held a gun to the head of irascible Captain Jonathan Thorn to prevent him from abandoning his uncle, David Stuart, for being late to the ship during a layover at the Falkland Islands. Reaching the churning mouth of the Columbia River on February 11, 1811, several men drowned under Captain Thorn's orders while trying to breach the violent outflow in small boats.

While Stuart and his trading partners were busy constructing Fort Astoria, Captain Thorn sailed north with twenty-three men to trade with the Indians at Clayoquot Sound on Vancouver Island. Captain Thorn had a vile temper and a hateful attitude toward anyone who crossed him, which to his mind was everyone. During negotiations with an Indian chief, Thorn became angry over what he considered a bad deal and smacked the chief across the face with a rolled up sea otter pelt before stomping out of the parley.

The next day, swarms of canoes sidled up to the *Tonquin* with hundreds of Indians holding sea otter pelts aloft in their outstretched arms. Greedy and eager to trade, Thorn allowed them to come aboard. Soon the decks were packed with Indians and too late, Thorn realized his error. When he ordered them off the ship, they pulled knives from beneath their pelts and began the slaughter. Only five men made it below deck, seizing their muskets and firing up through the hatches to drive the raiders away.

The next day, four men set south in a whaling boat, while the fifth mortally-wounded man prepared his revenge. When the Indians returned, he ignited nine thousand pounds of gunpowder, blowing the ship and two hundred Natives to kingdom come.

Only an Indian interpreter made it back to Fort Astoria alive; the four men in the whale boat had been captured and tortured to death.

In a terrible jam with no ship and little prospect of rescue, Stuart, now twenty-seven, was dispatched to cross North America overland to St. Lou is through unknown country. At the time of his journey, the High Plains were home to an estimated population of two hundred thousand Indians living in scores of tribal nations.

Stuart and a party of seven men acquired horses from the local Indians and made their way east via the renowned South Pass over the Rockies. Their discovery of the route would become the legendary Oregon Trail, soon to be followed by hundreds of thousands of settlers.

Returning home, Stuart served for a time as Astor's agent on Mackinac Island. Thereafter, he served as treasurer for the State of Michigan in 1840-41 before becoming a federal Indian agent.

As an agent, Stuart was said to be kinder than his predecessors when it came to the Indians' welfare, but there was a limit and he had been schooled in the hard-hearted practices of the fur trade.

Eyewitnesses to the treaty signing said that Stuart gave them little say in its terms. In the mode of a *mafioso* boss making an offer that couldn't be refused, he belittled the chieftains and warned that the government would seize their land whether they liked it or not if they refused to sign.

By tradition, Indian councils were held under a large tree or beneath a bower of limbs fastened to other trees, open at the sides so that all could see and hear. These were solemn events imbued with spiritual qualities, with hundreds of participants and onlookers seated respectfully on the ground as various orators and headmen stood and debated the issues at hand. Native dignitaries wore their best clothes, paid close attention to their hair, and considered the spoken word to be an inviolable promise rather than merely a starting point as perceived by the whites. For white negotiators used to snap judgements, these were excruciatingly dull affairs as dozens of formal speeches were countered with lengthy responses dragging on for days as a consensus was slowly cobbled together.

In his opening remarks on Sept. 29, 1842, Stuart outlined the Ojibwes' shortcomings:

"Last winter I visited your Great Father at Washington and talked with him about your circumstances - he knows that you are poor, that your lands are not good, and that you have very little game left to feed and clothe your women and children. He therefore pities your condition, and has sent me to see what can be done to benefit you. Some of you now get a little money, goods & provisions, others get none at all, because the government did not think your lands worth buying at former treaties."

Stuart went on to say that owing to the treaty signed with the Ojibwe in 1826, "you granted the right to carry away any minerals which might be found on your lands, so that they are now no longer yours: and the whites have been asking your great Father to give them permission to take away all they can find - but your Great Father wishes first to make a new treaty, and pay you well for those lands and minerals..."

Promising to provide "a little money" along with "Goods, provisions & tobacco," Stuart said he would also address the dismal performance of the white blacksmiths and farm instructors that the Ojibwe had been provided with in a prior treaty.

He then upbraided the Ojibwe for their lack of interest in the white man's form of education:

"From what I learn, I fear that you do not esteem your teachers & schools as you should - some of you seem to think that you may always live as you have done heretofore; but do you not see that the Great Spirit is changing things all around you? Formerly all the country down to Washington, and the Great Salt Lake, was owned and inhabited by the Red men. But now the whites fill the whole country, they are as numerous as the pigeons in the spring... whereas the poor Indians have died of poverty and drinking whiskey, and others have been sent west of the Mississippi to make room for the whites. The reason of this is not that the Great Spirit loves the whites more than he does the Indians: but that the whites have listened to their religious teachers & sent their children to school, so that they learned a great deal more than the Indians, and have become wise and rich, while the Indians remain ignorant and poor."

Stuart said he hoped the Ojibwe would open their hearts to the government-appointed schools. He also lectured them on their lack of interest in Christianity: "I see very few go to hear religious instruction from the Missionaries, altho' they are preaching every evening in the church, and very anxious that you should learn to become wise, from the good Book of the Great Spirit..."

As for being told by friendly white neighbors that they were being cheated on the true worth of their land, Stuart cautioned the Ojibwe not to listen to "fools" who were telling them "squaw stories."

The proposed cession of twelve million acres was rimmed in coercion. In stark terms the Copper Treaty contained threats of forced removal at the whim of any U.S. President, including this from Article II:

"The Indians stipulate for the right of hunting on the ceded territory, with the other usual privileges of occupancy, *until required to remove by the President of the United States...*" (Italics added.)

Elsewhere in Article VI of the treaty, the Ojibwe were advised that those, "residing on the Mineral district, shall be subject to removal there-from *at the pleasure of the President of the United States.*"

Gathered in council, the Ojibwe chieftains sat silently through Stuart's harangue, their dark eyes cold with anger, a sign that they did not agree.

Taken aback, Stuart hastened to claim without any authority that as long as they "behaved" the Ojibwe could live on their lands for the rest of their lives, a period of at least fifty to one hundred years. None of this, however, was written into the treaty ratified by the U.S. Senate.

The silence continued as Stuart fidgeted, waiting for a reaction. It was then that Chief White Crow of the Lac du Flambeau band stood up and spoke for all who were gathered there:

"I do not give you the land, it is the mineral only that I sell if there is any to be found on my land. *I do not cede the land!*"

Turning to his fellow leaders, White Crow heard a chorus of affirmation shouted around the room. "*Enh! Enh! Enh!*"

Here though, as in many other treaty negotiations, the Indians were at a disadvantage. White translators were often barely proficient in indigenous languages; nor did they grasp the subtleties of Indian metaphors and symbolism used in their councils. As historian and anthropologist Charles E. Cleland has noted: "These difficulties were the result of Indian emphasis on the spoken word, while Americans emphasized the final written document. Because of their training in listening to oration and remembering oral representations, Indians often came away from treaty sessions relying upon what American negotiators stated as bargaining positions. Often what they thought was included in a treaty was simply never written down and, more often, they had very little understanding of what the treaty actually stated."

Such was the case with the Copper Treaty, which was signed on Oct. 4, 1842 with an unsubstantiated promise on Stuart's part, guaranteeing the tribe's right to live within their ceded land for a lifetime. As the Indians were soon to discover, the U.S. Senate in far-off Washington, D.C., was never apprised of this promise, nor likely to approve it if it had been. The Ojibwe were also shocked to learn that they had traded away Isle Royale on the north shore of Lake Superior, having no idea that the 206-square-mile island was part of the deal.

In return for ceding their ancestral homeland and some of the richest mineral deposits on earth, the Ojibwe were promised annual payments for twenty-five years of $12,000 in specie (silver coin); $10,500 in goods such as axes, firearms, tools and clothing; $2,000 in food and tobacco; $2,000 to support two blacksmith shops; $1,000 to pay two farmers to teach agricultural skills; $1,200 to support two carpenters; and $2,000 to establish and support schools. Added to this was $75,000 to pay off existing debts owed by the Indians to traders and $5,000 for an agricultural fund. An additional lump sum of $15,000 was negotiated for the signers' "half-breed relatives." (The half-French *métis* Indians.)

Most of the $75,000 debt repayment went to Stuart's former employer, the American Fur Company. Although he had sold the company in 1834 and it had since gone out of business, the chief beneficiary of the repayment was John Jacob Astor, who demanded $37,994.98 owed by the Indians to the defunct company. He kept $23,696.28 for himself, dividing the balance with his agents. Stuart, who was a good friend of Astor, likely got a generous taste of the proceeds.

Stuart wrote that the Ojibwe were "highly delighted with the kind and generous dealing of the Government toward them." Many, however, expressed scorn for the treaty, which had been coercive and rushed. Chief Buffalo of the Madeline Island Ojibwe said he was "ashamed" of the signing, claiming that the Indians of central Wisconsin had also been cheated in the Pine Treaty of 1837. Another chief named Black Bird claimed that the Ojibwe had promised only the timber and mineral rights, and not the land on which they lived. The Ojibwe, he said, had been robbed.

These sentiments were echoed by Indian Affairs Subagent and Methodist minister Alfred Brunson even before the Copper Treaty's ratification. He noted that the Ojibwe had been paid less than eight cents an acre for the eleven million acres ceded in the 1837 Pine Treaty and would receive only a little more than four cents per acre for twelve million acres in the treaty of 1842. He made the bald claim that they were being cheated.

Speaking up on behalf of the Ojibwe didn't go well for Brunson. Commissioner Stuart arranged to have him dismissed for the "absurdity" of his claims, adding that Brunson was "not only deficient in head, but depraved in heart" for his "false and absurd accusations."

Stuart may have believed in his own false claim that the Ojibwe would be allowed to remain on their lands. Soon after the negotiations he wrote a letter to a reverend friend in Boston that, "I have the pleasure to state, that it is not expected the Indians will have to remove from their present locations, for many years to come." At most, he said, some of the Ojibwe might have to move a bit to the "right, or left" to make way for mining operations.

Yet eight years after the Copper Treaty was signed, government officials conspired to remove the Ojibwe of Michigan and Wisconsin to a new homeland beyond the Mississippi. The hatching of this plan in 1850 lured some four thousand members of various Ojibwe bands into a trap far from their homes.

Alexander Ramsey, Minnesota's territorial governor, is considered by many to be the chief villain in the affair, but he had help from Minnesota's Commissioner of Indian Affairs Orlando Brown, his subagent John Watrous, Secretary of the Interior Thomas Ewing, and his successor, Luke Lea.

Few whites living in Wisconsin and the Upper Peninsula were in favor of forcing the Ojibwe to move west. Newspaper editorials noted that the wilderness of western Lake Superior was of little use to white settlers; in fact there were only five hundred whites living in the region. *The Lake Superior News and Mining Journal* of Sault Ste. Marie opined that the Ojibwe were minding their own business, not bothering anyone, and deserved to be left alone.

Nonetheless, Gov. Ramsey and his supporters lobbied to have the Ojibwe removed to west of the Mississippi to the Minnesota Territory. If the plan succeeded, treaty payments and provisions would be delivered up the Mississippi from St, Louis, rather than via Detroit, giving the bankers and merchants of St. Paul a chance to skim a share. The Ojibwe would also have to spend their annuities at a remote trading post at Sandy Lake, instead of in Wisconsin or Michigan. Government funds spent on Indian schools and farms would also find their way into the region's economy.

The rationale for removal was said to be for the Indians' own good, in that it would remove them from the temptations of whiskey traders; prevent "injurious contact" with white settlers; relieve the "annoyance" of whites having to live alongside Indians; and congregate them in the west where they could advance toward "civilization and prosperity."

Unstated was the fact that whiskey traders were like fleas on a dog and would follow the Indians wherever they went, as would "annoyed" white settlers.

Adding pressure to push the Ojibwe west of the Mississippi, the newly-created Minnesota Territorial Legislature revoked the tribe's right to hunt, gather and fish on the lands they had ceded in the Pine Treaty of 1837, breaking a promise that had been guaranteed in the treaty.

Deliberating over all of this was President Zachary Taylor, who had earned the sobriquet, "Old Rough and Ready" for his actions fighting in the Second Seminole War in the late 1830s. A career soldier, he had also served in the Black Hawk War of 1832, and as commandant of forts at Green Bay, Wisconsin and in Minnesota. He had plenty of experience with the Indians, but primarily in fighting them. Taylor was also a hero of the 1847 Mexican War and was propelled to the presidency via the same military coattails as generals George Washington, Andrew Jackson, Ulysses S. Grant and Dwight D. Eisenhower.

Swayed by Ramsey's arguments, Taylor issued an executive order in February, 1850, requiring the Ojibwe of Upper Michigan and Wisconsin to move west beyond the Mississippi. The Indians were expected to begin their move that summer.

As might be expected, Taylor's decision didn't sit well with the Ojibwe, who protested the violation of the treaties they had signed. On Madeline Island, Chief Buffalo sent word to all of the bands in the region, asking if anyone had given white settlers any cause for complaint. Quite the contrary: many settlers, miners and lumberjacks were happy to have the Ojibwe as neighbors. Ojibwe men were serving as guides, hauling supplies, and providing fish and venison to miners and lumber camps, while

Many Anishinaabek chieftains used drawings of their clan totems to sign treaties that were written out by white translators. Detail is from the 1807 Treaty of Detroit.

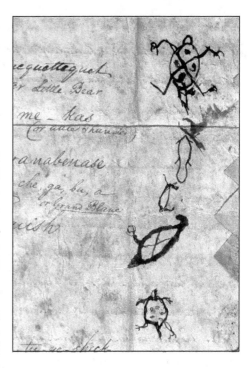

Ojibwe women offered fresh vegetables, corn, potatoes and other crops. And, with a scarcity of white women in Michigan's rugged Upper Peninsula, marriages between miners, loggers and Indian women were common.

A further complication lay in the fact that during the mid-1700s, the Ojibwe had invaded the Minnesota homeland of the Dakota Sioux and more than a century later the tribes were still fighting. Yet, now, the whites expected them to live alongside their mortal enemies.

The warriors of the Ojibwe were known as the Pillagers: *MukI'mduawininewug* (men who take by force), a society of warriors who were drawn from the Bear and Catfish clans of the tribe.

A large force of Pillagers swept into Minnesota during the mid-1700s, driving the Dakota Sioux to the west and capturing their territory at Sandy Lake, Leech Lake and other lakeside villages. This included attacking two major towns at Mille Lac, a twenty-five-mile-wide lake, rich in fish and game, that was in the heartland of the Dakota Sioux. Armed with guns supplied by the French, the Pillagers exterminated virtually everyone living in a village at Cormorant Point and then pushed on to a large Dakota town at the lake's outlet.

The Dakota had little access to firearms, which historically tipped the balance in favor of those who were so armed. Many hid in their earthen lodges, only to suffer the fate of flaming bags of gunpowder hurled through the smoke holes in their roofs. The survivors were driven west beyond the Mississippi, continuing a state of warfare and massacres that seemed to have no end.

Ojibwe historian William Warren wrote that a hunter passing through the border country between the Sioux and Ojibwe "moved through the dense forests in fear and trembling... expecting each moment that from behind a tree, an embankment of sand along the lake shore, or a clump of bushes on the river bank, would speed the bullet or arrow which would lay him low in death."

The French, the British, and then the Americans in turn had tried to stem the conflict for more than a century to no avail. This had included bringing the warring parties together in 1825 to sign a peace treaty that fell apart almost before the ink was dry. Commissioner Stuart had his own concerns as far back as 1842, writing that the government should mediate a treaty, "to put a stop to the horrible carnage which these Tribes are continually committing upon each other."

Even as late as 1896 during a stop with his Wild West Show at Ashland, Wisconsin, Buffalo Bill Cody convened a "peace jubilee" between the Sioux and the Ojibwe, who were still at loggerheads.

Thus, for the Ojibwe, the idea of moving west of the Mississippi into Dakota land was suicidal. In the mid-1800s the Ojibwe had no sense of pan-Indian unity or love of their neighbors. Their petition to Congress castigated "the wandering and vicious tribes which infest the plains and the mountains stretching from the Mississippi to the Pacific," adding that moving closer to their enemies would be tantamount to a death sentence.

Ojibwe leaders began a public relations campaign opposing their removal, writing to legislators in Washington and rousing support from local whites. A birch bark scroll depicting five clans opposed to the removal was sent to Washington in 1849. The tribe also sought the aid of those who stood to lose money upon their removal. Newspapers in Michigan and Wisconsin condemned the removal plan, with their stories reprinted by major newspapers back east. Many missionaries, traders, bankers, business owners and legislators also railed against removal.

Above all, the bands of Ojibwe across the U.P. and Wisconsin refused to move, and dispatching the U.S. Army to dislodge them had no support in Congress. The United States was still digesting the expense of the Mexican War of 1847 and grappling with what to do with the acquisition of California, Arizona and New Mexico. Add to that, gold had been discovered in California, which had entered the Union in 1849 as a free state, raising a clamor in Congress over the division of slave states and free. This resulted in the Compromise of 1850, which compelled the citizens of free states to assist in returning runaway slaves. In short, the federal government had more on its hands than coping with an obscure tribe in the northern wilderness.

Stymied, Gov. Ramsey and his fellow conspirators came up with a ruse to pressure the Ojibwe into moving to the Minnesota Territory. At their instigation, the annual payout of annuities and supplies was moved from La Pointe to a remote government substation 150 miles to the northwest at Sandy Lake. For many, this would mean a difficult canoe journey of up to 450 miles along winding rivers, including many arduous portages. Bureau of Indian Affairs subagent Watrous sent word to the Ojibwe that they had no other option but to make the trip if they wanted their cash and provisions, telling them to bring their families. The idea was to trap the Indians in Minnesota for the winter when the waterways would be frozen over and it would be impossible to travel home by canoe. This was intended to wear down their resistance to being relocated beyond the Mississippi.

Gov. Ramsey outlined his plan to incoming Commissioner of Indian Affairs Luke Lea in a July 16, 1850 letter, writing that he would induce the Ojibwe to gather at Fond du Lac near present-day Duluth,

"From that point we will convey them to Sandy Lake, and there, time the payment in such a way as to interpose obstacles to a return to the country they left."

Native peoples rarely made a move without lengthy councils, which could last for weeks before a consensus opinion was arrived at. As Michigan Territorial Governor Lewis Cass had noted in 1826, "the Government of the Indians, if it deserves a name, is a Government of opinion." There was no unified Ojibwe "nation" with one leader representing the whole; instead, each small band was a nation unto itself with the voices of many leaders inching toward consensus at a glacial pace.

This was the situation in early 1850 when many bands gathered to discuss their options, resulting in the neglect of their crops and a slim harvest. With few provisions on hand to get them through the winter, nineteen bands of the Ojibwe from throughout Wisconsin and the U.P. reluctantly made the long journey to Sandy Lake, expecting to receive their treaty cash and supplies on October 25. Some bands at Pelican Lake, Wisconsin, and those living in the Upper Peninsula at Ontonagon and L'Anse refused to make the trip.

The resulting disaster was a repeat of a annuity payment at La Pointe two years before in 1848, which like many government promises of food and cash, was long delayed.

A reporter on the scene at La Pointe for the *Cleveland Herald* wrote that "thousands of Indians traversed many miles of forest, wasted six weeks' time, and lost the crop of wild rice upon which they depended for their winter's subsistence." Traders at La Pointe also cheated the Indians by charging "exorbitant rates," requiring them to buy "dry goods and gew-gaws" and other "trash" as a prerequisite to obtaining supplies of pork and flour on credit.

As was the case elsewhere across the Midwest, annuity provisions often included items of no use foisted on the Indians by profiteers in league with government agents. The Indians were also forced to repay traders for their debts at the annual payouts. The *Herald* reported that the Ojibwe lost more than 85 percent of their annuity cash to the traders at La Pointe, coming away with the equivalent of one dollar each.

Typically, a family arriving at La Pointe on treaty payment day would have their name called and their identity verified by their band's lead-er. Family members, including children, received blankets, which were spread on the ground to receive their goods, along with supplies of pork and flour. Men would typically receive broadcloth for pants and calico or linsey-woolsey for shirts, along with a knife, gun, a comb, and lead for bullets, yet seldom any gunpowder. A woman could expect to receive a comb along with kitchen goods such as pots and pans along with sewing materials, including cloth, needles, scissors, thread and thimbles. Children received their own goods, and once the dole was complete the four corners of the blankets would be tied for the trip home.

But, as noted by the *Herald's* reporter, Indian families were often saddled with items that were little more than trash, including thin blankets and flimsy pots and pans. Scores of Indian hunters were also maimed or crip-pled by the explosion of poorly-made guns provided by the government.

The difference between the La Pointe fiasco of 1848 and that of Sandy Lake two years later was both geographical and purposefully cruel, with-holding the Ojibwes' cash and supplies for weeks while stranding them hundreds of miles from home in the teeth of winter.

Ramsey and Watrous knew that Congress had not even appropriated the allotment for the Ojibwe in the fall of 1850, yet they kept this a secret, both from local whites and the arriving Indians.

Watrous emerges as either incompetent or a particularly slimy character in his double-dealings. He was not even on hand when the Ojibwe ar-rived, having gone eight hundred miles down the Mississippi to St. Louis to secure federal funds for the payout, which hadn't been appropriated and didn't materialize. He then dawdled over personal business at St. Paul. It wasn't until November 24 that he showed up without the treaty funds, finding a disaster well underway.

History is sketchy as to how many of the Ojibwe traveled to Sandy Lake.

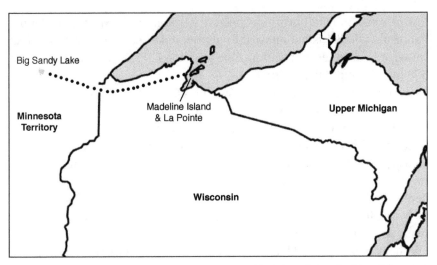

Moving treaty payments from La Pointe on Madeline Island 150 miles west to Sandy Lake in the Minnesota Territory meant making an arduous journey down tangled rivers and pathways that could double or triple the distance.

A monument erected at the lake puts the number at four thousand. This included 1,500 of the Mississippi Ojibwe and those of the region's Pillager band who were accustomed to receiving their allotments at the substation. Except for those who lived nearby, most of the arrivals were men who wisely left their families at home.

Bear in mind that it wasn't a straight shot down a roadway for any of the Ojibwe; rather, they traveled on foot or by canoe down winding tangles of rivers and paths that tended to vastly increase the distance to Sandy Lake and back.

Many of those who arrived at Sandy Lake were lightly dressed and ill prepared for the winter. Rolls of birch bark and mats needed to build temporary wigwams had been left behind to free up space in their canoes for annuity supplies. Nor had they brought much in the way of food, expecting to receive their cash and provisions in late October before making a speedy return home. Game was scarce in the swampy area around Sandy Lake and adequate shelter was also lacking, with many arrivals sleeping beneath their canoes in a waterlogged area.

Today, even the most experienced, well-supplied and well-fed outdoorsman would find camping to be a challenge in northern Minnesota in November, where temperatures range from a high of 35 degrees Fahrenheit to a low of 17. December, when the Ojibwe began their trek home, is far colder, with the average high temperature being 21 degrees and the average low being just 6 degrees. January, when many of the surviving Ojibwe reached home, is brutal, with an average high of 18 degrees and an average low of zero. Snowfall is also a concern, particularly in Michigan's Upper Peninsula where it's not unusual to get two hundred inches of lake effect snow, or sixteen feet per season. One year, the U.P. received a snowfall of 390 inches - more than thirty feet.

Given these dire conditions, along with an appalling lack of sanitation, disease began stalking those stranded at Sandy Lake. Many died from dysentery, caused by bacterial and amoeboid contamination of food and water, resulting in bloody diarrhea, fever and lethargy. Others died from measles, a particularly deadly disease among indigenous peoples. With no level of acquired immunity for protection, measles could result in massive hemorrhaging from every orifice of the body, often killing within a day or two. Cholera was also suspected by white observers, who reported as many as eight or nine Indians dying each day.

With the frozen ground locked as hard as the iron that Minnesota is known for, the starving, disease-wracked Ojibwe had no choice but to leave their dead wrapped in birch bark above ground, being too weak to dig graves. A few survivors remained behind to care for the sick and dying, only to succumb themselves as the winter wore on.

In the last week of November, Watrous scrambled to obtain a small amount of ammunition from local traders to allow the Ojibwe to hunt on the way home. But here, the traders showed their feathers as vultures, jacking up the price for gunpowder and shot. They also raised prices on food and supplies from three-to-six times what was charged in St. Paul and other trading posts, raking in $8,368.40 in credit from the forthcoming annuity cash.

Limited food supplies didn't arrive at Sandy Lake until December 2, consisting mostly of rotten pork and flour that was chalky green with mold. By then, thousands were stranded without adequate food, clothing, sanitation or shelter in a full-blown northern winter with a foot of snow on the ground. Many were convinced that the government was trying to poison them.

William Warren claimed that government contractors switched out the flour meant for the Ojibwe in order to line their own pockets:

"These same contractors, or those connected with them, took the best of the flour while lying in their store house, and sent it to the Winnebago Agency, returning in its stead, damaged Winnebago flour," he wrote. "These same contractors sold for the use of the Indians at Sandy Lake, *musty* Pemmican, which probably had lain in their store houses for years... This Pemmican aggravated immediately the disease among the Indians."

Add to this, the rivers had frozen over and many of the Ojibwe had burned their useless canoes for firewood. Packing their supplies on their backs, they set off on foot along snowed-over forest trails for hundreds of miles. Their only provisions were stores of bad food that Gov. Ramsey estimated couldn't have sustained them for more than three days.

Ojibwe leaders reported that 167 people died at Sandy Lake, including twenty who had been left behind to care for those who were too sick to travel. Another 230 died on the trek home, many being men who were the sole providers for their families. In all, up to 12 percent of the Lake Superior and Wisconsin bands died as a result of government malfeasance. Gone too was the bulk of their treaty cash for debt repayment to traders along with their precious canoes, which many depended upon for a livelihood.

Speaking before the Minnesota Territorial Legislature at St. Paul in early 1851, a young Chief Hole-in-the-Day the Younger of the Crow Wing Band railed that, "four, five and six people died every night and day" at Sandy Lake due to spoiled food. In a follow-up letter to the *Minnesota Pioneer,* Hole-in-the-Day wrote that, "two hundred Chippewa (Ojibwe) lost their lives eating rotten flour; and of that, only one pound was issued to each person for three days."

The chief added that even a dog had died from eating the government's rotten food. Nor did the Ojibwe receive their full allotment of provisions and supplies. Watrous had also refused to provide documents that would have worked in the Indians' favor on settling their debts with traders. "The Chippewa were compelled to sign papers (accepting their pay-out) through hunger and want."

Another condemnation of Ramsey came from Flat Mouth, age seventy-eight, of the Leech Lake band: "Tell him I blame him for the children we have lost, for the sickness we have suffered and for the hunger we have endured."

The Ojibwe also protested having to repay their debts, claiming that, in fact, the traders and the American Fur Company owed *them* for living in their lands rent-free and benefiting from cutting their trees for homes and firewood in addition to hunting their game for food. And, as Flat Mouth noted, many of the Ojibwe who owed debts had been killed while hunting in Sioux territory on behalf of the traders. "And they talk to *us* about paying our debts?"

Months later, Methodist Episcopal missionary John Pitezel visited the lake, finding that, "graves were to be seen in every direction, for miles distant, from Sandy Lake," including in the surrounding forest. Stricken with horror, Pitezel found signs of "a terrible calamity" everywhere, with sickness and death at every turn. "So alarming was the mortality, that the Indians complained that they could not bury their dead." Nor would they return to Sandy Lake, speaking of it as a haunted graveyard.

If Ramsey and Watrous had any remorse over the result of their disastrous scheme, they didn't show it. Ramsey wrote Commissioner Lea that, "except their money," the Ojibwe had received all that the government owed them, omitting to mention that this had included rotten food. He also blamed the Indians themselves, whose "thriftless habits" put them in hock to traders.

Ramsey and Watrous continued to insist that treaty payments and supplies be distributed further to the west, this time at Fond du Lac near present-day Duluth and at Crow Wing near Brainerd, Minnesota. Commissioner Lea had ordered the temporary suspension of President Taylor's Removal Order in the wake of the Sandy Lake disaster, but this was ignored by Watrous, who had the gall to request that troops be sent to La Pointe to forcibly remove the Ojibwe. This request was declined.

At La Pointe, Chief Buffalo and twenty-eight chieftains drafted a petition, blasting Watrous and claiming that it was he, and not President Taylor, who was behind the scheme to have the tribe removed west of the Mississippi. The petition also repeated Commissioner Stuart's pledge that the Ojibwe could live on their ceded lands for the rest of their lives, up to one hundred years without fear of removal. They also protested that they had "never shed the blood of the Whites; nor killed their cattle; nor done them any injury; and... are not in their way... why is (it) that we now hear this order to remove?"

The tribe's petition was sent to Indian Affairs officials in Washington, D.C., where it was roundly ignored. Incensed, and with the Ojibwe on the verge of a rebellion they could not win, Chief Buffalo resolved to make an illegal trip to the nation's capital against orders to speak to the president himself. It was a roll of the dice, upon which depended not only the fate of his people, but the threat of a prison sentence.

CHAPTER 2

THE WORLD IN THE 1850S

— Women are still largely the property of their husbands, denied the vote, control of their own bodies, and even custody of their children in the event of divorce. In 1848 Elizabeth Cady Stanton, Lucretia Mott and Susan B. Anthony had convened a convention demanding rights for women regarding the vote, divorce, child custody, property, and equal pay.

— There are nearly four million black slaves in America, enduring conditions that could include unbridled rape, beatings and sadism. Plantation owners, in turn, live in terror of a possible slave uprising. After failing to escape in 1856, runaway Margaret Garner kills her three-year-old daughter rather than see her raised as a slave.

— The Mexican-American War of 1846-1848 has resulted in the acquisition of California, Arizona and New Mexico for settlement, an area the size of Western Europe. In his memoirs, President Ulysses S. Grant, who served as a lieutenant in the war, stated that he, "to this day regard the war... as one of the most unjust ever waged by a stronger against a weaker nation."

— The guillotine remains popular in France. Employed on more than seventeen thousand people during the Reign of Terror in the 1790s, the head-chopping device will remain in service until 1977 as a humane form of execution. Author Charles Dickens observed a beheading in 1845 in Rome, describing a head rolling into a leather bag: "The executioner was holding it by the hair, and walking with it round the scaffold, showing it to the people, before one quite knew that the knife had fallen heavily, and with a rattling sound... Nobody cared, or was at all affected. There was no manifestation of disgust, or pity, or indignation, or sorrow."

— The expedition of Sir John Franklin hasn't been heard from in five years. Franklin and his ships, the *HMS Terror* and *HMS Erebus* left England in 1845 in search of the Northwest Passage in the arctic seas across the top of Canada in what was considered the best-equipped expedition in history. Eskimos later reported a band of starving white men wandering the rocky terrain of King William Island, never to be seen again.

— The Fugitive Slave Act requires citizens of the free states of the North to cooperate in returning runaway slaves to their masters. Abolitionists defy the law: "I never would obey it," states Reverend Luther Lee of Syracuse, NY, in 1855. "I had assisted thirty slaves to escape to Canada during the last month. If the authorities wanted anything of me... they could take me and lock me up in the Penitentiary on the hill; but if they did... I had friends enough to level it to the ground before the next morning."

— In 1852, politicians begin debating the idea of splitting the United States in two.

— More than eighty thousand Americans have braved the long trail west in the California Gold Rush. Some have traveled across the Great Plains and Rocky Mountains, others the dangerous sea voyage around Cape Horn or via the Isthmus of Panama. The mass extermination of California's Indians begins in earnest; in twenty years, 80 percent of California's Indians will be killed by disease or genocide. Many miners give up digging for gold for the more lucrative scalp bounties offered by the government, resulting in the murder of 9,000-16,000 Native people.

— Nathaniel Hawthorne has a bestseller with *The Scarlet Letter*, a tale of adultery among the Puritans of the seventeenth century.

— Mormon leader Brigham Young has led sixteen thousand of his followers to Utah from Illinois in the wake of the 1844 murder of the religion's founder, Joseph Smith, at the hands of a mob in Carthage, Illinois.

— Meanwhile, "King" James Jesse Strang and his Mormon followers are entrenched on Beaver Island in Lake Michigan. A low-grade war is underway between the Strangites and fishermen on the mainland.

— Harriet Beecher Stowe is at work on *Uncle Tom's Cabin*, a novel on the evils of slavery which Abraham Lincoln cited in half-jest as the spark which led to the Civil War. It sells 300,000 copies in its first year.

— Hermann Melville puts the finishing touches on *Moby Dick*, a novel which languishes with poor sales in 1851. It is rediscovered in the early twentieth century and hailed as the "Great American Novel," long after Melville died, a frustrated author.

— Isaac Merritt Singer invents the first sewing machine. A mechanic from Pittsburgh, his invention revolutionizes the textile industry.

— The nativist Know Nothing Party rages against the flood of immigrants from Ireland, Germany and other countries. The party is also virulently anti-Roman Catholic.

— A shipping boom is underway on the Great Lakes. At Grand Haven, a port at the mouth of Michigan's Grand River, observers report sighting as many as fifty sails per day by the late 1850s. A new canal and locks at Sault Ste. Marie opens in 1855, making it possible to ship ore and timber from Duluth all the way to the Atlantic Seaboard.

CHAPTER 3

THE DARING MISSION
OF CHIEF GREAT BUFFALO

Sometimes history pivots from disaster to salvation thanks to the deeds of a single individual who steps forth at a key moment in time. Such a man was Chief Great Buffalo, or Kechewaishke Pezheke, whose courage and skill as a negotiator marked him as one of the heroes of the Ojibwe.

Dates could be sketchy for Indians, especially in prehistoric times when calendars were unknown and the habit of marking years was haphazard. Many Indians had no idea as to how old they were and were given to a best-guess way of measuring the years, or recalling how tall they were as children when a notable event had transpired. An elder might say, for example, that he was as tall as his father's shoulder the year that the big tree near his village was hit by lightning, meaning that he was in his early teens at the time and could mark his age from then. Yet evidence indicates that Buffalo was born into the Loon clan at La Pointe on Madeline Island in 1759. One of his grandfathers was called Aandegwiiyaas - Crow's Meat - and this may have been the name of his father as well.

Given the Ojibwe's tradition of telling stories around their lodge fires, especially through the long winter nights, as a child Buffalo would have heard tales of a time before the arrival of the first white man on the shores of Lake Superior. He would have heard stories of great heroes, animals, monsters, spirits, far-off places, deeds of battle, trading routes and the oral history of his people, all mixed in with the earnest claims of Christian missionaries and the scuttlebutt heard around the trading post at La Pointe. He would have been familiar with the wars of the French, British and Americans and the Ojibwe's role in each conflict. On a darker note, he would have known of the genocide visited upon hundreds of tribes that had been exterminated over the course of two hundred years of conquest and disease. He would have heard of their removal west of the Mississippi to bleak reservations. These stories and his own experiences carousing with friends and fishing on Lake Superior would have shaped his outlook, and upon his maturity he emerged as a man of wisdom and common sense, worthy of being considered a chieftain - a Big Man among his people.

Traditionally, an *ogichiida,* or chief, had none of the powers we've come to associate with presidents or kings, not even that of a mayor or police chief. In Native societies, where individual freedom was an absolute given, a chieftain did not have the power to give orders. Instead, he led by persuasion and example. A war chief could rally men to smoke the war pipe, but he could not order them into battle. A village chief could direct the civic affairs of his band, but only with the support of its elders in council and those individuals who were willing to go along with his decisions. An *ogichiida's* tools lay in marshaling public opinion and convincing others of his wisdom as a leader, backed by consensus of the band. Even tactics in warfare might be crafted by a council of seasoned warriors, rather than by a general-like war chief, with punishments meted out for young hotheads who blew an ambush or attack. And if a war chief didn't succeed in bringing home his warriors alive, he could count on being quickly demoted.

The selection of an *ogichiida* involved a number of factors, including inheritance if one's father had been chief. Generally, an older man noted for his sense of caution and level-headedness was chosen by consensus to be a band's leader. His tools might include a sense of charisma, skill as an orator, and the traits of a "natural leader." He would likely belong to a large and influential family, have lucrative trading connections, have the backing of elders of both sexes, and the support of a powerful shaman, or in later years, missionaries. He may have led a war party or two in his youth, and thus, be feared as a man you wouldn't want to cross. These were the qualities which propelled Sitting Bull and Red Cloud to their positions among the Oglala Sioux and would have been expected among the leaders of the Anishinaabek.

Given the longevity of his leadership, Chief Buffalo surely had some of these traits along with an immense amount of energy and initiative. He began negotiating treaties on behalf of the Ojibwe starting in his sixties, including those of 1825, 1826, 1837, 1842 and 1854. Dressed in a military uniform complete with epaulets, a portrait of Buffalo reveals an avuncular man possessed of a direct gaze that is alive with intelligence and confidence. He wasn't the sort of man who could be easily manipulated.

In 1852, amid continuing pressure on the part of Watrous and Ramsey to force the removal of the Ojibwe to the west, the elderly Chief Buffalo decided to travel to Washington, D.C. to speak with the president directly. His companions included a savvy young chieftain named Oshoga, five other headmen, and Benjamin Armstrong, a frontiersman from Alabama who had married into the tribe and was considered a son-in-law. Armstrong served as the delegation's interpreter and guide.

The stakes were high, with rebellion brewing within the Michigan

Kechewaishke Pezheke - Chief Great Buffalo - negotiated numerous treaties on behalf of the Ojibwe and his band on Madeline Island.

and Wisconsin bands. Armstrong noted that, "To return without anything accomplished would be to rekindle the fire that was smouldering into an open revolt for revenge."

Buffalo began his trip in the spring of 1852 seated in the prow of a 24-foot-long canoe amid the lapping waves of Lake Superior, packing along supplies of sugar, coffee, crackers and a ceremonial pipe as a token of diplomacy. He was ninety-two at the time, an age where few, if any, men push their luck. Instead of sitting by a home fire wrapped in a blanket and listening to the prattle of great-great grandchildren, he was setting out on a journey that would have tried the skills of a man forty years younger. Nor did he know if he'd ever return; it was even possible that he'd spend his final years in a prison cell.

Buffalo and his team made the arduous ten-week journey by canoe, two schooner-rigged steamships and a train to Washington, D.C. He and his entourage were fortunate to have the wind of public opinion at their backs: news of the disaster at Sandy Lake and the subsequent Death March had created an uproar in the nation's press. A series of scathing editorials in the *Lake Superior News and Mining Journal* argued on behalf of the Ojibwe. One noted that the tribe "occupy a remote portion of the country... that would not, in all probability, have been settled for a hundred years to come."

Circulated in many influential East Coast newspapers, the *News* questioned the need for the tribe's removal:

"From time immemorial this people have occupied the northern region, and have become acclimated to its cold and rigorous climate; and by hunting and fishing, and the cultivation of their small patches of soil, they have lived comfortably and contentedly, causing little or no trouble to the United States and their neighbors. Until their little fields are needed for the accommodation of their white brethren, why should they be driven to

Chief Buffalo's delegation to Washington, D.C., was a daring bid to preserve the Ojibwe homeland. (Courtesy of the Wisconsin Historical Society, Wm. W. Bartlett, 1929.)

strange places, a prey to the designs of their worst enemies? They can live comfortably where they now are, but they will starve to death, as hundreds did last winter, in the miserable region to which the Government would remove them."

Bolstered by these sentiments, Armstrong circulated an Ojibwe petition to miners, settlers, lumberjacks, missionaries, and more importantly, to prominent businessmen. Thousands signed the petition, requesting that Zachary Taylor's removal order be rescinded.

The petition argued that the Ojibwe were "a peaceable and inoffensive race living chiefly by hunting & fishing," who had been "hardly and injuriously used by the Agents appointed to make their payments during the past two seasons," subjecting them to "cold & starvation."

Few of the petition signers, perhaps, had altruistic reasons for supporting the Ojibwe. They needed the tribe as much as the tribe needed them for support. The Ojibwe had become valuable assets as laborers, guides and providers of food for the mining and timber industries. That, and many businessmen and bankers wished to keep the Indians' treaty cash in Wisconsin and Michigan. The kicker in the petition stated that, "while their removal West would in Our Opinion be a great damage to them it would in no manner benefit the white population of the Country."

Armstrong had only a single dime in his pocket by the time the delegation reached New York City. With few options, Buffalo and his men were forced to put themselves on display to raise funds for their lodgings and onward journey. Exhibits of "wild Indians" were popular with paying crowds in the eastern cities, reaching a zenith with Buffalo Bill Cody's Wild West Show in the 1880s, featuring Oglala war chief Sitting Bull.

Reaching Washington, the delegation sought to arrange a meeting with President Millard Fillmore, who had gained the presidency after Zachary Taylor's untimely death. Taylor had succumbed to a stomach ailment after stuffing himself with cherries and iced milk at a fundraising event for the Washington Monument.

While Buffalo and his delegation waited in their lodgings, Armstrong made his way to the office of Indian Affairs Commissioner Luke Lea, hoping to arrange a meeting with the President. Lea and Secretary of the Interior Alexander Stuart turned him down flat.

"I want you to take your Indians away on the next train west, as they have come here without permission, and I do not want to see or hear of your Indians again," Lea said, according to a memoir Armstrong published forty years later in 1892. Armstrong added that he walked out of the meeting, "more discouraged than ever and could not imagine what next I could do."

The rebuke of Chief Buffalo and his party was somewhat unexpected, since Washington D.C., the "Federal City," was visited by many Indian leaders throughout the 1800s, generally at the invitation of the U.S. government. These diplomatic junkets benefited federal negotiators in that the long trip east was guaranteed to instill awe in the power and reach of the United States. For starters, Indian leaders who were barely out of the Stone Age would experience the almost unimaginable marvels of traveling by steamboat and train, passing through cities such as Chicago, Detroit, St. Louis and Philadelphia to see for themselves the vast population and troops of the United States. They would visit teeming cities lit at night with whale oil lamps, crowded with tenements, bustling with markets filled with wares from around the world and jammed with carriages, horses, immense piles of manure, and blizzards of flies. Once in Washington, Indian leaders would be treated with the honors of foreign dignitaries, yet cut off from their traditions of council and consensus and thus, easily manipulated.

Possibly, Buffalo's party encountered a group of Chickasaw emissaries who were also in town on a diplomatic mission. Two years later, in 1854, Washington D.C. would host a wave of tribal negotiators representing the Delaware, Omaha, Oto, Missouri, Shawnee, Iowa, Sauk, Fox, Kickapoo, Miami, Kaskaskia, Piankeshaw, Peoria and Wea nations.

Blessed with broad avenues designed by French-born architect Pierre L'Enfant, Washington was meant to arise from its swampy terrain to become a city "proportioned to the greatness which the capital of a powerful empire ought to manifest."

Yet Washington was still a small city in 1852 and a far cry from the bower of memorials and monuments we know today. Although the White House and other public buildings had been rebuilt after their destruction in the War of 1812, construction of the Washington Monument was stalled at 152 feet for lack of funds when Chief Buffalo and his party arrived; it had the appearance of a broken fang, less than one-third of its eventual height. Elsewhere, Buffalo's party would have witnessed black slaves and freemen extending the wings of the Capitol Building under the direction of Scottish stonemasons, a project that would take fourteen years to complete. The site was surrounded by ramshackle work sheds, piles of timber and marble, the shacks of slaves, stomach-turning latrines and an open sewer. The original Capitol Dome was in place - an ugly turtle shell of green copper that was widely disparaged for its lack of grace; construction on the 288-foot cast iron dome topped by the Statue of Freedom that we know today would not begin until 1859. Nearby, the party would have seen cows grazing on the Washington Mall and horse-drawn carriages skewering down muddy streets, yet none of today's familiar sights. It would be eighty-nine years before the construction of the Jefferson Memorial, and the notion of the Lincoln Memorial would have been considered laughable, since Abraham Lincoln was merely a radical and rustic young congressman from the backwater of Illinois and the Civil War was still nine years in the future. Construction of the Smithsonian Castle was almost complete, but the site of the National Archives and its Rotunda was a farm market. Much of neoclassical Washington with its wealth of monuments wasn't envisioned or built until well into the twentieth century.

For the most part, Washington City, as it was called, was a squalid town of brothels, gambling halls, cock fights, taverns and slave depots riven with muddy streets, swampy terrain, open sewers and slums. Its only businesses of note were boarding houses and the slave trade. Its unfinished roads, canals and appalling sewage problems had been neglected for decades by legislators from afar, who dragged their feet on voting to fund the city's infrastructure. When British author Anthony Trollope visited during the Civil War, he called the city "the empire of King Mud."

It wasn't all mud and squalor, however; the Treasury Building, Library of Congress and executive offices were neoclassical hints of things to come. Pennsylvania Avenue was a broad, tree-lined thoroughfare running more than a mile from the Capitol to the gleaming White House, which had been gutted by fire when British soldiers burned it in 1814. Constructed of Aquia Creek sandstone and sheathed in a brilliant whitewash, the interior of the "Presidents House" as it was called, had been rebuilt and looked much the same in 1852 as it does today. Washington also had its share of fine mansions, with some sprinkled around Capitol Hill. And for all its detractors there were also boosters. As far back as 1814, one of its few physicians, Dr. James Ewell, had compared Washington with "the noblest cities of the ancient world."

Then as now, Washington had a large black population, which included both slaves and freemen. Congressman Lincoln had introduced a bill in 1848 to abolish slavery in the District of Columbia, but it failed to pass. Slavery was a blazing issue in the halls of Congress, with many legislators carrying weapons to work and sometimes physically assaulting one-another. In 1856, U.S. Rep. Preston Brooks, a pro-slavery Democrat from South Carolina, attacked Republican Sen. Charles Sumner of Massachusetts with his walking cane in the wake of Sumner's fiery speech denouncing slavery. The savage beating drenched Sumner in his own blood and nearly killed him.

Proud of his savagery and hailed as a hero in the South, Brooks gave an account of the beating:

"I struck him with my cane and give him about 30 first-rate stripes with a gutta percha cane which had been given me a few months before... Every lick went where I intended it. For about the first five or six licks he offered to make a fight, but I plied him so rapidly that he did not touch me. Towards the last he bellowed like a calf. I wore my cane out completely but saved the Head which is gold. The fragments of the cane are begged for as sacred relics."

With legislators such as these in the U.S. Senate, what hope did the Indians have of mercy?

Added to this hostile political climate were diseases such as malaria, yellow fever and typhoid, engendered by Washington's sweltering, swampy location. Typhoid fever, caused by the contamination of food or water by sewage, would kill Lincoln's beloved twelve-year-old son, Willie, in 1862. A horde of legislators and bureaucrats fled the city en masse during the steamy summer months, returning to D.C.'s many boarding houses during more temperate weather.

One can only imagine what sensations ran through the minds of Chief Buffalo and his party as they made their way through the sweltering, muddy streets of Washington that June. But it is known that after they were refused an audience with President Fillmore, they retreated to their lodgings in despair.

Sitting down to dinner that evening under a cloud of gloom, Buffalo and his party knew that returning home empty-handed would call down the wrath of their people and a fight they couldn't hope to win. Near penniless and with their 1,200-mile mission to D.C. in a shambles, they had run out of options.

That would have been the end of things had it not been for the arrival of Whig Senator George Briggs of New York, who stopped by their inn to have his own dinner. The senator had befriended the delegation on their way east and their hearts must have lifted to see him again because he turned out to be what political fixers call an angel. Hearing their story, he invited them to take his own scheduled meeting with newly-elected President Fillmore, a fellow Whig.

Arriving at the White House, Chief Buffalo lit a long-stemmed calumet peace pipe and passed it around the room to the surprise of the President. Commissioner Lea and Secretary Stuart were also in attendance, possibly steaming that Buffalo had managed to work around them.

Buffalo had prepared a long list of grievances to present to "Great Grand Father" Fillmore, which was delivered in large part over the course of an hour by his spokesman, Oshoga. Today, it may seem appalling that the Indians referred to the likes of King George III and a succession of presidents as their "Great White Fathers," but to indigenous peoples who thought largely in familial terms this made perfect sense. Every man in a village of close-knit family ties was in a sense a brother, and every woman a sister. A headman or shaman of note had the honorific of being called a father or grandfather, and in Buffalo's case, he was simply one father speaking to another. A "father" was not the domineering boss of his "family," but rather, a guide and protector.

Employing a metaphor from nature, as was common among Indian orators, Buffalo compared his people to the "good trees" that are preserved whenever white men "begin to cut away the underbrush and bad trees... in order to make the land level and smooth so that nothing will come in contact to hurt their feet." Buffalo asked the President to allow the good trees of the Ojibwe "to stand and live in your domain." He also requested that the payment of annuities be reinstated to La Pointe.

President Fillmore had acted on behalf of a number of Indian causes and offered a sympathetic ear, but this alone didn't sway him. As it happened, he was the last Whig Party president elected to office and was well aware that many influential Whig businessmen and political allies had signed Armstrong's petition in support of the Ojibwe. After a day of consideration, Fillmore announced that he would rescind President Taylor's Order of Removal. He also promised to pay annuities that were in arrears and return the annual treaty payments to La Pointe.

Here, history gets muddy, for there is no known document rescinding the removal order. Nonetheless, it was never acted upon and there were huge celebrations once word got back to Michigan and Wisconsin that plans for the Ojibwes' removal were dead.

Two years later the U.S. Government came knocking at the Ojibwes' door once again, this time seeking the remaining land along the north shore of Lake Superior that had not yet been ceded. But having been suckered in prior negotiations the Indians were in no mood to play along. They flatly refused to sign any treaty until permanent reservations were created for Ojibwe bands ranging from Upper Michigan to Wisconsin and Minnesota.

Once again, Chief Buffalo was at the helm of treaty negotiations, raising his hand to silence a government interpreter and insisting that the Indians appoint one of their own choosing. "We do not want to be deceived any more as we have in the past," he said.

In the Treaty of La Pointe in 1854, Buffalo and the leaders of many scattered bands negotiated the establishment of eight permanent reservations in Michigan, Wisconsin and Minnesota, allowing the Ojibwe to remain in their traditional homeland. The reservations included Grand Portage, Fond du Lac, Red Cliff, Lac Courte Oreilles, Bad River, Lac Vieux Desert L'Anse, Ontonagon and Lac du Flambeau.

Under the terms of the treaty, Buffalo and forty-some Native families were evicted from Madeline Island, a home the Indians had occupied for centuries. In the tug-of-war between missionaries over the souls of Native peoples, Buffalo had joined the Catholic faith. He and other followers of the creed moved to the Red Cliff reservation on the mainland near Bayfield, Wisconsin; the Protestant faction of the island moved to the Bad River reservation near Ashland.*

---

*As if they didn't have enough troubles already, religious factionalism divided many Native bands across the country.

The following year, another eight reservations were created for the Pillager and Mississippi bands in Minnesota. Today, all of these reservations are still extant, representing a rare victory for Native peoples seeking to avoid removal to the west.

It wasn't a happy ending for everyone. It took twenty years before all of the proposed reservations were sited and surveyed. Some reservations had poor soil conditions for farming, while others had nebulous boundaries and were plundered of timber by local whites. The St. Croix and Sakaogan Ojibwe were left out of the 1854 negotiations, becoming known as the "Lost Bands" living as squatters until the Indian Reorganization Act of 1934 granted them legal title to reservation land.

Although the Ojibwe had retained something of their homeland, there was a heavy price to pay.

"On the darker side, from the Chippewa point of view, their reservations were too small to maintain a traditional hunting-fishing-gathering economy," noted author Edmund Jefferson Danziger, Jr., in his book, *The Chippewas of Lake Superior*.

"More than ever they were dependent on the white man's largesse. Their precarious economic position and confinement on reservations by 1854 also made them rather vulnerable to the BIA's program of forced acculturation... when chiefs touched their pens to the La Pointe treaty the bands began a new journey down the white man's road. For nearly a century it was a road without turning, a one-way street to cultural disintegration and crushing poverty."

As for Chief Great Buffalo - Kechewaishke Pezheke - he died September 7, 1855 of heart disease at La Pointe amid conflict over annuity payments. The Ojibwe blamed corrupt government agents and the threats of traders for the stress that led to his death at the age of ninety-five. On his deathbed he asked that his pipe and tobacco pouch be taken to Washington, D.C. as a sign of his commitment to the treaties he had negotiated. He was given a military funeral with volleys of gunfire discharged at intervals in his honor. He is buried beneath a small gravestone in the La Pointe Indian Cemetery on Madeline Island.

CHAPTER 4

WILLIAM WARREN
AND THE THREE FIRES OF
THE ANISHINAABEK

The history of the Anishinaabek - the Three Fires of the Ojibwe, Odawa and Potawatomi - was written on the lips of storytellers, passed down from one generation to the next while gathered around countless lodge fires over hundreds of years.

The tales told by Indians can seem inscrutable to those of us brought up in the traditions of Western literature. Often, there is no hero or heroine battling bad guys or overcoming challenges to save the day, as is common in English literature, but rather, a humble individual, even a fool or a demi-god trickster who succeeds by wit and kind-hearted choices, sharing what little he or she owns and doing what's right, even if it involves great peril. Sometimes the protagonist is anything but a good guy - killing a brother, for instance, over some slight or object of envy.

Few white newcomers to the Upper Great Lakes ever heard those stories or had the ability to understand them, much less the initiative to write them down. But one standout was William Whipple Warren, a young man of mixed blood who was gifted with a boundless curiosity and the talents of a journalist, ethnologist and historian.

A self-taught historian, Warren spent much of his tragically-short life collecting the stories of Ojibwe elders in the 1840s, leaving us one of the most remarkable books in all of American literature, the *History of the Ojibway People*.

It is thanks to Warren that we know of the roots of the Anishinaabek in stories passed down over hundreds of years, or as he wrote, "... the principal events which have occurred to the Ojibways within the past five centuries, as obtained from the lips of their old men and chiefs who are the repositories of the traditions of the tribe."

Warren was the son of an American fur trader and a mother of French-Ojibwe descent whose own mother was an esteemed member of the region's powerful White Crane Clan. He was born in 1825 on Madeline Island during the fractious period when the U.S. government had begun acquiring Native lands in the region. The Warren household spoke only Ojibwe, and young William heard his first stories at the knee of his mother, his Ojibwe grandmother, and her brother, Tugwaugaune, who was chief of the White Cranes.

Not for long, however, because at the age of six he was whisked off nearly four hundred miles to Mackinac Island and a succession of missionary schools where he learned to read and write English. By his early teens, Warren was enrolled at the Oneida Institute in Whitesboro, New York, studying grammar, geography, arithmetic, and even the Greek translation of Matthew's Gospel. He returned home in 1840 with his formal education completed at the age of fifteen. Two years later he found work as a translator with the Indian Affairs sub-agency at La Pointe.

Warren soon found himself with one foot in the white culture and the other among the Ojibwe, having to watch his step in both terrains. As a person of mixed blood he was considered a relative by the Ojibwe, but not a true member since blood ties were patrilineal and passed down on the father's side of the clan. Nor was he entirely accepted by white society, for Warren's trace of Ojibwe blood marked him as an Indian. Thus, Warren could neither claim to be truly an Indian or a white man.

So Warren - described by his sister as being "full of life, cheerfulness and sociability" - was a bit of a walking contradiction. He considered himself to be a white man by dint of his education, but was proud of his Ojibwe roots and was a lifelong friend, adviser and defender of the tribe.

So it was that Warren retained the support of influential chieftains, including Chief Buffalo, who was his grandmother's cousin. At a council of headmen at La Pointe in 1847, Warren announced his intention to collect stories of the Ojibwe elders, to which Buffalo gave his blessing. Buffalo's words in the self-effacing and metaphorical style of an Ojibwe orator are recounted in the introduction to Warren's book by historian and editor Theresa Schenck:

"My Grandson, you have now become as one of us, you have now arrived to the age of thinking and discretion, and can see far around you. You are able to watch and guard over the interests of your poor ignorant relatives. We have found in you a guide in our blindness, and a support to our weak and tottering footsteps.

"Since the white faces have come and resided among us our young men have become unsteady and foolish. They are fast forgetting the usages and customs of their fathers, and when the old men of the tribe who are fast falling into their graves, shall have disappeared, the traditions and customs of their fathers shall be buried with them. The ties of blood that connect

Considered a "half breed" in his day, William Warren compiled a history of the Ojibwe, including their legends and myths, while still in his twenties.

the wide spread band of the Ojibways will be forgotten... There shall be none to tell our little ones who are growing up, what our fathers have told us before they departed for the land of the Spirits."

Buffalo charged Warren with carrying on the tribe's torch with his writings.

"My Grandson, you have often asked me what I know of former times, but I did not open my heart to you, for you were then a child. You are now a man, you know how to write like the whites, you understand what we tell you. Your ears are open to our words and we will tell you what we know of former times. You shall write it on paper that our words may last forever."

Warren's book took a circuitous route to publication. In the late 1840s, Henry Schoolcraft, an ethnologist and former superintendent of Indian Affairs in Michigan, was enlisted by Congress to write a compendium of the nation's Indian tribes. Schoolcraft devised 347 questions entitled "Inquiries Respecting the History, Present Condition, and Future Prospects of the Indian Tribes of the United States." The questionnaire was the basis of Schoolcraft's six-volume study of the Indians. It was sent to Indian agents, missionaries, traders and Native spokesmen across the country, including to Henry Rice, a fur trader at Crow Lake in the Minnesota Territory. Rice, in turn, passed it on to his clerk, twenty-three-year-old Warren, who had already begun collecting the lore and history of the Ojibwe.

Warren took to his task like a duck to water, interviewing Ojibwe elders and filling in the blanks with stories told by his own family and friends. Rice was so impressed with his report that he passed it on to the *Minnesota Pioneer*, one of the territory's leading newspapers, which serialized his unedited findings. To Warren's surprise he found himself as a burgeoning author after newspaper editor D.A. Robertson urged him to write a book.

Frequently redundant, in need of trimming and criticized by Native and non-Native readers alike, Warren's book nonetheless shows respect for the Ojibwe's oral tradition and offers insights into their history as told by those who lived it. Its merits include an economy of prose, skirting the florid style of writing in the 1800s, and here and there a touch of skepticism that makes for a good journalist. Within its pages we find stories of the Great Walk of the Anishinaabek from the Atlantic seaboard to the Upper Great Lakes over the course of centuries, along with accounts of warfare with other tribes met along the way. There are tales of supernatural beings and the rituals of the *Mide-wi-win* shamans of the Ojibwe (literally, "the good-hearted ones"). It is also thanks to Warren that we have a deeper understanding of the clan and its role in Anishinaabek society. Imperfect though it may be, as source material little comes close to Warren's research.

One must also credit Warren for his diligence as an historian in that he recognized that the spinners of Indian tales often changed or embellished them from one generation to the next. At times Warren found the contradictions and fractured recollections of Ojibwe tale-tellers to be "a mess of nonsense." Thus, he took care to corroborate the accounts of elders with those of others to make his reporting as accurate as possible.

He also acknowledged his own shortcomings as an historian. Living in what was still a wilderness at the west end of Lake Superior where books were rarities, Warren wrote that he regretted being unable to compare his notes with other historical documents. He also noted that the Indians tended to be haphazard on chronological events, making it difficult to ascertain exactly when a battle or a migration occurred. He did the best he could with his own calculations of what constituted a generation among the Ojibwe.

Of note, there are a number of groaners in Warren's book, owing to the religio-pseudoscience of his time. Theories of evolution were being discussed in scientific circles, but it wasn't until 1859 that Charles Darwin published *The Origin of the Species*. Thus, Warren lived at a time in which many educated persons believed that Adam and Eve were the first humans and that the earth was only six thousand years old. And, at a time dominated by white supremacy, Warren subscribed to the belief that the various races of humankind sprang from separate origins around the planet. Some of this crept into his work, such as his speculation that the Ojibwe might be the enlightened Hebrew remnants of the Lost Tribe of Israel, while the Dakota Sioux more likely sprang from savage tribes out of Asia. Elsewhere, he refers to the Ojibwe as "simple children of nature" and the warriors of Pontiac's rebellion as "misguided savages."

On the other hand, he also defended the rites of the *Mide-wi-win* shamans from ridicule, pointing out that Catholic rituals seemed just as preposterous when the tables were turned.

Despite his youth, Warren had a number of accomplishments in his twenties beyond his work as a translator and historian. In 1850 he served as a legislator in the Minnesota Territory's House of Representatives. He was also enlisted by Indian Affairs subagent John Watrous to serve as a go-between during the disastrous events of 1850, when the government sought to remove the Ojibwe to the Mississippi.

In fact, Warren had been at Sandy Lake in October, 1850, staying there for two months as an interpreter. "I was witness to all the hunger, sickness and cold that they endured," he wrote. Warren claimed that Governor Ramsey had done all in his power to see that good provisions were sent to the Indians, but was stymied at every turn by traders seeking profit.

It was Warren who blamed the region's contractors and traders for the disaster, writing that they had swapped out good flour for bad from the Winnebago Agency to the south in order to glean a profit.

The region's traders attacked Warren's credibility at every opportunity, dividing the Ojibwe against him while attempting to bribe or corrupt him to no avail. He in turn had nothing but contempt for "these same contractors that have persecuted me for the past several years, because I would not be their tool and slave... They are, and always have been since they came into the country, the worst enemies the Chippewas have ever been cursed with."

Warren felt that the Ojibwe would indeed by better off moving west of the Mississippi to escape the negative influences of white society.

"It was his dream at this time to unify the Ojibwe into one strong tribe that could present a united front to the U.S. government," wrote historian Schenck, "but his efforts brought him into conflict with all the agents of the removal. When it was seen that the Ojibwe would not leave their lands, he was blamed for the failure of the removal."

This incurred the wrath of bureaucrats and businessmen in St. Paul, and even a close missionary friend turned against him. The 1851 uproar in the Minnesota press intensified a case of consumption (tuberculosis) which Warren had contracted five years earlier. Adding to his troubles was a battle with the Office of Indian Affairs to receive payment for his services.

Broke, bed-bound, and propped up on pillows, Warren struggled to complete his book as his body slowly ebbed away. We can imagine him gazing out the window of his home overlooking the Mississippi in St. Paul, coughing blood into a rag as he transcribed a hodge-podge of tales recounted by some of the most important chiefs and elders of his day. Sadly, his book remained unfinished. He managed to travel to New York and Chicago in search of a publisher over the next two years but was too weakened by illness to follow through; nor could he afford the $350 to print one thousand copies. Finally, he entrusted his manuscript to a businessman in

New York who had connections in the publishing world, asking only for one hundred copies as payment should he choose to pay for its publication. Barely twenty-eight years old, Warren died of his hemorrhaging lungs at his sister's home in St. Paul on the morning of June 1, 1853.

Thereafter, Warren's manuscript was passed on by friends and supporters who recognized its value. It was published in 1885 by the Minnesota Historical Society, thirty-two years after his death.

Let us look now over the shoulder of William Warren and hear the words of the Ojibwe elders, shamans and leaders. His sources included chieftains Buffalo, Flat Mouth, White Fisher, Hole-in-the Day-and his grandmother, Madeline Cadotte, for whom Madeline Island was named in 1828.

First, consider the term Anishinaabek. This is the plural form of "the true people" or "the original people," while to be Anishinaabe is to be an individual of the people. Thus, Chief Buffalo was Anishinaabe and he was of the Anishinaabek.

Warren believed that the Anishinaabek had no creation myth; no Yahweh breathing life into a man made of mud and then plucking a rib to create the first woman, or any of a thousand other creation myths dreamt up by the world's religions. He wrote that Anishinaabek meant "the spontaneous people," in that they had simply appeared out of nowhere. Schoolcraft believed that Anishinaabek meant "the common people," which Warren thought was belittling.

Whatever the case, primitive peoples around the world have generally called themselves some form of "the people" or "the human beings," as opposed to troublesome *Others* who lived over yonder. The Beothuk of Newfoundland, the Inuits of the Arctic and various tribes in the Southwestern U.S., among others, also called themselves "the people," while the Cherokee called themselves the Aniyuniwiya, which means the "real people." Yanomami means "human beings" in the language of the South American tribe, while the Hebrew tribesmen of ancient Israel famously called themselves "the chosen people." Add to this, familiar places that every village member knew were often known simply as "the big lake," "the long river" or "the lake with many reeds."

While there was no sort of Adam and Eve myth about the creation of the Anishinaabek, there are stories about the creation of the world.

Consider that science tells us that our own universe of trillions of galaxies containing trillions upon trillions of stars emerged from a space fall smaller than an atom under immense pressure and trillions of degrees of heat in the Big Bang explosion fourteen billion years ago. The Anishinaabek creation myth is no less astonishing. A much condensed version is as follows:

Long ago when there lived only spirits dwelling in the fog of time, the plants, animals and human beings were without form and had not yet come into existence, nor even the earth itself; and yet there appeared an old woman and her daughter.

One day the daughter felt the brush of a passing wind and soon found herself impregnated by a being that could only have been the Sun. She gave birth to Manabozhoo, the "first man" and the great uncle of the Anishinaabek, who was to guide them through all their troubles. A demigod in the mode of Hercules, a shape-shifter and trickster, Manabozhoo was a powerful spirit who had two bothersome brothers. These he killed in order to roam free, yet one of them, who had been born a rock, remained to create the spirit road to the afterlife, a one-way path that all living things would eventually travel.

As for Manabozhoo, he wandered off on many adventures, in time killing some nasty underworld spirits in the form of giant snakes. In revenge, the snake spirits flooded the world, forcing Manabozhoo to seek refuge at the top of the tallest pine tree on the tallest mountain that remained. There, the demigod begged an otter, a beaver and a muskrat to swim to the bottom of the drowned world to bring back a bit of earth. Only the humble muskrat succeeded, extending a paw filled with soil from which the earth was created with all of its mountains, plains, rivers and forests.

Taking a hand in all of this was the Great Spirit Kitchi Manito who helped shape the earth, the underworld, the sky and the realm of stars. Kitchi Manito is not a god in the Christian sense, but rather the "Master of Life" who oversees the affairs of an infinite number of the spirits. These spirits and their powerful *manito* cohorts created everything that Manabozhoo needed to live on earth.

Unexplained is how the spirits or Kitchi Manito created human beings, which was possibly the rub for Warren. At any rate, the spirits were quite busy thereafter, aiding and guiding the Anishinaabek, who, according to their oral history, were living along the Atlantic seaboard - perhaps on the Gulf of St. Lawrence - when the first clans of their people were created.

In this legend passed on to Warren, six radiant beings arose from Zhewita-ganibi - the Atlantic Ocean - entering a large town of the Anishinaabek. The gaze of one of the spirits was so powerful that a single glance from him resulted in the death of a passerby, "who instantly fell dead as if struck by one of the thunderers." Being too dangerous to be countenanced, his fellow spirits asked him to return to the depths of the ocean, which he good-naturedly obliged.

Thereafter, the five remaining spirits established the first five clans of the Anishinaabek. In time there would be at least thirty.

According to their traditions, sometime during the 1300s-1400s the Anishinaabek were induced to move west from the Atlantic Ocean on what was called "The Great Walk." Legend holds that prior to heading west the Anishinaabek lived in a large town that was so big that one standing on a hill at its center could not see the end of it.

We know of this migration thanks to pictographic records made on birch bark scrolls, the most famous of which is the 2.6-meter Red Sky Migration Chart created in 1960 by Eshkwaykeeshik (James Red Sky), one of the last Ojibwe shamans.

The chart depicts the Anishinaabek journeying from a sort of dream time along the Atlantic Ocean down the St. Lawrence Seaway to sites including Montreal, Niagara Falls, Detroit, the French River, Sault Ste. Marie, Chequamegon Bay, and wrapping up at Leech Lake, Minnesota, fulfilling a prophecy of reaching a place where "food grows on the water," in this case the staple of wild rice.

Warren overheard details of this journey while eavesdropping on a ceremony at the Great Medicine Lodge of the *Mide-wi-win*. This was an annual ceremony held in a temporary structure of bent trees walled by pine boughs measuring one hundred feet long and fifteen feet wide. Inductees into the *Mide-wi-win* gathered each year to hear what the shamans had to say.

Not understanding what he had heard, Warren approached a shaman the next day and asked him to explain. The shaman told of a time when the Anishinaabek were guided by the appearance of a huge, radiant cowrie shell (*megis*) that rose into the sky from the Atlantic and appeared thereafter whenever the tribe was imperiled by disease or warfare. These star-like shells prompted the shamans to move their Great Medicine Lodge to the west at every occurrence, with the Anishinaabek following suit.

No surprise, a brilliant celestial object guiding the way is a staple of many religions, including of course, the Star of Bethlehem.

Another story related by Warren is that a grand council was held when the Anishinaabek reached "the Third Stopping Place" near either present-day Detroit or the Mackinac Straits, with a decision made to divide their numbers into the Three Fires of the Ojibwe, Odawa and Potawatomi, who then scattered to the winds. (Elsewhere, the Anishinaabek are described as an alliance of three Algonquian tribes, and not a division,)

Prior to the arrival of the Europeans, the Anishinaabek didn't think of themselves as members of separate tribes constituting political, social and military units. Rather, they were simply "the people," identifying with their clan and the name of their band or village, such as the "people of the reed lake" or the "people of the big island." At best they thought in tribal terms when referring to their enemies or trading partners. The Odawa, for instance, would have recognized the Hurons as a distinct tribe with which they traded, whereas they disdained the Sioux and the Iroquois as being "snakes."

The division of the Anishinaabek into three distinct tribes was possibly the outcome of a catastrophic event. In his book, *Rites of Conquest*, anthropologist and historian Charles Cleland speculates that when bands of the Anishinaabek were driven to Green Bay on the western shore of Lake Michigan by Iroquois invaders in the mid-1600s, they found themselves strangers in a strange land, mixed in with the refugees of many other Native peoples. "People began to come together out of necessity to stay alive... Anishinaabeg bands independent and self-sufficient before the appearance of Europeans were fragmented and dispersed, but the surviving individuals, families, and sometimes larger groups were metamorphosed into the more inclusive social units that we now know as the Ottawa, Ojibwe and Potawatomi tribes... united by new social institutions and some measure of political integrity."

The Potawatomi settled in northern Indiana and southern Michigan where they farmed the "three sisters" of maize, beans, and squash or pumpkins. Slash-and-burn agriculture wasn't pretty, but it was effective. After burning a grove of girdled trees - which enriched the soil with potash and provided future firewood - corn, beans, squash and pumpkins were planted amid the charred, limbless timber. The corn provided a stalk for the beans to grow and the squash or pumpkins provided a leafy mulch to keep the ground moist for the corn. This symbiosis resulted in larger crop yields than was produced by European plowing methods and required less care in the way of cultivation and weed control.

The Odawa settled around the Mackinac Straits and at the northern end of Lake Huron on Manitoulin Island, Bois Blanc Island and thereabouts. Like the Potawatomi, they too had swidden gardens to supplement their diet. Like the Iroquois and Hurons, they lived primarily in their own form of longhouses with several families living within a bark lodge.

Odawa is synonymous with the term, "trader," and the tribe became the mariners of the Great Lakes. Their birch bark canoes were thirty feet or more in length, carrying up to eight thousand pounds of crew and cargo. They were the only tribe on the Great Lakes known to paddle beyond sight of the shore. One of their trade routes ventured from Escanaba in Michigan's Upper Peninsula down the Beaver Island Archipelago of islands in Lake Michigan to the southern mainland.

When the French arrived in the early 1600s, followed by the English in the 1700s, the Odawa quickly assumed the role of go-betweens as traders with more distant tribes. The Odawa played the English and French against one-another, juggling the balance of power on the Upper Great Lakes to their own advantage.

The Ojibwe established themselves at Boweting near present-day Sault Ste. Marie, with a number of bands edging west thereafter. They had a seasonal community spread for miles along the rapids of the St. Mary's River, harvesting whitefish with nets and spears. The fish was smoked and dried on racks by the shore, then packed away as provisions to get through the winter.

Although Boweting was not a town as we know it, the temporary villages along the river swelled to a gathering of thousands when the Ojibwe, Odawa and other friendly tribes were stockpiling fish. Given the worldwide tendency of indigenous peoples to hold festivals through every season of the year, the annual fish-gathering at Boweting may have been a time of celebration, perhaps with the inclusion of sporting events, shamanic ceremonies, theater, drumming, dancing, foot races, gambling, and the seeking of brides and grooms from visiting clans.

Warren wrote that the Ojibwe kept moving west well into the 1700s, migrating all the way to Minnesota where "food grew on the water." According to the legends, they displaced the Fox tribe in Michigan's Upper Peninsula and then the woodland Sioux of northern Wisconsin and Minnesota as they pushed on.

Warren's *History of the Ojibway People*, has been criticized for delving too much into the battles between the Ojibwe, the Fox, and the Sioux, but he had hoped to write more about their legends and customs before his untimely death. He wrote that a more peaceful branch of the Ojibwe established themselves north of Lake Superior, where there were few enemies to contend with. They were scorned by their more warlike cousins as bring *waabooz*, rabbits.

CHAPTER 5

CHIEF OSHKOSH
& THE MENOMINEE

Any discussion of the Ojibwe, Fox and Sioux in the lands west of Lake Michigan warrants mention of the Menominee tribe, which occupied central Wisconsin.

The Menominee were survivors, hemmed in by the Ojibwe and Dakota Sioux to the north and the Ho-Chunk, Sauk, and Fox tribes to the south and west. They lived in territory that ranged from Green Bay to beyond Lake Winnebago that was eyed by white settlers for its pine forests and farmland.

Their defender was Chief Oshkosh - Claw - who is revered to this day in Wisconsin.

Seeking to transplant the Oneida, Stockbridge and Munsee tribes from New York and Massachusetts to Wisconsin in 1827, Michigan Territorial Governor Lewis Cass lamented that there was no one among the Menominee who could speak for the tribe. "...like a flock of geese without a leader, some fly one way and some another," he complained.

One man noted for his oratory and decisiveness stood out in the negotiations, however, and thus Oshkosh was designated as the principal leader of the Menominee to negotiate with the Federal Government.

Over the course of nearly thirty years, Oshkosh would preside over the cession of ten million acres to the U.S. government. As with Chief Buffalo of the Ojibwe, he traveled to Washington D.C. in 1850 to meet with President Millard Fillmore to argue against moving the Menominee people to reservations beyond the Mississippi. Fillmore acquiesced and in 1854 the Wolf River Treaty created the 250,000-acre Menominee Indian Reservation just west of Green Bay.

But Oshkosh had also had a brush with controversy in the 1830 killing of O-ke-wa, the Pawnee slave of a *métis* ("half-breed") family living at Green Bay. O-ke-wa was stabbed to death by Oshkosh and two other men after killing a member of the Menominee in a hunting accident. While hunting in a marshy area near Green Bay, O-ke-wa had shot at what he thought was a deer wandering through some reeds alongside a creek. Discovering that

A drawing made from a daguerreotype of Chief Oshkosh in the 1850s. The image was appropriated by the Oshkosh Brewing company in the 1880s for marketing purposes.

he had killed a man, he took the body to Oshkosh in his canoe, only to suffer summary judgment and execution. In the resulting trial Oshkosh and the others were acquitted on the grounds that they had simply followed their own tribal law, which held that a slave could be killed for causing the death of anyone of the Menominee, even if by accident. Territorial Judge James Doty declined to meddle with tribal justice.

Oshkosh was no stranger to violence. As a young warrior he had sided with the British during the War of 1812 and took part in sieges and battles at Fort Meigs and Fort Stephenson in Ohio, and at Mackinac Island. In 1832 he signed on with three hundred Native troops allied with the U.S. Army, battling the Fox and Sauk in Black Hawk's War. That last bit underscores the fact that over the course of U.S. history, more Indians have fought as members of the U.S. armed forces than were ever killed by the same.

Much given to strong drink, Oshkosh was killed by two of his sons in a drunken brawl at Keshena, Wisconsin on August 31, 1858. It is believed that his remains are interred beneath a monument erected in his honor in the city that bears his name, though no one is quite sure that the chief's body is really there. In 1926, members of the Menominee claimed that his body had been switched out with that of another, and that the chief's corpse was still tucked away on the reservation he helped to create.

Book Two
From the Beginning

CHAPTER 6

THE FIRST PEOPLE

The first humans to visit the upper Midwest may have walked across lands which are now deep under water, perhaps on a high summer day up to thirteen thousand years ago. These would have been hunter-gatherers in search of caribou and other game, moving north up the shores of what were then the much-smaller Great Lakes.

Exactly how long ago humans visited the Upper Great Lakes is sketchy. Archeological sites with evidence of human visitors have ranged from 9,000-13,000 years. Some, perhaps, arrived when there were still mastodons wandering the tundra in the shadow of the region's retreating glaciers.

Today, we know from DNA samples and dental morphology that Indians are the ancestors of a people who lived in northeastern Asia, with the closest match being those living in the Altai Mountains of Siberia. Sometime perhaps 30,000 years ago, bands of these Asiatic people began journeying to North America by way of the Bering Land Bridge, which had been created by declining sea levels.

"How large this population was is a matter of debate and guesswork, with figures ranging from a mere seventy individuals to between 1,000 and 5,400 people," notes author Brian Fagan in *The First North Americans*.

Reaching present-day Alaska, these Stone Age emigrants wandered south, either via an ice-free corridor through glacial canyons, or perhaps by traveling down the Pacific coast in skin boats, or by walking along the shore. By fifteen thousand years ago, the newcomers had journeyed ten thousand miles to southern Chile.

The story of the Indians in the Midwest begins at the end of the last Ice Age, known as the Wisconsin Period. By then, the vast glaciers were retreating north after blanketing the land under more than a mile of ice off and on for nearly two million years. As the glaciers retreated, the land rippled and heaved under their weight, creating fluctuations in the depths of Lake Michigan and Lake Huron as roaring river channels to the far-off ocean came and went.

Ten thousand years ago, a lobe of the retreating glaciers carved a channel in present-day Ontario, extending to the St. Lawrence Seaway and creating a rapid drop in the level of Lake Michigan. Through the centuries, the lake levels fell as much as 180 feet lower than today, exposing millions of acres of boggy land. Even the five-mile-wide Mackinac Strait disappeared, replaced by the ancient and long-lost Mackinac River, the bed of which now lies deep under water at the bottom of the strait.

At its lowest ebb, Lake Michigan was reduced to half its size and divided into two lakes that drained through the Mackinac River. Lake Huron fell even further and was divided into three lakes. This was known as the Chippewa Phase in the development of the Great Lakes, a period of lower lake levels that stayed put for four thousand years.

Even today, the north end of Lake Michigan is shallow in depth; the present-day shoals running from Beaver Island to Waugoshance Point on the mainland are only about twelve feet deep on the average. At the end of the last Ice Age, the island was part of the mainland and appeared as a hill rising above marshland that was yet to be flooded by glacial runoff.

Indulge a Micheneresque fantasy and imagine a small band of travelers wandering along the lakeshore. Red Wing is their leader. He heads a band of twenty-six followers by dint of his charisma and initiative. A fight over a woman caused him to split from his father's band, and being younger and a more able hunter, he attracted followers. He and his people are Paleoindians who roamed North America in small bands for thousands of years as hunter-gatherers, almost continually on the move.

We might imagine their lives: Red Wing is a seasoned man of twenty-eight years and has two wives, Otter and Tall Grass, along with their three children. Otter was the first woman he took to, but he inherited Tall Grass following the death of his brother who died of his injuries after breaking his arm. Their faces are dark, Asiatic, burnished by the sun and wind.

Red Wing and his band have come from the south following the tracks of animals along the shoreline of Lake Michigan. Perhaps the sighting of a comet, an eclipse, or some other celestial event also influenced their journey to the north. They move every three-to-six days in an eternal quest for food. In a year's time, they might wander 220 miles or so.

Of course, it's one thing to wander the environs of the Great Lakes during high summer and quite another during the icy rains of spring and fall, not to mention the five months of darkness, snow and freezing temperatures of winter. Thus, although the Paleoindians are widely considered by anthropologists to have been highly mobile, they also established camps along rivers and lakes where fish, game and edible plants were abundant, huddling up during times of harsh weather in huts fashioned from animal hides and bark.

Red Wing and his band are a robust people, "ripped" by today's standards thanks to a diet which consists largely of edible plants, roots and nuts along with lean meat and fish. They know nothing of sugar or sweets, save for that derived from berries; it will be thousands of years before honey bees are introduced to North America by Europeans. The fat they consume comes largely from water fowl, fish, and marrow from the bones of animals. They have a "heart-healthy" diet, but this was of little benefit at a time when life-expectancy was in one's forties.

The Paleoindians began probing north out of Ohio as early as twelve thousand years ago as the vast glaciers retreated. The ancestors of Red Wing and his people would have been the last humans to have to have seen mastodons, mammoths, dire wolves and the short-faced bear. Red Wing's ancestors would have hunted the likes of the giant beaver, which measured six feet in length and weighed 275 pounds; the giant ground sloth, which measured up to twenty feet from tip to tail; and the stag moose, which stood six feet tall at the shoulder and had a candelabra of antlers that spread just as far. Known as megafauna, these animals went extinct some 10,000-12,000 years ago, possibly as a result of a colder and dryer era of climate change that eliminated their food sources. Their demise may have been hastened by the over-hunting of human predators.

No human remains of the Paleoindians have been found in the region of the Great Lakes, but this is not unusual, since very few remains have been found anywhere in North America. Nor do we have evidence of their hunting the megafauna of the Ice Age. Roughly three hundred mastodon skeletons have been unearthed in Michigan, yet archeologists have yet to find any spear points or markings on their bones to indicate that they were hunted in the Upper Midwest. With the passing of the megafauna, the people of what is known as the Early Archaic era were in pursuit of smaller game, in this case, herds of migrating caribou, along with the deer, elk, bison and the small mammals which occupy Michigan today.

Red Wing and the six men of his band carry only spears and clubs, since the bow & arrow was unknown to native peoples in subarctic North America until its introduction around 500 A.D. They are likely equipped with atladls, a spear-chucking stick with a notch on its end that whips a chert-tipped bolt forward with greater force than a man can throw freehand. In addition to their weapons, a brace of dogs surrounds the band as they move forward, aiding in the hunt and warning of intruders. The dogs are descendants of a long-extinct breed of prehistoric wolves, which were also the ancestors of modern wolves.

Their fluted spearheads and knives are created by a process called knapping, in which a hammer stone is used to create a rough shape from a piece of flint or chert, refining the blade with the flaking pressure of an antler, a length of hardwood, or a bone. They also likely have rudimentary sleds, snowshoes, deadfall traps and snares at their disposal.

At times the earth shakes with the thunder of thousands of caribou streaming by in their seasonal migrations; the band would also witness flocks of millions of birds flowing in a dark river across the sky for days on end.

But for the most part theirs is a silent world. Today, our lives are filled with so much noise that we've grown oblivious to it. The hum of a refrigerator, whir of an air conditioner, rush of a furnace, gurgle of a water heater, buzz of fluorescent bulbs, tick of our clocks, airplanes overhead and the rumble of traffic a block away, not to mention the TV, radio and incessant beep of those sending texts. We block out these and other noises as a matter of course. But in Red Wing's world there was only the sound of wind in the trees, the waves breaking on the shore and the cries of passing loons, crows, or a flock of geese. At night, they drum and sing, raising their voices in solidarity to break the deathly silence and show that they are not alone in this world. They have each other.

It would be a mistake to romanticize these people, however, whose lives were guided by the harsh realities of survival. What might they do with a deformed newborn, for instance? Or an elder who can no longer walk? What would they do with twins if there is only milk enough for one in a gaunt mother's breasts?

There are fewer men than women in Red Wing's band because, as remains the case in primitive societies today, this was a time of considerable violence. It's estimated that 15 percent of Paleoindians died at the hands of other men, compared to just 0.33 percent of people living worldwide today. Men were also prone to fatal accidents while hunting, sometimes being gored or trampled by their prey. And, as in the case with Red Wing's brother, a simple slip and fall on rocky ground or a patch of ice could be fatal at a time when there were no orthopedic surgeons or trauma centers on hand to repair a broken bone. A compound fracture was a death sentence, and a slow painful one at that. At times Red Wing may have had the unpleasant task of easing a hopeless band member into the afterlife by opening his or her veins.

Nor was this an easy time for women. Fossil evidence reveals that Paleoindian women were often mistreated and malnourished, perhaps being the last to be fed. When they were on the move, women had to carry their children until they reached the age of five.

Did Otter and Tall Grass love their mate? Love is universal and timeless, yet perhaps theirs was a more practical experience. Men and women were utterly dependent on each other for survival. Red Wing could no more live without a woman to tan and sew his leathers in addition to foraging for firewood, roots and edible plants than they could survive without him providing protection and the meat they prepared. And if he shared the same traits as latter-day Indians, then he would surely have died protecting his wives and children if called upon to do so.

Assuming that they shared the same habits of Stone Age peoples discovered within the past century in New Guinea and the Amazon, then everything in Red Wing's band is shared from birth to death, and every kill is prayed over and celebrated, giving thanks to the creature that gave its life so the band might survive. Stories, then as now, were important to them, including tales of supernatural beings, clever animals and great deeds. Perhaps they told stories of the animals their ancestors had known, with visions of mastodons and dire wolves passed down from one generation to another.

Little is known of the language that Red Wing and his people spoke. Amerind is the language which linguists have assigned to the Paleoindians, but there is widespread debate as to its geographic range and what it might have entailed, considering the hundreds of native languages which blossomed across the Americas thereafter. Over the course of thousands of years, the Algonquian, Iroquoian, Muskogean, Caddoan, Siouan and other language groups emerged as roving bands coalesced into tribes of people united by linguistics and settled by agriculture. But that was millennia to come after what was known as the Early Archaic period.

Judging by the few grave sites that have been found in southern California and the Andes, the Paleoindians had a sense of spirituality and a belief in the afterlife. Like the Indians who came after them, they may have taken their names from animals or places they inhabited. The petroglyphs they left behind tell us that they had an interest in art, and thus likely a sense of fashion and personal adornment.

Red Wing and his band keep to the coast because inland Michigan is still largely tundra and a boreal taiga of pines, cedars and spruce with little game. It will be another five thousand years or so before hardwood trees take root inland during a warming period from 6000-3000 B.C. This results in the mix of deciduous and coniferous trees that are common in the Midwest today, providing Native peoples with tons of nuts and acorns that were essential for surviving the winter.

Although no remains of Paleoindians have ever been found in the Midwest, we know that there were people living here, perhaps living in small settlements along the shores of the Great Lakes.

This, because in 2014, researchers from the University of Michigan discovered the remains of a nine-thousand-year-old V-shaped trap of stones arranged for hunting caribou. Called a drive lane, the trap was found 121 feet underwater in Lake Huron, about thirty-five miles south of present-day Alpena.

The site is located on what was once a bridge of dry land, called the Alpena-Amberley Ridge, which crossed Lake Huron nine thousand years ago when the lake was at its low ebb. Two parallel lines of rock-lined paths were found underwater, flanked by hunting blinds made of stone.

Herds of thousands of caribou were abundant in the ancient Midwest and communal hunting was the norm, with groups of men ambushing the herds during their fall migration to the south and then again during the spring as the caribou headed north to a cooler climate.

Imagine a line of thousands of caribou making their way north to where Red Wing's men lay hidden. Some are disguised as caribou themselves, cloaked in hides with their heads crowned with antlers. The herd funnels into the rock channel and as it narrows to twenty-five feet in width the boys of the band arise from the caribous' flanks with shrill cries and noisemakers. Panicked, the herd surges forward, with one animal collapsing in a tangle upon another as the hunters rise from behind their stone blinds to kill and kill again with spears, stones and clubs as the bucking, bleating animals rear and die.

From the encampment over a low rise come shrieks of joy as women and children pour down the hill to join in the butchering and celebration. That night brings dancing and feasting along with sacrifices to the spirits who smiled on the hunt. Days will be spent butchering the prey and hanging the meat to dry amid a blizzard of flies and the heavy stench of blood. Grimed up to their armpits in viscera and blood, the women of the band work half-naked, scraping the interior of the hides with tools of flint or chert. A mash of caribou brains and urine will be used to scrub the hides, making them soft and pliable for clothing.

Beyond the butchering circle a ring of wolves, coyotes, buzzards and eagles wait to scavenge their share. Perhaps a panther lolls on a nearby hill, content to watch the apex predators of the human race at work until it, too, can creep forward for a mouthful of entrails.

But the waiting scavengers may have found little to eat, because as with latter-day Indians who utilized every conceivable part of the buffalo, the Paleoindians would likely have done the same with the organs, intestines, antlers, hooves and hides of their prey. Caribou hides were especially useful for clothing and for constructing cords and tents. Lightweight, waterproof caribou hides have been shown to protect against temperatures of minus-55 degrees Fahrenheit thanks to their double layer of fur. A dense under-fur traps air beneath a thick guard layer of semi-hollow fur. This combination provided super-insulated clothing for those living in the Stone Age; even today, caribou garments are still preferred by indigenous hunters in the Arctic.

It's believed that there may be the remains of Neolithic villages and campsites all along the ancient coastlines of Lake Michigan and Lake Huron, but these lie underwater, miles out in the lake. Perhaps someday, scuba-diving archeologists using remotely-operated underwater cameras will find these settlements in the same manner that they found the caribou ambush site on Lake Huron.

Evidence of an ancient campsite was discovered in 2008 when amateur researcher Thomas Talbot found what is called a Clovis spear point while searching for arrowheads in a field at the Belson family farm in southwestern Michigan. The spear point was left by a Paleoindian band that roamed a small, ice-free zone of southwestern Michigan up to thirteen thousand years ago. This would have been a time when there were still mastodons, saber tooth tigers and other megafauna roaming the Midwest and larger spear points were needed for hunting.

Clovis spear points have a distinctive shape with a fluted channel carved down the middle of a length of chert, after which large flakes of the stone were knapped outward on either side, resulting in a razor-sharp weapon. This was a passing style of spear point construction which may have lasted only seven hundred years from 13,500 to 12,800 years ago, yet Clovis points have been found throughout much of North America, indicating that there may have been extensive trade routes or a sharing of Stone Age technology among Paleoindians that ranged across the continent. Spear points at the Belson site were made of Attica chert from a source more than 150 miles to the southwest.

Talbot thought his spearhead was a "once-in-a-lifetime find," but later that spring he found a number of other Clovis fragments, indicating that the field had once been the site of a Paleoindian camp. Eventually, he and a team of University of Michigan archeologists found more than twenty Clovis-era tools along with hundreds of other artifacts and debris at what became known as the Belson Clovis Site in St. Joseph County. With the bulk of Michigan still covered with glacial ice, this small, triangular section of dry land in the southwestern part of the state was the only habitable area along the coast of Lake Michigan during the late Ice Age.

In a paper published in the journal *PaleoAmerica*, researchers from the University of Michigan speculated that the campsite may have been occupied by no more than six or seven people along a bygone river. In addition to hunting caribou, these people may have survived as scavengers by driving saber tooth tigers and cave bears off their kills.

Red Wing and his band have such weapons, knapped over the long winter by the fireside as they share their stories, drum and sing. That spring, they wander north across the sandy plains and taiga along the lakeshore, an unknown people buried eons before written history. If they or people like them ever wandered the shores of Lake Michigan and Lake Huron, then the evidence of them is likely to be found deep under water.

Millennia passed as bands of Paleoindians coalesced into tribes, settlements, and eventually, civilizations. It was Native women who made this progress possible with the development of agriculture and the resulting establishment of farming villages and towns.

Women the world over are thought to have invented agriculture. Over the course of thousands of years in their role as foragers of edible plants and roots, women observed the value of propagation and grouping plants together. Camping along rich bottomlands, the vegetation of which attracted deer and other game, women became aware of groupings of edible plants. Gradually, they took to watering beneficial plants and clearing away weeds. "This simple process of encouraging, intervening, and deliberately planting harvested seeds, even on a small scale, marked the beginnings of deliberate cultivation," notes anthropologist Brian Fagan in *The First North Americans*.

Women also cultivated or knew of such plants as soapweed, which has detergent properties and can be used to kill fish; snowberry and willow bark for their medicinal properties; buckthorn vine for basket-weaving; cedar for insecticide, and many other useful herbs and plants.

Maize, the ancestor of modern corn, evolved from a tropical grass, *Balsas teosinte*, in central Mexico between 8,000 and 6,000 B.C. Its cultivation spread by 5,000 B.C. among foragers as a supplemental food source.

The mystery of how Native women discovered corn (which must be planted by human hands in soil that has been disturbed) and how it evolved from a weedy grass with few sickly kernels to the robust feeder of nations has never been solved, yet this is one of women's greatest gifts to humankind. Female agriculturalists also raised sunflower and now-forgotten crops of sumpweed, maygrass, knotweed and little barley.

Men in Asia, Europe and African morphed into herders based on their experience as hunters over thousands of years. Rather than attempting the mostly futile task of domesticating herds of caribou, buffalo, deer or elk, the Indians created game parks for ease of hunting. By one estimate, the game parks and farm acreage created in North America prior to the arrival of Europeans collectively encompassed an area the size of France.

Old-growth forests offer little forage for herbivores and the predators that follow them. Thus, as with the aborigines of Australia, the Indians of North America employed the judicious use of fire to create meadows, providing forage for wildlife along with easy hunting.

When the first expeditions of Spanish conquistadors and English colonists arrived in North America they were astounded to find park-like settings wherever they wandered. The "New World" was a land brimming with Native villages, carefully tended orchards and nut groves, thousands of acres of farmlands, hundreds of miles of trails and trading routes in every direction, monumental earthworks and game parks. European explorers couldn't believe their good fortune, reporting home of this ready-made Eden. Yet, as we shall see, within one hundred years of first contact between Native peoples and Europeans, much of this paradise was despoiled by the introduction of diseases such as smallpox and the resulting collapse of Native civilizations.

CHAPTER 7

THE COPPER AGE

Sometime around 200 B.C., a group of travelers gathered around a fire on Beaver Island, cooking their daily meal on a bluff overlooking Lake Michigan. The heat of the blaze cracked the rocks in their fire ring, leaving evidence of their visit twenty-two centuries later. Archeologists assume that theirs was a brief visit, since there is no sign of a nearby settlement.

What did they talk about around their fire? The animals they hunted, the women (or men) they lusted after, band politics, the weather. The outcome of a *baggitaywe* game played far to the north. The same things people talk about today.

By then, the diminished Ice Age levels of the lake had long since risen, obliterating the land bridge to mainland Michigan. What was once a low-lying hill became Beaver Island, thirty miles from present-day Charlevoix.

The identity of those fireside visitors remains a mystery, but there are several possibilities. Perhaps they walked across the ice to the island during the winter, following the tracks of moose, elk or deer. Or they may have been drawn to the island to take advantage of one of the richest fisheries on the Great Lakes.

Another theory is that early visitors may have used the Beaver Island Archipelago of fourteen islands as a trade route for crossing from the Upper to the Lower Peninsula. Possibly, these were traders from the north, bringing cargoes of furs and copper to trade with Indians living in agricultural communities far to the south. Their tribal affiliation, if any, is unknown.

Copper, in particular, has been identified as a trade item, which may have passed down the archipelago from pit mines located hundreds of miles north along Lake Superior. Radiocarbon dating has indicated that copper pit mines have existed on the shores and islands of Lake Superior up to 3,800 years ago.

On Isle Royale and other sites along Lake Superior, ancient miners grubbed at the earth with sticks and stone hammers, digging pits to expose veins of copper-bearing rock. The copper was extracted by smashing the rock with beach cobble stones weighing ten to thirty pounds. Another theory is that miners built fires beneath a copper vein and then dashed it with water to crack the rock, then smashing it with hammer stones to free the metal.

Mining engineers who visited Isle Royale in 1872 were astounded by pits up to thirty feet across and twenty-to-sixty feet deep, with some connected by underground drains cut through the rock. One sixty-foot drain was covered with timbers, long rotted away. The engineers also found excavations that extended for more than two miles at an inlet known as McCargoe's Cove. They noted that the amount of mining on three Native sites at the north end of Isle Royale, "is estimated to exceed that of one of our oldest mines on the south shore of Lake Superior, a mine which has been constantly worked with a large force (using modern tools) for over twenty years."

But copper by itself is a dead-end in its usefulness and unfortunately, the Indians never invented the bellows, which was arguably the single greatest invention in history.

Copper melts at 2,000 degrees Fahrenheit, but to reach (and sustain) that temperature a bellows is needed to fan the flames of charcoal or coal. A bellows is required to create alloys such as bronze, which is created by mixing roughly eight parts of molten copper to one part of tin. Without the bellows the human race would never have advanced beyond the Copper Age. No Bronze Age, no Iron Age, no steel, guns, automobiles, airplanes, rocket ships, not to mention millions of humbler things such as toasters, refrigerators, can openers and cutlery. Not even an iron nail could be created without a bellows.

Without knowledge of the bellows, Indian miners and craftsmen heated copper enough for it to be malleable and then used hammer stones to shape it into spear points, tools and jewelry.

Yet, unalloyed copper is a soft metal, which is useless as a cutting tool. As noted by one expert in metallurgy, "A pure metal has identical atoms arranged in regular layers. The layers slide over each other easily. Alloys are harder and stronger because the different-sized atoms of the mixed metals make the atomic layers less regular, so they cannot slide as easily."

For a simple analogy on the value of alloys, consider oatmeal. As a dry cereal it's a fluff that has nothing in the way of useful substance, but "alloy" it with water and it is transformed into an edible mush. Add heat and it can be baked as hard as a rock.

Metallurgy first took flight 5,500 years ago in Asia with the use of standing furnaces outfitted with clay tubes that allowed an updraft of air to create fires hot enough to smelt metal. Slaves blew into the tubes to fan the coals, but this of course, only took smelting metal so far and must have been hell on the tube-tooters. Enter the bellows.

Bronze weapons were good for stabbing people, but not sharp enough for slicing, and thus the advent of the Iron Age as man's march of folly embraced new weaponry, wars, kingdoms and empires.

The failure to advance in metallurgy was a tragedy for the Indians, because unlike the civilizations of Europe, Africa and Asia, they never experienced a Bronze Age or an Iron Age, which would have given them a leg up on the subsequent invasion of their continent. History would have been radically different if the Indians had mastered the creation of alloys. After traversing their own Bronze Age, they would have had access to the vast Iron Range of northern Minnesota. With the help of blast furnaces and the production of pig iron they would have progressed into their own Iron and Steel Ages; perhaps they would have invented guns, cannons and ironclad steamships, invading Europe in, say, 1492.

But that speculation is best left to the fiction of alternative history.

In any event, copper artifacts have been found in Indian mounds and the ruins of ancient villages from Lake Superior all the way to the Gulf of Mexico and Florida, indicating that continent-wide trading was commonplace for centuries before the arrival of European explorers. Inexplicably, copper mining ceased around 1600, a few decades before the arrival of the French on Lake Superior.

Isle Royale, at the northern end of Lake Superior, provided much of the copper mined by the Indians. Today, the island is a national park. Forty-five miles long and lying fifteen miles south of the Canadian shore, it is one of the few national parks which close from November 1 to April 15, owing to its harsh environment. Ninety-nine percent of the island is a wilderness of dense forest, swamps, marshland and rocks. Cold rains coming off Lake Superior wash over campers on the island, which is often too damp to enable a comforting fire at night.

What would induce hundreds of men to labor in the pit mines of such a place, hundreds of years before the advent of capitalism, wages and widespread markets? How would they feed themselves in a place which could not sustain agriculture? For the hunter-gatherers of Lake Superior, the quest for game and fish were full-time pursuits, which wouldn't allow much time for mining. And how did they ship tons of copper to the south, with their jewelry and implements found as far away as the Gulf of Mexico? It is fifty-six storm-tossed miles across Lake Superior to the Keweenaw Peninsula, or a journey of hundreds of miles along the coast.

The answer to these and other questions may be wrapped within another mystery: that of a people known as the Mound Builders, who flourished across the heartland of present-day America.

Centuries of increasingly sophisticated Native cultures known as the Adena (800 B.C.-100 A.D.), Hopewell (100 B.C.-500 A.D.) and Mississippian (800-1600 A.D.) ushered in the golden age of mound building. Archeologists have identified 200,000 mounds, mostly in the eastern half of North America. Often, these were at the site of palisaded towns, surrounded by moats and heavily fortified against attack by neighboring tribes.

Swidden agriculture had taken root during what was called the Woodland tradition that ranged from 1000 B.C. to 700 A.D. in what is now the eastern United States. But starting with the Adena Culture, Native peoples began taking agriculture more seriously, made advances in pottery, and built what we'd recognize as houses with wattle-and-daub walls and roofs sheathed in slabs of bark. They also got serious about creating mounds of monumental proportions. Among the Adena people in southern Ohio, many mounds doubled as tombs, with elites buried with copper jewelry, clothing, blankets and on occasion, tubular stone pipes shaped like animals with their mouths facing the smoker. The Adena, and likely those who came later, enjoyed getting high. Their tobacco had five to ten times as much nicotine as today's cigarettes and this mixture contained a number of hallucinogens.

The Adena Culture had everything an indigenous people could ask for: abundant deer, bear, turkeys, ducks, herds of woodland bison and other game, as well as the rich farmlands of the Ohio River Valley; add to that a fairly temperate climate. The succeeding Hopewell Culture built on their achievements, advancing in art, ceramics and trade along a network of rivers spreading out in all directions. They too carried on the tradition of building mounds, edging toward what we might consider a true civilization.

Mounds across the country range from gentle swells, barely six feet high, to the spectacular 1,348-foot-long Serpent Mound in Ohio. They served a variety of purposes; some contain the remains of human beings, buried with tools, jewelry, weapons and the human sacrifice of slaves for use in the afterlife; some were crowned by temples or the homes of rulers. Others contain scores of spear points, hammers, axe heads and other implements. Many are simply empty piles of soil. Aside from graves for important people, the mounds may have served as boundaries for hunting grounds, trail markers, or as speaking platforms for chieftains or shamans.

The mounds indicate the beginning of a caste system among Native peoples in which some were considered "more important" than others. At a Mound Builder community at Crystal River, Florida, for instance, lower-caste people - perhaps slaves or commoners - were buried without much more than a few pots in a low-lying mound, while elites were interred in a much grander mound with treasured objects.

Mound-building communities have been found throughout eastern North America, from Wisconsin to central Florida and from Arkansas to the Atlantic seaboard. This indicates that trade and a shared religion occurred on a continent-wide basis for more than two thousand years. How else would a community in Crystal River come to share the same mound-building impulse as the people who lived in Trempaleau, Wisconsin, 1,200 miles away at a time when there was no mass communication, highways or shared languages?

Burial mounds have been found in the Upper Great Lakes region which date back to the Early Woodland period of 1,000 B.C. This was a time when native peoples were beginning the first tentative steps toward agriculture, cultivating a few plants to supplement their hunting and gathering.

In Grand Rapids, Michigan, for instance, there were nearly thirty mounds in the downtown area, all leveled in the nineteenth century as the city expanded. Nearby on the Grand River is a collection of thirteen mounds in a city park, ranging from five to fifteen feet in height, all that remain of the thirty-five or so which once stood there. Constructed around 100 A.D., the people who built these mounds used digging sticks and hoes fashioned from the shoulder blades of large animals, such as elk, to deposit one basketful of dirt at a time for their construction.

Excavations in 1874 and the mid-1960s uncovered burial chambers filled with human and animal remains, including the jawbones of wolves and bears along with elaborately decorated pottery, various tools and exquisite arrowheads.

The mounds found in Grand Rapids were modest compared to those further south. Outside present-day Detroit, the Great Mound of the Rouge River was three hundred feet long and two hundred feet wide, standing twenty feet tall. Like many mounds found in urban areas it was leveled to the ground many years ago.

The agricultural communities of the Mound Builders were especially robust along the Mississippi River and its tributaries, with people living in hundreds of fortified towns and villages.

The Mound Builders weren't a unified civilization with a central government, but rather a collection of many different peoples connected by trade, ritual, agriculture and artistry. Similarities between their pottery and implements can be found throughout the heart of North America. They also traveled widely, trading for copper and silver from Lake Superior; mica from Alabama and the Appalachians; tortoise shell, shark teeth, stingray spines and marine shells from the Gulf Coast; galena (a lead ore for pigment) from Missouri; tobacco from Virginia; pipestone from Minnesota;

and obsidian from as far west as Yellowstone. Many of these items were interred in their burial mounds, indicating pan-Indian religious beliefs.

In an age without maps or any modes of travel other than on foot or via canoe, Indian traders made epic journeys. Hundreds of pounds of razor-sharp obsidian, for instance, have been found at Mound Builder sites in Ohio, originating 1,700 miles to the west at an obscure mountain of volcanic glass known as Obsidian Cliff in Yellowstone National Park. The sharpest natural material on earth, obsidian was used to create knives, axe heads, spear and arrow points. Native peoples began mining the site 11,500 years ago, indicating a continent-wide trading network. Today, one has only to make the three-day drive from Ohio to Yellowstone to appreciate the fortitude and endurance of prehistoric traders.

Uncovering the mystery of the Mound Builders has occupied explorers and archeologists for more than two hundred years. Dr. Henry Gillman, for instance, was an ethnologist and expert on Indian mounds in Michigan in the early 1870s. He passed through Beaver Island while investigating the ancient Indian copper mines of Isle Royale and found a number of mounds just north of the town of St. James.

Excavating the mounds, Gillman found "highly wrought stone implements, many of them being of uncommonly skillful workmanship... These consist of axes, chisels, fleshing tools, spear points, arrowheads, etc., formed of a great variety of stone. One of the handsomest stone axes I ever saw was taken out of this place."

One of Gillman's finds was an implement made of greenstone, which is found only on Isle Royale and the Keweenaw Peninsula.

In his report on "The Mound Builders of Michigan" to the Detroit Scientific Association in 1874, Gillman speculated that the vast numbers of men needed for the mines of Lake Superior may have been slaves of the Hopewell Culture centered in Ohio, Illinois and Indiana.

Slavery was common among Native peoples (indeed, all over the world), but, other than in Mexico, not on the scale indicated by the mining operations of Lake Superior. Still, Gillman's musings offer food for thought:

"The discoveries on Isle Royale throw a new light on the character of the Mound builders," he wrote. "The copper... must have been conveyed in vessels, great or small, across a stormy and treacherous sea (Lake Superior), whose dangers are formidable to us now, being dreaded by even our largest craft, and often providing their destruction. Leaving their homes, these men dared to face the unknown - to brave the hardships and periods of the deep and of the wilderness...

"How did these people become aware of those mineral deposits at so isolated a point? How did the men become present in such large numbers as is implied by the extent of the works discovered? How did so great a population support life in such circumscribed limits while still carrying on their mining operations? ... Did any or all of them remain throughout the severe northern winter, or was the work prosecuted during the summer months only? These are questions not easily answered.

"It is evident that such extensive operations as are here described required a system and an organization of no mean order for those days. The island probably abounded in game... However, we have hitherto supposed that the Mound builders were essentially an agricultural people, largely dependent on cereals for subsistence. If grain food was used by them, as is probable, it was most likely transported to the island in sufficient supply from a more southern latitude.

"The question will not fail to suggest itself: Were these vast operations accomplished through slave labor? That a conquered people were kept at this isolated place by their victors, and in this thralldom obliged to work the copper mines, is an opinion, however, which cannot be received without further confirmation."

Gillman wondered if a centralized government of the Hopewell Culture may have held sway with an "autocratic power" over its people and those it conquered.

Problematic with Gillman's theory is that the Hopewell Culture was characterized by similarities in pottery, agriculture, ritual, and trading networks rather than the creation of a pan-Indian empire. For what it's worth, the nineteenth century was riddled with crackpot notions, with some believing that the Indians were descendants of the Lost Tribes of Israel; that Irish monks had settled among the Mandan tribe of Upper Missouri; or that Vikings had made their way up the Great Lakes to Minnesota. This was a time when many educated people believed that there was a warm sea and a tropical paradise beyond the frigid, arctic seas at the North Pole and that the earth was hollow with a sunny land at its center.

Setting aside the idea of slavery, a sunnier notion is that perhaps the Hopewell Indians of the Midwest simply flocked to Isle Royale during the summer as a lark in the spirit of treasure hunters. Once their crops were planted in the spring, young men often took to raiding their enemies in other tribes, leaving their women at home to tend the crops. During times of peace (or a disinclination to go raiding) perhaps some set their sights on digging for precious metal in the far north for its trading value. There's a corollary to this notion in that Native peoples often traveled hundreds of miles to mine the Red Pipestone Quarry located in southwestern Minnesota. Pipestone (catlinite) was highly valued for the carving of calumets found across North America.

Whatever the case, there is evidence that the Hopewell people had trading connections to Isle Royale during their heyday from 100 B.C. to 500 A.D. Many ornaments of Lake Superior copper have been found in Hopewell burial mounds in Ohio, Indiana and Illinois. Copper mining camps from the Hopewell period have been found on Isle Royale at Indian Point, Chippewa Harbor, Merritt Lane and Washington Island, among other sites.

The Hopewell Culture dissipated around 500 A.D., about the same time that bow and arrow technology finally reached all of North America. (Bows had been present in the Arctic as far back as 3000 B.C.) As is the case with all innovations in weaponry, the spread of the bow and arrow resulted in a corresponding rise in violent warfare.

The Hopewell Culture gave way to the Mississippian Culture, which hastened the rise of what are called chiefdoms. Typically, a chiefdom might include a capital of several thousand farmers with a number of outlying towns and villages of 500-2,000 residents each. Its area of influence might encompass thousands of square miles, inhabited by tens of thousands.

During the Mississippian Era, the Indians established dozens of chiefdoms, particularly in what is now the southeastern United States.

Historian Charles Hudson, one of the most knowledgeable experts on the Mississippian Culture, noted that a chiefdom fell somewhere between the political organization of a decentralized tribe and that of a highly-centralized state. "In a state wrongs against individuals are punished by legitimate agents of the state," he wrote, "but in a tribe wrongs are punished by the individual's kin group, and this often causes feuds among the kin groups which weaken the social fabric."

Thus, a state maintains social order through strict rules and officials charged with carrying them out, while the leaders of tribes led at best by persuasion and influence. Chiefdoms, as the name implies, were led by chiefs, along with a council of elites. And as Hudson noted, everyone knew where they stood "in terms of a strict hierarchy, from highest to lowest, partly with respect to age, and partly with respect to their accomplishments as warriors, leaders of men, and as religious and medical practitioners."

Some notable chiefdoms included the Casqui people of northeastern Arkansas, whose capital was a walled city on the St. Francis River with twenty-one outlying villages. Another was Coosa, centered in northern Georgia, which held sway over fifty thousand Indians in a realm spanning four hundred miles from Alabama to Tennessee. Typically, the capitals of these chiefdoms were dominated by earthen pyramids rising fifty feet or more, atop which the elites lived and ceremonies were conducted. Lording it overall would be what anthropologist Marshall Sahlins called a "Big Man," or chief, along with a caste of nobles, likely including women.

If we were to stop by a typical Mississippian-era community we'd find a town of about five hundred farmers whose homes are gathered around a plaza dominated by a central pyramid where the chief and his family live, along with several smaller mounds, including a district for the elites. Our hosts show us their winter home: it is constructed of wooden posts driven into the ground, between which they have woven branches and cane; plastering the web-work over with mud or clay - what is called wattle-and-daub. Their house is ten feet wide, thirty feet long, and its floor has been excavated a foot or two to make it easier to heat in the winter. In the summer they might move to an airier, temporary structure that requires little care.

At Moundville Archeological Park in Alabama the excavation of artifacts such as carvings and pottery revealed that life was good for the chief dwelling at the top of a central pyramid. He was served the choicest cuts of meat with no one allowed to watch him eat. His people prostrated themselves in his presence, and he was borne about on an elegant litter carried on the shoulders of muscular slaves with his feet never touching the ground. Swathed in a feather headdress, a fine cotton robe, and ornaments of copper and marine shells, he carried a jeweled stone axe, mace, or an obsidian sword as a mark of his authority. But woe betide him if successive droughts or floods ruined the crops for a number of years, because as Scottish anthropologist James Gordon Frazer noted in his 1890 book, *The Golden Bough*, it was the rulers of ancient communities who were scapegoated for such disasters, often assassinated, deposed or sacrificed to appease the gods.

The greatest chiefdom of all, possibly attaining the level of a state, was that of Cahokia, whose ruins can be visited in Illinois across the Mississippi River from St. Louis. Inhabited from 700 to 1250 A.D., Cahokia was home to 12,000-15,000 people and was as large as London during its heyday. (Hudson puts the figure at up to 38,000 living in the region around the city.)

Surrounded by a two-mile-long stockade of 20,000 timbers with guard towers placed every 70 feet, the city featured 120 mounds. Its 40-acre Grand Plaza was the site of public gatherings, sporting events, a market, festivals and executions.

An exhibit at Moundville Archeological Park in Alabama depicts life among the elites, in this case the arrival of a young bride-to-be.

The plaza was dominated by a 100-foot-tall pyramid crowned by a wooden temple that may have risen another 50 feet. Covering fifteen acres and larger than the base of Egypt's Great Pyramid of Cheops, the four-level pyramid was constructed with twenty-two million cubic feet of soil, deposited one basketful at a time by thousands of workers.

Cahokia likely had a caste system that included slaves, the common people, craftsmen, warriors, priests and rulers. Cottonwood canoes up to one hundred feet long crowded its port, bringing copper, firewood, shells and meat along with diplomats from far-off tribes and the city's own warriors. Its women were likely tattooed and clothed in cotton gowns, draped in feathers, shells and jewelry. Its sporting events would have included hundreds of men taking part in massive games on the central plaza. Visitors from "the sticks" would surely have been blown out of their sandals to witness such splendor.

Cahokia was the only Native city ever established north of the Rio Grande, and perhaps its founders were inspired by the civilizations of Mexico. But a few standout communities before and after its establishment were certainly a step above mere towns.

At Poverty Point in present-day Louisiana, a massive community laid out in six horseshoe-shaped earthworks flourished from 1700 to 1100 B.C. We know little of the people who lived here, nor what they called their home, but it was likely the heart of a trading network that extended along the Mississippi to the Red, Ohio, Arkansas and Tennessee rivers. Seen from the air, the concentric earthworks of Poverty Point are so strikingly modern in appearance that they would not be unusual in a science fiction film depicting a colony on another world. It was home to up to five thousand people roughly fourteen hundred years before the establishment of Cahokia.

Similarly, Moundville along the Black Warrior River in northern Alabama arose around the time that Cahokia lapsed, reaching its height from 1250 to 1500 A.D. Covering more than 185 acres, surrounded by a 1.5-mile palisade and dominated by a sixty-foot-tall pyramid, Moundville was home to perhaps one thousand residents with another ten thousand living in the vicinity. As with Poverty Point and Cahokia, it too melted away for reasons that are unknown, although we know from their lavish funerary rites that the rulers most likely lorded over their people to the point of being *persona non grata*. Its demise was also concurrent with infectious diseases spread by Spanish explorers.

No one knows why Cahokia was abandoned sometime around 1300 A.D., although there are several theories. Built on a flood plain below the confluence of the Mississippi and Illinois rivers, the city and its farmlands may have been frequently underwater. Its sanitation problems were immense, possibly resulting in epidemics. Another theory posits the lack of firewood due to deforestation and the destruction of wildlife habitat for hundreds of miles around. Additionally, the prevalence of buffalo along the Mississippi in the 1200s may have induced its people to follow the herds onto the western plains.

One of the more intriguing theories is that social disorder contributed to Cahokia's demise. Riots, regicide, the tossing of priests to their deaths from the heights of pyramids - that sort of thing.

Only eighty mounds survived the arrival of white settlers, and many have not yet been excavated. But one, Mound 72, yielded grisly discoveries that shed light on the brutal religious practices of old Cahokia.

Mound 72 was first excavated in 1967 by archeologist Melvin Fowler, who discovered five mass graves containing anywhere from twenty to fifty bodies. He found numerous other graves with bodies buried singly and in groups, sometimes atop the mass graves. Overall, he identified 272 bodies over the course of five excavations, including many who appeared to be sacrificial victims, with all of the burials occurring during Cahokia's most robust period between 1000 and 1200 A.D.

Initially, the most important grave in the mound was thought to be that of a tall man in his forties, believed to have died around 1050. His bones rested on twenty thousand conch shell beads of immense value at the time.

Beneath him and his layer of shells lay another body and nearby were six individuals who may have been retainers who volunteered to join him in the afterlife (or were made an offer they couldn't refuse). The grave included nearly eight hundred exquisite arrowheads attached to shafts that had long since disintegrated. Two bushel baskets of mica were also found, a mirror-like mineral that was considered a huge treasure in its day.

The discovery was thought to be a testament to male dominance in ruling Cahokia. This theory was upended in 2016 when a new study revealed that a female of high status had been buried along with the man, with the two bodies lying atop one-another. Further investigation revealed other male-female burials, indicating that women were likely among the nobility of Cahokia, if not rulers themselves.

Elsewhere were found the bodies of four men with their heads and hands inexplicably cut off in addition to fifty-three young women between the ages of twelve and twenty-five, who were either strangled or buried alive. Were the women strangled one at a time atop a pyramid to send a message of obedience to the onlookers below? Or did their families look on as they were buried alive? Perhaps few in the crowd were happy to endure the loss of a beloved daughter or wife, even if it meant that she might live on as a servant or concubine in the afterlife.

Some of the mass graves in Mound 72 were awash in violence, with victims tossed willy-nilly into a pit with evidence of dismemberment, beheadings, skull fractures and arrow wounds. Possibly they were relatives who protested the sacrifice of their loved-ones, political rivals, victims of a crushed rebellion, or captives taken in battle.

What is known, however, is that people started fleeing Cahokia in droves around the same time that the mass graves began filling with victims.

Flooding, disease, bad water, dwindling resources, a shit-storm of bad sanitation and an autocratic theocracy - all may have contributed to Cahokia's demise.

Hundreds of years passed before French Trappist monks discovered the ruins of Cahokia in the mid-1700s, bestowing the name, Monk's Mound, on its central pyramid. They found no trace of the people who had once lived here, nor any idea of their language or even what they called themselves. Those who once lived here came to be known as Cahokians after a small sub-tribe of the Illinois Indians migrated to the area from the east in the 1600s. Only the ghosts of this long-dead civilization can tell us who the original people were and how they fell, but they're not talking.

Possibly, those who abandoned the city resurfaced as a people called the Quapaw. A buffalo hide painted by the Quapaw in the seventeenth century seems to depict a map of Cahokia, with people shown leaving the city. The

Quapaw were later known as the Osage, Omaha, and Kansa tribes who lived west of the Mississippi.

"The odd thing about Cahokia is that... the epic stories of a founding city seem to be missing in the eastern woodlands," notes historian Timothy R. Pauketat in *Cahokia - Ancient America's Great City on the Mississippi*. "It should have been commemorated in tales and songs (yet) in the eastern United States, there are no oral-history references to Cahokia."

Nor have historians, archeologists and anthropologists been able to find references to Cahokia among tribes located further south or on the Great Plains. Pauketat writes that perhaps those who left Cahokia simply wished to forget a place that had spiraled out of control into anarchy and degradation.

But here's another thought; it's possible that with the passage of centuries, wandering nomads in pursuit of buffalo herds across the rolling plains simply couldn't get their heads around the idea that once there had been a city of thousands dwelling beneath a pyramid that aimed to touch the sun. Perhaps four centuries after its collapse, Cahokia was simply beyond its descendants' imagination.

CHAPTER 8

THE NEW FOUND LAND

Sometime around the year 1,000 A.D., a Viking trader named Bjarni Herjolfsson got lost in a storm-driven fog while trying to sail from Iceland to Greenland.

Herjolfsson had never been to Greenland, which had been settled by the Norsemen only fifteen years before, yet he hoped to make his mark there as a trader serving the new farmstead communities of sod and stone houses on the east and west coasts.

If he survived the trip.

The Vikings sailed by the stars and sun, and by observing the flow of the wind, the flights of birds, and other natural phenomena. It's believed that they, or the Irish, discovered Iceland by observing the effects of volcanic eruptions far over the horizon, surmising that there must be land to the west; and perhaps this is how they also discovered Greenland.

But blinded by the fog, Herjolfsson and his men were utterly lost. For days their ship was buffeted amid the murk and towering swells of the North Atlantic. Most likely, he and his men were traveling in a *knarr*, a heavy, freight-carrying ship, the stability of which saved their necks. These blue-water vessels were quite unlike the shallow-draft dragon boats of popular imagination, which were used for coastal raiding and gliding up rivers to attack inland towns. A *knarr* could weigh eight tons and range up to sixty feet in length and fifteen feet in width, with sixty men working the oars and managing the sail.

In those days, five hundred years before Native peoples introduced Christopher Columbus to the hammock, seamen slept on the deck of their ships, wrapped in furs and exposed to the elements. For Herjolfsson's crew the first voyage to North America would have been marked by chill, soaking misery; the spectre of sea monsters and icebergs; and the terror of knowing they were hopelessly lost. The North Atlantic itself was a vast gray monster upon the back of which the men slithered helplessly to the west in their frail craft.

At last the storm lifted and the crew spied a green, timbered land to the west, yet with none of the glaciers known to exist in Greenland. Sailing north, Herjolfsson came upon a barren shore of rock slabs backed by snow-capped mountains. Although Herjolfsson's men begged him to put ashore, he declined every request. He was a trader, not an explorer, and had a valuable cargo at risk. Who knows? Perhaps there were monsters or demons lurking on this unknown shore; perhaps it was even the realm of the afterlife. Whatever, Herjolfsson wasn't taking any chances, and eventually he and his crew made their way back east to the settlement of Brattahild in Greenland.

News of the discovery created a sensation among the Greenlanders, who were in dire need of timber to construct their homes. Eirik the Red had settled Greenland around 985 A.D. during a time of favorable climate conditions, which had also enabled the settlement of Iceland more than one hundred years prior. His son, Leif Ericsson, purchased Herjolfsson's ship and set sail with thirty-five men. This time they set foot on the new land, becoming the first Europeans known to have reached North America. They were elated to find white beaches, shallow seas and green meadows backed by immense forests.

We know of the Viking incursions because of the *Vinland Sagas* of both Greenland and Iceland, which were written down by unknown monks in the early 1200s. This was more than two hundred years after the events of the sagas and differences between the two works often mix up various characters along with their deeds and chronologies. Whatever, the *Sagas* report that interactions between the Vikings and Native peoples clearly had their troubles.

Ericsson established an outpost at what is now L'anse aux Meadows at the northern tip of Newfoundland. Today, it's a Canadian national park at the tail end of a highway called the Viking Trail offering reconstructions of the sod houses and rock walls built by the Norsemen. In 2021, researchers used carbon dating on the rings of felled trees at the site to determine that Ericsson's camp had been built exactly one thousand years ago in the year 1021. In time, a small complement of women joined the men here, along with a few pigs and cattle.

Thereafter, Leif's brother, Thorvald, took to exploring the new land on expeditions that may have ranged as far west as present-day Quebec and south to Long Island, a place they called Vinland after its grapes.

It was on one of these voyages that Thorvald and his men became the first Europeans to encounter Native peoples, setting the template for centuries of animosity and murder. The Vikings had met Inuit peoples in Greenland, whom they called Skraelings, but the Indians of "New Found Land" were clearly something else.

Following is a transcription of the *Saga of the Greenlanders*, detailing

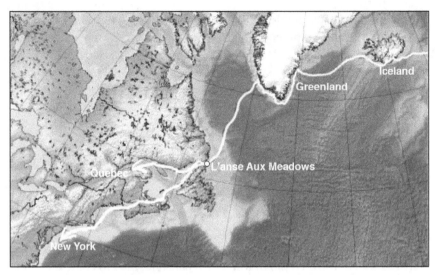

Possible explorations of the Vikings one thousand years ago. Map detail, Wikipedia Commons.

the Vikings' first encounter with the Indians. After running aground and wrecking the keel of their ship during their second summer of exploration, Thorvald and his men repaired the damage and pushed on:

"They then left to sail to the east of the country and entered the mouths of the next fjords until they reached a cape stretching out sea-wards. It was covered with forest. After they secured their ship in a sheltered cove and put out gangways to the land, Thorvald and all his companions went ashore.

"He then spoke: 'This is an attractive spot, and here I would like to build my farm.' As they headed back to the ship they saw three hillocks on the beach inland from the cape. Upon coming closer they saw that they were three hide-covered boats, with three men hiding under each of them. They managed to capture all of them except one, who escaped with his boat. They killed the other eight and went back to the cape. On surveying the area they saw a number of hillocks further up the fjord, and assumed them to be settlements."

The next day, "A vast number of hide-covered boats came down the fjord, heading toward them." Thorvald was struck by an arrow in his armpit in the ensuing battle and died of his wound. In one account it is a one-legged being that kills Thorvald - a uniped - which the Vikings claimed to have encountered in other parts of the world. Curiously, the Cree of northern Canada also believed in the existence of a uniped named *Paija*, a gobbler of men's souls whose single leg sprang from her enormous hairy belly.

Thereafter, trade commenced between the Norsemen and the Indians, possibly the Mi'kmaq or Beothuk of present-day Nova Scotia and Newfoundland. Initially, the Norse offered strips of red cloth in exchange for furs. Soon, however, the Indians demanded the iron weapons of the Vikings, having seen the effectiveness of their weapons. To the Indians' disgruntlement, the Vikings forbade any trade in iron.

This created problems.

The story of a couple named Thorfinn Karlsefni and his virtuous wife Gudrid illustrates the dilemma faced by the Norse in their relations with Native peoples. Declining to trade their iron for furs, the couple offered milk and cheese instead. But on once occasion, a Native attempted to seize a weapon and was killed by a servant.

Thereafter, the couple (whose son Snorri was the first European born in North America) fortified their farm with a palisade, only to come under increasing attacks. Frightened and under siege, they fled back to Greenland the following spring.

Some historians speculate that L'anse aux Meadows was simply an outpost or a boat repair station and that a larger settlement may have been established further south where the Norsemen could graze their cattle. Butternut shells have been found at L'anse aux Meadows, along with references to grapes in the sagas. But both of these grow much further to the south, leading to speculation that the Viking's main settlement may have been in Nova Scotia, Maine, or even New York. If so, its ruins have yet to be found.

Timbering between Greenland and the forests of southern Labrador continued into the 1300s. Yet the Norse abandoned their farms and outposts in Newfoundland within one hundred years of their arrival in the wake of repeated Indian attacks and cold weather brought on by climate change. Even Greenland was abandoned by the early 1500s after the climate turned too cold to sustain farming. Ice-clogged seas made it dangerous to sail from Norway to Iceland, let alone Greenland or North America.

But the Vikings carried more than timber home from the New World. In 2022, evidence of Native DNA was discovered in Iceland, indicating that Viking men may have brought their Indian wives home with them from North America.

What the Vikings brought to North America, however, was something that would bedevil the Indians for centuries: the practice of primogeniture.

Under the rule of primogeniture, an eldest son inherited all of his parents' real estate and possessions upon the death of his father. This could range from a simple farm with a half-acre plot to a castle with a sprawling kingdom. Succeeding sons received nothing and lived at the pleasure of their eldest brother. Woe betide the daughter who failed to marry, for she of course received nothing either in the way of inheritance.

As a result, the first Europeans to set foot at L'anse aux Meadows were likely second, third and succeeding sons out to make their fortunes with nothing to lose and everything to gain.

The same laws of primogeniture held sway in France, Spain, Germany and the bulk of Europe. Thus, the fourth son of a farmer in Extremadura, Spain in the sixteenth century had ample motivation to join the expeditions of conquistadors in the hope of gaining treasure and land in the New World. Primogeniture filled the armies and navies of Europe with younger sons who had few other options.

Those who crossed the ocean to the Americas did so under the lash of desperation and with a chip on their shoulders. Primogeniture was banned in Virginia in 1785, but the practice in lieu of a will continued in Great Britain until 1925.

Indian tribes had their own sense of inheritance flowing to either male or female descendants, depending. With as many as five hundred tribes, sub-tribes and major clans existing in Pre-Colombian America there were many differing ways of passing on family treasures.

But in the main, the prehistoric Indians lived communally, sharing everything they hunted, fished and farmed so that everyone could survive and thrive. The idea of owning land seemed as odd to the Indians as the idea of owning the sun, the sky, wind, water or clouds.

Yet land was everything to European peasants, who were not only dependent on the largesse of their eldest brothers, but also on the whims of nobles and landlords. The very idea of a poor farmer owning land was novel, radical, since all European peasants owed a landlord rents for their hovels and a patch of ground upon which to grow their crops.

During the sixteenth and seventeenth centuries, the nobility of Europe began privatizing the "commons," which was land that was available for everyone in need of water, firewood, building materials, foraging for edible plants, and pastures for grazing livestock. Once landlords began evicting their tenants in the early 1800s in order to raise more profitable cattle, the allure of America, where one could become a virtual baron overnight, became irresistible.

Thus, primogeniture and lust for land sparked fire to the heels of many an adventurer to the New World, with little concern for its Native inhabitants.

Within five hundred years of the Vikings' departure, explorers from a dozen European nations began probing the Americas for land and treasure. This included the likes of the Basques of northern Spain, whose fishing fleets swept over the Outer Banks of the North Atlantic, sweeping up cod by the millions to be salted and sold in Europe. The sea route to the Basques' fishing territory was a closely-guarded secret handed down from father to son over the centuries, but evidence of their presence can still be found at Channel Port aux Basques at the southern tip of Newfoundland.

Foremost among the newcomers were the Spanish, who thought of themselves as having God's blessing when it came to murdering and enslaving the Indians en masse. Having driven the Moors out of the Iberian Peninsula after seven hundred years of Muslim rule, the Spanish felt entitled, even obligated, to force their brand of Christianity on indigenous peoples wherever they found them.

CHAPTER 9

THE NEWCOMERS IN BRIEF

One day in October more than five hundred years ago a young mother searching for shellfish along the shore of a small island in the Caribbean looked up to find three immense creatures heading her way over the sapphire sea. Dazed, she could hardly believe her eyes.

Seizing her infant daughter sitting on the beach and running for the safety of the trees, she called to her son: "Run and tell your father that there are big birds coming over the water, taller than the trees! They mean to eat us - *run!*"

Soon the beach was crowded with people running down from the village to witness a spectacle beyond their imagination. As the creatures drew near, the islanders discerned that they were mammoth canoes, plumed with what appeared to be the wings of great birds, and atop these vessels were crowded a host of creatures which resembled men.

But what men! Hairy-faced like beasts and as white beneath their clothes as the dead; perhaps they were ghosts themselves. Unlike the islanders, who were completely naked except for their ornaments, tattoos and paint, the newcomers were comically swathed in wrappings usually reserved only as blankets. Some were carapaced in a strange metal as if they were turtles or crabs. And not a single woman was seen among them. How could such beings have been born without women?

Some of the braver islanders paddled out and were rewarded with a few trinkets and bits of red cloth tossed from the ships. Tentatively at first, a few more swam or paddled out to the ships until their numbers swelled to more than a hundred, surrounding the strange beings from the sea.

The Arawaks of San Salvador may have been the first Caribbean Indians to encounter Europeans in 1492, but their experience would hardly be unique in the years to come. Over and over in hundreds of landings, Native peoples were confounded by sights they had never seen or imagined as the multi-sailed vessels of Europe and their hair-faced crews landed on their shores. With their ships often mistaken as monsters, huge swans or fish, many Native peoples were unsure as to whether the newcomers were ghosts or gods.

They were soon to learn that the Europeans were neither.

Christoforo Colombo, or Christopher Columbus as we call him, set the mold for brutalizing the Indians.

Arriving Oct. 12, 1492 after sixty-one days at sea with a company of ninety surly and rebellious men, Columbus soon found himself in a new Eden of lush islands, "like April in Andalusia." In his log written expressly for Queen Isabella and King Ferdinand of Spain, Columbus grew giddy rhapsodizing about the islands, their tropical birds, majestic trees and gentle people. He wrote that, "All these islands are so green and beautiful that I don't know where to go first."

Thousands of islanders flocked to his ships as he passed through the Bahamas to Cuba and Hispaniola, showering his men with gifts and greeting them as if they were gods. "By the signs they made I think they were asking if we came from Heaven," he wrote. He added that the first people he encountered, "go about as naked as the day they were born," although some painted themselves in a variety of colors. He marveled that the islanders seemed docile, friendly, and appeared to have no weapons or warlike spirit.

On the very same day that he landed at San Salvador, Columbus began cogitating on how to convert and enslave the Indians.

"I want the natives to develop a friendly attitude toward us because I know that they are a people who can be made free and converted to our Holy Faith more by love than by force," he wrote.

Noting that the Indians he met suffered enslavement by tribes from other islands, Columbus opined that they might just as well do the bidding of

Spaniards:

"They ought to make good and skilled servants, for they repeat very quickly whatever we say to them. I think they can easily be made Christians, for they seem to have no religion. If it pleases Our Lord, I will take six of them to Your Highnesses when I depart, in order that they may learn our language."

Reaching Hispaniola (present-day Haiti and the Dominican Republic), Columbus wrote that the islands were there for the taking.

"... all that is needed here is to build a town and order the Indians to do your bidding ... I and the few men I have with me could go anywhere in these islands without opposition... (The Indians) have no weapons, they're totally defenseless, they in fact know nothing about arms, and they are cowards. A thousand of them could not face three of us. And for this reason it's easy to order them about and make them work, to sow and to do whatever else might be necessary, such as having them build houses and be taught to wear clothing and to take up our customs."

In other writings, Columbus is enraptured by the Indians: "They are such a loving, docile, peaceful people, that I swear to Your Highnesses, there can be no better people or land in the world. They love their neighbor as themselves. Their speech is sweet and cheerful, and always delivered with a smile."

At one point, the islanders told him of a continent to the west, which he surmised was the land of the "Great Khan" of China.

Soon enough, Columbus learned that not all of the islanders were "sweet and cheerful," particularly that of a tribe known as the Caribs, who were alleged to be cannibals and prone to showering the Spanish with poisoned arrows shot by men and women alike.

On Christmas Day, 1492, Columbus's flagship, the *Santa Maria* ran aground on a sandbar after its pilot turned the tiller over to a ship's boy for the night. Loathe to pack all his men aboard the leaking *Niña* and *Pinta*, Columbus used the wreck of the *Santa Maria* to build an outpost called La Navidad on Hispaniola, promising to return the following year. Forty men lusting for gold and Native women volunteered to stay behind while Columbus sailed back to Spain on the *Niña*.

Delirious with possibilities and hoping to help launch a new Crusade to the Holy Land with the gold he anticipated finding, Columbus left instructions for his men to search for gold and keep their hands off the local women, an injunction which was quickly ignored.

"I hope to God that when I come back here from Castile... that I will find a barrel of gold, for which these people I am leaving will have traded, and that they will have found the gold mine, and the spices, and in such quantities that within three years the Sovereigns will prepare for and undertake the conquest of the Holy Land," he wrote.

When Columbus returned a year later, however, he found his mens' bodies decomposing all along the coast with the fort having been destroyed. The Indians told him that the Spaniards had begun seizing their women for pleasure and had paid a price in blood.

Soon enough, the Spaniards paid the Indians back ten-thousand fold.

As was the case with many European explorers, Columbus seized native peoples to be shipped home as curiosities and slaves. On his return from his first voyage with a handful of prisoners, he promised that he could deliver "slaves in any number, all from the ranks of the idolaters." On his second voyage to the Caribbean he returned with thirty prisoners. On his third voyage, Columbus himself was shipped back to Spain in chains along with his two brothers for bungling affairs in Hispaniola, driving its colonists to the brink of revolt.

The newcomers had a religious justification for lording it over the Indians. Their pope - held to be God's representative on earth - said that any heathen land that was not Christianized was fair game for conquest and seizure.

In 1493, Pope Alexander VI issued a decree (known as a bull) to settle a squabble between Spain and Portugal over the right to colonize and plunder the New World. The *Inter Caetera* drew a meridian through South America, granting Portugal rights to the east of the line and Spain to the west. As a result, Portugal obtained the rump of eastern Brazil, where Portuguese is spoken to this day, while Spain was granted the lion's share of North and South America.

Pope Alexander also granted Spain and Portugal dominion over what would have been fifty million or more Indians living in North and South America. Implicit in the *Inter Caetera* was the right of Christian explorers to do whatever they wished with the indigenous peoples they encountered:

"... we make, appoint, and depute you and your said heirs and successors lords of them (the Indians) with full and free power, authority, and jurisdiction of every kind..."

In an outrageous ruling more than three hundred years later in 1823, the U.S. Supreme Court used this bull and two other papal decrees known as the "Doctrine of Discovery" to justify its ruling that Native peoples had only the right to occupy the lands on which they lived, and not the ownership of the land. It wasn't until 2023 that the Vatican under Pope Francis repudiated the Doctrine of Discovery, more than five hundred years after its promulgation. By then of course, the genocidal damage had been done worldwide, including the dispossession of the Indians under the United States government.

Give their temperament, the Spanish would have run rough-shod over the Indians, papal bull or not. The Spanish peasantry had been brutalized by their own nobles for centuries and the expectation of cruelty and arrogance was endemic in their culture, from the ghettos of Barcelona to the desert of Tabernas. But the *Inter Caetera* made any action justifiable, no matter how cruel.

As governor of the new lands Columbus and his brothers set about turning paradise into hell. They established the *encomienda* system, which granted large tracts of land to Spanish colonists, enslaving all who lived on the property. Tens of thousands of Indians were forced into slave labor on Spanish plantations and within their gold mines. One practice was to cut off the hands of any man over the age of fourteen who didn't produce a hawk's bell (thimble-full) of gold every three months. Other practices included the severing of noses as a common punishment, wanton beheadings, rapes, and massacres for the sport of it. In *la Monteria infernal*, "the hellish hunting," Indians were literally thrown to the Spanish attack dogs to be torn to pieces or used as dog food.

We know of these hideous practices thanks to the work of Bartolome de las Casas, who arrived in Hispaniola as a colonist in the sixteenth century and became a slave-owner himself before growing horrified by the actions of his fellow Spaniards. De las Casas become a Dominican friar, then a priest, and ultimately a bishop, freeing his slaves and abandoning his *encomienda*. But his lasting achievement was his authorship of *A Short Account of the Destruction of the Indies*, which chronicled the atrocities committed by the Spanish in excruciating detail. The book became a best-seller and was widely read, taken up as anti-Catholic propaganda by Protestant Europe.

De las Casas' opponent, Spanish theologian Juan Gines de Sepulveda argued that the Indians were "inferior beings" and "slaves by nature," while Spaniards were given to "prudence, intelligence, magnanimity, moderation, humanity," and the mercies of the Christian religion.

Sepulveda opined that the Indians were little more advanced than animals and insects:

"It is true that some display a certain talent for craftsmanship, but this is not proof of human intelligence, for we know that animals, birds and spiders do kinds of work that no human industry can completely imitate."

European interlopers were squarely in the corner of Sepulveda over the next few centuries, depicting Indians as soulless subhumans and an inferior race until well into the twentieth century.

There were up to eight million people living on Hispaniola alone when the Spanish arrived, yet all but a few thousand were exterminated through a combination of slavery in the mines and cane fields, diseases such as smallpox and measles, and outright massacres. Faced with a declining population of Indians, the Spanish hit upon a new scheme, importing African slaves from the Portuguese. Black slaves out of Africa were accustomed to farm labor and had more resistance to the infectious diseases of the Old World. Then too, they were utterly disoriented and demoralized by their shipment across the ocean to a foreign land with no chance of escape.

The Spanish decimated the Caribbean before doing much the same in Mexico. There were an estimated twenty million Indians living in Mexico when the conquistador Hernán Cortés arrived in 1520, yet only two million survivors by the year 1600 in the wake of widespread epidemics, slavery and massacres.

A reader might ask, what did Cortés have to do with the Native peoples of the Midwest? In short, the ripple effect. To employ a pathenogenic metaphor, Cortés was "Patient Zero" in the extermination of tens of millions of Indians across both North and South America. His story bears repeating because his plundering of Mexico unleashed hordes of disease-bearing conquistadors across two continents who, as he said, had "a sickness that can only be cured by gold."

Inspired by Cortés, conquistador armies shattered Native civilizations, including the robust chiefdoms of the southern United States, resulting in millions of deaths and refugees. Boring into the American South like worms in a ripe apple, the conquistadors left disease, slavery and ruin in their wake. Trade was disrupted throughout what is now the eastern United States, from the Gulf of Mexico to the northern shores of Lake Superior.

The survivors of the fallen chiefdoms of the Southeast coalesced into remnant tribes such as the Creek, Chocktaw and Natchez. Refugees also fled to the Shawnee and Cherokee, and many tribes became allied with the Indians of the Great Lakes three centuries later. If Cortés had found nothing but cornmeal, chocolate and turkeys among the Aztecs instead of packing galleons gunwales-deep with gold and silver, the history of North America would have been radically different.

Cortés, thirty-three, landed on the Mexican coast with 508 troops, 100 sailors and 16 horses. Equipped with swords, pikes, crossbows, matchlock firearms and cannon, some of his men were sheathed in metal armor, but more often in *cuiraisses* of heavily-padded cotton and leather which allowed for greater mobility.

Faced with the threat of a mutiny by a hostile faction of his troops, Cortés famously scuttled eleven of his ships near present-day Veracruz and sent his small army on a do-or-die mission, marching over the coastal mountains toward the Aztec capital of Tenochtitlan. Believing them to be gods and awed by the conquistadors' armor, steel, firearms, horses and dogs of war, tens of thousands of warriors from the vassal states of the Aztecs quickly joined Cortés, hoping to destroy their hated overlords. Native warriors, bearers and women marched west with their numbers swelling to more than one hundred thousand by the time they reached the cities ringing Lake Texcoco, the heartland of the Aztecs.

Tenochtitlan was a metropolis of three hundred thousand, located in the middle of Lake Texcoco and linked to the mainland by causeways. It was said to have been the most beautiful city in the world, rivaling Paris and Naples in size, which were the largest cities in Europe at the time. Taking the utterly confused Aztec ruler Montezuma prisoner as a "house guest," Cortés began lording it over the Aztecs until their patience ran out. Virtually every man, woman and child among the Aztecs vowed to fight to the death rather than face being sacrificed to the bloody gods of Cortés's allies. What followed was house-to-house urban warfare with every palace, temple and home in the city leveled to the ground.

As luck would have it, one of the Spaniards' slaves was infected with the smallpox pathogen, and this more than anything led to the fall of Tenochtitlan, in addition to wreaking havoc on Cortés's allies. Tens of thousands died in the resulting plague, including Cuitlahuic, the ruler who replaced Montezuma after he was either murdered by his own people or stabbed to death by Cortés's men.

By the end of the siege, Cortés was also unable to stop his 150,000 Tlaxcalan allies from engaging in what historian Kevin H. Siepel called "an orgy of slaughter."

"Our allies accompanied us with swords and shields, slaughtering right and left, whether on land or water," Cortés wrote in his memoirs. "On that day they slew or took prisoner more than forty thousand souls. Not a man among us remained unmoved by the wailing and shrieking of the women and children, a sound to break the heart of anyone. We expended greater efforts in dissuading our allies from their murderous and cruel behavior than we did in battling the enemy. No nation has ever witnessed the level of unnatural cruelty practiced by these people. And our allies took much plunder that day, which we could by no means stop. After all, we were only some nine hundred men and they were 150,000."*

Cortés's conquest spurred the Spanish to a fever of exploration. Yet, further north, they were far less successful, with many of their expeditions to what is now the United States ending in disaster.

Juan Ponce de Leon, who discovered Florida in 1513, died in Cuba eight years later after being struck in the thigh with a poisoned arrow. De Leon landed in southern Florida in 1521 with more than two hundred men and fifty horses, planning to establish a colony in territory that was held by the powerful Calusa tribe. There were an estimated 100,000 Indians living in Florida at the time and by 1521 those living along the coasts had been the victims of Spanish slavers. Florida's natives were also alerted to Spanish atrocities among their trading partners in Cuba and Hispaniola. Warnings of the white devils were no doubt issued by tribes throughout the peninsula and the Calusa were reputed to be a particularly warlike tribe. Attempting to site his colony near their capital, De Leon and his men were quickly overrun and slaughtered. He retreated to Havana where he died of his wound.

Then there was the expedition of Panfilo de Narváez, which was a disaster from start to finish.

An enemy of Cortés, Narváez and a force of eighteen ships and nine hundred men were sent to Mexico in 1520 to rein in the Captain of Castile, only to be defeated in a surprise attack in which he was blinded by a pike thrust to one of his eyes. Thereafter, all of his men were enlisted in Cortes' march on Tenochtitlan, while Narváez was imprisoned for two years.

That gave him plenty of time to think and brood. Once freed, as governor of Cuba, Narváez had the wealth and ambition to attempt making his own mark in New Spain, hoping to outshine Cortés in the lands to the north.

After a perilous crossing beset by a hurricane and contrary winds, Narváez landed near present-day St. Petersburg in the spring of 1528. He then made the fatal blunder of splitting his command. Narváez headed into the dense jungles, swamps and dunes of Florida with three hundred men and fifty horses, sending his ships north along the coast for a rendezvous. Instructions for the meet-up were vague, however, and the pilots steering his ships had no idea as to what lay ahead.

Narváez and other Spanish explorers hoped to find an Indian empire similar to that of the Aztecs or Incas, dripping with gold, silver and jewels

* Cortés and his men had conducted a massacre of their own early on against a people called the Cholulans, slaughtering thousands of unarmed citizens on suspicion that they were plotting against them.

in the lands north of Mexico. They were often encouraged by the tribes they met during their rambles; seeking to get rid of the interlopers, Native chieftains avowed that, yes indeed, there was much gold and treasure to be had far away in the land of our enemies. Now go and leave us alone.

Such was the case with Narváez, who was told that the treasure he sought could be found hundreds of miles to the north in a town called Apalachee. Central Florida's Indians were even able to produce golden trinkets validate their story, neglecting to mention that these had been taken from Spanish galleons that had been shipwrecked along the coast.

Narváez was noted for his cruelty. Legend has it that early on, he was angered by a chieftain of the powerful Timucuan tribe and sliced off the man's nose. He then threw the chief's elderly mother to his dogs of war, who tore her to pieces. Today, when we say that someone has been "thrown to the dogs," there are literally precedents dating back to ancient times.

But the Timucuans got even because some who had been seized as guides took Narváez's army through the most dangerous terrain of swamps, jungle, sand hills and rivers that they could find, with constant attacks by Indians along the way.

Months later, starving, half-naked and wracked with exhaustion the Spaniards reached Apalachee only to find a humble village with not a speck of gold in sight; only a few mortars with a sprinkling of corn. Worse, reaching the coast south of Tallahassee the tattered army found that their ships were nowhere to be found. One-by-one, they butchered their horses along a stretch of the Gulf Coast that is still called the Bay of Horses. Starving and desperate, the remnants of Narváez's army constructed crude rafts, planning to sail for Mexico despite the fact that there wasn't a single sailor or carpenter among them. They reworked their iron weapons and armor to make nails, used their shirts to make sails, and braided ropes from their horses' tails.

Packed nearly fifty men to each low-riding raft with sea water slopping over the gunwales, the survivors set out for the northernmost Spanish town of Panuco in Mexico, thinking it was perhaps one hundred miles away. Actually, it was about 1,500 miles and many died of thirst and starvation on the voyage. After two months at sea about one hundred survivors washed up on Galveston Island in November, with many quickly dying of exposure. The survivors were enslaved by the fierce Karankawa Indians of the Texas coast, with many killed after the appalled Indians discovered that the Spaniards had devoured their dead to survive. Cannibalism was a taboo which the Karankawa could not stomach.

In the end, out of three hundred men who landed in Florida, only four survived after wandering nearly naked across Texas and the deserts of the

In 1535, French explorer Jacques Cartier made it all the way up the St. Lawrence Seaway to the Iroquois town of Hochelaga (present-day Montreal), pictured here in a print from 1850. His search for gold and diamonds ended in disappointment.

southwest for eight years. One of them was a black slave named Estevanico.

As for one-eyed Narváez, he and his raft were last seen swirling into the darkness one night in a storm off the Texas coast, never to be seen again.

It wasn't just Spaniards who were smitten with dreams of riches in the New World. Sailing for France in 1535, Jacques Cartier traveled up the Saint Lawrence Seaway as far as present-day Montreal in search of the Northwest Passage to China. (The suburb of Lachine - *la Chine*, French for China - owes its name to the winter he spent there.) Thereafter, like Narváez, De Soto and Coronado, Cartier caught wind of the "Kingdom of Saguenay" after a local chieftain told him of a land that was rich in gold and diamonds far up the fjord of the same name in Quebec Province. For once the Europeans actually found the place, sending a ship home to France that was packed with tons of what turned out to be fool's gold and quartz.

CHAPTER 10

THE LOST CENTURY

Sometime during the summer of 1541 the farmers of a small village near present-day Knoxville, Tennessee began hearing ominous news from the capital of their chiefdom of Coosa more than 170 miles to the south.

Runners from the main town of Coosa in what is now northwestern Georgia told of a strange disease that was sweeping the capital, killing hundreds, including the elites who lived atop its earthen pyramids. Sacrifices had been made, the gods had been beseeched, powerful medicine had been invoked by the most knowledgeable shamans in the land, but all in vain.

First the elderly and very young had been stricken with the strange, scarring disease, which left its victims covered with pustules and twisting in agony, only to die within days. Even the warrior class was afflicted, leaving the frontiers of Coosa defenseless against its enemies.

For months all that anyone could talk about in the village was of the army of ghostly white men and the terrifying beasts upon which they rode, who had appeared at the capital after much hullabaloo about their arrival from the sea more than five hundred miles to the south. Unlike the people of Coosa who dressed in cotton, adorned with ornaments, tattoos and paint, the newcomers were comically-swathed in a strange metal and wrappings of many colors. They stank horribly from their practice of never bathing and a long train of strange animals followed in their wake, attended by hundreds of miserable Indian slaves.

The elites of Coosa had marched out to meet the men from Spain, with the chief himself borne on the couch of his ornate covered palanquin, carried by the nobles of his town, with hundreds of musicians, singers, warriors and townspeople trailing in his wake. Through signs and awkward attempts at speech, the chief learned that the leader of the expedition was named Hernando de Soto, whose army stayed more than a month at the capital before heading to the south.

They had left behind a man who was ill to be cared for by Coosa's medicine men. But soon even the physicians were sick and dying, and now hundreds of refugees were streaming out of the capital, running for their lives. Even now they were appearing at the palisade walls of the village in Tennessee.

Historians have long been mystified as to why Native peoples abandoned their copper mines along the north shore of Lake Superior around 1600 A.D. Why, after 3,400 years of continuous mining, would the Indians of the Upper Great Lakes stop digging for a metal they considered to be as precious as the diamonds and gold that we value today?

Following the dots, one possible reason that the Indians of Lake Superior gave up mining might be because most of their trading partners in the chiefdoms far to the south were dead. Or, that the Indian miners of the Midwest were themselves decimated by European diseases.

The 1500s have been called the "Lost Century" because of the apocalyptic ruin visited on the many Native civilizations that ranged from the heartland of North America to the jungles of the Amazon. Diseases such as smallpox, measles and influenza introduced by European explorers swept the continents, exterminating chiefdoms with populations ranging into tens of thousands. This period is literally a blank page in history, as lost to us as the blackest years of the Dark Ages.

Other than archeological discoveries, knowledge of what transpired in America's southern heartland from 1540 to 1700 is largely guess-work. Given the Indians' oral tradition, no written accounts have been passed down to us other than the journals of wandering conquistadors.

When we imagine the end of the world through nuclear holocaust, an asteroid strike, or an environmental breakdown giving rise to bands of marauders, warlords and desperate refugees fleeing from one place to another, we have the same conditions faced by the collapse of Native chiefdoms in the 1500s.

It was these civilizations that imported copper from Lake Superior along trade routes that had existed for thousands of years. Owned by the elites of chiefdoms such as Ocute, Coosa, Calusa and Cofitachequi, copper was highly prized as a trade item. It's likely that furs, hides, fishing nets, dried meat and other items from the north were traded as well, since these played a role in inter-tribal commerce in later centuries. Coincidentally, copper mining ceased along the shores of Lake Superior once the southern chiefdoms disappeared.

The Lost Century is a misnomer in that this helter-skelter period lasted for at least 150 years, with European colonists finding none of the vibrant civilizations that had been described by conquistador De Soto in his 1539-1543 rampage across the South. "Almost one and one-half centuries passed between de Soto's *entrada* and the time when the Southeastern Indians... entered the historic era," wrote historian Charles Hudson.

De Soto's fleet landed at Tampa, Florida in 1539 with an army of 600 men, 100 seamen, 100 slaves, servants and camp followers, 243 horses

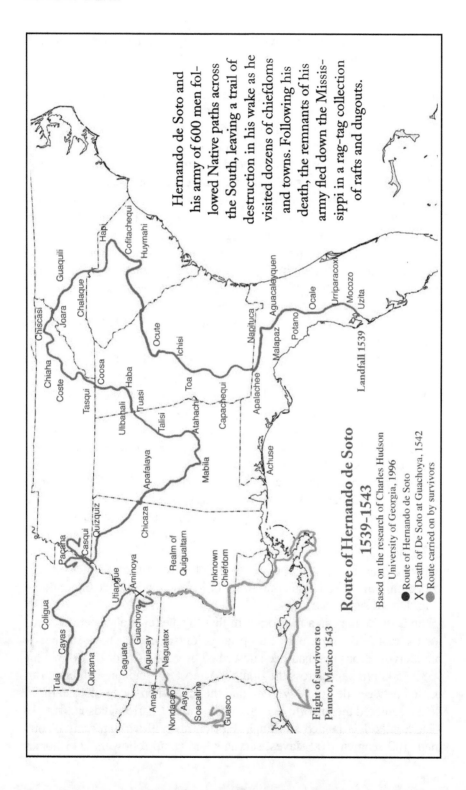

Hernando de Soto and his army of 600 men followed Native paths across the South, leaving a trail of destruction in his wake as he visited dozens of chiefdoms and towns. Following his death, the remnants of his army fled down the Mississippi in a rag-tag collection of rafts and dugouts.

Route of Hernando de Soto
1539-1543

Based on the research of Charles Hudson
University of Georgia, 1996

● Route of Hernando de Soto
X Death of De Soto at Guachoya, 1542
● Route carried on by survivors

and a herd of hundreds of disease-carrying pigs. De Soto was a veteran of the conquests of Nicaragua and Panama, and had become fabulously rich in Pizarro's conquest of the Incas - he was a billionaire by today's standards. It was glory, rather than riches, that sent him and his army rampaging for thousands of miles across the South in an expedition that ranged as far north as Tennessee and as far west as Arkansas. De Soto wished to be appointed a marquis in Spain and that was the expected reward if his expedition succeeded.

One of the foremost chiefdoms De Soto visited was Coosa, a collection of eight large towns that held sway over many smaller chiefdoms. Coosa, the name of both the capital and the chiefdom itself, held sway over 50,000 people, ranging for four hundred miles along the western slope of the Appalachians from Tennessee through Georgia to Alabama. Conquistadors described its capital as being as large as Mexico City with "innumerable" inhabitants. "The country, thickly settled in numerous and large towns, with fields between, was pleasant and had a rich soil with fair river margins," wrote one eyewitness. De Soto and his army were greeted by the principal chief, borne on a litter "in great state" and accompanied by hundreds of warriors. Soon, the chief and his lieutenants found themselves bound with heavy iron collars around their necks, as lowly as slaves and forced to carry loads of baggage as De Soto moved on.

De Soto and other Spanish explorers such as Francisco Vázquez de Coronado and Ponce de Leon were inspired by a Christian myth of vast riches to be found in the New World.

Spanish legend had it that eight hundred years earlier in 711 A.D., seven Catholic bishops had fled Portugal when the Islamic Moors crossed over from Africa and conquered the Iberian Peninsula. It was taken as gospel that the bishops had fled across the Atlantic with an immense treasure to an island called Antillia where they established seven Cities of Cibola paved with gold.

The churchmen and scholars of Spain avowed that North America could indeed be Antillia and that the descendants of the bishops would likely be willing to part with a generous share of their riches to any enterprising Christian who might happen by.

The corker for this preposterous legend was an eyewitness in the form of Friar Marcos de Niza, who set out from Spanish Mexico in 1538 to probe the Southwest in the company of the aforementioned slave, Estevanico, who had survived the expedition of Panfilo Narváez. Estevanico was killed by the Zuni Indians during their trip, possibly for his habit of being grabby with the tribe's women, but Friar Niza returned to Mexico, claiming that he had seen a golden city high up on a hill during his travels.

Although Niza hadn't entered the city himself, he described it as being as large as Mexico City.

Bolstered by this good news and concurrent with De Soto's expedition, Coronado set out in 1540 with a force of 400 soldiers and 1,500-2,000 Mexican Indians in search of the treasure.

Coronado managed to discover the Grand Canyon but never found any cities - only sand, cactus and gila monsters. Most likely, what Friar Niza had spotted from a distance was a cliff dwelling of the Anasazi, shining like towers of gold in the setting sun.

Questing for the Cities of Cibola or an Indian empire rich with gold and treasure, De Soto and his army ranged from one chiefdom to another. For the most part he found only freshwater pearls of poor quality and things that only the Indians valued, such as copper, mica, feathers and shells. On the march he set about enslaving thousands of Indians, demanding women for sex slaves, burning towns for the hell of it and stealing Native food supplies. Indians who didn't submit were threatened with torture, mutilation and death. Many slaves tasked as porters died from exposure while being forced to march half-naked in chains without blankets or protection from the cold. A common tactic was to hold the leaders of a town hostage, evicting its residents to the harsh winter while pillaging their stores of corn, nuts and other foods before moving on. With meat being scarce, the Spanish took to eating the Indians' dogs.

Five hundred Indians also became willing servants, only to be abandoned west of the Mississippi, hundreds of miles from their homes amid the territory of hostile tribes when the expedition began to break down.

Cultural misunderstandings abounded. On one occasion a young warrior struck a conquistador on the back with his bow and took off running, thinking that the Spaniard would give chase in what was a traditional bit of Indian play-acting, mimicking warfare. If the Spaniard was unable to catch him, the young warrior would score a victory in this game of tag. But of course the offended conquistador didn't grasp that this was simply a game; thinking he'd been attacked, he set an Irish wolfhound attack-dog on the warrior's trail.

De Soto's expedition was attacked repeatedly along his route, but Native warriors were no match for firearms, cavalry, armor, weapons of iron and steel, and armored dogs of war.

As was the case in Europe's medieval wars, De Soto's cavalry swept through ranks of Native warriors as if they were dandelion fluff. The Indians were terrified of the "big dogs" of the high-riding Spanish, assuming that horses were capable of eating a man alive. De Soto had told them so

Legend has it that De Soto was welcomed to Cofitachequi in Georgia by the beautiful niece of the chiefdom's female ruler. Dressed in an exquisite gown of white mulberry fibers, she arrived in a canopied canoe, followed by a retinue of attendants. One smitten Spaniard compared her to Cleopatra, being "brown but well-proportioned." She presented De Soto with a small fortune in pearls, only to be taken captive. Fortunately, the "Lady of Cofitachequi" was able to escape a month later. Thereafter, De Soto lost all of his pearls in the Battle of Mabila.

himself. They soon learned to target horses with their arrows, ushering the beginning of the end for De Soto's army. Yet as Native warriors would discover in the centuries ahead, superior military technology almost always prevailed, even against overwhelming odds.

At a major battle at Mabila in present-day Alabama, the conquistadors were ambushed with their guard down. Swarmed by thousands of warriors, De Soto's men scrambled for their weapons for a counter-attack, killing anywhere from 2,500-6,000 Indians while suffering the loss of only eighteen men and seven horses. That's one account; a memoir written in 1557 by a Portuguese knight named the Gentleman of Elvas, who accompanied the expedition, claimed that 200 Spaniards were killed, with another 150 suffering serious wounds, of which twenty soon expired. Yet another account claims that only two of De Soto's men were killed. Who knows? All accounts agree that almost every Spaniard was seriously wounded, with many dying after the battle.

De Soton died of a fever in the village of Guachoya in what is now Arkansas after discovering the Mississippi River. To perpetuate his legend as a god and prevent the Indians from desecrating his grave, his corpse was stuffed into a hollow log and dumped in the muddy Mississippi. He never found the gold he was seeking, but did leave behind a herd of seven hundred pigs.

Thereafter, his army was ground down by hunger and continuous attacks. The survivors tried to make their way to Mexico by land across the dry and dusty plains of Texas, hoping to encounter the expedition of Coronado, but found no Indians to plunder for food, nor any water. Turning back, the conquistadors engaged in a running battle against a massive flotilla of warlike tribes down the Mississippi, fleeing south in makeshift boats and rafts. By then the survivors were dressed in rags and animal skins and had been forced to melt down their armaments to make the nails that held their rafts together; they cowered behind bulwarks of reeds, enduring a rain of spears and arrows. More than half of the army died during its four-year rampage, along with all of 243 of its horses.

De Soto was the first and last European to see many of the great chiefdoms that spanned hundreds of miles across the South. As had been the case with the conquest of Mexico by Cortés, De Soto's expedition included a man who was infected with the smallpox pathogen. Left behind in Georgia, the sick man sparked a contagion of disease that swept across the South, wreaking havoc and ruin everywhere.

Coosa was utterly destroyed in the wake of De Soto's visit. Twenty years later, a group of starving colonists under Tristan de Luna searched for the chiefdom in vain in the hope of finding food and guides. Coosa's towns had been abandoned, its fields were overgrown, and its population had been reduced by tens of thousands.

"The arrival of the Spaniards in former years had driven the Indians up into the forests, where they preferred to live among the wild beasts who did no harm to them, but whom they could master, than among the Spaniards at whose hands they received injuries...," wrote a chronicler of the expedition.

Similarly, the Caddo people of Arkansas and East Texas had a civilization of 200,000 people with towns filled with earthen pyramids, plazas and vast markets. By the time Sieur de La Salle arrived in 1682, however, only 8,500 Caddoans had survived the diseases and devastation left by De Soto.

The refugees of these, and many other ruined chiefdoms, coalesced into remnant tribes which European colonists encountered a century later. The people of Coosa resurfaced as the Creek Confederacy, which included the Choctaw, Catawbas, Chickasaw and Muskogee. Also impacted were the Cherokee on either side of the Appalachians, the Natchez west of the Mississippi, the Shawnee ranging from Tennessee to South Carolina and many other Native peoples.

Then too came the sudden disappearance of the Fort Ancient people, who were likely the ancestors of the Shawnee. Dwelling on both sides of the Ohio River and arising from the Hopewell Culture, the Fort Ancient people built huge earthworks and lived in palisaded towns. Two thousand years ago, they constructed a huge ceremonial center fifty miles north of Cincinnati along the Little Miami River which included more than three miles of low earthen walls surrounding a one hundred-acre complex of mounds and astronomical facilities. Now a state park near the town of Lebanon, the site is the largest prehistoric enclosure in the country. As with the civilizations to the South, the Fort Ancient people also dispersed around 1600, coinciding with the spread of European diseases.

The collapse of the southern chiefdoms likely had an effect on the tribes of the Midwest and Great Lakes, if only by disrupting trade. But the truth is that archeologists don't know for certain what happened to the refugees of the Lost Century, where they fled, and what tribes they joined or formed. Although tribes living far distant from the southern epidemics may have been slaughtered by way of contact with Indian traders and refugees, diseases such as smallpox and measles would have quickly gone extinct without large populations to serve as hosts.

The newly-configured tribes were a shadow of the chiefdoms that had come before them, giving rise to the belief existing to this day that the Indians were, in Andrew Jackson's words, nothing more than "a few savage hunters" sprinkled here and there through a dense wilderness. Gone were their civilizations with populations rivaling Europe, along with all of the towns, farmlands and trading routes which once sustained them.

As for the capital of mighty Coosa, it was dubbed Little Egypt by the explorers who came after its fall. Today its ruins lie deep beneath Carters Lake in Georgia.

CHAPTER 11

A PLAGUE OF PATHOGENS

"Infinite thousands" is how Jesuit Father Martin de Murua described the death toll from smallpox among the Incas in the 1500s. The Incans had an empire of up to twelve million people in South America when Spanish conquistadors arrived bearing deadly pathogens, killing nine out of every ten who were infected.

Smallpox, measles, diphtheria, viral hepatitis, mumps, flu, cholera, typhus, scarlet fever, influenza and whooping cough were the unstoppable horsemen of a pathogenic apocalypse, descending on Native peoples across North and South America with the arrival of European explorers and settlers.

Smallpox covered its victims in bubbling pustules, sometimes blinding them. Immobilized, all its victims could do was lie in an agonized state of near paralysis. Those who survived were often scarred for life. Native peoples who contracted measles might die within a day or two, hemorrhaging blood from every orifice. Infectious diseases were the equivalent of biological nuclear bombs.

European diseases had a devastating effect of the social order of the Indians. Despair rained down on hundreds of communities, shattering religious beliefs and the authority of respected shamans and healers who were powerless against the white man's diseases. The death of Native leaders and elders left survivors without guidance at a time when they needed it most. The extermination of a tribe's warriors left them fair game for their enemies, some of whom had nursed grudges for generations.

During the 1950s and '60s anthropologist Henry F. Dobyns conducted archival research into Native death rates based on ledgers compiled by Spanish priests dating back to the 1500s. Over more than a decade of research he estimated that there had been 90-112 million people living in the Americas when European explorers arrived. If true, then based on epidemic models from Europe and Asia, the introduction of infectious diseases may have killed between 80-100 million.

"... in most areas, around 95 percent of the tribal population died during the early contact period," wrote Ojibwe historian Anton Treuer in his *Atlas of Indian Nations*. "Making matters worse, those deaths often occurred at the same time that Europeans came to take their land or enslave their people. The combination crippled resistance and toppled many tribal political systems."

Dobyns has had critics and supporters arguing back and forth over the indigenous population ever since he published his findings in 1966; later studies have ratcheted population figures down to fifty million. Who knows? Whatever the indigenous population was prior to 1492, we do know that death rates from disease thereafter were atrociously high.

Native peoples first experienced the horrors of smallpox with the fall of Tenochtitlan in 1520. An Aztec account, written down by Spanish monks, described the carnage:

"... a great plague broke out here in Tenochtitlan... and lasted for seventy days, striking everywhere in the city and killing a vast number of our people. Sores erupted on our faces, our breasts, our bellies; we were covered with agonizing sores from head to foot. The illness was so dreadful that no one could walk or move. The sick were so utterly helpless that they could only lie on their beds like corpses, unable to move their limbs or even their heads. They could not lie face down or roll from one side to the other. If they did move their bodies, they screamed with pain.

A great many died from this plague, and many others died of hunger. They could not get up to search for food, and everyone else was too sick to care for them, so they starved to death in their beds."

Similarly, there were tens of thousands of the Timucuan people living in northeastern Florida when the Spanish arrived in the early 1500s, but by 1698 less than one thousand had survived the epidemics brought by the interlopers. The last known Timucuan died in 1767.

New England had up to 90 percent of its Native population eradicated by disease, and the death rate among the Iroquois and Hurons sparked a diaspora that drove dozens of tribes fleeing all over the map of the Great Lakes.

"An unidentified epidemic or epidemics caused the Winnebago in Wisconsin to suffer a population drop from about 20,000 possibly to a low figure of 600 between 1634 and 1670," wrote Helen Tanner in her authoritative *Atlas of Great Lakes Indian History*.

Smallpox also utterly destroyed the Mandan civilization of the Upper Missouri. There were twelve thousand Mandans living in earthen homes in well-ordered towns encompassing fifteen acres surrounded by dry moats when the first white explorers and trappers arrived in the early 1800s. By 1838, there were only three hundred survivors. Many of the afflicted leapt from the cliffs over the Missouri River to end their agony.

Add to this, the rats we see today in urban areas did not exist in the Americas prior to the arrival of Europeans. The arrival of Norway rats (aka brown rats, sewer rats, etc.) on European ships unleashed hordes of scavengers on Native food caches at a time when the sick were in peril of starvation. They played a significant role in the extermination of the Mandans, who were ironically happy to see them at first, thinking they would prey on bothersome field mice.

Tanner noted that historians have attributed smallpox to most epidemics afflicting the Indians, and while this pathogen swept the Great Lakes in virtually every decade from the 1630s on, measles and cholera were also leading causes of death among Native peoples.

This roulette wheel of infectious diseases is why early colonists were surprised to find relatively few Indians waiting to greet them when they arrived decades after the first explorers. Thousands of Native towns and villages had been swept from the earth in the wake of introduced diseases. English colonists found the rotted tatters of villages and "heapes of bones" when they arrived in New England. In 1682 the French explorer Sieur de la Salle expected to find fifty Native towns along a two-hundred-mile stretch of the Mississippi that had been described as a vibrant civilization by Hernando de Soto 140 years earlier. Not a single town or village remained. Instead he found, "a solitude unrelieved by the faintest trace of man."

So although it's widely known that Native peoples had little resistance to the disease brought by Europeans, few of us seem to know the reason why.

The answer is quite simple. The most devastating diseases that plague the human race jumped species from animals to humans after the development of agriculture and herding eight thousand years ago. Europeans, Asians and Africans had thousands of years to develop a small measure of immunity to diseases such as smallpox and measles, but not so for the Indians whose ancestors crossed over from northern Asia twenty thousand years ago, long before these pathogens evolved.

Pathogens that jump from animals to humans are called zoonotic diseases, which comprise six out of ten infectious diseases. These include rabies, Lyme disease, brucellosis, West Nile, and the coronaviruses.

Ebola virus is thought to have originated from fruit bats in Africa. Measles jumped species from cattle. Smallpox may have originated from camels or gerbils in Africa, with the first outbreak reported in Egypt in 3,700 B.C. And if we are to believe the Chinese, then Covid 19 didn't originate in a biological research lab in Wuhan, but rather, from the consumption of

A fanciful meeting between a Jesuit "Black Robe" and the Odawa depicted in a stained glass window at the Little Stone Church on Mackinac Island. The Indians were skeptical of priestly claims of Christianity, which seemed dubious at best. Some played along to gain favorable trading privileges. Unfortunately, many well-meaning missionaries introduced infectious diseases which killed tens of thousands of their intended converts.

half-raw pandolins, raccoon dogs or bats sold in that city's "wet" market.

In the Old World, the domestication of the horse around 3500 B.C. and the camel around 2500 B.C. allowed infectious diseases to spread over wide distances by way of trade and conquest. Additionally, the establishment of cities in Egypt and Mesopotamia created the large populations which infectious diseases require in order to survive their own extinction. Measles, for instance, requires at least 500,000 people living close together in order to keep on keeping on. By 1000 B.C., Thebes, the capital of Egypt, had a population of 120,000, as did Babylon in Iraq. Rome would be the first city on earth to achieve a population of one million by 100 B.C. These cities were sugar plums for diseases such as smallpox and were frequently swept of their citizens in the tens of thousands.

Europeans diseases were easily spread. Smallpox, for instance, has an incubation of twelve days, meaning that a Native trader carrying the pathogen could infect far-off villages. The clothing he wore or the blankets he traded could be contagious with the smallpox pathogen for up to a month. With this lengthy incubation period, those managing to flee could infect even more.

With their belief in evil spirits as the cause of disease, Native peoples initially huddled together in large council houses, erroneously believing that there was safety in numbers and hoping to scare off the demons of disease by posting frightening masks at the entry ways. This only made things worse. Among the Iroquois, the "false face" ceremony was an attempt by shamans to summon healing spirits and scare away the demons of disease, again with no effect other than to undermine Native confidence in their medicine men, fracturing their society.

Smallpox also had the unintended effect of Christianizing many Indians. Many Europeans carried the smallpox pathogen without ever getting deathly ill or dying (typically, only a third of infected Europeans died). The Aztecs saw their Spanish enemies surviving while they were dying by the tens of thousands. Ditto for the Hurons dwelling among the disease-bearing "Black Robes" of the Jesuit missionaries. Many tribes attributed this to the beneficence of the Christian god protecting his people while their own gods were powerless to resist.

Book Three
King Beaver

CHAPTER 12

MARRIED TO THE ANIMALS

The Ojibwe were barely beyond the Stone Age when the first European trade goods reached their territory on the Upper Great Lakes in the mid-1600s. It was trade in the lowly beaver that catapulted them the cultural equivalent of thousands of years into the future.

A little background:

As any backpacker can tell you, the forests along the shores of Lake Superior don't look like they'd be survivable for long. Terrific winds blow from off the lake, bringing arctic cold and snow drifts up to twelve feet high. Nor do the dark pine forests look like they'd yield much in the way of food, if any. Yet it was here that the Ojibwe lived and thrived.

"Snowshoe Dance at the First Snowfall" 1835 by frontier artist George Catlin performed by the Ojibwe at Fort Snelling, MN. Courtesy of the Smithsonian American Art Museum.

The Ojibwe - indeed, all Indians - were masters of many things we've long forgotten. Their women had an encyclopedic knowledge of edible plants and those with medicinal properties. Women were also expert in the tanning of hides, which involved scraping away the last bits of flesh and then massaging a mash of greasy brain matter and urine into the leather to make it pliable. A woman would then spend hours seesawing the hide around the smooth bark of a maple tree to make it even more pliable. Her other duties would have been collecting tons of firewood for the long winter ahead, foraging for berries and digging for roots, all with her baby strapped to her back on a cradle board. After the men had bowed the saplings for the creation of a wigwam, she was in charge of covering it with reed mats, birch and elm bark. She fashioned her family's clothing using bone needles, repaired her husband's moccasins every night during the winter hunt, made the day's only meal, tended the garden and wove mats from the reeds she collected in the marshes. It was tough being a woman.

Men, being the providers, were at risk of an early death from the hazards of hunting and fishing: slip-and-falls resulting in broken bones; falling through the ice while fishing or crossing a lake; being gored, crushed or bitten by prey; or killed by skulking raiders. Speaking of which, every able-bodied man had to be a paramilitary warrior, ready to respond at a moment's notice if his village was attacked.

As with women, men had specialized skills. It takes days to carve a bow strong enough to take down a deer with only stone tools to work with; then fashioning arrows from shoots of dogwood, ash or birch; then braiding a bowstring from the sinew of a snapping turtle's neck or the rawhide of a black squirrel's pelt. Over the long winter nights, men would knapp arrowheads and spear points by the score from chert and flint. A man also knew how to start a fire through the friction of wood-on-wood or sparks from a chunk of flint; how to make a gill net and fish weir; and how to spear fish through the ice by using a wooden decoy shaped like a sturgeon. Men and women worked miracles with tools of bone, antler, stone and wood.

As for children, they were raised by the example of older kids, roaming at large and playing games that would serve them in the hunt or the lodge as they grew older. Europeans were astounded to find that Native children were never subjected to corporal punishment; the Indians believed that children had strong guardian spirits who wouldn't take kindly to the beatings and child abuse that were common in Europe.

But these talents alone did not account for the Anishinaabek thriving on the Upper Great Lakes.

Today, we have the myth of the rugged individual going it alone, as celebrated in popular media: the survivalist with his gun, Rambo and Mad Max the Road Warrior, all toughing it out solo. Yet as reality television shows such as "Naked and Afraid" or "Alone" demonstrate, even highly-trained survivalists with metal tools at their disposal often turn into frightened wrecks, filled with despair and sobbing for their loved-ones within weeks of being dropped into environments similar to that of Lake Superior.

Native peoples would have scoffed at the notion of the rugged individual, knowing that no one can survive for long without the help of family and friends. Although each band had its own clearly-defined hunting, wintering and gardening grounds, everything that was gathered was shared in their communal societies so that all could survive. An infant might nurse at the breast of any woman who had milk to spare, while children might spend the night at the lodge of anyone in the village. Everyone was considered a relative, cherished or at least tolerated by everyone else.

Worse than a death sentence in some tribes was banishment for a crime such as murder or cannibalism. Cast into the forest, a person who was banished would be terrified of the evil spirits that lurked in the night, with slow death from starvation or exposure being certain. Then, one's bones would be eaten and scattered by animals making it impossible to live on as a whole being in the Spirit Land.

The Anishinaabek believed they had a sacred bond with the animals that approached blood ties, as reflected in their myths of shape-shifting and transmogrification, with, for instance, a bear or wolf becoming human and vice-versa. They didn't see themselves as having "dominion" over the animals as taught in the Bible; rather, they were all-one with all that existed. In a metaphorical sense they were married to the animals: brothers and sisters to the deer, wolf, eagle and other creatures, while recognizing that there was a hierarchy among predators and prey, and that it was entirely natural to kill for food. When a hunter took a deer, he gave thanks to it for sacrificing its body so that he and his family might live. Failing to do so could incur bad medicine, such as rheumatism. A bear, *makwa*, the most revered of animals, might be decorated and have tobacco smoke blown into its mouth as a way of saying thanks.

Their clans sprang from the animals from which they were named; they knew that the *Migizi* clan had been hatched from an eagle's egg, while the *Mooz* clan of "twig eaters" had been calved in the marshes.

Also called totems or *dodems*, a clan was a form of an extended family, often possessed of a specialty, such as warfare, leadership or healing. In the patrilineal society of the Anishinaabek, clan membership flowed from the father's side of the family, with all of his children belonging to his clan and not the mother's. Typically, a village included a number of clans, including those made up of captives adopted from other tribes.

Advantageous marriages were often arranged by parents or grandparents in order the strengthen the family, although persons from the same clan were forbidden to marry under the strictest taboo.

Thus, no matter how much his heart might pine for her, a young man of, say, the Moose clan, could never wed a Moose maiden, which would be akin to marrying a sister. Of note, the Australian aborigines also mandated that marriages be between those who were "three skins away" to avoid the troubles inherent in incest, with the punishment being spears thrust through the legs of errant Romeos.

Everything had an essence or spirit that unified all of creation - every rock, tree, human, war club, drum, pot, lodge and animal. Today, we can get a sense of what the Anishinaabek might have felt with the vibe we get from a dream car, a favorite guitar or piano, a photo of a departed loved-one, a beloved leather jacket, a wedding dress, or the shiver that crawls up an arm when we cradle our grandmother's jewelry. Any biker knows there is a powerful spirit within the guts of his Harley.

Spirits that were especially strong were *manitos* inhabiting places of power, such as a cave, a resplendent tree, or a boulder where one sat to watch the sunset. The sun, moon, grandmother earth and powerful forces of the natural world were among the strongest *manitos*, prayed to and giv-

"Chippeway Woman and Child" by Charles Bird King, 1838. Native women have often been ignored in history books, yet many held powerful leadership roles in tribes such as the Iroquois and Potawatomi. Revered as elders, grandmothers often held the purse strings and the family lodge was a wife's domain in which her husband was a guest. Painting courtesy of the Smithsonian American Art Museum.

en sacrifices. A *manito* could be helpful or extremely dangerous, watched over by Kitchi Manito, the Great Spirit. Mild and remote, Kitchi Manito was not all-powerful like the Judeo-Christian God, but rather the "Master of Life" who offered some guidance at times (or not) to the *manitos* under his watch. Or as one Ojibwe observer prosaically noted, "He is like the captain on a steamboat."

Shamans visited the spirit world through a trance state, seeking out beneficial *manitos* to save their people from the malicious ones who spread disease or bad luck. Each individual also had a guardian spirit in the form of an animal, bird or fish. (One finds a corollary in the Catholic belief in guardian angels.) At around the age of twelve, boys, and often girls, would be sent on a spirit quest, fasting for days to reach a point of delirium where it was hoped their guardian spirit would seek them out. Thereafter, the spirit would serve as their benefactor in love and war, hunting, fishing and matters of fate.

The Ojibwe tended to establish their villages on islands or peninsulas, close to good fishing, easily defended, and less prone to surprise attack. Given the ferocious nature of black flies in the north woods, they varied their settlements throughout the summer, moving camp to either the breezy shoreline or the interior woodlands to avoid the temperature-sensitive flies. They were fishermen and hunter-gatherers, relying on fish and nuts for most of their protein. Fishing for sturgeon, trout, perch, whitefish and other species was conducted in every season, including through the ice in the winter.

Their food sources included extensive groves of nut trees, which provided hundreds of baskets of what is called mast - a mix of acorns, hazel nuts and hickory nuts - in order to survive the winter. These jealously-guarded groves also provided hunting opportunities for deer and bear that came to feast on acorns each fall. A cache of nuts buried in a vault lined with rocks and timber could also assure a band's survival when they returned from their winter hunting grounds in the spring. Additionally, groves of sugar maples were tapped each spring, with the boiled sap used to make candies and to sweeten everything from pemmican to dried fish.

As was the case with their Ice Age forebears and the tribes of the Great Plains, the Anishinaabek also resorted to game drives in communal hunts. Moose, deer and other prey were driven onto peninsulas or into V-shaped thickets of branches and brambles where men lay hidden with spears, clubs and arrows. French explorer Samuel de Champlain told of Hurons howling like wolves to send the terrified deer bolting into the enclosures where the were cut down. "... in the thirty-eight days that we were there, they captured one hundred and twenty deer, with which they made good cheer," he wrote, "keeping the fat for the winter and using it as we do butter..."

Explorer Louis Lahontan noted that "a good hunter sometimes kills as many as a dozen animals in a day." He also witnessed carefree Indians, "from time to time bringing into their village some enormous bears, tamed in the course of their hunting; they drive them before them with switches, like sheep driven to the slaughterhouse."

The French quickly became *bons amis* with Native peoples on the Great Lakes, providing trade goods and marrying into Indian families. Ilustration: "Father Jacques Marquette and Louis Joliet Discover the Mississippi, 1763," by John Clark Ridpath, 1893.

CHAPTER 13

FIRST CONTACT

The Ojibwe could hardly believe their good fortune upon first meeting the French, who wanted nothing more than beaver pelts, which were widely available, in exchange for such wonders as iron hatchets, knives, kettles, needles and glass beads. Initially, the French would not provide muskets and ammunition, but eventually even this hurdle was surpassed. In addition to making life infinitely easier, these high-status goods boosted a family's prestige and elevated any chieftain who could secure trade.

Although the Ojibwe had always hunted beaver for food and clothing, they never took more than they needed and were amused that the Europeans cared so much for the beaver that they would part with things that the Indians considered treasures. As an Algonquian quipped to a Jesuit missionary in 1634, "The English have no sense; they gave us twenty knives like this for one beaver skin."

For their part, the French and English thought their cheaply-made trade goods were little more than junk, meaning that both they and the Indians felt they were coming out on top.

"When they discovered that all the Europeans wanted in exchange for their goods were relatively common furs, the Indians launched themselves

wholeheartedly into this trade, much to the detriment of local animal populations," notes historian Eric Jay Dolin in his book, *Fur, Fortune and
Empire*.

But this arrangement drove the beaver to the brink of extinction along
with the unintended consequence of devastating the Indians across the
continent. There were an estimated four hundred million beaver in North
America when the white man arrived, yet most were gone within two
centuries, with the invisible hand of the capitalist market crushing Native
peoples under its thumb thereafter for lack of furs to trade.

In Europe, beaver hats were expensive status symbols in much the same
way that the sneakers of basketball stars and rappers are today. But it
wasn't just fashion that drove the beaver trade. The years between 1680
and 1730 were the frozen heart of the Little Ice Age, a five-hundred-year
period of low solar activity from 1300 to 1850. Sea ice made a good deal
of shipping and fishing impossible; summers grew anemic and shrank by a
third; famine spread across Europe; and glaciers crept down from the Alps
threatening the towns below the slopes. It was in short, pretty damn cold,
and everyone needed a hat. As it happened, hats made from the hyper-in-
sulated pelts of the beaver were the warmest head coverings available and
it didn't hurt that they were also stylish. Beaver hats were also symbols of
prestige and achievement, since the kings of old had forbidden the wearing of furs to all except for the nobility along with high-ranking merchants
and bankers who made the cut. Thus, everyone who was anyone wanted a
beaver hat and was willing to pay dearly for one. A lowly chimney sweep
who managed to score a beaver hat was a prince among his peers, for as
long as he could hang onto it, that is.

We know a good deal about the Native peoples of the Upper Great Lakes
during the seventeenth and eighteenth centuries thanks to the journals kept
by French explorers and Jesuit missionaries who apparently loved writing as much as they did paddling into death-defying scenarios. Samuel de
Champlain, who founded Quebec and visited the Hurons in 1615, wrote
Voyages of New France; fur trader Nicolas Perrot, who explored the Upper
Mississippi Valley in the 1660s, wrote an extensive memoir; and the Jesuit
fathers wrote copiously of their time among the Algonquians and Hurons
in a series of letters called the *Relations*. Ardent journalists with an eye for
detail, many other explorers added to what we know today. The spelling
of tribal names and many other things in these texts tend to be all over the
map, given that the writers were going on their best judgment of what they
heard, but even so, it's not hard to determine, for instance, that the Out-
avois, Outaouaks, Ottawa and Odawa were all one in the same.

This trove of information came to light thanks to the work of many scholars during the depths of the Great Depression. Over the course of 1935-'36 the archives of Montreal, Quebec, Ottawa, Chicago, Detroit, Ann Arbor and Washington, D.C. were scoured for information on first contact between the French and Native peoples of the western Great Lakes, churning up hundreds of volumes of information.

Through their trade connections, the Ojibwe were likely aware of European explorers for seventy years before they actually met any of the "shadow men" who had no color. They had long envied the Odawa and Huron go-betweens who had secured trade agreements with the strangely-dressed, bearded men they called *Wemitigoji*. A young Frenchman named Étienne Brûlé is said to have been the first European to meet the Ojibwe at the Mackinac Straits in 1614.

Brûlé fit the mold of a swashbuckling adventurer, and was the first in a line of French *coureurs de bois,* or "rangers of the woods" who scoured the Upper Great Lakes in search of pelts and trade with the Indians.

Born in Paris in 1592, he traveled to the wilderness of Canada at the age of sixteen and became a protegé of Samuel de Champlain. Seeing promise in young Brûlé, who begged to live among the Indians in order to learn their language and customs, Champlain sent him to the Hurons in 1610 with orders to report back within a year. It was likely a suicide mission, but to Champlain's surprise, Brûlé returned in 1611 dressed in Huron fashion, bringing vital information on establishing trade with the Indians. Thereafter, he was dispatched again, disappearing for four years without a word back home as he wandered to the west as far as the Mackinac Straits. He was likely the first white man to see all five of the Great Lakes.

On one occasion, Brûlé was traveling with a small party of Hurons when they were attacked by the Seneca Iroquois. Abandoning his mates, Brûlé plunged into the wilderness only to find himself completely lost. After wandering for days and on the brink of starving to death, he came across three Seneca hunters and gave out a hearty halloo, despite the risk. The hunters took him to their village where everyone crowded around to see a "Man of Iron," referring to the metal implements of their French enemies. Brûlé danced around the subject, dissembling that he was of a "better nation than the French," meaning a subset of the Hurons who desired to make peace.

Not believing him, the Seneca tied him up, seared him with firebrands, bit his fingernails out with their teeth and plucked out his beard. It looked like curtains for Brûlé, until they came to the silver cross hanging on a necklace around his neck. The agonized Brûlé told his tormentors that if they took the crucifix and killed him, "you will all die - you and all your kin."

Then in an account worthy of a chivalric romance novel, "darkness brooded o'er the scene," obscuring the sun, followed by thunder and lightning "so violent and long-continued that it was something strange and awful."

According to his report to Champlain, the villagers fled en masse, only to be called back by Brûlé, who promised he would intervene on their behalf to the Great Spirit if they would play nice. They nursed him back to health and sent him on his way.

Returning to Quebec, Brûlé was confined for a year for consorting with renegade French traders, among other slights. While there, he taught Jesuit priests the Huron language before departing for France and a short-term marriage. In 1628 while sailing with a French fleet, he was captured by the British and taken to London before being returned to New France. A year later he was accused of spying on Quebec, which was captured by the British in the Anglo-French War of 1629.

Thereafter, Brûlé returned to the Hurons, where he met his end at the age of forty-one. One legend has it that he was too free with the Huron ladies and was knocked on his head, boiled and eaten for his indiscretion. The more accepted version, however, is that a faction of the Hurons were suspicious of Brûlé's escape from the Senecas and accused him of trying to establish trade with their enemies. He was stabbed and dismembered, initiating a schism with other Hurons who opposed his death.

Sadly, for all of his adventures, language skills and insights into Native societies, Brûlé left no written records of the things he had seen and done.

Brûlé's visit was followed up twenty years later by Jean Nicolet in 1634, a *coureur de bois* alleged to have been the first European to explore Lake Michigan.

Like Brûlé, Nicolet was one of a number of young men who Champlain sent to live among the Indians in order to learn their language, habits and to encourage trading ties. He had spent two years with the Algonquians and eight years with the Nipissings to the north of Lake Huron. As Champlain's interpreter, he was well suited to lead an expedition to the mysterious "People of the Sea" living beyond the Mackinac Straits. Champlain thought it possible that this unknown land might lie on the brink of Asia.

Few men were better suited for this trek. On his many adventures with the Indians, Nicolet had at times gone up to eight days without food; once living for seven weeks on little more than lichen and the bark of trees. He had also led a party of four hundred Algonquians on a successful peace mission to the Iroquois.

Writing in 1642, his friend and admirer Father Barthelemy Vimont told Nicolet's story: Setting out with seven Odawas as an escort (elsewhere they are referred to as Hurons) Nicolet would hang presents on poles wherever he landed so that the locals would know he was friendly. The Menominee of northern Wisconsin enthusiastically sent word on ahead of the "wonderful man" heading south to the Ho-Chunk Sioux.

He famously landed at Green Bay wearing "a grand robe of Chinese damansk, all strewn with flowers and birds of many colors," Father Vimont wrote. "No sooner did they perceive him than the women and children fled at the sight of a man who carried thunder in both hands — for thus they called the two pistols that he held. The news of his coming quickly spread to the places round about, and there assembled four or five thousand men. Each of the chief men made a feast for him, and at one of these banquets they served at least six score (120) beavers."

The irony is that Nicolet hoped to bump into Asia, but geographically speaking, he was himself from the "far east" as far as the Ho-Chunk were concerned. He went on to explore Wisconsin, traveling almost as far as the Mississippi River. Alas, he never found China.

In recent years some historians have cast doubt on whether he even made it to Lake Michigan or met the Ho-Chunk; and that his cloak of many colors may also have been sheer fabrication, pun intended. But one may be forgiven for choosing to believe the more colorful story.

Trade with the Ojibwe began in earnest a few years thereafter. In 1641, Jesuit fathers Isaac Jogues and Charles Raymbault attended a Feast of the Dead among the Nipissings in Ontario, a magical rite which was attended by two thousand Natives from many tribes. They were blown away by what they saw: "so mighty were the combats, so virile the games, so plaintive the chants, and so agile the dances of these barbarians... under the guise of mourning their dead they displayed many feats of valor and indulged in hearty feasts."

At the feast they met a company of Ojibwe who invited them to visit their village at Boweting three hundred miles to the west near the outflow of Lake Superior. The Ojibwe hoped to learn something of the magical powers of the Black Robes and establish a trading partnership.

Arriving at Boweting after seventeen days of paddling in birch bark canoes, fathers Jogues and Raymbault found two thousand Indians busy fishing along the St. Marys River. Fishing for souls themselves, the Jesuits returned in 1668, with Father Marquette establishing a mission at the Sault, which is the French word for rapids. The Jesuits had already established a mission among the Hurons of Georgian Bay in Ontario, which they called Sainte Marie after the mother of Jesus. Building on the name, they called their new mission Sault Sainte Marie, designating the Ojibwe of the area as *Saulteurs* - the people of the rapids. Thus, the neighboring Sault Ste.

Marie cities in Michigan and Ontario are known to this day.

An invalid, Father Raymbault died at Quebec in 1642 a year after his visit to the Ojibwe. Father Jogues was captured and tortured by the Iroquois while returning home. After securing his release he foolishly returned to Iroquoia at a later date, hoping to establish a mission. Instead, he died there as a martyr.

Word of a wilderness rich with fur-bearing animals led French traders Medard Groseilliers and Pierre Esprit Radisson to establish a trading post at Chequamegon Bay in western Lake Superior in 1658, engaging the Ojibwe, Odawa, Cree and many other tribes in trapping the beaver to the north and west. The two returned to the town of Trois Rivières in New France in 1659 with nearly a hundred canoes packed with thousands of beaver, lynx, martin, mink and wolverine pelts only to be thrown into jail for operating without a license from the king of France. Their furs, worth millions, were confiscated. But Radisson and Groselliers got even by going on to help the British launch the fabulously successful Hudsons Bay Company, which bloodied the French nose.

Many *coureurs de bois* disappeared into the wilderness, preferring the freedom of life among the Indians to the suffocating mores of the Old World. But others dreamed of returning dazzlingly rich to France as the owners of chateaus, horse-drawn liveries, and attended by coachmen, servants and perfumed mistresses.

Native peoples hunted beaver in the winter when their pelts were thick and luxurious and it wasn't until the late 1700s that they acquired metal traps. English trader Alexander Henry, who spent the winter of 1763-'67 hunting with a family of Ojibwe on a river somewhere along the east coast of Lake Michigan, offered an account:

"The most common way of taking the beaver is that of breaking up its house, which is done with trenching tools during the winter, when the ice is strong enough to allow of approaching them and when, also, the fur is in its most valuable state.

"Breaking up the house, however, is only a preparatory step. During this operation the family made their escape to one or more of their washes (a cavity under the ice where beaver surfaced to breathe). These are to be discovered by striking the ice along the bank, and where the holes are a hollow sound is returned. After discovering and searching many of these in vain we often found the whole family together in the same wash... From the washes they must be taken out with the hands; and in doing this the hunter sometimes received severe wounds from their teeth."

In another account by a French trader, the Odawa drove beavers into nets as they scuttled into their washes, after which they were clubbed to death.

A simpler method was to chop a hole in the ice with an iron axe and wait for a beaver to swim up for a breath of air. The waiting Indian trapper would plunge his hands into the icy water, grasping the startled beaver by its front legs and jerking it onto the ice where it could be clubbed and skinned.

Getting bitten by a beaver was as serious as a knife wound, and possibly even fatal given the pathogens in its mouth. A large beaver can measure up to four feet long, weigh seventy pounds, and has inch-long orange incisors powerful enough to chisel its way through tree trunks more than two feet in diameter. Its four curved incisors are edged with extremely hard enamel and never stop growing. If a beaver were to stop gnawing trees, its ever-growing teeth would eventually curve back and penetrate its brain.

Yet this risk was outweighed by the beaver's commercial value as a stylish warmer-upper. As noted by historian Dolin, the fur of a beaver "comprises two types of hair: the longer, coarser guard hairs, and the softer, woollier undercoat, which together achieve astounding densities ranging from 12,000 to 23,000 hairs per square centimeter (about a half inch)." Perhaps only the caribou with its double coat of hollow fibers provides better insulation.

A dirty and dangerous business, trapping beaver for trade goods also necessitated slaying them in the hundreds. Typically, an Indian trapper would accrue packs weighing one hundred pounds, about eighty beaver pelts.

Henry said he enjoyed the taste of beaver while living with the Ojibwe, but upon returning home he "could not relish it." He also added this intriguing detail: "Beavers, say the Indians, were formerly a people endowed with speech, not less than with the other noble faculties they possess; but the Great Spirit has taken this away from them lest they should grow superior in understanding to mankind."

The trade in beaver gave the Indians of the Upper Great Lakes entrée into the modern world of metal tools, manufactured clothing and other conveniences, but it also made them unwitting victims of ruthless capitalism and the laws of supply and demand, giving rise to the so-called Beaver Wars and decades of anarchy and migration.

CHAPTER 14

EMPIRE OF THE IROQUOIS

Dawn rose on July 4 of 1648 with hideous shrieks beyond the palisade of Teanauustaye, a Huron town of two thousand souls on the Georgian Peninsula in Ontario. Beyond its ragged pine wall raged an army of hundreds of Iroquois warriors, the age-old enemies of the Hurons.

The morning sky turned from day to night amid the thunder and powder smoke of hundreds of muskets as the Iroquois hacked their way through the pine stockade, setting it ablaze with their torches of pitch and flax. Soon, the tattooed and painted warriors surged through the maze of the town's longhouses, intent on seizing captives and cutting down its defenders.

Hiding in the chapel of St. Joseph with his flock of converted Hurons was Jesuit Father Antoine Daniel. He hurriedly baptized a few last-minute converts in the hope of meeting them in Heaven and then turned to the raiders at the doorway with an upraised crucifix, buying time for his converts to flee. The Iroquois were startled by the black spectre creeping towards them with an upraised cross, but only for a moment. Father Daniel was shot multiple times, after which his mutilated corpse was tossed into his burning chapel.

Armed with muskets obtained from the Dutch at Fort Orange and New Amsterdam, the Iroquois far outgunned the Huron defenders, who had been denied firearms by their French allies. By the time the smoke cleared, 1,300 Hurons lay dead, with the remaining seven hundred taken captive, mostly women and children.

A cloud of fear settled over Huronia, a confederacy of six tribes of Native farmers connected by clan ties and a military alliance. Ironically, the Hurons were a virtual mirror of the Iroquois, speaking an Iroquoian dialect and sharing many customs. Yet these two civilizations had warred against one-another for generations.

Dwelling south of Lake Erie and Lake Ontario, the Iroquois were also a confederacy of five tribes. The League of Five Nations, included the Mohawk, Seneca, Oneida, Onondaga and Cayuga. (In 1722 the Tuscarora

Recreation of a longhouse and palisade at the Huron Traditional Site north of the City of Quebec. Heavily-sheathed in bark, a longhouse could be more than 150 feet long and 30 feet high, sheltering a number of families.

were admitted to the League after being driven out of North Carolina by the British.) As with the Hurons, the Iroquois were a farming people, raising corn, beans, squash, sunflowers, pumpkin, tobacco and arcane vegetables such as goose foot and pigweed. Both the Iroquois and Hurons were matrilineal societies with inheritance and clan membership flowing from the woman's side of the family. Female leaders had a strong voice in guiding the civic affairs of the tribes, although a council of men took precedence in matters of warfare.

Both the Hurons and the Iroquois lived in fortified towns, dwelling in immense domed longhouses thirty feet high, sheathed in bark and divided into apartments. In his 1615 visit to the Hurons, Samuel de Champlain wrote that their homes were 150 to 180 feet long and thirty-six feet wide with a ten-foot-wide passage running down the center. "On both sides is a sort of platform, four feet in height, on which they sleep in summer to escape the annoyance of fleas of which they have many... Pieces of wood are suspended on which they put their clothes, provisions and other things for fear of mice which are in great numbers. In one such cabin there will be twelve fires, which make twenty-four households, and there is smoke in good earnest, causing many to have eye problems... for there is no window nor opening except in the roof by which the smoke can escape."

One can only imagine what a fire trap such a bark lodging would be!

Watchtowers were erected along a town's walls to guard against approaching enemies or to spot animals raiding the adjacent fields, which spread for miles. Typically, there was also a maze of thorny branches within the town's only entrance to confuse and delay attackers.

Arising from the agricultural communities of the Finger Lakes region in upstate New York around the year 1000 A.D., the Iroquois began building their towns on hilltops for better defense between 1300 and 1600. An Iroquoian town of up to two thousand residents could encompass ten acres surrounded by a palisade. A large town might hold sway over 600,000 acres of farmland and game parks. A French explorer traveling through Iroquois lands in 1669 reported that each town was surrounded by six square miles of cornfields.

Jon Parmenter, an associate professor of history at Cornell University and the author of an Iroquoian history, *The Edge of the Woods*, notes that these towns were abandoned every ten or twenty years with a new site planned by female leaders. Aside from soil and game depletion, the primary reasons for upping stakes and moving on appear to have been, "motivated by the declining availability of local building materials and firewood, physical deterioration of bark long houses and log palisades, the accumulation of refuse, and possible infestation by rodents and insects."

As was the case with many Indian tribes, the Hurons and Iroquois were given the names we know today by white interlopers, who often opted for a neighboring tribe's unkind description of their enemies. The Hurons called themselves the Wendat, or a similar approximation, but received the name we know today by dint of a their bristling, upswept hair style that reminded the Jesuits and *voyageurs* of the tufts of a wild boar, or *hure*, in French. Disparaging of the Wendats and their wretched meals of cornmeal mush, *huron* was French slang for a ruffian hick. Nor did the French like staying in the Hurons' crowded longhouses, which were overrun with dogs, mice, fleas and lice in addition to the pervasive smoke.

For their part, "Iroquois" was either Basque fishermen jargon for "killer people" or a mash-up of French and Algonquian for "snakes." As with the Hurons, it was not a name the Iroquois gave to themselves; by tradition they called themselves the "original men" or "the men of men." They were also known as the Haudenosaunee, "people who build a lodge."

The formation of the Iroquois League, which they called the great Tree of Peace, was the outcome of a myth known as the *Deganawidah Epic*, of which in typical Native fashion there several versions.

The story goes that around the year 1000 A.D., five tribes living along the shores of lakes Erie and Ontario were locked in an endless cycle of warfare, spurred on by a tradition of revenge and blood feuds. Into this hairball of violence came a Huron shaman, Deganawidah, in a canoe of white stone. Born of a virgin maiden, Deganawidah brought a message of peace, but due to a problem speaking, he hooked up with a famous Onondaga orator, Ayenwatha, otherwise known as Hiawatha. This is this same Hiawatha who served as the protagonist in Henry Wadsworth Longfellow's epic poem. Deganawidah and Hiawatha had many adventures as they traveled among the tribes of the Mohawks, Oneida, Onondaga, Seneca and Cayuga. In one telling, Jigonsaseh, the "mother of nations," agreed to stop feeding warriors so that the warpath could be transformed into a path of unity.

In another story, Tododaho, a powerful shaman and ruler of the Onondagas, killed Hiawatha's three daughters. Tododaho had a frightening persona, manifesting evil and weaving live snakes into his hair. Yet in the spirit of mercy, Hiawatha declined to seek revenge, vowing that no parent should have to suffer the loss of a child. (Subsequent Iroquoian war parties were not as empathetic.)

While four of the tribes agreed to an alliance at a council held in upstate New York, Tododaho and the Onondagas were holdouts. To convince them, Deganawidah invited Tododaho to try breaking an arrow. This was an easy matter for the skeptical shaman, but when Deganawidah asked him to try breaking a bundle of five arrows, he found it impossible. Thus, the point was made that a League of Five Nations would be far stronger than any tribe going it alone. Tododaho agreed after witnessing a solar eclipse which confirmed the celestial favor of the deal, but with the stipulation that an Onondaga town at present-day Syracuse would be designated as the capital of the League. The sun god smiled down on his people from his realm in the sky and the great Longhouse of the Five Nations was born.

The creation of the League gave rise to one of the first parliamentary governments in the history of the world. "Only Iceland's *Althing*, founded in 930 A.D., is older," noted Charles C. Mann in his book, *1491*.

By tradition, Deganawidah established the Iroquois' Great Law of Peace, a constitution of 117 codicils which laid down the powers of government, but also its limitations and the guarantee of individual freedom. Fifty male *sachems*, or chiefs, were appointed by the female heads of various clans to govern the League. While there may have been more *sachems* participating in council from a particular tribe (such as the powerful Mohawks), this made little difference in that only unanimous decisions were valid to a government that valued consensus among all else. Imagine the U.S.

Congress coming to a unanimous decision on anything; even the 1941 declaration of war against Japan in the wake of Pearl Harbor had a single holdout in the House.

The Iroquoian form of government inspired numerous writers, statesmen and philosophers, including Paine, Jefferson, More, Locke, Montaigne, Franklin, Washington and Rousseau, and its divisions of power contributed to the creation of the U.S. Constitution and Congress.

The Iroquois may have achieved peace among themselves, but that was hardly the case when it came to their dealings with other tribes. Their culture was rife with revenge as a motivating force, and they often assumed that any death from sickness, heart failure, a hunting accident, falling off a palisade wall, or any seemingly-unrelated cause was due to the influence of far-off enemies and witches, which must be avenged. Jesuits missionaries, in particular, fit the M.O. of witches perfectly in the Iroquoian mind, as did the Hurons who hosted them.

"Whether a child died young or an elderly parent died of cancer at an advanced age it was nearly always somebody's fault and revenge was an appropriate response," noted anthropologist Dean R. Snow of Pennsylvania State University.

In that respect, the Iroquois were similar to the Waorani of eastern Ecuador, one of the most violent people on earth, whose belief in causality also assumed that virtually any death was the work of an enemy, requiring revenge. Spiralling out of control, it was this epic cycle of blood feuds, raids and counter-raids that prompted the five tribes of the Iroquois to form their league and abide by its great Law of Peace, at least among themselves.

But the Iroquois were certainly not alone in their dread of occult forces. Concurrent with their era, Europe was convulsed with fears of witches and the devil for a 250-year period, resulting in the death of tens of thousands.

"... no man thought himself secure, either in his person or possessions, from the machinations of the devil and his agents," wrote nineteenth century author Charles Mackay of the "witch mania" that swept France, Italy, Germany, England, Scotland and Scandinavia. "Every calamity that befell him he attributed to a witch. If a storm arose and blew down his barn, it was witchcraft; if his cattle died of a murrain - if disease fastened upon his limbs, or death entered suddenly and snatched a beloved face from his hearth - they were not visitations of Providence, but the works of some neighbouring hag, whose wretchedness or insanity caused the ignorant to raise their finger and point at her as a witch."

European witches, sorcerers and wizards were said to have signed a pact with the devil in blood, selling their souls without any chance of redemption. Their "confessions" were typically produced under torture, such as on the rack. Mackay notes that in some German cities it was common to execute six hundred witches per year - nearly two per day, aside from Sundays. To this day, one can find witch-burning poles in the squares of almost every town in Germany, considered jolly cultural artifacts, but once the scenes of fire and blood.

It wasn't all revenge and mayhem for the Iroquois, however. They had immense festivals throughout the year, trading networks which spanned hundreds of miles, and undoubtably a strong sense of community. Spirituality was a powerful guiding force in every aspect of their lives, with both men and women inducted into their priesthood. They believed that every individual had a protective inner power called an *orenda*, whose magic combatted evil spirits, both for the self and for one's people. "Although an individual's *orenda* was small, it contributed to the total *orenda* possessed by a family group or clan, " noted historian Alvin Josephy, Jr., in *500 Nations*. "When a person died, the group's total *orenda* was reduced and was often replenished by the adoption of a captive or a member of another tribe to acquire his or her *orenda*."

It's no stretch to consider the Iroquois' influence and extent as being that of a Native empire, albeit one that was short-lived and limited to plunder and slaves. Barely a step beyond the Stone Age, they could field armies of more than a thousand warriors, nearly exterminating entire tribes. Given the demise of the Aztecs and Mayans, they were likely the most powerful military force in all of the Americas in the 1600s.

"Iroquois movements from 1534 to 1701 occurred over a vast range of eastern North America from the shore of Hudson Bay to the palm groves of South Carolina, and from the coastal waters of Newfoundland to the lower Mississippi River valley," noted Parmenter.

Often, raids by the Hurons and Iroquois consisted of 500-600 men who crept into enemy territory, splitting into cells as small as five men to lurk around a village in the hope of killing or capturing a passerby. These same tactics were used in the 1700s by the Shawnee and Delaware to terrorize isolated settlers in the valleys west of the Appalachian mountains.

Over the course of decades, the Iroquois had come to covet the rich farmland of Huronia. For one, the soil was sandier there, and easier to work in the planting of corn. Huronia was also surrounded on three sides by the waters and bays of Lake Huron, making for good fishing. It was also the gateway to the northern tribes of the Odawa and Ojibwe who traded dried meat, furs, copper, animal hides and other necessities for corn and tobacco. The Hurons also had a pipeline for trade down the French and Ottawa rivers to Montreal. In short, it was a plum target for the Iroquois who had depleted many of their own resources.

They also had an axe to grind; in the summer of 1639 the Hurons had captured 113 Iroquois, burning them alive after the prerequisite tortures. It was this sort of back-and-forth ferocity that put the two civilizations on a fatal track.

Initially more numerous than the Iroquois, the Hurons were also notable warriors and apparently relished their eternal battle. Historian John Witthoft wrote that Huron and Iroquois men may have craved battle to bolster their humdrum lives as farmers and to prove themselves as warriors, rather than mere dirt scratchers.

In addition to the expertise as farmers the Hurons, Iroquois and other tribes had a fabulous cult of the dead. Every ten or twelve years they would collect the bones of all who had died during that period, carefully scrub them clean of any remaining tissue, and hold a mass burial ceremony, filling a common pit grave with the collected bones and immense treasures of every sort, including furs, jewelry, fine pottery and weapons. Several days of celebration, dancing, drumming and other festivities would follow.

They had plenty of bones to bury once the white man arrived. The Hurons were crippled for decades by deadly epidemics of smallpox and other diseases introduced by traders and the "Black Robes" of the Jesuits, who established eleven missions among them. Accounts vary wildly, but when the Jesuits first encountered the Hurons in 1615 they estimated that there were 30,000 to 40,000 living on Ontario's Georgian Peninsula. Similar numbers lived among the neighboring Neutral (Attiwandaronk) and Tionontati tribes to the south. Yet, two out of every three members of these tribes lay dead thirty years later from diseases such as smallpox, measles, whooping cough and the flu. Between 1615 and 1641 the combined population of the Hurons, Neutrals and Tionontati plummeted from 90,000-120,000 souls to only 24,000 survivors.

The Iroquois were also helpless against diseases introduced by the Dutch and English. Smallpox swept through the Five Nations in 1634 killing 60 percent of those it touched, with more epidemics to follow. These events led to what were called "mourning wars" as the Iroquois struggled to appease the angry spirits of their ancestors and rebuild their population by taking captives. By the 1640s, the Iroquois and Hurons each had populations of around 12,000.

As with the Aztecs of Mexico, Iroquois warriors were more intent on taking captives than slaughtering their foes. Instead of seeking captives for sacrifices, however, the Iroquois sought new recruits to replenish their numbers. Typically, an Iroquoian family that had lost a loved-one to disease or warfare would seek a captive as a replacement. Thousands of captives taken from tribes such as the Huron, Odawa, Illinois, Tionontati, Potawatomi, Erie and others were incorporated into Iroquoian families, often becoming warriors in military campaigns against their own people.

Adoption into an Iroquois family could include some preliminary torture as a way of humbling captives, possibly having their fingernails ripped out by the teeth of their captors, or a finger or two lopped off as a way of showing dominance. This invoked the phenomenon of Stockholm Syndrome in which newcomers were perversely eager to cleave to their new families in order to avoid an even grimmer fate.

Historical accounts of the Iroquois and Hurons never fail to mention the hideous tortures inflicted on their captives, particularly male prisoners, which could last for a single night or up to six days with everyone in town participating. "Caressing" a victim with firebrands over every inch of his or her body was a commonly-cited method, giving the victim time to rest and recover before starting the torture anew. Care was taken that no victim died before sunrise so that the sun god would have a chance to witness the work of the tormentors. A victim might also suffer having his genitals, fingers, or strips of his flesh carved away with a knife or sharpened shell, followed by a command to eat up. (After having a thumb lopped off by his captors, Father Isaac Jogues quickly threw it away in order to avoid being forced to eat it.) Scaffold tortures atop platforms were commonplace to allow hundreds of onlookers to enjoy the spectacle, and the grand finale of the show came as dawn broke, at which time the victim was finished off. Through all this, a victim worth his salt was expected to sing his death song, mocking his tormenters and begging them to do their worst as he kicked at the coals he was forced to walk upon or endured the firebrands thrust into every orifice of his body.

That said, historian William Brandon noted in his book, *Indians*, that it's possible that Iroquoian torture was simply better documented and more notorious than what was going on at the time, "considering that most of their neighbors indulged in similar delights." The Iroquois may also have received more than their share of what we'd call bad press from the French, who were much given to compiling journals they called the *Relations*.

Also worth noting, Iroquoian warriors were not known to rape their female captives, a common enough practice among Slavic and Asian armies to this day. This, perhaps, because the warriors of a number of tribes took pride in sexual abstinence, believing that copulation would damage their war medicine.

As a counterpoint to torture, the French claimed that the Hurons were extremely hospitable to visitors and also warm and loving to their neighbors, despite living in crowded conditions. "Although the Hurons manifested a great deal of hostility toward their enemies, their behavior in their homes and villages was noted for its gentleness and tranquility," wrote Bruce G. Trigger, a chronicler of the tribe. "... The Huron were famed for their generosity. Any visitor to a village, unless he came from a hostile tribe, was welcome to food and lodging."

Historians hasten to claim that the Indians were amateurs at torture compared to the horrific practices of European Christians, particularly during the religious wars of the Old World. (Popular "torture museums" throughout Europe can attest to this.)

Examples of European atrocities are legion: Across the ocean in "civilized," Christian, London, for instance, during the mid-1600s an execution might involve being dragged through the filthy, cobbled streets on a wooden frame until one's skin was ripped to shreds; then strangled while hanging until nearly dead, pulled down, slowly castrated, and forced to watch as one's intestines were unraveled and burned along with one's genitals. After this bit of showmanship for the admiring crowd would come a beheading before being ripped into four quarters by teams of horses. Typically, the heads of the executed were spiked on poles to be picked at by crows.

Incredibly, this nearly identical practice of drawing-and-quartering was sentenced on some rebellious farmers who rose up against crippling taxes in Colonial Virginia as late as 1771 (though likely not carried out).

Also concurrent with the Iroquois' heyday, during 1643 the Dutch played football with the severed heads of eighty Wappinger Indians in the streets of New Amsterdam, after which they tortured thirty Natives to death as a public entertainment, *including infants* that were bound to boards prior to their torment.

That, and in Britain's army, navy and penal colonies, punishment could include as much as 500 to 1,000 lashes with a cat-o'nine-tails - with a man being essentially skinned alive and filleted down to his rib cage and spine before hundreds of onlookers standing at attention; the practice endured into the early 1800s. And of course, the lynchings widely practiced in the American South into the twentieth century were spot-on for cruelty, with torture witnessed by thousands of cheering spectators.

All of the above would have been cold comfort to those who endured the tortures of the Iroquois or Hurons, however. Torture rituals were described by the Jesuits in great detail (some suffered direct experience), but there were some practices that they found too gruesome to put in print.

Aside from its entertainment value for bored Iroquois and Huron farmers, torture served both practical and ritual purposes. For the former, it served as a caution not to mess with our people; for the latter, the suffering of a captive under firebrands and slow roasting might satisfy Areskoui, the god of war and hunting. The more stoic a captive endured his fate, the more satisfying was his sacrifice; perhaps he would serve his captor as a slave in the afterlife. Afterward, it was common to devour a heroic captive's heart or some portion of his flesh in order to absorb some of his valor.

The practice of ritual torture, which seemed quite sensible to the Iroquois and other tribes, came back to haunt them in wake of the French and Indian War of 1754-'63, when hundreds of white settlers were captured on the frontier. While many were eventually ransomed, or were treated quite kindly and preferred to remain as adoptees with their Native families, many male captives suffered death by torture, the lurid tales of which burned through the pages of the colonial press, dooming even the most peace-loving Indians as devils in the eyes of the whites.

Obtaining captives was not the only mission of the mourning wars. By the 1640s the Iroquois had depleted all of the beaver and fur-bearing animals in their territory which were needed to trade for muskets, kettles, iron axes, needles, clothing and other goods from the Dutch and English. As would later be the case with the Ojibwe and Odawa, the Iroquois were also egged on by traders to over-hunt their territory, allowing no time for the beaver to rebound.

To the north, however, the Hurons had long been trading partners with the Odawa, Nipissing, Algonquians and other tribes, exchanging agricultural crops for furs, fish nets and other goods from the northern forests. The furs amounted to immense trading riches. Partnering with the French, the Hurons had developed a trading route along the Ottawa and French rivers from Montreal to Lake Huron, cutting the Iroquois out of the action. It was along these rivers that the Iroquois began attacking convoys of canoes bearing their valuable cargoes of furs and trade goods.

In their quest for captives and dominance in the fur trade, the Iroquois began pushing north and west in the so-called the Beaver Wars. On the morning of March 16, 1649, a force of 1,200 Iroquois launched an unheard-of winter attack against the Huron town of Taenhatenteron, which was also the site of a Jesuit mission.

Native warriors in general never conducted military campaigns in the winter for good reason. For one, rivers were often iced over and not possible to navigate by canoe or dugout. Then too, tracks in the snow could lead vengeful foes along the fleeing warriors' trail, and bare trees made it impossible to sneak up on enemies. Winter was the season for planning and gathering warriors for a summer campaign, not for raiding.

The Iroquoian campaign of 1649 was singularly different. Armed with a four hundred muskets supplied by the Dutch at Fort Orange in New York, an army of Mohawk and Seneca warriors set out from upstate New York in the fall of 1648, crossing the St. Lawrence River near present-day Kingston, Ontario. For more than four months they made their way slowly west, hunting, fishing and living off their stores of parched corn.

Completely surprised, the Hurons of Taenhatenteron awoke to the sound of Iroquois warriors hacking at the walls of their fortified town with iron hatchets. The Iroquois' muskets were thrust through the gaps, firing on the town's residents. As with the attack on Teanauustaye the previous year, the town's defenses were quickly shattered. Killing or capturing four hundred Hurons, the Iroquois pushed on, attacking three more villages that hosted the Jesuit missions of St. Ignace, St. Louis, and Sainte-Marie, Ontario. At St. Louis, Ontario Jesuit Fathers Jean de Brebeuf and Gabriel Lallemant were tied to stakes, scalped, "baptized" with boiling water and slung with necklaces of red-hot axe heads. Father Brebeuf died bravely, uttering not a word under torture. His tormentors ate his heart as tribute to his courage.

Of note, the Black Robes of the Jesuits fully intended to die - and often did - as martyrs among the Hurons in their mission to spread the word of God. Eight priests were declared saints after their martyrdom at the hands of the Iroquois. Unfortunately for them, many Hurons and Iroquois considered the Jesuits to be witches and sorcerers. Who else would spread frightening stories of Christ rising from the dead and his gruesome depiction on the cross? That, and the latent cannibalism of the communion host, the descriptions of hell, and other Christian beliefs smacked of witchcraft. Native peoples everywhere were also given to sharing in a communitarian spirit of survival, and those who hoarded their goods, ie., the Jesuits, shared that selfish trait with witches. It also seemed no coincidence that horrendous diseases followed in the Black Robes' wake, yet seemed to not affect them. Many Huron converts played along simply to gain better trading opportunities with the French, who gave special privileges to Christian converts. Other "converts" were baptized as dying infants or adults faced with death who hoped to land in the Christians' heaven.

Believing that occult forces were behind every death and injury that they incurred, the Iroquois viewed the widely-scattered Jesuit missions as a sign of Huron treachery and witchcraft, making them plum targets for attack.

Smoke billowing from the burning long houses of Taenhatenteron alerted other Hurons of the Iroquois' army. The following day, an attack on the Jesuit mission of Sainte-Marie on March 17, 1649 sealed the Hurons' fate. While the Iroquois suffered roughly one hundred casualties, they managed to slay the town's eighty defenders. Thereafter, they tied undesirable captives to stakes within the town's longhouses and set the huge buildings ablaze. The resulting fire storm created a pillar of flame and smoke more than a thousand feet into the sky, turning the sundown blood-red that evening. Loading the surviving captives down with booty in the manner of packhorses, the Iroquois began their long trek home. Those who could not bear up under their loads were killed and tossed by the wayside.

With fifteen of their towns destroyed, the surviving Hurons scattered to the winds. Several thousand fled to Gahoendoe Island (aka Christian Island) in Georgian Bay where most succumbed to starvation and the harsh rain, snow, and cold winds coming off Lake Huron. Those who made it to the mainland across rotting ice in the late winter were picked off by lurking Iroquois. Reduced to eating bark and fungus, only about six hundred survived. Half made their way to Quebec that summer. Others fled to southeastern Michigan or to the north among the Odawa on Manitoulin Island and the Mackinac Straits. Over the next few decades between 1,600 and 2,800 Hurons were adopted into Iroquois families, soon to find themselves fighting other tribes, and even their own, on behalf of their captors.

By 1651, Huronia was utterly smashed and abandoned, yet the onslaught was far from over.

CHAPTER 15

THE GREAT DIASPORA

Swelled by warriors adopted from many conquered tribes, the raiders of the Iroquois swept across eastern North America in the late 1600s, throwing thousands of square miles into chaos as Native peoples everywhere fled for their lives. Meanwhile, in New France, extending from Quebec to Montreal, three hundred colonists quaked in their boots as their lightly-defended territory fell under attack.

Iroquoian raids were sporadic, however, and punctuated by times of peace. Often, it was a single tribe of the Iroquois that went to war - such as the Mohawks battling the Mahicans in the Hudson River Valley - rather than all five tribes of the League.

For nearly seventy years from 1634 to 1701, the five nations of the Iroquois were literally all over the map, first assailing the tribes of eastern Canada, Pennsylvania and the Atlantic states; then those living north of lakes Ontario, Erie, and Huron; and even beyond Lake Michigan as far west as the Mississippi. Unlike the Romans or other empires, which sought to hold territory for tribute and vassals, the Iroquois tended to strike hard and return home with captives, leaving their enemies in ruins. As an Onondaga leader named Teganissorens claimed, when the Iroquois went to war against another people, the goal was "to destroy them utterly."

They also had it in for the French, an animosity that lasted off and on for 150 years. While exploring the lake that bears his name in 1609, a party of Algonquians suckered Samuel de Champlain into attacking 250 Iroquois who were passing through. Champlain killed two prominent Iroquois chieftains with a single blast of his arquebus, while one of his companions killed a third. Never having experienced the thundersticks of the white man, the Iroquois turned and fled, but they had long memories. Another battle against the Mohawks the following year cemented bad relations between the French and Iroquois that were never fully resolved. The Iroquois would back their English allies against the French for the next 150 years.

Like the Aztecs, whose weapon of choice was the obsidian-edged club, the Iroquois went into battle with tomahawks supplementing their muskets. These were war clubs with a stone ball or iron hatchet affixed to the end. In 1634 Plymouth settler William Wood described an attack by the Mohawks, who came:

"... running, and fiercely crying out, *Hadree Hadree succomee succomee, we come we come to sucke your blood*, not fearing the feathered shafts of the strong-armed (English) bowmen, but like unruly headstrong stallions beate them downe with their right hand. Tamahaukes be staves of two foote and a halfte long, and a knob at one end as round and bigge as a football... one blow or thrust with thee strange weapons, will not neede a second to hasten death, from a Mohackes arme."

Wood added that the Mohawks much preferred sporting events to warfare, "in which they are more delighted and better experienced."

For decades the Iroquois were intent on rounding up Huron refugees either through diplomatic means (ie., trading French hostages for Hurons) or via conquest. In their quest to absorb the fleeing Hurons, they gathered Native peoples from many other nations. By the late 1660s the Onondagas alone had adoptees from twenty defeated tribes.

Hot on the heels of smashing the Hurons, an army of 1,200 Iroquois all but exterminated the so-called Neutrals, who lived to north of Lake Erie

Warlike and well-armed with muskets, the five tribes of the Iroquois were literally all over the map in the 1600s, driving many other tribes as far west as the Mississippi. Up to 10,000 refugees gathered at Green Bay, Wisconsin. Many tribes were driven back to the east by the Sioux.

around Niagara Falls. (The French had dubbed them Neutrals for the position they took in avoiding the conflict between the Hurons and Iroquois.) Captives of the Iroquois included many members of the Potawatomi and Mascouten tribes from Michigan. They, in turn, had been taken captive by the Neutrals in the tribe's own mourning wars of 1641-'43.

Pushing north to Georgian Bay, the Iroquois swept the Tionontati "Tobacco People" before them and then fell upon the Odawa living along northern Lake Huron in 1651. But this was only the beginning.

It seemed that nothing could stop the well-armed and organized Iroquois, who out-gunned, out-generaled, and out-fought much larger forces standing against them.

In 1653, the Erie tribe living south of Niagara Falls launched a preemptive attack on the League, burning a Seneca village and slaughtering a force of eighty Onondagas. The Iroquois gathered their forces, pitting an army of 1,800 warriors against 3,000-4,000 Eries, who were known as the People of the Panther. Although they were outnumbered and driven off repeatedly, the Iroquois regrouped each time, destroying a major Erie town near present-day Erie, Pennsylvania. Warfare between the tribes continued over the next two years until the Erie were shattered by an army of 1,200

Onondagas. It's believed that some of the survivors made way to the Sa-
vannah River in South Carolina, where they became known as the Westos,
becoming active in the slave trade, raiding other tribes to sell Indian captives to European planters.

While Indians preferred the ease of traveling by canoe or dugout, they
also had a network of trails extending for hundreds of miles; these were of
use to Iroquoian warriors and refugees alike.

The Great Trail was a network of pathways that crisscrossed present-
day New England, eastern Canada and the mid-Atlantic states, extending
all the way from Chesapeake Bay to the Mississippi River. Other trails
branched out to various Native towns and villages. For instance, in Michigan, there were well-known trails from the Detroit area to Grand Rapids,
and from Traverse City to Cadillac. Stranded explorer Robert Cavalier
Sieur de La Salle and his party of traders used some of these Native pathways when they became the first white men to cross Lower Michigan in
1680. La Salle's ship, *La Griffon*, a forty-five-ton barque equipped with
seven cannon, had been lost on Lake Michigan after leaving Green Bay
with a load of furs. La Salle and his men had been waiting for the ship far
down the Michigan coast when they heard of its disappearance. Rather
than canoeing home all the way around Michigan, he opted to hike nearly
two hundred miles across the base of the peninsula, skirting Iroquoian
raiders to the south.

Native trails were used primarily for trade and hunting expeditions, but
also figured as warpaths and evacuation routes for those fleeing raiders.
Many were used by colonial armies to attack the Indians in later decades
and were eventually adopted as roads by settlers, in time becoming major highways. It was along these trails and canoe routes that the Iroquois
pressed their onslaught.

Imagine the excitement of a young Seneca warrior heading north through
southwestern Ontario in 1651. He carries the musket passed down to him
by his father, who used it in the attack on Teanauustaye only three years
before. His scalp has been plucked for war, leaving only a strip of hair
three fingers wide down the crown of his head with a scalp lock topping
its crest. Now, he and an army of more than a thousand warriors make
their way through the deserted lands of the Hurons. The vast cornfields of
their enemies' blackened towns are already overgrown with maple shoots
and aspen, quickly returning to the forest. Here and there, gaunt survivors
peer at them from the forest, quickly scuttling to safety as the throng of
warriors, nearly a mile long, makes its way north. One night, feeling a jab

at his back, he rolls over in his blanket to discover that he is lying on the bones of a Huron skeleton, half buried by leaves and debris.

By day he makes his way along, holding his musket by the barrel with the stock slung at a jaunty angle over the bedroll on his shoulder. A rawhide bag bears his provisions of roasted cornmeal, which must sustain him for up to six weeks, along with whatever he and his mates can hunt along the way. A medicine bag filled with protective charms is draped by a cord around his neck.

Before leaving his village south of Lake Ontario, our young brave promised his wife that he would return rich with captives and plunder. Such was often the case for Iroquoian warriors, who might expect to return home with up to five captive women and a number of children. As is the custom, his wife and the women of the village will tend the crops and civic affairs throughout the summer while their men are off raiding. The women will also decide which male captives will be adopted or die under torture.

Now, making his way north along the Bruce Peninsula with its spectacular pillars of stone rising from Lake Huron, the young Seneca's heart beats like thunder as he spies Manitoulin Island across the water with its necklace of Odawa villages and their swidden fields spread along the shore. His will be the first of many attacks on the Odawa, pursuing them to the west. His own son will return in the winter of 1669 with an army of six hundred Seneca and Cayuga warriors to attack the Odawa once again in Michigan's Upper Peninsula.

In his *History of the Ottawa and Chippewa Indians of Michigan*, Chief Mack-e-te-be-nessy (Blackbird) claimed that a war party of Seneca raiders wiped out a small tribe that once lived on Mackinac Island. He added that the Senecas were especially troublesome to the Odawa at the Mackinac Straits while vouching for the valor of his people: "Quite often the Iroquois would attack them, but the tradition says that in almost every battle the Ottawas would come out victorious over the Iroquois."

No doubt the Odawa won a few, but in the main they fled to the west in a hurry, abandoning Manitoulin Island and the Mackinac Straits. With them came remnants of the Hurons and the Tionontati, the "Tobacco People," also known as the Petun Hurons, who lived at the base of the Georgian Peninsula. It was these refugees who settled among the Ojibwe on Madeline Island at Chequamegon Bay in 1661.

Historian Helen Tanner, who compiled a brilliant *Atlas of Great Lakes Indian History*, wrote that the journey to Madeline Island took a roundabout route: "In 1657, Huron and Ottawa on Rock Island, at the entrance to Green Bay, prevented an attack by a party of 1,200 Iroquois through the vigilance of scouting parties." Fearing another Iroquoian war party, the Odawa, Huron and Tionontati fled west to the Mississippi River before migrating back east to Madeline Island in 1661.

Owing to their loose cohesion, Indian tribes didn't flee en masse, but rather as individual bands. Some of the Odawa wandered as far west as the Mississippi, where they were welcomed by the Sioux at first for their French trade goods, but inevitably came into conflict with them and fled back east. Others settled at the Mackinac Straits, northern Lower Michigan, and in the Saginaw River Valley, battling it out with Iroquois war parties for decades. Still others fled to Green Bay on the west side of Lake Michigan, along with refugees from many other tribes, including the Potawatomi, Tionontati, Fox and Mascouten.

Jesuit Father Paul Le Jeune claimed that Iroquois warriors might travel anywhere from 600-900 miles, spending a year or more away from home. He noted that rudiments of their language were understood within a 1,200-mile radius of their homeland, making it easier to adopt captives.

Lower Michigan was "hollowed out" in the 1650s as the Iroquois fell on Potawatomi, Mascouten, Sauk and Odawa villages. Tribes armed with bows and arrows were no match for the Iroquois, who were well-armed with muskets from the Dutch and British and renowned as marksmen. The thunder, flame and smoke of hundreds of black-powder muskets also served as terrifying psychological weapons against Native peoples who had rarely encountered firearms. Nor could small, isolated Native villages prevail against attacks by hundreds of Iroquois warriors. The default in such raids was for the women, children and elders to run for the safety of the woods while their men attempted to delay the attackers. But this made for easy pickings once the defenders were slain.

Yet, despite their superior firepower and tendency to field whole armies of warriors, the Iroquois didn't win every fight. Almost comically, in 1655, a huge army of Iroquois set out to attack Mitchigami ("big lake"), a stronghold of the Potawatomi in the Green Bay area, but were starving by the time they had traveled more than seven hundred miles to their destination. The story goes that they begged the Potawatomi for food, who obliged by giving them poisoned corn. Smelling a rat, most of the Iroquois retreated to Illinois where they were slaughtered. A separate party of one hundred Iroquois traveled north where the Ojibwe finished them off at the St. Marys River near Sault Ste. Marie.

To this day, the Ojibwe also celebrate a battle in the spring of 1662, in which they, along with some Odawa hunters, came upon an encampment of one hundred Mohawk and Oneida warriors at a point on Lake

Superior near present-day Brimley, Michigan. Led by an Ojibwe chieftain, they attacked at dawn the next morning, killing them all. Located near the Bay Mills Indian Reservation, the battleground is still known as Iroquois Point.

By the late 1600s, Green Bay, Wisconsin was home to an estimated ten thousand refugees from the Odawa, Huron, Tionontati, Potawatomi, Mascouten and other tribes fleeing the Iroquois. The Ho-Chunk Sioux (Winnebago) who lived at Green Bay were powerless to resist the tide of newcomers. They had been decimated by a smallpox epidemic and their force of fighting men was almost nil. In a legendary attack on the neighboring Fox tribe, an armada of Ho-Chunk canoes had been caught far from shore on Lake Winnebago in a violent storm, resulting in the drowning of five hundred warriors.

During the same decade the Iroquois were hammered by a French invasion of their homeland in 1666, with troops and militia burning towns and rampaging through the countryside at a time when there were few warriors available to fight back. The native Iroquois were so depleted by warfare and disease that they were minorities among the captive peoples in their own country.

It looked like curtains for the Iroquois when their people among the Cayuga and Seneca tribes were attacked by the far more powerful Susquehanna of Maryland, Pennsylvania and Virginia. The Susquehanna were almost jolly at the prospect; they had been armed by the British and Swedes for decades and unlike the tribes to the west, were no pushovers. Yet on the verge of wiping the Iroquois out of existence they were decimated by an epidemic. Weakened by disease and famine, the Susquehanna were easily defeated. They too were rounded up, with the survivors adding new blood to Iroquoia.

As the power of the Iroquois waned, the Odawa, Potawatomi and other tribes were driven out of Wisconsin and Minnesota by the Dakota Sioux and began filtering back to their former homelands in the east. In 1671 the Odawa and Huron established a community at St. Ignace on the southern shore of Michigan's Upper Peninsula, while others returned to Manitoulin Island. In the 1700s they established a community called Waganawkezee, twenty-five miles south of the Mackinac Straits at the site of L'arbre Croche, an immense crooked tree which served as a landmark for Native mariners and French *voyageurs*. Waganawkezee included two major villages and some smaller settlements extending fifteen miles or more.

Meanwhile, the Potawatomi resettled northern Indiana and southern Michigan, while Ojibwe and Odawa villages were established in the Saginaw River Valley and south of Detroit. The Miami and Shawnee filtered back into Ohio and many Huron refugees settled in the Detroit area, where they were dubbed the Wyandots by the British.

Some tribes were all but obliterated in the Great Diaspora. In 1680 a war party of eight hundred Senecas joined by several hundred Miami and Shawnee warriors attacked the Illinois tribe (also known as the Illini), taking up to 1,200 captives. Fleeing north, the Illinois were attacked again in 1684 and 1689. Subsequent attacks in the eighteenth and nineteenth centuries by American soldiers, the Sioux, Fox and other tribes drove the Illinois to the point of extinction.

Yet by the 1680s the Iroquois were over-extended, bled dry and in retreat. Reinforcements of French troops arrived at Montreal and Quebec and began a series of punitive raids, circling Lake Ontario and burning Iroquois villages. An alliance of Ojibwe, Odawa, Mississauga and Huron warriors also went on the attack, sweeping the Iroquois from the north shore of Lake Ontario.

Now better-armed and emboldened, the western tribes of the Great Lakes secured their trade routes to Montreal, driving the Iroquois out of Michigan. In the spring of 1696, a fleet of Odawa and Potawatomi warriors attacked a Seneca hunting party in the Saginaw River Valley, taking thirty scalps and thirty-two captives, with an additional forty Senecas drowned in a naval battle of canoes on Lake Huron.

Bled white by warfare and disease, the Iroquois began suing for peace as their fortunes began to flip. Odawa war chief Sagimau dealt a number of punishing blows to the tribe; some Seneca captives were incorporated into the Odawa as the Forked Clan.

All was not lost for the Iroquois; they had taken the Delaware tribe of Pennsylvania and factions of the Shawnee in Ohio under their wing, serving initially as powerful protectors and allies.*

In 1695 Iroquoian diplomats met with their Odawa and Ojibwe counterparts at the Mackinac Straits to discuss trading issues and the cession of hostilities. Then on August 4, 1701, the French hosted a huge peace conference at Montreal. Some 1,200 delegates from 40 nations met with 300 Iroquois counterparts to bury the hatchet, celebrating with an ox roast, cannon fire and fireworks. Now buddies, the chieftains vowed that their tomahawks, spears and arrows were buried in a pit so deep that they would never be found, and that from then on all parties would be considered brothers. The French established a fort at Detroit to serve as a way-station

---

*Soon enough, the Iroquois would betray these and other tribes to the west in the 1744 Treaty of Lancaster, in which they ceded all of the Ohio country to colonial Virginia by right of conquest. It was the first of a number of under-handed giveaways.

for trading with the Iroquois and the tribes to the west.

That same year the Iroquois also met with the British in Albany, pledging eternal peace. As with the Germans and Japanese after World War II, the five tribes of the Iroquois vowed to give up their warlike ways for a policy of strict neutrality that lasted for more than fifty years.

That wasn't the end of the Great Diaspora, however. The Iroquois had shuffled the chessboard of neighboring tribes after nearly seventy years of conflict, but many of the refugees were still seeking their place in the world decades after peace came to the Midwest. Beginning in the 1740s, bands of the Odawa began making their way up the Grand River in Michigan, just north of their cousins among the Potawatomi. The soil was rich, the area was filled with game, and the river emptied into Lake Michigan for ease of travel and trading. Odawa villagers would enjoy life there for more than eighty years before white settlers and speculators cast covetous eyes their way.

CHAPTER 16

THE SAUK, THE FOX
& THE FOUNDING
OF DETROIT

Saginaw is variously thought to mean "Land of the Sauks" (*O-Sag-e-non*) or "*Sag-in-a-we*," meaning to flow out, in reference to the river flowing into Michigan's Saginaw Bay and Lake Huron. Long before the white man arrived, this rich river valley was the scene of Indian-on-Indian violence.

Anishinaabek oral legend has it that prior to the arrival of the white man - possibly the early 1500s - the Saginaw River Valley and the three rivers that flow through it was home of a warlike people called the Sauk, along with a lesser tribe known as the Onottoway. Far to the north at the Mackinac Straits, the Ojibwe and Odawa coveted the valley as a winter hunting ground, They conspired with bands of the southern Odawa living in the Detroit area to stage an attack on two fronts.

"The invaders entered the country of the doomed tribes in two columns," wrote local historian Alan Teelander, in his history of Flint, Michigan. The southern Odawa paddled north from present-day Detroit, meeting up with the Ojibwe and northern Odawa who arrived from the Straits, "paddling by night, and lying concealed in the woods by day."

Reaching Saginaw Bay, the war party made for shore and split up, with half landing on each side of the Saginaw River. "Then, in darkness and stealth, the two detachments glided up through the woods on both sides of the river, and fell upon the unsuspecting Sauks like panthers upon their prey."

What followed was a bloodbath at dawn with the unsuspecting Sauk and Onottoway peoples set upon with tomahawks and a rain of arrows and spears. The fleeing survivors made it to an island in the Saginaw River, thankful that their enemies had left their canoes behind. Legend has it, however, that a hard freeze that night made it possible for the enemy war party to cross the ice, killing all but twelve women. Thereafter, the island was so littered with bones and skulls that it was named Skull Island, a moniker it bears to this day.

The victorious warriors pushed on to attack other Sauk villages near present-day Flushing and Bridgeport, including a last stand at a place called Beacon Hill. Survivors fled to Wisconsin where they regrouped with their relations among the Fox tribe, also known as the Mesquakie.

But the bloodshed was far from over.

When the Odawa fled the invasion of their territory by the Iroquois in the 1650s, they established a tidy business supplying French kettles, axes, muskets and trade cloth with the tribes of Wisconsin and Green Bay, including the Ho-Chunk Sioux and the Fox. Friendly relations soon went sour, however, in part because the Odawa passed on shoddy goods at exorbitant prices in exchange for furs. French explorer Nicolas Perrot said these included "old knives, blunt awls, wretched nets, and worn-out kettles." Beleaguered, the Odawa appealed to the French to help them fight their former customers among the Sioux and Fox, only to learn that their allies had done an end-run around them and were trading directly with their newly-acquired enemies.

Angered, the Odawa threatened to turn to the English as trading partners, crippling French trade on the Upper Great Lakes. In response, the French dispatched Sieur de Antoine de La Mothe Cadillac to establish the trading center of Fort Ponchartrain at Detroit ("the straits - *De Troit*") in 1701, just as the long war with the Iroquois was winding down. As noted earlier, the fort was meant to be a neutral meeting ground and trading center for the

Fort Ponchartrain (later Detroit) as it may have looked in the 1700s, based on a map drawn by French military engineer Joseph Gaspard Chaussegros de Lery in 1749. Illustration courtesy of the Detroit Public Library.

tribes of the Great Lakes, including the Iroquois.

Cadillac then sent out a blanket invitation to all of the tribes of the Upper Great Lakes to settle near Detroit, after which he was relieved of command. Soon, villages of Odawa, Ojibwe, Miami, Potawatomi, Mascouten, and Wyandot were sprinkled throughout the region.

"The attempt to concentrate 6,000 Indians in the vicinity of Detroit strained resources and tempers," wrote historian Helen Tanner in her *Atlas of Great Lakes Indian History*. "Intertribal animosities flared..."

This powder keg reached a flash point when the French invited the Fox to settle in Detroit, thinking this would help cement their trade relations in Wisconsin and mediate a peace with the Odawa. By 1710 the invitation had attracted one thousand or so Fox, Sauk, Kickapoo and Mascouten who began pushing into the Saginaw River Valley; this however, was the prime winter hunting grounds of the Odawa and Ojibwe.

The Odawa were also alarmed that the Fox and Sauk, being "the most savage and unreasonable of the nations" would now be able to purchase French guns, shot and powder to be turned against them.

Thus a war of extermination began, first against the Mascouten, a small Michigan tribe that had long been at odds with the Odawa. Then, enlisting the support of the local Wyandot, the Odawa managed to convince Detroit's gullible new commander, Charles Renaud Dubuisson, that the Fox were conspiring against the French. Dubuisson ordered the Fox to pack up and leave. They declined to do so, opting to besiege Detroit for nineteen days. Beaten off, they retreated only to suffer a massive attack by the Odawa, Wyandot, Potawatomi and French, who killed hundreds of men women and children, with many of the survivors sold as slaves to the French. The few who managed to escape back to their relatives in Wisconsin spread word of French treachery, dashing any hope of France trading beyond the barrier of Wisconsin. Defeating several French expeditions against them, some bands of the Fox and Sauk were eventually forced across the Mississippi in 1734.

Nearly one hundred years later they would meet their doom in Black Hawk's War.

But in the meantime, life in Wisconsin was apparently good for the Sauks and their cousins, the Fox. English explorer Jonathan Carver had a high opinion of the Sauks upon visiting the "Great Town of the Saukies" on the Wisconsin River in October, 1766. "This is the largest and best built Indian town I ever saw," he wrote. "It contains about ninety houses, each large enough for several families. These are built of hewn planks, neatly joined, and covered with bark so compactly as to keep out the most penetrating rains. Before the doors are placed comfortable sheds, in which the inhabitants sit when the weather will permit, and smoak their pipes. The streets are regular and spacious; so that it appears more like a civilized town than the abode of Savages. In their plantations, which lie adjacent to their houses, and which are neatly laid out, they raise great quantities of Indian corn, beans, mellons, etc., so that this place is esteemed the best market for traders to furnish themselves with provisions, of any within eight hundred miles of it."

Book Four
War in the Forest

CHAPTER 17

THE FIRST WORLD WAR

World War I is commonly held to be the first global war, but as Winston Churchill noted, it was actually the Seven Years War of 1756-'63 that holds that distinction.

Known as the French and Indian War on this side of the pond, the conflict pitted Great Britain, Prussia, Hanover and Spain against France, Russia, Sweden and Austria, with the Indians of North America backing either the French or the British. Fought in North America, Europe and India, the war claimed one million lives.

And, although they won the war, it was the beginning of the end for the British in America.

The Anishinaabek of the Upper Great Lakes played a role in sparking the war. On June 21, 1752, some 250 Odawa, Ojibwe and Potawatomi warriors attacked a fortified British trading post at the Miami Indian village of Pickawillany on the Great Miami River in central Ohio.

The war party was led by Charles-Michel Mouet de Langlade, a *métis* war chief born of an Odawa mother and French trader who was the head of a powerful trading family at the Mackinac Straits. Threatened by British and Miami attempts to divert the fur trade from their French trading partners, the Anishinaabek killed thirteen of the fort's defenders. Vastly outnumbered with only twenty survivors left to defend their wretched palisade, the remaining villagers watched as a British blacksmith was dragged from the fort and stabbed in a glimpse at what lay ahead. "As he lay dying, his assailants ripped his heart out and ate it," wrote historian Michael A. McDonnell in the introduction to his book, *Masters of Empire*. Thereafter, the raiders killed the village chief, Memeskia, and then boiled and ate his body in front of his family.

Faced with a hopeless situation, the Miami bargained for their lives in exchange for the British traders. Satisfied with the burning of the post, Langlade's warriors made their way to the French at Detroit with four surviving traders along with furs worth $300,000 in today's currency.

From their perch in Canada, the French were delighted with the outcome of the attack, which was seen as the key to unlocking the lands of the Ohio River Valley. The soil west of the Allegheny Mountains in Pennsylvania and Ohio was fabulously rich and the region teemed with fur-bearing animals. Both the British and the French realized that whoever controlled the Ohio River would control the future of North America. Accordingly, the French and their Indian allies swept down from Canada, attacking British trading posts all along the frontier. They also established a string of forts all the way from Montreal to New Orleans.

Into this scenario was thrust a young social climber, George Washington, a twenty-one-year-old with no military experience whatsoever who managed to set the world on fire.

Washington had grown up in genteel poverty in rural Fredericksburg, Virginia with few prospects. His father had died when he was eleven, leaving his mother to raise five children without any resources. Fortunately, his wealthy half-brother Lawrence stepped in to save the family, becoming a surrogate father to young George and mentoring him in the social graces and ways of the world. Much-loved and admired, Lawrence had been educated in London and had secured a post as a colonial officer in the British Navy in addition to commanding Virginia's militia. He also owned the estate of Mount Vernon, which George would one day inherit. But Lawrence died of tuberculosis at the age of thirty-four, leaving twenty-year-old Washington stricken with grief.

Washington was an atrocious speller, but good at math, and this helped him to launch a career as a land surveyor while still in his teens. Although he had no military experience, he applied to fill Lawrence's post as head of Virginia's colonial militia in order to honor his brother's legacy. Exceptionally tall, blessed with a noble bearing and a ramrod-straight posture, Washington looked the part of a military man, even if he was clueless; perhaps this and fond memories of Lawrence secured him an officer's commission. This in turn led to a secret mission on behalf of Virginia's lieutenant governor, Robert Dinwiddie.

In 1753 young Washington was dispatched to spy on the French in Pennsylvania and enlist the aid of the Iroquois through the Half King Tanaghrisson, an elderly chieftain of the Senecas. Half kings were emissaries of their people, empowered to deliver the diplomatic messages of their councils and report back, without the power to make binding decisions. Tanaghrisson was intent on scuttling French power in North America, however, undermining the wishes of the Iroquois' grand council at Onondaga to remain strictly neutral.

Traveling with Tanaghrisson, Washington was charged with informing the French that they were trespassing on British land; in particular, the land claimed by the Ohio Company, a powerful group of speculators that included his own family. He was politely rebuffed by the French and sent packing.

A year later, Lieutenant Colonel Washington's Virginia Regiment and a party of the Seneca Iroquois were sent to the Forks of the Ohio where the British were building a fort at present-day Pittsburgh. His mission was to hack a road through the wilderness to supply the fort. But by the time he arrived the French had evicted the Brits with a force of one thousand Indians, Canadians and regulars who had marched down from Quebec. In response, Washington built a small, circular stockade called Fort Necessity about sixty miles to the south.

Then, on May 28, 1754, although there was no state of war between England and France, twenty-two-year-old Washington took it upon himself to conduct a surprise attack on thirty-five French soldiers camping in a ravine now called Jumonville's Glen in western Pennsylvania. He and his force of forty militia and twelve Seneca warriors attacked the sleeping French at dawn, killing thirteen and capturing twenty-one prisoners. Among the dead was the young French commander, Joseph Coulon de Jumonville,

By one account, Jumonville was on his knees before Washington and pleading that he was simply on a diplomatic mission to tell the British they were trespassing on French territory when Tanaghrisson split the his skull with a hatchet and washed his hands in the Frenchman's brains as a way of saying that the Iroquois and tribes of the Ohio country had washed their hands of the French, whether they liked it or not.

Washington was likely shaken to his core by the barbarity of what he witnessed; normally prone to writing volumes in his journals, his official account was brief to the point of being an afterthought and he rarely spoke of the battle thereafter. Not understanding the French terms of his surrender, he also implicated himself in the assassination of Jumonville, which made him notorious on both sides of the Atlantic.

After what was basically a massacre, Washington retreated to Fort Necessity and waited for the French to respond. But Tanaghrisson derided the tiny stockade as an indefensible joke and withdrew his warriors, knowing that Washington was doomed. The fort was sited in a low-lying meadow where the enemy could blast the defenders from the surrounding trees and the French did just that in the resulting battle on July 3, 1754. Taking hundreds of casualties under heavy fire in a pouring rain, Washington surrendered, but managed to negotiate an armed release (the French erroneously believed that he was about to be reinforced with five thousand British troops). Sending Washington and his men on their way back to Virginia, the French went on to complete what they called Fort Duquesne.

The battle, which shook the ministries of London and Paris alike, whetted young Washington's appetite for war. As would later be echoed by the likes of Teddy Roosevelt and Winston Churchill, he was "charmed" at being shot at without result.

"I fortunately escaped without any wound," he wrote, "for the right wing, which I stood, was exposed to and received all the enemy's fire... I heard the bullets whistle, and, believe me there is something charming in the sound."*

Together with conflicts between Prussia and Austria over contested territory, the resulting hostilities sent armies marching in North America and Europe, along with a naval attack on the French port of Pondicherry on the southeastern coast of India.**

Although the hapless Washington was ultimately blamed for "setting the world on fire," historian Colin G. Calloway notes in his book, *The Indian World of George Washington*, that more likely it was the elderly and obscure Seneca chieftain, Tanaghrisson, who lit the fuse that killed one million people worldwide.

The French and Indian War was a continuation of barbaric frontier raids between the French and British dating to the late 1600s, including King Williams War (1688-1697), Queen Anne's War (1702-1713), and King George's War (1744-1748).

One might wonder; what would possess Anishinaabek warriors from as far north and west as Lake Superior and Green Bay to paddle hundreds of miles across the chop of the Great Lakes and down a network of winding rivers to aid the French in far-off Pennsylvania? It was because by the

---

* Reading Washington's account, British King George II sniffed that the upstart might not be so "charmed" if he was shot at more often.

**Central Pondicherry looks much like the French Quarter of New Orleans with its wrought iron balconies, colonial-style homes and bright colors. Both were constructed by the French during the same period in the 1700s.

1750s, protecting their trade with the French had become a life-and-death matter of survival. Having long since forgotten or forsaken the skills of hunting with bows and arrows, the Anishinaabek needed trade guns and ammunition to survive. The Odawa, Ojibwe and Potawatomi feared British hegemony, and many also had familial ties with the French built over decades of trade and friendship. For their part, the British were backed largely by the Cherokee and Mohawks.

Initially, the tide of war favored the French. One of the war's most infamous battles was that of Braddock's Defeat in 1755.

British General Edward Braddock had led a seemingly invincible army of three thousand men from Fort Cumberland in Maryland to attack the French at the newly-built Fort Duquesne. Braddock expected an easy victory, after which he planned to push on, sweeping French forts and trading posts all the way to Quebec.

Sixty-year-old Braddock had four decades of experience fighting fixed-formation battles in Europe, but none in North America where guerrilla tactics were the norm.* He wasn't shy about expressing his disdain for Native warriors and colonial militiamen; he considered them an incompetent rabble compared to his crack British regulars and refused to take any advice. "He was full of pride and ignorance," opined an Iroquois chieftain named Monacatoocha. "(He was) a bad man when he was alive; he looked upon us as dogs, and would never hear anything that was said to him."

Disgusted, many of the Mohawks allied with the British departed, leaving Braddock to his fate.

Similarly, a Delaware chieftain named Shingas was rudely rebuffed when he offered to provide Braddock with some warriors and scouts, which might have warned of the danger ahead. When Shingas asked what the general planned to do with the Ohio River Valley once the French were driven out, he was told that it would become British territory. Shingas then asked if the Indians who had been friendly to the British would at least, "be permitted to live and trade among the English and have hunting grounds sufficient to support themselves and families?" To this, Braddock arrogantly replied that, "No savage should inherit the land." Stung, Shingas told the general that, "if they might not have liberty to live on the land, they would not fight for it." Once word got around, many warriors

---

* Today, many wonder why European armies stood in ranks of hundreds, firing at one-another across open fields, but the answer is quite simple. A British soldier was trained to load and fire his musket up to four times per minute, alternating with a line of soldiers behind him. This created the effect of a colossal human machine gun, firing tens of thousands of rounds per minute against enemies who were not as adept.

At left, Odawa/French war chief Charles de Langlade exhorts his warriors while in the distance, George Washington reaches out to mortally-wounded General Braddock in this painting by Edwin Willard Deming. Indians from as far west as Green Bay, WI journeyed to New England to fight the British.

immediately switched sides to the French. As Shingas and his warriors were leaving, Braddock is said to have taunted him by shouting "that he did not need their help and had no doubt of driving the French and their Indians away."

As they neared the fort after weeks of brutal effort hacking a road through the wilderness, Braddock split his command into a 1,300-man "flying column" meant for rapid advance, with eight hundred men left beyond to manage the supply wagons.

Once again, Odawa/French war chief Charles de Langlade of the Pickawillany attack played a key role. Knowing that the French and Indian forces were badly outnumbered, he urged the French commander to go on the attack while the British were in disarray after crossing a ford of the Monongahela River.

Fearing their doom under bombardment by British cannon, 250 French regulars and Canadian militia, along with 640 Indians stormed out of Fort Duquesne and attacked Braddock's disorganized column, which had barely finished crossing the river. French soldiers and militia blocked the road ahead while warriors including the Odawa, Ojibwe and Potawatomi, attacked from the cover of the forest on either side with a murderous crossfire. More than nine hundred British troops and colonial militia were killed or wounded. Native warriors also reveled in the riches garnered from the abandoned supply train. It's believed that the Potawatomi and Wyandot obtained their first horses as spoils of the battle.

The victory was credited in large part to the leadership of Langlade. He would go on to lead Native warriors in other battles along the frontier, including the capture of Fort William Henry on Lake Champlain in 1757. The surrender of that fort and the ensuing massacre of its departing troops was depicted in the Daniel Day-Lewis film, *Last of the Mohicans*, based on the novel by James Fennimore Cooper.

As for Braddock, he was mortally wounded, perhaps by friendly fire, dying three days later with enough time to reflect on his hubris. "Who would have thought?" he said upon being shot. He was buried in the middle of the road his men had cut through the forest, with Lt. Col. Washington presiding over his funeral. Thereafter, heavy wagons and the tramp of horses and oxen packed the earth over the grave to keep it from being discovered and defiled by the Indians.

During the fight, Washington had two horses shot out from under him, with musket balls tattering his uniform at close range. Thus began the legend of Washington being blessed by a lucky star, escaping several times from being shot at point-blank range.

Most tribes living in Ohio, Pennsylvania and Kentucky had attempted to remain neutral during the French and Indian War, waiting to see which nation would come out on top; nor did they wish to antagonize the Anishinaabek tribes supporting the French. Why, they wondered, didn't the British and French fight in their own lands far across the sea? Obviously they were vying for Indian lands, and while the Indians were eager to have traders in their territory, they didn't want any more settlers. The Delaware, Shawnee and several Iroquoian tribes assumed that the French and British were battling for their homeland, with the winner taking all. A tug-of-war commenced between the British and the French, seeking Indian allies with promises to leave them unmolested after the war.

Inevitably, a number of tribes were dragged into the conflict. More than eight hundred colonial settlers and their black slaves were captured by various tribes during the war. Many were adopted by their captors, with women and children often treated kindly and accepted into Native families. Men, however, risked being tortured and killed. In the Shawnee culture, for instance, a warrior was free to decide whether he wished to kill a captive or not, and his wife could decide whether to have him tortured.

Of those who were adopted, many chose to remain with their Indian families, preferring the freedom and permissiveness of Native society. Most notable was Mary Jemison; captured by the Shawnee at the age of fifteen and adopted by the Seneca, she chose to live with the tribe until the age of eighty-one. Others managed to escape. One celebrated escapee was Mary Draper Ingles, a twenty-three-year-old mother of two living on the Virginia frontier, who was captured by the Shawnee. Her sons were adopted by the tribe at their village near Chillicothe, Ohio, but Mary escaped along with an elderly woman. She spent forty days in the wilderness as fall turned to winter, following a network of rivers five hundred miles to home.

After many defeats the British began to gain the upper hand. In 1758 a force of 150 British ships and 13,100 troops captured the mammoth French Fort Louisbourg in Nova Scotia, cutting off supplies and reinforcements to New France. Then, at 4 a.m. on September 13, 1759, three companies of light infantry under Col. William Howe scaled a 170-foot cliff in a commando raid on Quebec, overcoming a French outpost. This cleared the way for 4,500 British soldiers to attack the French fortress spread across a plateau called the Plains of Abraham. Montreal fell the next year, and with the British navy blockading the entrance to the St. Lawrence Seaway, the French were choked off from their holdings and called it quits.

Native peoples on the Upper Great Lakes faced an even more fearsome enemy than the British, however. An outbreak of smallpox hit the French and their Indian allies in 1757, possibly contracted from dead or captured British soldiers in the battlegrounds of New York and Pennsylvania. That fall, returning warriors among the Anishinaabek infected their villages at Detroit, Michilimackinac, St. Joseph and Green Bay to devastating effect just as winter was coming on. The Potawatomi of Wisconsin were almost wiped out, while hundreds of Odawa died in the villages of Waganawkezee at L'arbre Croche in northern Lower Michigan. Horrified by the cascade of death at Waganawkezee and, "nothing but dead bodies lying here and there in their lodges," Native warriors refused to resume the battle in the east. And, as was the custom, the Odawa demanded restitution for their dead from the cash-strapped French, whose "bad medicine" was to blame for the epidemic.

With their supply lines cut and their angry Indian allies in retreat, the cause of New France was lost. At the Treaty of Paris in 1763, the French gave up their territory in North America, including Quebec, Ontario, the Upper Great Lakes and the Ohio River Valley. Spain was granted the French city of New Orleans and the Louisiana Territory in an attempt to keep it out of British hands. Within a few decades Spain would return the city and territory to the French under Napoleon.

For their part, the Native peoples of the Upper Great Lakes were strapped with the hated British as a trading partner, whose parsimonious policies soon turned the peace pipe upside down.

CHAPTER 18

PONTIAC'S WAR

Word of the peace treaty at Paris was late coming to the Upper Great Lakes and the ink was not yet dry before thousands of Native warriors rallied to the war belt, taking up the tomahawk and musket again to resume the fight in Pontiac's War. Simply put, the Indians were not happy with the British, who committed a series of diplomatic blunders well before the French and Indian War ended.

The Indians were used to receiving "presents" from the French, which might include blankets, ammunition, liquor, tools, cloth, kettles and other goods three or four times a year. Ammunition, in particular, was vital in the fall when Native peoples were moving to their winter hunting grounds, with powder and shot weighing the difference between starvation and survival.

But Britain's national debt had nearly doubled with the staggering costs of the war, so corners were being cut. Many of the authorities in newly-conquered Canada also craved revenge against the tribes that had sided with the French. From his governing post in Canada, Major General Sir Jeffery Amherst took it upon himself to strangle the pipeline of gifts and ammunition to the Indians just as the British began assuming command of French territory.

Pugnacious by nature and full of resentment, Amherst was a dandy given to dressing in a scarlet greatcoat with gold epaulets, even posing for a portrait in a suit of medieval armor. He was intent on punishing the Indians, "for they can never be considered by us, as a people to whom we owe rewards," he wrote. "It would be madness to the highest degree ever to bestow favors on a race, who have so treacherously & without any provocation on our side, attacked our posts."

His wrath extended to genocide and germ warfare. "Could it not be contrived to Send the Small Pox among those Disaffected Tribes of Indians?" he wrote to a subordinate, Colonel Henry Bouquet. "We must, on this occasion, Use Every Stratagem in our power to Reduce them."

A Swiss mercenary, Bouquet took the hint and distributed smallpox-infected blankets to a party of Odawa at a peace talk held at Fort Pitt (the renamed Fort Duquesne). The blankets were old, however, and the pathogen had died off.

If it were within his power, Amherst said, there would not be "an Indian settlement within a thousand miles of our country; for they are only fit to live with the inhabitants of the woods, being more nearly allied with the brute than the human creation."

For their part, Native warriors felt anything but conquered. They had come home from the war with hundreds of scalps and canoes filled with plunder. They had captured many British forts and given their foes a good beating, and despite the presence of a few isolated and vulnerable outposts, they still held all of the land ranging from Kentucky to Lake Superior and beyond. As one Ojibwe chieftain told a British trader: "Englishman, although you have conquered the French, you have not conquered us. We are not your slaves!"

Yet Native peoples were justifiably alarmed by the hordes of settlers flooding into their territory. The British had promised that Fort Pitt would be abandoned; instead its garrison was strengthened and the future site of Pittsburgh became a magnet for settlers streaming over the Alleghenies. Settlers were also flooding into the rich hunting grounds of the Ohio River Valley, with frontier militias and vigilantes burning villages and slaughtering Natives in revenge for their part in the war.

By contrast, French settlements and trading posts had been few and far between, with little interest shown in colonizing North America. French *voyageurs* and traders tended to live with the Indians through the winter and married into their families, becoming valuable trading assets. The French also offered better trading terms than the British newcomers. But now, it was *adieu* to these *bon* companions.

At the Mackinac Straits, 2,500-3,000 Odawa and Ojibwe also felt insulted, snubbed and threatened when the British chose to negotiate with the southern bands of the Odawa and the Wyandots at Detroit, cutting the northerners out of the action. The British assumed that the Indians living three hundred miles to the north were all of one piece with their southern cousins and would fall in line with the negotiations in Detroit, failing to realize that these were separate peoples with separate priorities.

So, no presents, no ammo, a rising tide of settlers and empty British promises delivered with a like-it-or-lump-it approach that included heavy-handed threats. Into this powder keg stepped Pontiac - Bowondiac - a savvy, energetic Odawa whose political skills and oratory united the factions of many tribes behind the belief that all was not lost with the French, who would surely make a comeback with the help of their Indian allies.

In fact, in the metaphor-heavy thinking of the Indians, King Louis XV of France was only sleeping, ready to rouse and roar like a lion with a bit of encouragement.

Minavavana, the Ojibwe war chief of a band at the Straits put it this way: "Englishman, we are informed, that our father, the king of France, is old and infirm; and that being fatigued with making war upon your nation, he is fallen asleep. During his sleep you have taken advantage of him, and possessed yourselves of Canada. But his nap is almost at an end. I think I hear him stirring, and inquiring for his children, the Indians; and when he does awake what must become of you? He will destroy you utterly!"

Pontiac bought into this rosy scenario, which, if successful, would assure the resumption of trade with the French. The son of a minor Odawa chieftain and an Ojibwe woman from Lake Superior, he was born in the mid-1720s into a band living along the Maumee River in Ohio. Tall and muscular, by 1757 he was a veteran war chief.

Described as having "an uneven face" and being "proud, vindictive, warlike, and easily offended," Pontiac was passionate in his hatred of the British. He was on the scene in November, 1760, when the British landed at Detroit to take command from the French, likely sizing up the fort's weaknesses.

In 1762, he and Seneca war chief Kysutha began circulating black wampum war belts among the western tribes, calling for an uprising against the British forts acquired from the French. Their cause was bolstered by the teachings of Neolin, a Delaware Indian prophet who called for a return to traditional values and clean living to revive Native fortunes. Neolin, who had a habit of weeping dramatically as he went from town to town, preached against the corrupting influence of the whites, particularly that of their liquor, which was the ruin of Native men and women alike. He also called for an end to adultery, polygamy, sorcery, infighting and dependence on trade goods as a way to promote Native unity and get rid of the whites. Instead of reliance on medicine bags, which every warrior carried for protection, he advised praying directly to the Great Spirit. He also advised returning to the bow & arrow and foregoing the musket. And instead of rum, he recommended drinking a bitter, vomit-inducing herbal tea as a way to cleanse the body and spirit of white witchcraft.

Some of his ideas didn't fly, such as his advice to limit sexual intercourse to a minimum and the notion that devotees should rub sticks together to light their fires, rather than using steel and flint. Nor were warriors inclined to give up their precious muskets. Nonetheless, Neolin guaranteed that if his prescription was followed, the Great Spirit would cleanse the land of whites, bring back game in abundance, and establish an earthly Native paradise.

Neolin's old-time religion captured the imagination of thousands, rallying the warriors of many tribes who were already in an uproar over the clueless British.

At a council of four hundred chieftains held outside of Detroit in April,

Intricately designed belts of wampum crafted from shells were emblems of diplomacy for many Indian tribes. A wampum belt could signal an alliance, a bid for peaceful coexistence, a call to war, a token of friendship, an agreement on trade, and the division of hunting grounds, among other negotiations. Dashing a wampum belt to the ground or ripping it apart was a clear sign of rejection.

1763, Pontiac shared the words of Kitchi Manito as delivered to Neolin. Of note, in his condemnation of the whites, the Great Spirit - via the medium of Pontiac - took pains to exclude the French, who were in fact, quite "dear" to the god:

"The land on which you live I have made for you, and not for others. Why do you suffer the white men to dwell among you? As for these English, these dogs dressed in red, who have come to rob you of your hunting grounds, and drive away the game - you must lift the hatchet against them. Wipe them from the face of the earth, and then you will win my favor back again, and once more be happy and prosperous. The children of your great father, the king of France, are not like the English. Never forget that they are your brethren. They are very dear to me, for they love the red men, and understand the true mode of worshiping me."

Pontiac was nervous but optimistic as he led three hundred warriors to the gate of British-held Detroit on May 7, 1763. A week earlier, he had staged a ceremonial peace dance at the fort so that his spies could reconnoiter its defenses, powder room and store houses. He had told commander Major Henry Gladwin that he would return for a peace talk within a few days, and now, after revving up his warriors with a war dance and promises of plunder and an easy win, he was ready to strike. Elsewhere, the war chiefs of many tribes were poised for a coordinated attack on British forts spanning an area of more than five hundred miles.

Pontiac's warriors included the Odawa, Ojibwe, Huron, Potawatomi, Mascouten, Wyandot and Shawnee. Each had concealed a tomahawk, knife or sawed-off musket beneath his shirt or blanket. As for Pontiac, he carried a ceremonial belt of wampum to be presented to Major Gladwin as a sign of peace and unity. But there was a hitch: if Pontiac was sure of victory, he would flip the belt over and hold it aloft for his warriors to see the other side beaded all in green. This signal would green-light the attack on the garrison's 120 soldiers, catching the British completely by surprise.

But as Pontiac entered Detroit's eastern gate he was met by the stern-faced major and his officers, backed by every soldier armed and on alert, along with the doubling of sentries in the blockhouses and all of the storerooms securely locked. The major had been warned of the impending attack by either a friendly Huron woman or a French trader who had witnessed the war dance.

Pontiac and a handful of subordinates were invited into a room to speak with Gladwin, but his warriors were barred admittance to the fort. Realizing that the jig was up, he backpedaled in high dudgeon, scowling at Gladwin for his unfriendly welcome and claiming that, "some bad bird had given you ill news of us." The proposed peace talk turned sour, and after accepting a few token presents, Pontiac and his war party skulked back to their camp where he was bitterly condemned by the hot-heads among his warriors for not pressing the attack.

He made another attempt to enter the fort two days later, but now thoroughly on guard, Gladwin would allow only small numbers of Indians within the palisade. Thus began a six-month siege in an attempt to starve the fort into submission, killing anyone caught outside its walls. Many of those who were captured were tortured within sight of the fort, yet beyond the musket range that would have ended their suffering.

Elsewhere, his warriors were far more successful. Within days, Pontiac's alliance struck thirteen British forts, including those at present-day Fort Wayne, Sandusky and Lafayette, Indiana; St. Joseph and Michilimackinac in Michigan; and Fort Pitt in Pennsylvania. Fort Edward Augustus at Green Bay, Wisconsin, was abandoned by its frightened soldiers, who fled east to the Mackinac Straits where they were captured. In every case, Native attackers used a *ruse de guerre* of the sort as time-tested as the Trojan Horse, entering each fort on a peaceful pretext before slaughtering its garrison. In less than two months, Native warriors had captured nine forts. Only the British forts at Detroit, Niagara and Pittsburgh held out.

We have an idea as to how things went for the unfortunate British soldiers and traders at these forts thanks to the journal of Alexander Henry, an English trader who lived among the Ojibwe for more than a year after his capture at Fort Michilimackinac. Henry's journal makes for a gripping account, not only of the battle and his eventual deliverance, but also of the winter he spent hunting with the Ojibwe family who took him in.

Today the re-created fort with its pine palisade, wooden blockhouses, cannon and fourteen buildings is a tourist attraction standing by the northern shore of Lake Michigan just shy of the five-mile-long Mackinac Bridge. Millions of tourists flock to the area each year to browse the fudge and t-shirt shops of Mackinaw City, embarking on a fleet of boats to Mackinac Island, just east of the "Mighty Mac." With only bicycles and horse-drawn wagons for transportation, Mackinac Island is glutted with restaurants, bars, souvenir shops and high-end hotels. A popular pastime is cycling eight miles on a pathway around its perimeter.

It's a far cry from what was once known as the Great Turtle Island, a sacred gathering place, where in ancient times the shamans and chieftains of the Ojibwe and Odawa gathered for high-level councils.

Mackinac Island was the navel of the world for the Ojibwe and Odawa for good reason: From this island at the nexus of Lake Superior, Lake

Michigan and Lake Huron one could travel by water all the way to the Atlantic Ocean; or up through Lake Superior to the fur country of Manitoba; or down a network of rivers to the Mississippi and the Gulf of Mexico; or along the same route to the Missouri and west to the Rocky Mountains.

The island became the Gibraltar of the New World once the British, and Americans built a fortress there, with its cannons barring the way to Lakes Michigan and Superior. By the early 1800s Mackinac Island would serve as the headquarters of the American Fur Company, with more than 400 clerks supervising the efforts of 2,000-3,000 trappers and boatmen. Up to 3,000 Indians camped along its shore, supplying the pelts that filled the company's barter room.

But long before Mackinac Island's heyday the French had established Fort Michilimackinac in 1715 at the northern tip of Lower Michigan. The fort served as an important trading post and was a source of income for Odawa farmers and hunters who kept its troops in provisions. The French had passed the fort on to the British, who were newly-arrived in 1763 and had no clue as to their impending fate.

On June 4, 1763, the ninety British soldiers who garrisoned Fort Michilimackinac were busy celebrating the birthday of King George III, with festivities that included a lively game of *baggitaywe* (lacrosse) played outside the fort walls between the Ojibwe and some visiting Sauks. The rough-and-tumble of today's football and hockey pales before the violence of *baggitaywe*. Played with four-foot-long rackets with a hoop net attached to the end, these games often involved hundreds of men who were free to slash, punch and stomp one-another, with the only rules being that one could not kill an opponent or blind him. Severe lacerations and broken bones were liabilities for the players.

Thrilled at the sight of scores of Indians battling with their rackets for the leather ball, many soldiers and traders watched the game from outside the fort walls. At one point the ball soared over the pine palisade and the players rushed through the open gate in hot pursuit. Joining them were their women with weapons concealed beneath their blankets. Within minutes four hundred warriors under the leadership of Ojibwe war chief Matchekewis took the fort by complete surprise. At least seventy British soldiers and traders were killed in the bloodbath that followed, with only twenty survivors. Looking on "calmly" were nearly three hundred French Canadians, who escaped harm.

As for Alexander Henry, he hid in the attic of a *métis* home as the fort was searched for survivors. Ironically, the home was that of Charles de Langlade, the war chief who had led many battles against the British during the prior war, but, seeing which way the winds of trade were blowing, had now switched sides.

Gazing through an opening at the violence below, Henry observed what likely took place at a number of captured garrisons: "The dead were scalped and mangled; the dying were writhing and shrieking under the unsatiated knife and tomahawk; and from the bodies of some, ripped open, their butchers were drinking the blood, scooped up in the hollow of joined hands and quaffed amid shouts of rage and victory. I was shaken not only with horror, but with fear."

Discovered at last, he was stripped naked and placed in a canoe with four other captives with the intention of taking them to Beaver Island where they would likely have been executed. Several miles to the south, however, a flotilla of Odawa hailed their canoe as they were passing Waugonoshance Point on Lake Michigan. The Odawa were either angry that they had missed the attack, or else enraged that the Ojibwe had pressed it against their wishes. In any case, Henry was taken back to the fort for an uncertain fate.

Then something on the order of a miracle happened. A year earlier, an Ojibwe headman of around forty-five years of age named Wawatam - Little Goose - had approached Henry to be his adopted brother. In his journal, Henry described the sequence of events:

"Shortly after my arrival at Michilimackinac, a Chippewa named Wawatam began to come often to my house, betraying in his demeanor strong marks of personal regard. After this had continued for some time he came bringing his whole family, and at the same time a large present, consisting of skins, sugar and dried meat. Having laid these in a heap, he commenced a speech in which he informed me that some years before he had observed a fast, devoting himself according to the custom of his nation to solitude and the mortification of his body in the hope to obtain from the Great Spirit protection through all his days; that on this occasion he had dreamed of adopting an Englishman as his son, brother, and friend; that from the moment in which he first beheld me, he had recognized me as the person who the Great Spirit had been pleased to point out to him for a brother; that he hoped that I would not refuse his present, and that he should forever regard me as one of his family."

Now, a year later, Little Goose flew to the rescue, taking his adopted brother under his wing and protecting him from harm.

Henry's fortunes improved a great deal thereafter as he joined Wawatam and his extended family for the following year. Much of his writing is evocative of his time hunting with the band that winter midway down the Michigan peninsula, possibly along the Big Sable River at present-day

Ludington, Michigan. Looking over Henry's shoulder, a reader learns how the Indians hunted deer, bear, beaver, raccoons and other animals. With a country brimming with game, winter was a time of plenty for Wawatam's band. On one occasion, they took a five-hundred-pound bear, the oil of which "filled six porcupine skins." During the Moon of Crusted Snow, in February when it was difficult for deer to run, "it frequently happened that we killed twelve in the short space of two hours. By this means we were soon put into possession of four thousand pounds of dried venison." This, he added, had to be dragged seventy miles to their canoes on Lake Michigan.

It's important to note that even in the midst of Pontiac's War and that of many others, for most Native families life went on through the rhythm of the seasons just as it had for thousands of years. Henry's journal reminds us that for most Indians, the seasons for hunting, growing, fishing and gathering continued unabated, attended by celebrations, festivals and sacrifices. History books, including this one, tend to be filled with warfare, dastardly deeds and mayhem, ignoring the pedestrian, pastoral side of life along with the balancing role of women. If history was nothing but a stew of violence and warfare, none of us would be alive to read about it.

Eventually, Henry, along with Fort Michilimackinac's surviving officers and those captured at Fort St. Joseph and Green Bay were taken to Montreal by Charles Langlade and the Odawa as a show of good faith, an event which did much to brighten British hopes for peace.

As for Pontiac, he had a small victory on July 31, 1763 when his warriors ambushed a company of men led by Captain James Dalzell, who planned to attack the Indian's camp more than two miles north of Detroit. Capt. Dalzell and his men crept out of Detroit at 2 a.m. only to find Pontiac's warriors waiting for them. Dalzell and twenty-one men were killed in an ambush along a stream that became known as Bloody Run. Today it is the site of Detroit's Elmwood Cemetery.

By October, 1763, Pontiac's 870 warriors began drifting home to begin the winter hunt, disillusioned by their failure to take Detroit, which was continually resupplied despite their best efforts. Some left in disgust, protesting the torture and ritual cannibalism of captives, which went against the teachings of Neolin. Elsewhere, Native warriors abandoned the forts they had taken, having no use for them, and the alliance gradually drifted apart.

Unlike the armies of Europe, Native warriors had no supply lines of ships or wagon trains bringing arms and provisions to help them withstand a long siege or hold a position. Nor did they wish to hold and govern territory in the tradition of the Romans or the Mongols. They had wives and children waiting for them in their far-off villages, where they were urgently needed as hunters, defenders, and to bring in the fall harvest. Striking a British fort or trading post tended to be a one-and-done proposition, with the ruins left to the locals.

Another blow came that fall when Pontiac was thunderstruck to learn that a peace treaty had been signed between the British and French in Paris. Now, to his great surprise, the French were begging him to give up the fight so as not to upset the apple cart between the nations. Pontiac quickly dashed off a letter to commander Gladwin at Detroit:

"My Brother, the word that my father has sent me to make peace I have accepted; all my young men have buried their hatchets. I think you will now forget the bad things that have taken place for some time past. Likewise I shall forget what you may have done to me, in order to think of nothing but good. I, the Ojibwa, the Huron, we are ready to speak with you when you ask us. Give us an answer. I am sending this resolution in order that you may see it. If you are as kind as I, you will make me a reply. I wish you a good day, Pontiac."

Pontiac followed up by sending a peace belt to Detroit, but by then, Gladwin had been recalled. Believing that Pontiac was beaten, the new commander, Col. John Bradstreet (who had reinforced the fort with 1,200 soldiers), hacked the belt to pieces. This breech of diplomacy was an intolerable insult, prompting Pontiac to redouble his efforts. He rallied the Indians of Illinois and secured pledges from the Ojibwe and Miami to continue the fight. In the end the British realized they couldn't simply dismiss a war chief capable of rallying thousands. Peace talks were held at Detroit in the summer of 1765, where Pontiac finally buried the hatchet.

During the two-year course of Pontiac's War, his warriors managed to kill five hundred British soldiers, inflicting casualties on up to two thousand colonists, while barring British access to their newly-won French holdings in the Illinois country for up to three years. Innocent Native peoples also suffered, with vengeful colonists burning villages, massacring their residents and burning their crops. In the end, as historian Charles Cleland has noted, Pontiac and his allies won every battle, yet still lost the war.

As for Major Gen. Amherst, he was recalled to London in disgrace, where he was blamed for igniting the war by way of his skinflint policies and callous diplomacy. Forever after, he has been infamous for his proposal to spread smallpox among the Indians.

In its aftermath, the expenses of the French and Indian War were so great that King George III of Britain was compelled to raise taxes on the American colonies to pay the debt, which became a major cause of the American Revolution. Pontiac's War only deepened the debt, accompanied by pleas from the colonies for protection from the Indians. This in turn prompted the British to continue the deployment of ten thousand troops in North America, creating even more expense, estimated at £214,340 per year (totaling more than $47 million annually today, by one calculation). The British vowed to pay the first year's installment, but after that the burden would be on the Thirteen Colonies.

British Prime Minister George Grenville, who created the infamous sales tax levied through the Stamp Act, thought it quite rich that the Americans asked for British protection from the Indians on one hand, while being infuriated over the taxes to pay for it on the other. In his biography of King George III, historian Andrew Roberts notes that every penny raised in the taxation of the colonies went to pay for their protection. The colonists thought otherwise, believing that their taxes were, in fact, paying for troops meant to keep them in line.

Pontiac's War also spurred the frightened British to bar settlement west of the Appalachians in a much-despised "Proclamation Line."

On that score, one could argue that it was Odawa war chief Pontiac who was the true "father of our country" - or at least the stepfather - for stimulating British taxes and prompting the hated Proclamation Line, both of which spurred on the Yankee Doodle Dandies of the American Revolution.

The quintessential tough guy, Pontiac came to an ignominious end. In 1766 he attended a council of chiefs at Fort Niagara, where he vowed to support the British, "in the name of all the nations to the westward whom I command." The British took him at his word, elevating him to the status of king of all of the western tribes. Full of himself, Pontiac agreed.

This was on par with farting in a crowded room to his proud war chief allies, who by then in bald terms considered Pontiac to be a loser who'd stirred up a heap of trouble with little to show for it. Others felt that he had betrayed the cause by giving in to the British. Even his young Odawa warriors turned against him. Disgraced, in 1768 he went to live with his relatives among the Illinois tribe, where he received a cold welcome: two years earlier he had knifed a major chieftain of the Illinois to death in a drunken fight in the streets of Detroit.

An English trader paid an Indian of the Illinois tribe to murder Pontiac. On April 20, 1769, Pontiac visited a French trading post at Cahokia. Exiting the post, his companion clubbed him from behind and stabbed him to death. Hearing the news, his old friend, Minavavana, set out for Cahokia, seeking vengeance. But by then of course, only a legend remained.

CHAPTER 19

THE FLOODGATES OPEN

When newspapers from London arrived via a fast schooner from Britain in late 1763, twenty-year-old Thomas Jefferson and twenty-seven-year-old Patrick Henry could hardly believe their eyes. The government of King George III had issued a proclamation which put the Indian country west of the Appalachians completely off limits to their side hustle as land speculators. Along with their partners George Washington, Benjamin Franklin and members of Virginia's powerful Lee family, these young patricians and would-be land speculators blasted the Proclamation of 1763 as utter tyranny. Outrage ran through the Thirteen Colonies like an electric shock.

The recently concluded French and Indian War had been infamous for its extreme violence. Women and children had been slaughtered by Native war parties; infants ripped from their mothers' arms and brained against trees; many colonists had been burned alive. Yet now King George was going to reward his Indian enemies and deny the colonists the spoils of war? The colonists ignored the fact that many of the same cruelties had been visited on the Indians, including those committed to peace. In fact, rather than adopting many of their captives as the Indians did, white soldiers were notorious for killing their captives.

Added to the burden of British taxes, the Proclamation of 1763 set the fuse for the American Revolution.

Hastily written without much thought for the consequences, the proclamation had been issued by Lord George Halifax, the First Lord of Trade and Plantations overseeing the colonies, who had been severely rattled by Pontiac's uprising. His Line ran down the mountain spine from Lake Champlain to the Gulf of Mexico. Those who had already settled west of the Appalachians were told "forthwith to remove themselves."

The rationale for the Proclamation Line was strong. During the prior war, the French had been backed by a coalition of the Abenaki, Mi'kmaq, Delaware, Ojibwe, Odawa, Shawnee and Wyandot, among others. As the British quickly learned, the Indians could field thousands of guerrilla warriors who struck in small, highly mobile units that were impossible to defeat on their own turf.

Bled dry of his treasury and troops, King George and his government promised their Indian allies and foes alike that there would be no settle-

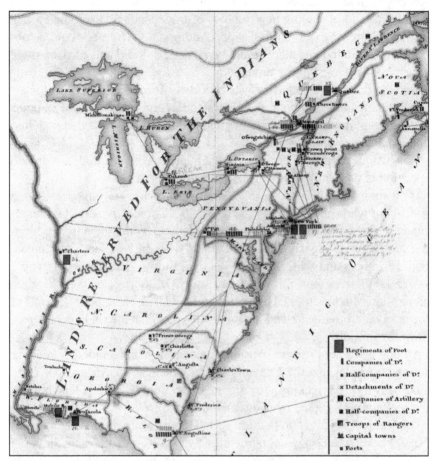

The gray stripe above was King George III's hated Proclamation Line depicted in an 18th century map, barring the way west over the Appalachian Mountains. The line would soon be moved to the west along the Ohio River.

ment on the western side of the Appalachians. In return, the Indians would allow the Brits to garrison the eleven French forts that had surrendered or been abandoned. The king provided Native leaders with large silver peace medallions to demonstrate his good intentions and promised to send troops to root out illegal settlements. The Proclamation Line was intended to create "one gigantic Native American reserve where no American colonial settlement would be permitted," wrote Andrew Roberts in his biography of George III, *The Last King of America.*

More than just assuring peace with the Indians beyond the mountains, Britain's Board of Trade believed the barrier would expand their lucrative fur trade with the Indians, a bonanza taken from the French. It would also force American colonists to continue purchasing goods manufactured in Britain instead of finding new sources of trade, such as from the French or Spanish by way of the Mississippi. Additionally, if peace could be obtained with the Indians there would be no need to build and garrison more expensive forts west of the mountains.

But the mandated boundary was a disaster from the get-go. Colonists seeking new land chaffed at the proclamation and many ignored it, pouring over the mountains to seize the rich farmlands of Pennsylvania, Ohio and Kentucky.

This included a plague of professional hunters, whiskey traders and land speculators with little or no regard for Native territories.

At the time of the proclamation, George Washington was a rapacious land speculator who sometimes worked under an alias, scheming to claim thousands of acres over the mountains that were held by the Indians. Washington started surveying land in the wilderness when he was barely seventeen, both for others and with an eye to his own future. Late in life, he would own 54,000 acres outright, with a share in 70,000 acres of West Virginia alone for resale to settlers. His tactics included squeezing poor veterans of the prior war, buying up land grants "for a trifle" that the soldiers had been awarded for their service.

Among his other projects, Washington and fifty shareholders, including Jefferson, Henry and the Lee family, had launched the Mississippi Land Company in 1763, seeking a royal grant of 2.5 million acres of land beyond the mountains occupied by tribes including the Delaware and Shawnee.

The company planned to petition King George to grant each shareholder 50,000 acres free of any tax burden for twelve years, with each allotment to be settled by at least two hundred paying families. With the land already spoken for, the idea was to keep non-paying, impoverished squatters from flooding over the mountains. As for troublesome Indians, the company proposed the construction of two forts on the Ohio and Mississippi rivers in the hope of overwhelming Native resistance to the land-grab.

The Proclamation Line put the kibosh on the plan before its promoters had a chance to present it to the king. One can hear the echo of their frustration in the Declaration of Independence, in which Jefferson wrote that all men had the right to "life, liberty and the pursuit of happiness," the last of which - "pursuit of happiness" - has been suspected of being a veiled allusion to the right to settle Native lands without the meddling of the British government. Or, perhaps, an obscure hint at the right to own slaves.

Washington, who was bitterly disappointed over the dashing of his scheme, opined that the proclamation was merely a sop to "quiet the minds of the Indians & must fall of course in a few years." As with many other speculators, he simply ignored the line, telling his land agent to carry on. He promised his agent a future percentage of any farmlands he claimed for him in the Ohio territory.

In any event, settlers had been pouring over the mountains since the 1740s like water through a sieve, and continued to do so despite the Proclamation Line. And who was there to stop them? King George was four thousand miles across the ocean and his troops were spread thin across a global empire. With turmoil brewing in Ireland, India and continental Europe, he had bigger things to worry about than chasing roughneck pioneers over the Appalachians. As with the Chinese proverb, "The mountains are high and the emperor is far away," many colonists felt they could safely thumb their noses at daft King George.

Washington's prediction that the Line would fall came to pass just five years later with the first Treaty of Fort Stanwix, which opened the floodgates to Indian country beyond the Appalachians.

Gazing from the bastion of Fort Stanwix in 1768, Sir William Johnson must surely have been impressed, and perhaps a little anxious, at the sight of more than three thousand Iroquois camped beyond its sagging palisade and overgrown defensive ditch.

Johnson spoke the Iroquoian language and had led British and Mohawk forces against the French during the recent war, winning many battles and taking a musket ball in his hip that remained there for the rest of his life. He was infamous for paying the bounties of New York's Scalp Act of 1747, despite knowing that the scalps included those of Native women, children and noncombatant men aligned with the French. A ladies man, he had numerous children by Mohawk and immigrant women alike. He was just the sort of diplomat needed to grease a deal that had rotten consequences for Native peoples thereafter.

Located near present-day Rome in upstate New York and laid out in a four-pointed star, the sixteen-acre fort had been abandoned by the British in 1765 and was so run-down that a new council hall and lodgings were built to conduct negotiations with the Iroquois. A decade later the fort would be reoccupied by American rebels during the Revolution, gaining fame as "the fort that never surrendered."

The fort's environs were well known to the Iroquois. For thousands of years Native peoples had followed a water route and portages connecting the Atlantic Ocean and Lake Ontario via the Hudson and Mohawk rivers, Wood Creek, and a chain of lakes. The fort was located in the homeland of the Oneida people and had been used to stage attacks on the French in Canada. It was adjacent to the *Deo-Wain-Sta*, a mile-long portage between the Mohawk River and Wood Creek known as the Oneida Carry. Other than the St. Lawrence River and the Ottawa/French rivers far to the north, this ancient trading route and war path was the only feasible link between the Atlantic and the Great Lakes.

Now, Johnson, the British superintendent of Indian affairs in the colonies, had come to purchase an immense territory from the Six Nations of the Iroquois, who were staunch allies and still the most powerful Native force in North America. Hundreds of chieftains from all six tribes were on hand to hammer out a treaty that would replace the boundary set by the Proclamation of 1763.

The Proclamation Line had been an abject failure and had only managed to infuriate the Thirteen Colonies who saw it as a British stranglehold meant to keep them down. Hoping to ease tensions and quell rampant violence along the frontier, the British decided to create a new barrier that would be more accommodating to colonists. Thus, the Treaty of Fort Stanwix moved the boundary of settlement four hundred miles further west of the Appalachians. It drew a new line from the fort to the confluence of the Kanawha and Ohio rivers in West Virginia, then proceeding down the Ohio River to the Mississippi. Under the treaty, all of the land north of the Ohio River was declared Indian country, while millions of acres to the south and west were ceded to the British Crown for settlement.

Johnson cut a self-serving deal with the Iroquois against the wishes of his superiors in London. It allowed him and his friends to purchase thousands of acres of land freed up by the new treaty.

Even so,the new boundary was plum pudding for the Brits, who gained all or part of West Virginia, northeast Tennessee, and western Pennsylvania, Kentucky, Maryland and Virginia.

Signed by the Iroquois in November 1768, the treaty was the grandfather of bad deals afflicting the Indians, setting the precedent for land-grabs authorized by chieftains who had no right to grant their approval.

In ceding the land of many other Indian tribes the Iroquois hoped to preserve their own homeland from settlement in New York and Pennsylvania. They claimed to own all of the territory west of the Appalachians by right of conquest in the 1600s. They also claimed to own the land as far south as Tennessee, which was a surprise to the British, who had purchased much of Tennessee from the Cherokee that year in a separate Treaty of Hard Labour.

On the losing end of the stick, the treaty funneled settlers into the homeland of thousands of Delaware, Mingo and Shawnee, whose chieftains attended the treaty talks, but had no say in the negotiations. Considering themselves the "elder brothers" to the tribes further west, the Iroquois felt entitled to speak for all.

Needless to say, this did not sit well with the tribes that had been dispossessed with the stroke of a quill pen, especially since the new treaty was considered a sweepstakes by European colonists, sparking a land rush of settlers and speculators. The giveaway incited widespread anger among tens of thousands of Indians living in the lands of the Great Lakes and the Ohio River Valley, holding the line against two million colonists east of the mountains.

In return for their treachery, the Iroquois received £10,460 in gifts and cash, which was the most that the Brits had ever awarded to an Indian tribe. Converting the currency of the past is notoriously difficult, but a rough guess is this amounted to nearly $2.4 million in today's currency.

The Shawnee and Mingo (who were an offshoot of the Seneca Iroquois) rightly considered the treaty to be outrageous and refused to abide by it, renouncing the Iroquois as their brothers. They began attacking flatboats on the Ohio River along with settlements in Kentucky under the leadership of Shawnee war chiefs Cornstalk and Blackfish. Over the next twenty years a mighty alliance of Indian tribes would coalesce to defend Native territory.

As for Sir William Johnson, he dropped dead of a stroke six years later while delivering a rousing speech to the Iroquois on July 11, 1774.

CHAPTER 20

A LAND BEYOND THE LAW

To the Iroquois, the O-hee-yo was "the beautiful river," and other Native peoples called it the same. Nearly one thousand miles long and roughly a mile wide, the Ohio River flows through the heart of America, serving as the eastern branch of the riverine tree of the Mississippi. Its bottomlands were, and are, among the richest in North America, providing a bounty of food and game to all who lived along its banks. It also served as the great river highway of early America, leading to the fulfillment of riches and dreams for all who journeyed along its course.

Yet that journey was also a gauntlet, jealously guarded by those who had lived along the O-y-o's valleys, forests and meadows for thousands of years.

Prowled by angry war parties, frontier thugs, vigilantes, militias and the dueling armies of France, Britain and the United States, the Ohio River Valley and Kentucky came to be known as the "dark and bloody ground," a lawless place where both Native peoples and white settlers lived suspended in terror. It was a gauntlet for those who took their lives into their hands, sweeping down the river on flatboats, canoes, rafts and barges brimming with livestock, tools, luggage and families in the hope of settling territory that Native peoples relied on for hunting.

This frontier was also the "line in the sand" for Native peoples who would go to any extreme to protect their homeland. What happened in the Ohio River Valley would resonate all the way to the shores of the Great Lakes.

A mix of desperation and hope inspired thousands of settlers to risk their necks at isolated cabins and pathetic forts along the frontier, where a dozen young men painted black and eager to prove their worth as warriors might appear with fire and hatchets after midnight on any given evening. The terror was so great at Boonesborough in Kentucky that its residents were unable to grow crops for fear of leaving the safety of their fort. They relied on salted venison to survive.

Ambush, terror and subterfuge were prime tactics for Indian raiders. On the Ohio River, white captives were ordered to beg for help from passing boats, which were overwhelmed by hidden warriors when they drew ashore. Elsewhere, attacks on farmers in broad daylight were far more common than night raids. Forced to work his fields from dawn to dusk with the tree line close at hand, a lone farmer might be able to get off one shot if he could reach his musket in time and steady his shaking hands, but he was no match for an attack from all sides. This is exactly what happened to Abraham Lincoln's paternal grandfather, also known as "Captain" Abraham Lincoln. In May 1786 he was shot by a Native warrior while working his field in the company of his three sons. His eldest son seized a musket and killed the intruder before his younger brother could be spirited away.

Native warriors painted themselves before battle to look as terrifying as possible, often paralyzing white militia and settlers with fright. Used for close-quarter combat, their tomahawks were gruesome weapons, the hammer-blows and centripetal force of which could split a skull, splashing blood and brains everywhere. Historian Peter Silver notes in his book, *Our Savage Neighbors*, that raiders would amplify terror by staging horrific scenes, placing mutilated corpses in the middle of roads to frighten travelers. These same macabre tactics were quickly adopted by Virginians in their war with the neighboring Cherokee, leaving the mutilated bodies of Indian victims along trails used by Native peoples.

While Europeans assumed that the "rules of war" (devised after their own horrific religious wars) forbade the killing of noncombatants, Native societies had no such inhibitions; rather they aimed to create the maximum possible terror in order to end a conflict quickly, with women and children being fair game (though they were mostly taken captive for ransom or adoption).

Huddled into forts or barricaded within their homes, settlers were overcome with free-floating anxiety over attacks that might come at any moment, or perhaps not for weeks, if ever, dragging on the agony of anticipation. There were many instances of well-armed settlers and militias who far outnumbered their Indian foes, yet were so terrified that they were frozen with fright and easily overcome. Any hint of an attack on the frontier could spark an exodus that jammed the roads back east to the safety of Philadelphia. On a trip west in that period, Benjamin Franklin was shocked to see the road jammed with settlers rushing pell-mell to the east.

Imagine the situation of a poor Irish immigrant in the New Land. On their way across the ocean he and his wife ate rats to survive and endured beatings from the crew on their disease-ridden ship, then spent three years in bondage to pay for their voyage. Now, he, his malaria-stricken wife and their three children are squatters in the territory of the Delaware Indians in Pennsylvania, living in a wretched lean-to of logs and pine boughs with a clay hearth, the sum of which isn't much more than an animal's burrow. At night he is accustomed to hearing the howl of wolves and the throaty hoot of owls. But one night, while smoking his pipe on a stump outside his home, he hears a wavering "death hollow" coming from the direction of a neighbor's camp. This is a long "*Aahooooooooo*" signifying the scalping of an enemy. The Delaware have been friendly to now, but he's seen none of them since a band of white frontier ruffians attacked one of their villages and knows very well that revenge can take the innocent as well as the guilty. What is he to do?

Native peoples faced terrors of their own. Women left behind to tend their crops and villages while their husbands were gone off hunting were easy prey for roving gangs of white outlaws who attacked undefended villages in addition to pillaging cabins abandoned by fleeing settlers. At best, Native women might gather their children and run for the shelter of the forest, an age-old refuge for primitive peoples to avoid being raped and murdered. Outlaws were such a problem on the frontier that posses of white "Regulators" were frequently dispatched to bring them to the gallows.

In advance of the settlers came a plague of market hunters who left the corpses of deer, buffalo and bear to rot by the thousands, taking only their hides. Armed with a Kentucky long rifle, a good marksman could kill anywhere from ten to thirty whitetails on an average day, accruing several hundred hides in a season. Packing up to 250 pounds of hides on his horse, he could expect a payday of $1,000, or about $40,000 in today's currency. The hides were used to make leather breeches, gloves, shoes and hats worn in the Colonies and exported to Europe.

Market hunting in Kentucky enraged Native peoples. The Shawnee, Chickasaw, Iroquois and Cherokee had spent hundreds of years creating forage for bison, deer, bear and other species with the judicious use of fire to establish game parks in the region. There was a loose agreement on their respective hunting territories, along with the stipulation that no tribe could establish a village in another's preserve.

Yet who could resist these easy riches? The Cherokee and other southeastern tribes quickly got into the act, slaughtering tens of thousands of deer for the hide trade. Market hunters and the settlers who came in their wake to gobble up the game parks for their farms became an existential threat for Indians living west of the mountains.

Kentucky takes its name from *Kantake*, an Iroquois phrase for a town they called "place of the meadows." This was a large town of Shawnee farmers at a salt spring, who called their community Skipakithiki, meaning Blue Lick after the salt gathered there.

Long before flatboats filled with settlers began coursing down the Ohio River, the land of *Kantake* over the mountains was *terra incognita* to the English, Scotch and Irish living along the Eastern Seaboard. It was professional hunter and explorer Daniel Boone who hacked a road over the mountains, leading the way west for hundreds of thousands.

Boone and legions of men and women who followed in his footsteps had been seduced by visions of endless game and rich farmland amid the bluegrass meadows of *Kantake*. He was entranced by the tales of trader John Findley, who had made his way down the Ohio river in 1738 with four companions and a canoe full of English goods. Coming across a party of Shawnee hunters, they had been invited to Skipakithiki, where they found other traders from Pennsylvania and a lively commerce in furs and the hides of deer and bear.

That winter, Findley and one of his assistants barely escaped with their lives after a war party of French and Indian marauders fell upon the town, killing three of his men, kidnapping others and stealing hundreds of their pelts and supplies. Nonetheless, he brought back tales of a paradise brimming with buffalo, deer and bear beyond count, along with fertile meadows and river valleys, rich enough to fulfill the dreams of generations.

Findley had filled Boone's ears with these tales in 1755 when he was a twenty-year-old teamster serving in the ill-fated army of British Gen. Edward Braddock. With the battle turning into a disaster, wagoneer Boone had escaped by cutting his lead horse loose and galloping across the ford of the Monongahela River to safety.

Nearly fifteen years after the battle, Findley and Boone happened upon one-another again, reviving the old tales of paradisiacal *Kantake*. To the hard-worn settlers of western North Carolina, "Kentucke" sounded like a promised land of milk and honey, and though Findley was no pathfinder, he proposed making their way there via the Great Warriors Trail of the Cherokee through a notch in the Cumberland Mountains.

It was through this gap in May of 1769 that Boone and five others made their way as one of many bands of market hunters who quickly upset the balance of hundreds of years of Native hunting traditions.

Boone went on to broker the purchase of virtually all of Kentucky from the Cherokee for the Transylvania Company of North Carolina. The purchase was later declared illegal, but by then settlers were pouring through the Cumberland Gap to get their share.

Despite their fears, many settlers risked their lives as squatters on Indian land because of the high prices sought for land elsewhere. The Transylvania Company asked as much as $40 for one hundred acres in 1775 at a time when the average workingman made thirty-three cents per day. Given the price of tools, supplies, and a wagon or boat to make the trek over the mountains or down the river, many couldn't afford the rates of land speculators and chose to push their luck on Native lands instead.

Standing about five-foot-eight, Boone had a level gaze that was not easily disconcerted. Although he was self-conscious of his short stature, he was said to be "built like a pony" and strong as a horse, with a thick chest, arms and legs. A hunter since boyhood, he loved nothing more than to disappear into the wilderness for months on end, slaughtering game for the markets back east. Near his home in North Carolina, Boone is said to have killed ninety-nine bears in a single season along what became known as Bear Creek. On another occasion, he shot thirty deer in a single day.

He did much the same in Kentucky, slaughtering thousands of deer and other animals for the markets back home while risking his neck to avoid angry warriors. Once, he and a partner were captured by a jovial group of Shawnee hunters who took their haul of nine hundred deerskins and a large pack of furs, letting them go with a warning to leave Kentucky and never return. Boone returned to North Carolina broke and in debt with nothing to show for his six months in the bush.

In the decades ahead, market hunters such as Boone would scrub North America clean of game from the Appalachians to the Rocky Mountains, a practice which eventually starved more Indians to death than all of those killed by the U.S. Army.*

The market for deer hides, and later buffalo, played a huge role in frontier economies. As historian John Mack Faragher noted in his biography of Boone, more than 30,000 deer hides were exported from North Carolina in 1753 alone, not counting the thousands more used locally to create leggings, moccasins and other clothing. A "buck," meaning a deer hide, was the standard of trade, and by 1750 the term became a synonym for hard cash, and then the U.S. dollar, which in turn was a bastardization of the German term for currency, *thaler*.

A far grimmer source of income for heartless pioneers was the trade in Native scalps. During their colonization of Ireland in the early 1600s, the English had paid a bounty for Irish heads, later accepting the scalps and ears of their victims as being more expedient. Taking heads as trophies of war was known to the Indians (and perhaps most peoples on earth at the level of barbarism), but there's controversy to this day as to whether the practice of scalping was widespread prior to the arrival of white invaders. Whatever the case, it was the British, followed by the Americans, who made it a thriving trade from New England to California. By the 1780s, Native scalps were fetching thirty dollars each in Cincinnati, with no questions asked as to whether the victim had been man, woman, child, or of a friendly tribe.

Despite their best efforts, the Shawnee lost all of Kentucky and much of West Virginia in the aftermath of a barroom massacre that led to Lord Dunmore's War.

By the early 1770s the Shawnee were attacking settlements and flatboats all along the frontier. In early 1774 a force of ninety men under George Rogers Clark and Michael Cresap took it upon themselves to declare war on the Shawnee and set off on punitive raids in present-day Ohio. Twenty-one-year-old Clark planned to attack the Shawnee capital at Chillicothe, home to hundreds of warriors. He was wisely dissuaded by the more savvy Cresap.

On April 30, 1774, two dozen vigilantes led by Daniel and Jacob Greathouse split off from Clark's expedition and lured four peaceful Mingo Indians to a sit-down at Bakers Tavern on Yellow Creek, forty miles west of Fort Pitt. After a convivial drink and some small talk by the Greathouse

*Of the sixty million bison that roamed North America in the 1700s, for instance, only three hundred survivors were recorded in the wild by the dawn of the twentieth century.

brothers, the butchering began with their men bursting from an adjacent storeroom. The party murdered two young men and two young women, one of whom, Koonay, was heavily pregnant. During the subsequent mutilation of the corpses, Jacob Greathouse sliced open Koonay's abdomen and ripped her unborn son from her body, scalping the fetus and impaling its tiny body on a stake.

Enraged, Mingo and Shawnee warriors terrorized the frontier under the leadership of Cornstalk - Hokoleskwa - a reluctant but resolute war chief, who said at one point, "better for the red men to die like warriors than to diminish away by inches. Now is the time to begin. If we fight like men, we may hope to enlarge our bounds."

Indian raids prompted Virginia's royal governor, Lord Dunmore, to raise an army of three thousand militia. In part, Dunmore hoped to keep Virginia's able-bodied men busy so as not to join the rebels of New England who were agitating for independence from Britain.

A staunch supporter of Britain, Dunmore would later offer freedom to any black slave who joined the British cause in the American Revolution. Somewhere between 800 and 2,000 slaves accepted his offer, with many becoming soldiers in Dunmore's Ethiopian Brigade. Dunmore also raised the ire of patriot Patrick Henry, who famously shouted "Give me liberty or give me death!" after the governor refused to give the rebels powder, guns and shot.

At the Battle of Point Pleasant on October 10, 1774, Cornstalk's warriors attacked two columns of militia totaling three hundred men, and although they gave a good account of themselves and killed more Virginians than their own casualties, it sank in that theirs was a lost cause, considering the endless number of troops that could be thrown at them. At the subsequent Treaty of Camp Charlotte in late 1774, the Shawnee and their allies under Cornstalk ceded all of their lands south of the Ohio River, including Kentucky and West Virginia. They also promised to end their attacks on the river. In return, they were granted all of the territory north of the Ohio River, but as events would soon show, this promise was quickly forgotten.

Cornstalk's towering presence made a powerful impression at Camp Charlotte where he hammered home the injustice to the Shawnee in a speech to Lord Dunmore. Virginia Col. Benjamin Wilson reported that, "I have heard the first orators in Virginia, Patrick Henry and Richard Henry Lee, but never have I heard one whose powers of delivery surpassed those of Cornstalk on that occasion."

Yet not every faction of the Shawnee agreed to abide by the treaty. Many insisted that the hunting grounds of Kentucky were sacred and theirs alone. Thus, white squatters kept pouring into Indian territory and attacks by bands of roving Indians carried on as usual.

Eager to field a proxy army of Indians against the American rebels in the Revolution, the British began arming their Indian allies at Detroit in 1776. Native warriors were given guns, ammo, scalping knives, food, and promises of eternal fealty. The goal was to create a western front in the war that would pin the rebelling colonists between the Indians and the Redcoats.

Growing weary of warfare and its futility, Cornstalk, his son, and two Shawnee elders were murdered by a mob of white militiamen three years after the battle of Point Pleasant at a fort built on the spot. They had come to warn the Americans that the British were raising the Indians against them.

As for Boone, he sat out the American Revolution, yet had an unwitting role in thwarting British ambitions.

In February, 1778, he talked thirty of his men into laying down their arms without a fight after they were surrounded by 120 Shawnee warriors while working at a salt spring in Kentucky. Led by war chief Blackfish on a mission to avenge the death of Cornstalk, the Shawnee were on their way to attack the starving residents of Boonesborough, who were barely hanging on behind a ramshackle palisade. They desperately needed salt in order to preserve the venison that kept them from starving to death.

In order to forestall the attack, Boone promised Blackfish that he would surrender the fort the following spring. But first, as a sign of good faith, his men would lay down their arms and march one hundred miles through the snow to the Shawnee town of Chillicothe on the Little Miami River.

In a narrow vote of sixty-one to fifty-nine, the Shawnee allowed Boone's men to be held for ransom or adoption instead of being executed. Considered a great prize and honored for his skill as a hunter, Boone was taken all the way to Detroit and dangled before the British as a trophy, though Blackfish declined to give him up. Thereafter, the captives were adopted by Shawnee families who had lost sons or husbands; others escaped the following spring.

After running a gauntlet at Chillicothe*, Boone was given a thorough scrubbing by the women of Blackfish's band and had his hair plucked clean except for a scalp lock decorated with ribbons and feathers. He was given a new name, Sheltowee, or Big Turtle, and adopted by a Shawnee family. Yet he soon escaped, riding an Indian pony to its death from exhaustion and fording the mile-wide Ohio River on a patchwork of logs and vines to lead the defense of Boonesborough.

Blackfish was understandably dismayed and disappointed at the treachery

---

* Boone's gauntlet ordeal was apparently meant for show, rather than harm. He was only lightly abused in a ritual that could be deadly for many.

of his adopted "son." He had saved thirty whites from death in exchange for Boone's help in the peaceful surrender of Boonesborough and felt that a deal was a deal. Backed by the British, he laid siege to Boonesborough for eleven days in September, 1778, but by then Boone had strengthened its flimsy defenses and the attack flopped. This also dashed British hopes of establishing a southern front with their Indian allies over the mountains against the American rebels of the Revolution.

Unfortunately for Blackfish and the Shawnee, Boone's escape provided information on the whereabouts of their previously-unknown village and trading center at Chillicothe. In a counter-raid the following year, Blackfish was shot in the leg and died soon thereafter of infection.

It wasn't all good times and high adventure for Boone, however; he also suffered heartache over the violent deaths of two children along with his younger brother, Ned. One of his sons, James, was infamously tortured to death as a boy, while another, Israel, was shot through the neck during a skirmish. Yet biographer Faragher claimed that, unlike most frontiersmen, Boone never grew to hate the Indians. Perhaps his time among the Shawnee and a life spent in the wilderness gave him a deeper understanding of Native issues than most. Eventually, he wearied of the frittering away of Kentucky; within a few decades of his carving a road over the mountains some 300,000 settlers had followed in his footsteps, and that was too close for comfort. He moved his family across the Mississippi to Spanish-held Missouri, where he died in 1820 at the age of eighty-five.

Like Davy Crockett from neighboring Tennessee, Boone became a pioneer legend. In 1964, actor Fess Parker played him on NBC's hit series, *Daniel Boone*, which ran for six seasons. Ed Ames starred as Mingo, a Cherokee friend who always had Boone's back. Parker wore a coonskin cap on the show, out of character with the legend who preferred a tall hat to heighten his short stature.

***

Notable victims of the American Revolution were a peaceful band of Moravian Delaware Indians who had been converted to Christianity by Moravian missionaries. In March, 1782, a militia of 150 American rangers captured a starving group of ninety-six Moravians as they were foraging for corn at Gnadenhutten in southeastern Ohio. Although they were sworn to peace and neutrality, the Moravians were locked in their mission house overnight while the Pennsylvanians debated their fate. The next morning, they were bound, gagged, and bludgeoned to death one-by-one. Killed, scalped, and tossed into their burning mission were 39 children, 29 women and 28 men. The rangers loaded eighty horses with Indian plunder before torching the village and pushing on. This too only served to amp up more

Indian attacks on settlers.

Following the Revolution, the infant United States signed the second Treaty of Fort Stanwix in 1784, this time informing the vanquished Iroquois that the British had ceded all of their holdings south of Canada to the new nation, *including Iroquois territory*. Having sided with the British, they were now punished by the American victors. Under the new boundaries the weakened Six Nations would be confined to a much smaller reserve in upstate New York and Pennsylvania. Their westernmost boundary was limited to what is roughly the eastern border of Ohio.

During the negotiations, the Iroquois continued to insist that they spoke for all of the tribes to the west by right of conquest in the 1600s, stating that: "We are the only persons adequate to treat of, and conclude a peace, not only on the part of the Six Nations, but also on that of the Ottawas, Chippewas, Hurons, Potawatomies, Messasagas, Miamis, Delawares, Cherokees, Chicasas, Coctas, and Creeks, and establish peace in the name of them all (sic). Whatever conclusion is made at this treaty will be strong, and... communicated throughout the various tribes."

None of these tribes were on hand at the second Treaty of Fort Stanwix, and the Iroquois, having claimed to speak for their "younger brothers," were instructed to deliver the bad news: the American victors planned a new boundary line that would allow settlement deeper into their territory, robbing them once again.

But the six tribes of the once-mighty Iroquois inexorably lost all of their land as well in treaties signed in 1783, 1784, 1785, 1788, 1790 and 1795. It was only in the Treaty of Canandaigua, signed in 1794, that the Seneca gained more than a million acres of their land back in return for gaining their cooperation in seizing what was left of Ohio from the Shawnee and Miami. Yet even this land at the western end of Lake Ontario was taken by the U.S. once again in treaties signed in 1797 and 1842.

CHAPTER 21

THE NORTHWEST TERRITORY

Deep in debt and desperate for cash, the leaders of the young American republic saw the sale of real estate to settlers as a way out of their troubles. The fact that the land belonged to the Indians seemed of little consequence. Besides, there was ample reason to believe that God Himself wanted the new nation to succeed. After all, hadn't the scrappy Continental

American Progress, painted in 1872 by Prussian-born John Gast captured the spirit of Manifest Destiny as the United States pushed west against the fleeing Indians. At the National Gallery in Washington, D.C.

Army defeated the most powerful military on earth against all odds in the Revolution? Many Americans felt that God was clearly on their side and these notions of divine intervention would soon coalesce into the credo of Manifest Destiny: the belief that America was so good, so morally right and so blessed that it should hold sway from sea to shining sea.

More than that, in their creation of a democratic republic, the Americans had embarked on one of the noblest and most radical experiments in history. As Thomas Paine had written in *Common Sense*, "We have it in our power to begin the world over again."

All that stood in the way of this dream were a few Indians, yet these proved even more difficult than the British.

So, if not by conquest, how would Americans obtain the land of the Indians who had lived there for thousands of years? Perhaps in the manner of the cowbird, which lays its eggs in the nests of songbirds, whereupon its hatchlings crowd their smaller mates out of the nest.

In 1783, George Washington had espoused this cowbird strategy to New York State Senator James Duane, claiming that the Indians, "will ever retreat as our settlements advance upon them, and they will be as ready to sell as we are to buy."

Treaties with the Indians were nothing new in North America. The British, French, Spanish and Dutch had been signing treaties since the 1600s; witness the purchase of Manhattan Island for a chest of glass beads in 1626. Washington and the Founding Fathers knew that negotiating treaties was far less costly than kicking up in a hornets' nest of angry Indians north of the Ohio River.

Considering that the United States would spend $5 million fighting Indians from 1790-'96, or five-sixths of its total expenditures, buying Indian land at far less expense made more sense than trying to seize it by conquest.

Washington, who was a great one for run-on sentences and a mangled syntax rivaling Yoda, added this regarding the purchase of Indian lands: "That is the cheapest, as well as the least distressing way of dealing with them, none who is acquainted with the nature of an Indian warfare, and has ever been at the trouble of estimating the expense of one, and comparing it with the cost of purchasing their lands, will hesitate to acknowledge."

Elsewhere, he had this to say, betraying a lack of empathy for the Indians he hoped to displace: The flood of American settlers would, "as certainly cause the Savage as the Wolf to retire: both being beasts of prey, tho' they differ in shape. In a word there is nothing to be obtained by an Indian war but the soil they live on and this can be obtained by purchase at less expense, and without that bloodshed, and those distresses which helpless women and children are made (victims) in all kinds of dispute with them."

Since the newly-formed Confederation Congress had no power to levy taxes for revenue, acquiring Indian lands for resale to settlers was seen as the best way to raise capital in a hurry. Congress passed the Land Ordinance of 1785, which created a system for settlers to purchase undeveloped land in the west.

This was followed by the Northwest Ordinance of 1787, which called for establishing several new states north of the Ohio River in the heart of Indian country whenever their respective territories reached a population of 60,000. The Northwest Territory included all of present-day Michigan, Ohio, Indiana, Illinois, Wisconsin, and a portion of northern Minnesota. Beyond it lay British Canada and *terra incognita*, referred to at the time as the Great American Desert.

The Northwest Ordinance empowered the federal government to admit new states to the union, rather than allowing the likes of Virginia and the Carolinas to extend their borders all the way to the Pacific Ocean. It also forbade the ownership of slaves north of the Ohio River, not out of any sense of humanity, but in order to keep northerners from obtaining their

The Northwest Territory of 1787, including the borders of what eventually became six U.S. states.

own slaves to compete with politically-powerful growers of the slave-owning South.

Written by Thomas Jefferson, Article III of the Northwest Ordinance made the following vow, which has the ring of a schoolboy, promising to be good:

"...The utmost good faith shall always be observed towards the Indians; their lands and property shall never be taken from them without their consent; and, in their property, rights, and liberty, they shall never be invaded or disturbed, unless in just and lawful wars authorized by Congress; but laws founded in justice and humanity, shall from time to time be made for preventing wrongs being done to them, and for preserving peace and friendship with them."

In virtually no time at all, the United States managed to find rationales for "just and lawful wars" against the Indians of the Northwest Territory.

Several coercive treaties and military raids by the Americans led to the creation of what historians have called the Northwestern Confederacy, an alliance of the Shawnee, Miami, Potawatomi, Wyandot, Delaware, Mingo, Odawa, Ojibwe, Kickapoo and other western tribes. It was as if the United States was twisting a tiger's tail to see if it would roar.

The intentions of the United State vis-a-vis the Indians were hammered home in Pennsylvania at the Treaty of Fort McIntosh in 1785. Signatories from the Odawa, Ojibwe, Wyandot and Delaware agreed to cede the area around the forts at Detroit and the Mackinac Straits in addition to returning captives. But the most stinging aspect of the treaty opened settlement to the lower two thirds of Ohio, granting Native peoples only the northwestern third of the state, pulling the homeland of the Shawnee and Miami out from under their feet and raising more hell along the frontier.

Just one year after the Treaty of Fort McIntosh came the 1786 Treaty of Fort Finney, signed at a rough blockhouse west of Cincinnati. The treaty was inked by a few moderate Shawnee chieftains who had no right to speak for the tribe as a whole. It called for establishing a new, much smaller reserve for the Shawnee and Miami peoples in northern Ohio. The treaty enraged those who hadn't signed, kicking up war parties that struck settlements ranging from Kentucky to the Mississippi.

In response, in 1786 a militia of eight hundred Kentuckians swarmed up the Mad River in Ohio, murdering Natives, taking captives and burning towns and crops. The victims included those who had signed peace treaties. An elderly chief named Moluntha, who flew the American flag outside his home and had signed the peace treaty at Fort Finney, was murdered by an unhinged militia major, who struck him on the head with an axe and took his scalp. This outrage only encouraged more warriors to join the growing alliance of tribes.

By the late 1780s there were eight American forts established along the Ohio River, three of which had been constructed on the north bank in Shawnee territory. There was also a smattering of outposts delving deep into Native territory and ten thousand settlers floating west down the river each month on a hodge-podge of boats and rafts.

Yet the Indians of the Northwestern Confederation would have nothing to do with the treaties signed at forts Stanwix, McIntosh and Finney. Armed by the British and gathering strength, the alliance would soon orchestrate the darkest hour in U.S. military history.

CHAPTER 22

THE BATTLE
OF 1,000 SLAIN

George Washington had a lot to think about in December, 1791. Elected as the first president of the United States only two years before in 1789, he faced several ongoing crises, not the least of which was paying down the nation's towering debt, incurred in the Revolution. America was stone broke with a storm of trouble on every horizon.

Overseas, the Barbary pirates were attacking American ships on the Mediterranean and enslaving their crews in North Africa, while French privateers were plundering hundreds of ships on the high seas and in the Caribbean. West of the Allegheny Mountains were the stirrings of the

Whiskey Rebellion, with farmers chaffing under the very first tax imposed by the nation's new Congress. Many farmers used their surplus wheat, rye, barley and corn to make whiskey, which was non-perishable and easily transported. As such, the new excise tax on the manufacture of whiskey was an outrage to veterans of the Revolution who had fought against the levying of taxes in general. Three years later, in 1794, five hundred armed men stormed the fortified home of an excise tax collector and Washington himself led a militia of 13,000 men to put down the rebellion.

Further afield, the British remained entrenched in six forts throughout territories that had been ceded to the United States in 1783, thumbing their noses at the infant nation and continuing to arm the Indians. These included forts at Mackinac Island, Detroit, Niagara and near present-day Toledo. It was no secret that the forts were arming and agitating the Indians against the Americans. Yet with an empty treasury and the dismissal of the Continental Army, it was impossible to evict the British.*

But the most alarming crisis facing Washington and the U.S. Congress was the slaughter of an army led by Gen. Arthur St. Clair on the Wabash River in the Ohio Territory.

Today, if asked, most Americans would likely cite Custer's Last Stand as the greatest battle ever waged by Native peoples. That was indeed a big fight. After tracking as many as ten thousand Sioux and their Cheyenne allies to their winter camp on the Little Bighorn River in Montana with the help of Crow scouts, Lt. General George Armstrong Custer of the 7th Cavalry split his command and got the bright idea to attack the camp's 2,500 warriors with a force of 210 men. Quicker than you can say Arrow Shirt, the 7th found themselves pinned down on a hill-top behind the bodies of their dead horses and surrounded on all sides. Over the course of twenty minutes the sky turned black as tens of thousands of iron-tipped arrows rained down on their position, not to mention thousands of rounds from Indian firearms, killing every defender.

Afterwards, while stripping the corpses of the defeated 7th Cavalry, the Sioux and Cheyenne warriors were astonished to find that many of the troopers had shot themselves in the head to avoid capture.

Again, the Last Stand was a big fight, but in terms of casualties, it paled against many battles fought by the tribes of the Midwest and Great Lakes, including Braddock's Defeat and Tecumseh's slaughter of five hundred Kentuckians outside Fort Meigs in Ohio in 1813. Almost unknown is the

* The forts were surrendered to the U.S. in the Jay Treaty of 1794, with some retaken in the War of 1812.

defeat of Lt. Gen. Arthur St. Clair, who suffered nearly five times as many casualties as Custer in the so-called Battle of 1,000 Slain.

Few, if any of the western tribes had knuckled down under the dictates of federal treaties, which aimed to push them further north and west. Under Shawnee chieftain Blue Jacket - Weyapiersenwah - and Miami leader Little Turtle - Meshekinnoqquah - they had instead assembled the second great alliance of tribes after Pontiac.

The Miami - Myaamia - are thought to be the descendants of the Mississippian Culture. They fled the Iroquois in the mid-1600s, settling in Wisconsin before returning to their homeland in northern Indiana, Ohio and southern Michigan around 1700. Like the Anishinaabek, they too called themselves "the people" - *Mihtohseeniaki*.

The ever-wandering Shawnee, whose name may mean the "southern people," are thought to have arisen from the Fort Ancient Culture of Ohio. The most powerful Native force after the Iroquois, they had no particular homeland, but ranged from West Virginia and Kentucky to Ohio and Indiana. One faction lived beyond the Mississippi River in Missouri, hoping to skirt problems with the white man.

By the mid-1700s many of the Shawnee began to coalesce in Ohio alongside the Miami. Both tribes lived in towns of up to one hundred bark lodges and were adept as farmers.

The Shawnee and Miami were the principal organizers of the alliance of tribes aiming to stop the nascent United States in its tracks, but their leaders reportedly loathed one-another. Blue Jacket was a dandy and a wheeler-dealer trader who wore a scarlet frock coat, huge dangling earrings and silver-spangled deerskin breeches. One of his wives was of French descent, he owned black slaves, and lived in a cabin of a sort owned by a well-off frontiersman, complete with European furniture. By contrast, Little Turtle was a hero of the Miami for his military exploits. He dressed simply, stood more than six feet tall, and was taciturn and cautious - a bit of a sphinx. His second wife was a captive American woman and he had also adopted William Wells - Eepiihkaanita - who had been captured at the age of thirteen from a prominent Kentucky family.* In a portrait, he appears draped in a simple blanket with a necklace of claws adorned by a medallion bearing King George's likeness. Yet both men swallowed their differences to serve as superb generals in marshaling their forces.

Strapped for cash, the U.S. Congress had entered into a real estate deal with the land speculators of the Ohio Company, which had built the town

---

*Wells married Little Turtle's daughter and fought with the Indians at St. Clair's Defeat, going on to serve in the U.S. military, carrying messages back and forth from Vincennes in Indiana to Native forces in northern Ohio.

of Marietta (named for Marie Antoinette) on the north bank of the Ohio. Under the deal, and against the rotten value of the nation's paper currency, the company acquired 1.5 million acres of Indian land for just nine cents per acre, with an option to purchase an additional 3.5 million acres. Other speculators were surveying their own plats all along the river in the land rush following the Revolution.

Historically, not all land grabs were driven by greed; some were rooted in the creation of religious sanctuaries, others in search of utopias.

The foremost example of this was the grant of all of eastern Pennsylvania and much of New Jersey to William Penn in 1682. Penn was a wealthy Quaker who forgave a hefty loan to King Charles II of England in exchange for land in the New World. His aim was a "holy experiment," creating a colony where religious and civic freedom would be guaranteed. Although the land was occupied by the Delaware (also known as the Leni Lenape), King Charles claimed ownership by dint having evicted the Dutch with a fleet of English warships in 1664.

A more dubious experiment was that of a group of French nobles who hoped to establish a refuge for beleaguered Queen Marie Antoinette at the height of the Reign of Terror. They established the community of Asylum on 1,600 acres in the wilds of northeastern Pennsylvania, which included the construction of a "chateau" for Antoinette (a two-story log structure). They planned to spirit the queen away to the American ship, *Sally*, at the port of Le Havre, where she would sail to freedom; but the plot was either bungled or too late. The richest woman in the world, Antoinette had her hands bound behind her back, her head shaved, and was led through Paris in an open cart to the cheers and bombardment of a jeering crowd, losing her head to the guillotine on October 16, 1793.

Within sight of Marietta was Fort Harmar, established to protect the flood of settlers. Built on land the Shawnee considered to be their own, the establishment of Marietta and Fort Harmar struck the Indians as bald evidence of American treachery.

Northwest Territory Governor St. Clair had busied himself pursuing the country's policy of purchasing Indian land and punishing those who didn't go along. In 1787, he had received a letter signed by the chiefs of many tribes requesting that the boundary line against settlement be returned to the Ohio River, as agreed upon by the British at Fort Stanwix in 1768. That idea was off the table; instead Congress ordered St. Clair to simply purchase the land.

In 1788, St. Clair invited the Iroquois and the western tribes to meet him at Fort Harmar to hash out boundary issues. Few attended.

Undismayed by the small gathering, St. Clair informed the attendees that the U.S. government regarded the tribes as sovereign nations empowered to sell their land, but the land must be sold to the government, pronto.

The deal was brokered by Mohawk war chief Joseph Brant, whose Iroquoian name was Thayendanegea. In 1775 Brant had been received at the court of King George III in London, who sought the aid of the Iroquois in putting down the American Revolution. In his spare time Brant enjoyed translating the Scriptures into Mohawk, an ironic pastime considering he'd been the terror of the frontier during the Revolution, "with all his howling desolating band" raiding New York and Pennsylvania. American General Benedict Arnold called Brant and his warriors "A *banditti* of robbers, murderers and traitors."

Brant hoped to reaffirm the Iroquois' pan-Indian "Longhouse" and their status as the elder brothers of the western tribes. But his attempt to create a new boundary that would satisfy both the western tribes and the Americans was flatly rejected by both parties. Discredited, he left the negotiations in a huff, advising the western tribes to boycott the meeting, who did just that. The tribes also blasted the Iroquois for continuing to claim that they owned the land on which the Shawnee, Miami and other tribes had lived for hundreds of years.

Nonetheless, St. Clair mustered a small turnout of two hundred friendly Seneca Iroquois chieftains and other compromised Native leaders, wrangling them into signing the Treaty of Fort Harmar, which simply reaffirmed prior treaties that aimed to push Native peoples off their lands.

Rather than re-establishing the Ohio River as the northern barrier to settlement as Shawnee and Miami leaders wished, the U.S. government continued to insist that they move north to an area that was less than half of their original homeland.

Smitten with his own pipe dream, St. Clair reported to Congress that he had purchased millions of acres of Shawnee and Miami land from the Iroquois for $23,000 and that all parties were satisfied with the deal.

The Harmar Treaty had the effect of rubbing more salt in the wound for outraged Shawnee and Miami militants, who redoubled their raids on settlers while strengthening their alliance.

Two years later in 1790, St. Clair authorized a "mopping up" operation to "chastise" Ohio's Indians, sending 1,500 troops under Josiah Harmar from Fort Washington at Cincinnati to strike Kekionga, the homeland of the Miami. Located at the confluence of the St. Joseph and St. Mary rivers at present-day Fort Wayne in Indiana, Kekionga was a major trading

Miami war chief Little Turtle rivaled Red Cloud and Sitting Bull in his exploits, defeating a French expedition in 1780; then the armies of Josiah Harmar and Arthur St. Clair in 1790-'91 with the aid of Shawnee war chief Blue Jacket. Thereafter he led the negotiations at Fort Greenville after the Battle of Fallen Timbers. He went on to conduct peace negotiations with presidents Washington, Adams and Jefferson.

center in a region of villages, cornfields, orchards and hunting preserves. It was far from the troubling reach of the white man and about as close to an earthly paradise that any Indian could ask for.

Blue Jacket had moved his Shawnee militants to Kekionga in 1786 after his villages on the Mad River had been destroyed by the Kentuckians. The combined Shawnee and Miami made a plum target and it was here that St. Clair planned to clean out the *banditti* as hostile Indians were called. This "flying strike" was meant to be akin to a *blitzkrieg*, destroying villages, crops, granaries and orchards while capturing women and children to be used as pawns in negotiations. It was the first military expedition authorized and funded by the new U.S. Congress and approved by President Washington.

In blunt terms, St. Clair talked tough, informing the Indians of their fate unless they surrendered:

"Your warriors will be slaughtered, your towns and villages ransacked and destroyed, your wives and children carried into captivity, and you may be assured that those who escape the fury of our mighty chiefs shall find no resting place on this side of the great lakes."

But the Miami and Shawnee played rope-a-dope with the invading force, evacuating their women, children and elders and burning their own towns. Harmar's troops managed to burn several villages, destroying corn crops and orchards, but they found only ashes at Kekionga and nowhere to bivouac. Returning south, Harmar's men got sloppy and overconfident just as the forces of Little Turtle and Blue Jacket came together in a vice, picking them off in a series of hit-and-runs. The Shawnee also surprised an elite militia of Kentucky cavalry, who were considered the pride of America's military, cutting down dozens and forcing them to flee for their lives. Their horses added to the Indians' own war effort.

Harmar was ambushed by Little Turtle's warriors on October 22, 1790. With most of his men fleeing without firing a shot, Harmar retreated back to Fort Washington claiming victory, but with 183 men dead or missing the expedition was clearly a defeat and a national disgrace.

Thereafter, St. Clair was ordered to "liberate" the Ohio country, this time leading the troops himself to teach the *banditti* a lesson. In response, the Shawnee and Miami retreated forty miles east to northwestern Ohio, quickly building new villages in a region called the Glaize, a bottomland of rich farmland that had once served as a wallow for buffalo.The Glaize was a natural fortress, surrounded by the formidable Black Swamp, which stretched for many miles in every direction.

Obese and stricken with an agonizing case of gout, St. Clair was carried in a hammock strung between two horses as he and his army of 1,700 regulars, militiamen and teamsters made their way north along the Wabash River. Many of the militia were naive farm boys or the dregs of society, recruited for two dollars a month from taverns, brothels, prisons and trading posts. They expected to elect their own officers and were inclined to walk away from a fight if they had a notion to get clear. Largely untrained, filthy, undisciplined, ill-equipped and hungry, the militias of early America were better known for drinking than fighting; certainly not "well regulated" as proscribed by the Second Amendment. Washington had cursed the militia as being the near wreck of his fight against the British in the Revolution, puncturing the myth of the sturdy "citizen soldier," rushing to mow down Redcoats with his fowling piece.*

St. Clair had also recruited the better part of the country's "regular" troops on short-term enlistments. The regulars were splendidly dressed in blue coats and white trousers, better trained than the militia, yet not quite the force he might have wished. There was no U.S. Army in 1791, owing

---

*Twenty-three years later in 1814, an army of mostly 10,000 militia would flee in terror of 4,000 British soldiers at the Battle of Bladensburg, north of Washington D.C., allowing the White House, U.S. Capitol, Naval Shipyard and all public buildings to be torched in the War of 1812. In the history of the U.S. military, only the "Bladensburg Races" of fleeing militia rivaled St. Clair's defeat for ignominy.

to the fact that the American revolutionaries feared that a standing army could be employed against the citizenry by some future tyrant. They had the example of British Redcoats, often drafted from the dregs of society or prisons and compelled to brutalize anyone, anywhere, at the bidding of their king.

Having frequently failed to pay their troops, state legislatures were also anxious to dissolve the Continental Army before its angry soldiers could stage an insurrection. The entire army of up to 48,000 men was disbanded on Nov. 2, 1783 following the American victory against the British, with only twenty-five privates retained to guard the storerooms at Fort Pitt and fifty-five soldiers for the same duty at West Point. Congress reluctantly created the one-year enlistments of "regulars" in reaction to Indian attacks on the frontier, but even these were drawn from the militias of four states and stood at just seven hundred men in 1791. Many of them were on the trail of doom with St. Clair.

Prior to his departure, St. Clair had met with Washington at the Presidents House in Philadelphia. Washington repeatedly warned him to beware of surprise attacks. For his part, Secretary of State Thomas Jefferson gushed like a frat house schoolboy over the impending victory, saying: "I hope we shall give the Indians a thorough drubbing this summer, and then change our tomahawk into a gold chain of friendship."

St. Clair slowly made his way seventy miles up the Wabash, hacking a road alongside the river to accommodate his lumbering oxcarts filled with supplies. Following along with the supply train were up to one hundred women and children, including laundresses, prostitutes, girlfriends and wives.

Hidden in the forest on either side of the column were Native warriors, picking off stragglers, hunters, deserters and anyone who wandered too far into the woods to relieve his bowels.

Setting out in the fall was a bad idea. Soaked to their bones from the chill rains of October, with their clothing and boots in tatters and supplies running low, the morale of St. Clair's army dissolved along with its discipline. This didn't escape the Indians, whose runners made daily reports to Blue Jacket, Little Turtle and Delaware war chief Buckonghahela, who had been gathering warriors for months. Nonetheless, St. Clair was flippant, telling his officers that, "The savages if violently attacked will always break and give way and when once broke, for the want of discipline, will never rally."

A greater fear for St. Clair was that the *banditti* of the Shawnee and Miami would slip away before they had been properly chastised.

What he didn't know was that on the evening of November 2, 1791 somewhere between 1,400 and 2,000 Native warriors painted black and red for war were having a huge war dance to the sound of thundering drums just over the horizon, preparing their weapons, finalizing strategy and receiving the blessings of shamans by the light of massive bonfires. The following afternoon in blistering cold weather, they advanced to the shelter of the trees two miles from St. Clair's camp on the Wabash River and spread out in a crescent formation. Heedless of Washington's warning to beware of surprises, St. Clair had taken no steps to fortify his camp, which was attacked the next morning amid the aching cold. St. Clair's troops were caught in a net with the Shawnee, Miami and Delaware forming the base of the crescent and the warriors of the Ojibwe, Odawa, Potawatomi, Kickapoo, Wyandot and other tribes making up the horns.

Unable to form a line and return fire, discipline collapsed in a thunderclap, with the militia troops flinging down their heavy muskets and running for their lives. Officers among the regulars who tried to rally them to the defense were shot down by the score from the cover of the trees.

Making a last stand, General Richard Butler of the regulars was shot through an arm and then toppled from his horse. Propped up against an oak tree with no chance of fleeing, he ordered his brothers, Captain Edward Butler and Colonel Thomas Butler to leave him. It was the only chance to save Thomas, who had suffered two broken legs. With men being killed, scalped and mutilated all around him, General Butler was left to his fate with two loaded pistols.

The army was cut to pieces on the battlefield, with the slaughter including almost every woman and child among the camp followers.* Fleeing soldiers raced back down their rough-hewn road, with many cut down by pursuing Indians for up to four miles to the south; some had been scalped, yet survived, with their heads and faces painted thick with blood. Over the long day and night ahead, the terrified survivors stumbled along their root-and-stump-littered trail to Fort Jefferson, a pathetic log structure that was only ten-by-ten feet square, meant to serve as a supply depot rather than a fortification. Exhausted but fearing for their lives, the men began an all-night retreat through the forest, heading for the safety of Fort Washington, eighty miles to the south. By morning they were strung out for five miles along the forest track, open to attack at any moment. Only the chance to plunder their belongings had saved them as their Indian pursuers turned back to get their share of tents, horses, weapons, clothing and other riches.

---

* Too weak to carry her baby onward, the sole surviving woman was so exhausted during the retreat that she abandoned the infant on the trail and pushed on alone.

As for General St. Clair, he escaped on an old plow horse, jouncing painfully down the path to ignominy, later claiming that he'd been overwhelmed by superior numbers and defeated by the cowardice of the men he'd failed to discipline.

By the end of the three-hour battle, the warriors of the Northwestern Confederacy had killed an estimated 870-900, including almost all of the camp followers, with more than three hundred suffering from ghastly wounds. Native casualties were less than one hundred.

Washington, famed for never blowing his cool, was livid when the news reached him at what was then the capital at Philadelphia. He raged that St. Clair had left him with "my last solemn warning thrown into his ears, *and yet!* To suffer that army to be cut to pieces, hacked, butchered, tomahawked — *by surprise!* The very thing I guarded him against!" St. Clair, he said, was "worse than a murderer! The blood of the slain is upon him! The curse of widows and orphans! *The curse of Heaven!*"

Washington demanded St. Clair's resignation in the spring of 1792, but he nonetheless carried on as governor of the Northwest Territory.

The battle resulted in the loss of one-third of the nation's armed forces and in percentage terms it was the greatest defeat ever suffered by the United States military. The only beneficial result of the disaster was a change of heart by the young Congress, which finally listened to Washington's plea to create a standing army. Thus came about the creation of the U.S. Army, known in its first iteration as the Legion of the United States, organized by a very tough customer in the form of General "Mad" Anthony Wayne.

Even then, fears of a standing army and navy persisted for decades, inflamed by the intense partisanship of Jefferson, Adams, Madison, Burr and Hamilton fighting over the direction of the nation. Republicans under Jefferson (no relation to today's GOP) favored militia forces of "citizen soldiers," while the Federalists led by Alexander Hamilton and Washington argued for a professional fighting force. By the War of 1812, the United States had a standing army of just seven thousand men and a navy with a core of only six frigates to protect a nation of 7.2 million, yet the military was all but strangled in its crib for lack of supplies, uniforms and munitions, along with virtually no training. By comparison this was at a time when Napoleon commanded 400,000 troops and Britain had a navy of more than 800 warships.

CHAPTER 23

THE BLACK SNAKE COMETH

In the wake of St. Clair's appalling defeat, President Washington and Congress finally got a clue that the western tribes weren't happy with the fraudulent sale of their land by the Iroquois.

Two peace envoys pretending to be traders were sent north under the naive notion that the Shawnee and Miami would be satisfied if it was simply made clear that the U.S. Government intended to pay up and make things right. Both emissaries were killed and scalped before they reached Keki-onga and the Glaize, however, and at any rate, the tribes weren't interested in selling off their homeland. Washington called the killings a "lamentable proof of Indian barbarity," vowing that if diplomacy failed there would be no alternative but "the sword."

By now the Glaize in northwestern Ohio and Kekionga in Indiana were brimming with a virtual United Nations of tribes drawn from the Shawnee, Miami, Odawa, Ojibwe, Delaware, Wyandot, Potawatomi, Sauk, Creek, Fox, Cherokee, Kaskaskia, Kickapoo, Conoy, Mahican, Nanticoke, Peoria, Mascouten and Piankashaw, along with representatives from the Iroquois of New York and Algonquians from Canada.

Working through British, Mahican and Iroquois intermediaries, the United States offered to abandon a number of military outposts north of the Ohio River, provide $50,000 in trade goods, pay an annuity of $10,000 per year, and recognize Indian sovereignty over the bulk of Ohio if the tribes would sell their lands around Cincinnati and the Scioto and Muskingum rivers. The Shawnee nixed the deal, suggesting that the U.S. use the funds to resettle squatters encroaching on their lands instead. A peace delegation of fifteen Native men and three women from several tribes also traveled to Philadelphia with a wampum peace belt, dining at the Presidents House and smoking calumets with Washington and Secretary of State Thomas Jefferson. Jean Baptiste DuCoigne, a *métis* chieftain of the Kaskaskia, presented Jefferson with some painted buffalo hides and laid out the Indians' appeal to maintain the Ohio River as the barrier to settlement.

"Father, your people of Kentucky are like mosquitoes, and try to destroy the red men, but I look to you as to a good being," DuCoigne said. "Order your people to be just. They are always trying to get our lands. They come on our lands, they hunt on them, kill our game and kill us. Keep them then on one side of the line and us on the other. Father, you are rich. You have all things at command, you want for nothing. You promised to wipe away our tears. I commend our women and children to your care."

But it was mum's the word from Washington, who professed to be uninterested in obtaining Indian land in Ohio and Indiana while planning to do just that. Nor was he necessarily a "good being" to the Indians; although he had met hundreds of Indians and entertained most of their leaders during his lifetime, he also prided calling himself Conotocarious, an Iroquois word meaning "Town Destroyer" or "Devourer of Villages," a moniker inherited from his grandfather.

Thus, at loggerheads, another military campaign was authorized by Congress as a "just and lawful war" to be conducted by the new Legion under Anthony Wayne.

A hero of the Revolution who'd been the toast of high society for his daring exploits, Wayne had endured a long slide into scandal and bankruptcy following his departure from the Continental Army in 1783. Georgia had awarded him a Tory's rice plantation in thanks for his service fighting the Creek Indians who sided with the British, but it needed years of clearing and ditching to become profitable and Wayne had gone far out on a limb purchasing slaves on unsecured credit from Dutch bankers who were too strapped for cash to lend him anything.

Deep in debt and fearing prison, Wayne managed to wriggle free of his obligations only to find himself charged with election fraud by the Second American Congress for stealing votes and other chicanery. The House voted unanimously to strip him of his seat as a congressman from Georgia. Shortly thereafter, to his great surprise he was called back into service by President Washington to head up the Legion. Considering that Wayne never cared for farming but had been entranced by warfare and tactics since his boyhood, this was a golden ticket. Having a reputation as a strict disciplinarian, it's likely that Washington chose Wayne as being just what the yahoos and layabouts of the new federal army needed to shape up. He spent the next three years doing just that.

He was labeled "Mad" Anthony Wayne by a n'er-do-well private who'd been jailed during the Revolution. When Wayne declined to help set him free and promised to have him flogged if he acted up again, his sometime acquaintance spouted "Anthony is *mad!*" The nickname stuck and gained traction with his troops, appalled by Wayne's mad devotion to endless drilling and discipline.

Handsome and something of a ladies man, Wayne was thin-skinned and even whiny when he felt slighted. He had also been impetuous to the point of being reckless during the Revolution, noted for charging in when oth-

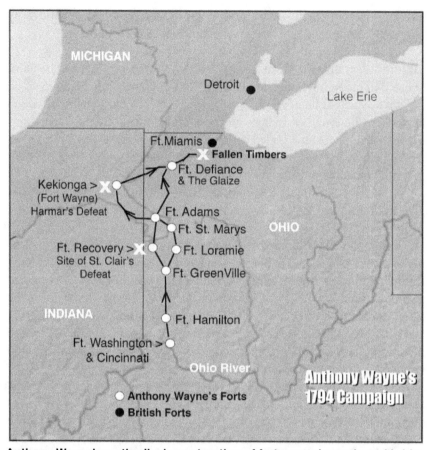

Anthony Wayne's methodical construction of forts, supply roads and bridges allowed him to creep into the territory of the Northwestern Confederacy of tribes over the course of two years, burning their villages and seizing their crops along the way. Native forces met their doom at the Battle of Fallen Timbers, betrayed by their British allies at nearby Fort Miamis.

ers were in retreat. His most notable exploit was a midnight commando raid on Stony Point, a British outpost occupying a heavily fortified 150-foot bluff over the Hudson River. Wayne ordered his men to empty their muskets prior to the attack so as not to lose the element of surprise due to a misfire. Their bayonet attack took out the sentries at the base of the cliff, allowing his 1,500 hand-picked troops to scale the heights and fall upon the sleeping British. Wayne was grazed in the head by a musket ball, but kept on fighting and by the battle's end, his troops had captured 472 Redcoats.

Two years earlier, more than two hundred of Wayne's own troops had been massacred in a nighttime bayonet attack at Paoli's Tavern outside

Philadelphia. A British bayonet was seventeen inches of razor-sharp steel, and most of Wayne's men had been killed while they lay sleeping; thus his victory at Stony Point was sweet revenge.

But, nine years after the war's end, Wayne took a far more deliberate tack in his campaign against the Indians. He'd been seriously wounded during the war, and now in his late thirties, was suffering from gout and malaria. Arriving in Pittsburgh in 1792, he found its poorly-sited fort impossible to defend. Add to this, Pittsburgh was a "Gomorrah" of vice, taverns and brothels that played hell on army discipline. As a remedy, Wayne established Legionville at a distance from town and began recruiting troops, who soon found themselves in the grip of iron discipline and constant drilling in a virtual prison. Disobedience resulted in flogging, or in the case of two soldiers who fell asleep on guard duty, execution by firing squad.

Thereafter, Wayne moved his troops to Fort Washington near Cincinnati and began constructing a series of forts up the Wabash River, with headquarters at the dreary outpost of GreeneVille deep in Indian country. Moving forward, each camp was surrounded by a chest-high breastwork for defense, guarded by round-the-clock sentries. Watching from afar over the course of two years, the Indians began calling Wayne "Black Snake" - Sukachgook - for his restless vigilance.

Arriving at the site of St. Clair's defeat, Wayne's troops found hundreds of skeletons, skulls and broken military hardware scattered across the battlefield. Included were the remains of General Butler, whose skeleton was identified by an old broken leg wound. A mass grave was dug within the walls of a new fort called Recovery. Thereafter, the fort was attacked several times by up to 1,200 warriors under Little Turtle without success, disheartening the Miami leader and convincing him that the cause was lost.

One hundred and fifty miles to the north, the British had constructed Fort Miamis on the Maumee River near present-day Toledo. Fort Miamis barred the way to Detroit, which lay another seventy miles on, serving as a supply depot for the distribution of weapons, ammunition and provisions to the Indians. The British had been waging a proxy war with the United States in the wake of the Revolution by way of their Indian allies, egging them on and supplying them with weapons.

But inexorably, Wayne drew closer, establishing Fort Defiance at the confluence of the Maumee and Auglaize rivers within the Indians' stronghold of the Glaize itself after constructing bridges and roads across the formidable Black Swamp.* His troops swarmed through Native villages,

---

* One soldier complained that the mosquitoes in the Black Swamp were "very troublesome, and larger than (I) ever saw." Forging through the mud of the swamp required building bridges up to 225 feet long.

seizing their crops and burning what they could not consume. One town alone was surrounded by one thousand acres of cornfields - food that Native peoples needed to survive the winter.

Even so, as Wayne's 3,300 troops drew closer, many Native warriors were confident that the British would aid them in a crushing blow, similar to the fate of St. Clair.

Little Turtle was not as sanguine. His adopted white son-in-law, William Wells, had traveled to Fort Washington to seek the freedom of some Miami captives, including his wife and child. Wells reported home that the whites had gathered an overwhelming force. Thus, at a council of chieftains at the Glaize in August, 1794, Little Turtle recommended suing for peace.

"The Americans are now led by a chief who never sleeps: the night and day are alike to him," Little Turtle said. "And during all the time that he has been marching upon our villages, notwithstanding the watchfulness of our young men, we have never been able to surprise him. Think well of it. There is something whispers to me that it would be prudent to listen to his offers of peace."

Scorned as a coward, Little Turtle gave up his dual leadership, while promising to fight in the coming battle.

Going into the fight, Blue Jacket had 1,100 warriors including those of the Shawnee, Miami, Delaware, Kickapoo, Odawa, Ojibwe, Potawatomi, Mingo and Wyandot, along with two companies of Canadian volunteers and a few Brits disguised as Indians. Yet outnumbered three-to-one, his warriors had the added disadvantage of hunger. As was a common practice, they began fasting well before the battle in order to have their bowels empty in case they were gut-shot. But the battle was two days in arriving, by which time the famished warriors were weak from hunger. Many had peeled off to eat a breakfast when Wayne's troops arrived.

Blue Jacket had arranged his warriors in the same crescent formation that had been so successful against St. Clair, but this proved futile in the disarray of his warriors, along with the impediment of marshy terrain washed over by a downpour. Flustered, the warriors fell back to a tangle of trees that had been uprooted in a tornado, but even this shelter proved worthless as Wayne ordered a bayonet charge. With a heavy line of blue-coated soldiers bristling with steel approaching them en masse the Indians broke and ran for the safety of Fort Miamis downstream.

Here the British showed their treachery, meeting their anguished allies with fixed bayonets and muskets at the gate and refusing to let them shelter in the fort. Recognizing that engaging Wayne's army would mean certain defeat and the risk of sparking a new war with America, British promises to their Indian allies evaporated as soon as they saw the warriors on the run. As Blue Jacket said bitterly thereafter, "It was then that we saw the British dealt treacherously with us."

Some of Wayne's troops went berserk. "The American army have left evident marks of their boasted humanity behind them," said British agent Alexander McKee. "Besides scalping and mutilating the Indians who were killed in action, they have opened the peaceful graves in different parts of the country, exposed the bones of the consumed and consuming bodies, and horrid to relate, they have with unparalleled barbarity driven stakes through them..."

The Battle of Fallen Timbers broke the spirit of the Northwestern Confederation and had devastating consequences thereafter as Wayne's "big knives" conducted a scorched-earth campaign, burning many square miles of cornfields and scores of Native towns, chopping down orchards and killing livestock. Wayne burned the revived Miami capital of Kekionga to the ground and established Fort Wayne on the site. Refugees in their own land, Native peoples starved through the winter with little in the way of shelter, surviving on what they could glean from their devastated fields or from British handouts.

The total wreck of Native fortunes came on August 3, 1795 when ninety-nine chiefs signed the Treaty of Greenville, with the U.S. represented by Wayne, future president Henry Harrison, and future explorers Lewis and Clark, among others. For starters, the treaty required the return of white captives, with ten chiefs to be held as hostages until all were returned.

Surprisingly, the would-be peacemaker Little Turtle was the sole chief objecting to the cession of Native territory, only to be told by Wayne that the Miami didn't actually own their land: the British had ceded it to the U.S. when they lost the Revolution. In Wayne's telling, the United States were being the good guys by offering to pay for Indian land, rather than simply seizing it.

Thus, Little Turtle reluctantly went along and the chieftains surrendered two-thirds of Ohio, as had been demanded at the treaties signed at forts Stanwix, McIntosh, Finney and Harmar. The new Greenville Treaty Line boxed the Shawnee and Miami into a small territory in northwestern Ohio. In return the chiefs divided around $20,000 in goods and cattle, with promises to award them $500-$2,000 annually to support their individual bands.

Soon enough, even the Indians' new territory would be gobbled up by more treaties to come.

The Treaty of Greenville and all that followed turned Native peoples into wards of the state, making them dependent on government handouts, which, as noted earlier, often included goods of poor quality, useless trash items and spoiled food, if the annuities arrived at all. The constriction of their hunting grounds also had the effect of undermining the self-esteem of Native men, who recoiled at the government's aim of turning them into Christian farmers. A man who could no longer return to his wife and family with venison and tales of the hunt felt diminished, emasculated, and bereft of the camaraderie of fellow hunters. Initially, Native peoples also found themselves in thrall to their own chieftains who facilitated government handouts and could play favorites with who got what.

More than that, the treaty was a prelude to shuttling the Shawnee and Miami west beyond the Mississippi to "Indian Country" in Kansas and Oklahoma on prairie land that was of little use to the whites.

Today, the Fallen Timbers battlefield is a state park honoring the last stand of the Northwestern Confederacy. Elsewhere, generals Wayne and St. Clair are honored as the namesakes of various cities, universities and counties throughout what was once Indian land. These include Wayne County, Wayne State University, the city of St. Clair Shores and Lake St. Clair in southeastern Michigan. Hamtramck, an enclave of Detroit, was named after one of Wayne's generals. Kekionga, the beloved home of the Miami, is now the city of Fort Wayne, with the remnants of many Native villages and cornfields buried beneath it suburbs. This, and "Mad" Anthony was considered such a folk hero for more than a century after his exploits that actor Marion Robert Morrison changed his name to John Wayne to come across as more of a tough guy.

Yet, other than the eponymous city of Pontiac in Michigan, nowhere will you find Blue Jacket and Little Turtle honored in the same spirit. At a time when Confederate statues have been torn down throughout the South, along with universities, military installations and highways stripped of the names of high-ranking Rebels, the persecutors of America's Indians remained unscathed in their memorials.

General Wayne had scant time to enjoy the celebrations in his name. While traveling home to Pennsylvania two years after the Battle of Fallen Timbers he fell ill and died at the age of fifty-one.

As for Little Turtle, he traded his tomahawk for a peace pipe and became a diplomat on behalf of the Miami, visiting Washington, D.C. several times to speak with presidents Washington, John Adams and Thomas Jefferson. He died of natural causes at the age of sixty on July 14, 1812, with the baton of mighty Indian alliances passed to another heroic leader, Tecumseh.

CHAPTER 24

1807 & 1812

Indian land had been under the carving knife of European explorers and colonists since they first set foot in North America, but it was nearly three hundred years after the 1513 discovery of Florida by Ponce de Leon before that blade reached the Michigan Territory.

A strip of land ranging along the Detroit River from Lake Erie to the northern end of Lake St. Clair was ceded by the Indians to the United States as an area of strategic importance in the 1795 Treaty of Greenville. Other cessions included land at the Sault and around forts at present-day Chicago, Fort Wayne and Toledo.

But the carving of the Michigan Territory began in earnest with the Treaty of Detroit, signed in November, 1807. Revolutionary War hero, General William Hull, signed the treaty with thirty chieftains of the Odawa, Ojibwe, Potawatomi and Wyandot, ceding a pie-slice of southeastern Michigan extending from present-day Toledo north to the state's "Thumb" and then skirting west to what is now the city of Jackson. (See map on p. 204)

For this massive purchase of eight million acres, the U.S. Government paid just .0012 dollars per acres - a little over one-tenth of a cent - possibly the equivalent of about two-and-a-half cents per acre today.

Hull was the governor of the new Michigan Territory as well as its superintendent of Indian Affairs. Written out in elegant script on two pages of parchment and approved by President Thomas Jefferson, the 1807 Treaty of Detroit guaranteed the Indians small parcels of land to live on within the ceded territory and also provided them with "ten thousand dollars, in money, goods, implements of husbandry, or domestic animals..." The funds were to be paid in installments and split four ways, with the Odawa and Ojibwe each receiving $3,333.33, the Potawatomi granted $2,400 and the Wyandot $1,666.66. An additional $2,400 would be divided between the tribes annually, "forever."

The tribes were promised the services of two blacksmiths for a ten-year period. They were also guaranteed hunting and fishing rights on the ceded land, "as long as they remain the property of the United States."

The treaty became a template for many treaties to come throughout the Midwest, promising acreage to individuals and families, services such as blacksmiths and farm instructors, installment payments in coins (referred to as specie), and inviolable hunting and fishing rights. It also became a template for broken promises.

One might wonder why Native peoples opted to cede their ancestral lands when the threat of removal was still more of a rumor than a reality. Simple economics forced the issue in 1807. Egged on by traders, the Indians had scoured southeastern Michigan clean of fur-bearing animals and there was nothing left to trade for muskets, kettles, blankets, tools and other necessities except for their land. Then too, they had little understanding as to how many white settlers were waiting in the wings, or what ceding their land would actually mean. To some it may have seemed as nonsensical as the idea of ceding the sun or the wind; what could it hurt? In time, Native emissaries would travel to New York, Philadelphia and Washington to learn to their dismay that the whites were as numerous as the leaves of the forest, but the ramifications of this onslaught may not have been anticipated by the Indians in 1807.

Some of the Native signatories sided with the British soon thereafter as part of Tecumseh's alliance in the War of 1812, while others stayed neutral, taking a wait and see approach as to which side would come out on top, the Brits or the Yanks.

Sealing the deal in 1807 was one of the high points of Hull's career. He had arrived in Detroit only two years earlier just after the whole town burned down as the result of sparks flying out of a baker's pipe and igniting a pile of hay. Together with newly-arrived judge Augustus Elias Brevoort Woodward, the two master-minded the rebuilding of Detroit, with Woodward designing the streets arranged like spokes from the waterfront. From this pinnacle of achievement Hull's career and reputation plummeted to the bottom five years later when he was duped into surrendering Detroit to a lesser force of the British and their Indian allies during the War of 1812.

The war had a number of causes. For years the British Navy had been kidnapping sailors off American merchant ships on the slimmest of pretenses, and then even from a U.S. warship, impressing them into lives of virtual slavery aboard their own ships. American trade with Europe was also suppressed amid the Napoleonic Wars, causing economic turmoil at home. Add to this, the Brits were rabble-rousing the Indians, who raided American settlements from the safety of British Canada. The administration of James Madison declared war after Britain refused to end its practice of plundering American ships. Unfortunately, news that Britain intended to end the impressment of American sailors arrived weeks after the war got underway.

The capture of Detroit was preceded by the bloodless surrender of Mackinac Island on July 17, 1812.

In mid-July, fort commander Lieutenant Porter Hanks noticed that the normally-friendly Odawa had developed a certain "coolness." A friendly Odawa also told him that large numbers of Indians from many tribes were gathering at the British fort on St. Joseph Island lying thirty miles to the north. Hanks dispatched Michael Dousman, the captain of the local militia company, as a "confidential person" to find out what was going on.

Dousman had paddled his canoe about twelve miles across the gray-green waters of Lake Huron when he spotted an armada of seventy war canoes flying pennants of eagle feathers and streamers of cloth and willow fronds, filled with six hundred warriors painted for war. Accompanying them were fifty British soldiers aboard the schooner *Caledonia* and ten *bateaux* bearing 150 Canadian militiamen. Taken captive, he was pumped for information by British Captain Charles Roberts, whose force landed on the north end of the island at 3 a.m.

Wishing to avoid bloodshed, Captain Roberts sent Dousman to warn the residents of the town below the fort to take shelter, making him promise not to spill the beans to the American troops. Roused at 6 a.m. by Dousman knocking on their doors, the townspeople fled to a stout distillery for safety. Their flight was reported to Lt. Hanks by the post's surgeon, who lived in town. Hanks mustered his troops and prepared to make a stand.

Meanwhile Captain Roberts and his force made their way along a rough track across the island to the heights above the fort, setting up a 6-pounder cannon, which was capable of firing an iron ball about the size of a softball. Easily maneuvered and capable of knocking down walls, firing shrapnel or canisters full of slugs like a giant shotgun, or skipping a ball across a field of troops, the 6-pounder was the artillery of choice in battles ranging from the Revolution to the Civil War. Even so, its 870-lb. barrel and carriage of several hundred pounds hauled without the aid of horses or oxen made for a tough slog up the rough trail to the heights above the fort.

Down below, Lt. Hanks and his sixty-one men had seven cannon, but all of them were trained on the harbor, and in any event, their cannon could not fire uphill even if they'd been wheeled around. Nor was withstanding a siege possible, since the fort's only well was located outside its walls. Later that day, three townspeople arrived and talked Hanks into surrendering - an easy decision, considering the odds. He and his men didn't even know that war had been declared. As was a common practice at the time, Hanks and his men were set free by Captain Roberts after swearing a gentleman's agreement that they would not take up arms against the British.

Weeks later in August, British Major General Isaac Brock laid siege to Detroit with a force of 1,300 soldiers, 600 warriors, and two gunships, bombarding the town from across the river in Canada. For his part, American General Hull had 2,500-3,000 troops and militia and 700 civilians sequestered behind Detroit's palisaded walls. Alas, their supply lines were cut off and they were far from any hope of rescue.

Hull had accepted the order to secure Detroit with great reluctance, and then only because no other general was available. His orders included attacking the British Fort Malden at Amherstburg across the river in Canada. The American strategy called for conquering Canada in order to end Indian attacks on U.S. soil from their sanctuary beyond the border.

But Hull was the wrong man for the job. Nearly sixty, he had suffered a stroke and was debilitated by additional health problems and personal tragedies. With supplies from Ohio cut off by Tecumseh's warriors and British troops, Hull began to crack, speaking in a trembling voice and dribbling tobacco juice down his beard and clothes. Worse, four hundred hand-picked men, the cream of his troops, had gone off to try re-opening the supply lines to Ohio and had elected not to return to Detroit's defense.

Psychological warfare played a major role in the siege of Detroit. General Brock had arranged for a British courier to be captured along with a bogus document, which claimed that five thousand Indians were preparing to attack the fort. Learning that the fort at Mackinac Island had been taken, Hull said its defeat "opened the Northern hive of Indians, and they were swarming down in every direction." In a panic over the Indians and his blocked supply lines, he abruptly canceled the attack on Fort Malden, outraging his officers and crushing troop morale. "He is a coward and will not risque his person," said one of his soldiers.

Huddled behind the log palisade of Detroit, Hull and his men watched as long lines of Tecumseh's warriors paraded past the fort, uttering hideous war cries and gesturing with their weapons before sneaking around unseen behind a low bank of earth to repeat the charade. One can imagine the warriors had a good laugh back in their camp as the subterfuge went on.

Prior experience with Indian warfare had shown that native warriors might be content to simply plunder their foes and knock them about a bit if they surrendered, but a bloodbath was almost certain if they took losses in battle. Native war chiefs were far less cavalier about the loss of a single man compared to commanders in the Napoleonic and American Civil wars, who sent tens of thousands to their deaths in mass attacks and then slept well at night. The loss of a single warrior was devastating to his family and his band, for who then would care for his wife and children? A war chief was judged by how many men he brought home safely, perhaps even more than the victories he scored.

Revenge was also deeply ingrained in a warrior's psyche, requiring lethal payback for any casualties incurred. This trait played out in the surrender of Fort Dearborn at present-day Chicago.*

Prior to the siege of Detroit, Hull had ordered the evacuation of Fort Dearborn against the wishes of its officers and citizens, who were up against a force of five hundred Potawatomi.

Angered by the death of some of their warriors during a fifteen-minute battle, the Potawatomi attacked their unarmed captives on the march out of the fort, killing twenty-six soldiers, twelve militiamen, two women and two children. The killings were partly in revenge over the burning of their home, Prophetstown, following the Battle of Tippecanoe in Indiana ten months earlier. More on this later.

Of course, the slaughter of innocent non-combatants was hardly confined to that of Native warriors. Across the ocean amid the war with Napoleon, hundreds, if not thousands of unarmed Spanish citizens who refused to surrender to the British were killed by Lord Wellington's troops at the towns of Badajoz and San Sebastian in an orgy of mass rape, murder and arson that went on for days even while the war in America was being waged. An appalled British officer wrote that, "Men, women and children were shot in the streets for no other apparent reason than pastime; every species of outrage was publicly committed in the houses, churches and streets, and in a manner so brutal that a faithful recital would be too indecent and too shocking to humanity."

Surrendering to the Indians in the hope of being spared was a reasonable option, and Hull would have learned that not a soul was harmed by the warriors at Fort Mackinac. Gen. Brock played on well-known fears of a massacre, advising Hull that he had little control over his Indian allies, whose blood was up. "It is far from my inclination to join in a war of extermination," he wrote to Hull, "but you must be aware, that the numerous body of Indians who have attached themselves to my troops, will be beyond control the moment the contest commences."

"*My God!* What shall I do with these women and children!" Hull exclaimed on receiving Brock's message. Horrified at the thought of a bloodbath, he was bamboozled into surrendering Detroit on August 16, 1812 without firing a shot or even consulting his officers. Outnumbered two-to-one, Brock had nonetheless crossed the river with 330 British regulars, 400 militia and 600 Indians. His force captured 2,500 American troops, thirty-three cannon and the *Adams* brig of war, including the entire Michi-

---

* Chicago derives its name from the Algonquian word, shikaakwa, meaning "onion," owing to the many wild onions and leeks that grew in the area.

gan Territory. An admiring Tecumseh exclaimed, "Now *this* is a man!" But a man for only for a short time; Brock was killed in battle at Niagara two months later.

Hull later claimed that Detroit had been running low on ammunition and cannon balls, but Brock's troops were astonished to find more than five thousand pounds of powder and huge quantities of shot at the fort. Hull was court martialed in 1814, convicted of cowardice and dereliction of duty, and sentenced to die by firing squad. He dodged those bullets, however, after President James Madison pardoned him in lieu of his age and service in the American Revolution.

One of the ironies of the fall of Detroit was that three days later, Hull's nephew, Captain Isaac Hull, would capture the British warship, *Guerriere* while commanding the *U.S.S. Constitution*, sending shock waves through the British Empire. Isaac Hull was hailed as a national hero, while his uncle's reputation went "hull down."

CHAPTER 25

THE SKY PANTHER, TECUMSEH

From the moment of his birth, the Shawnee diplomat and war chief Tecumseh was destined for great things. Born into the Panther clan of the Shawnee in 1768 under a shooting star, Tecumseh was the fourth son of the war chief, Puckeshinwau, who had died in Cornstalk's battle at Point Pleasant on the Ohio River.

Prior to his birth, Tecumseh's family had lived among the Creek tribe of central Alabama. They moved six hundred miles north to the Ohio River Valley in 1759 at a time when the far-flung Shawnee were unifying as a people. With his legendary father killed when he was six years old, Tecumseh grew up with big moccasins to fill, and when he was only fifteen he participated in the first of many attacks on the flatboats of settlers heading down the Ohio River. On that occasion he spoke out against the roasting of the sole white survivor, tongue-lashing the warriors as the victim screamed in pain and shaming them into promising they would never burn another prisoner. As a young man, he once shot a prisoner in the head to spare him the anguish of a fiery death at the hands of a startled war party that wouldn't listen to his reasoning. The sparing of prisoners from torture became a lifelong trait, earning him the admiration of even his white enemies.

As a teen, he also had several white friends: Benjamin Kelly, Philemon Waters and Stephen Ruddell, who had all been captured by the Shawnee and adopted into the tribe. In fact, it was fifteen-year-old Ruddell who lured the flatboat to shore in Tecumseh's first battle. Ruddell claimed that, "when prisoners fell into his (Tecumseh's) hands, he always treated them with... much humanity. No burning, no torturing. He never tolerated the practice of killing women and children."

Tecumseh also distinguished himself as a hunter. Like other Shawnee boys, he was taught to use a bow and arrow from an early age and was expected to provide for his own food as a rite of passage. At the age of sixteen he killed sixteen buffalo with only a bow in one of the last hunts of the declining herds in Kentucky.

Another quirk was an alleged bout of celibacy as a young man. The Shawnee culture encouraged men to delay sexual liaisons until well into their twenties, at which time their mothers initiated them into the mysteries of mounting and pleasing a wife (!). Tall and handsome, Tecumseh is said to have disdained relations with many more-than-willing women for a considerable dry spell before doing a turnaround as a sexual libertine, acquiring one girlfriend after another before dumping them on the slightest pretense.

In the only known sketch of him we see that Tecumseh wore his hair loose to his shoulders and had a long, narrow face with a patrician's nose. Like other Shawnee, he wore a head scarf wrapped like a turban, a linen shirt and a silver nose ring. Shawnee men were also fond of huge silver earrings dangling from their split earlobes along with silver-spangled breeches and jackets.

Perhaps he would have blossomed into a daring but obscure war chief were it not for the influence of his younger brother, Lalaawethika, later known as the Prophet Tenskwatawa - He Who Opens the Door.

Blind in his right eye, thin and debilitated by drink, young Lalaawethika was held to be a braggart and drunken fuck-up who lived on hand-outs and was smitten by his own importance, despite all evidence to the contrary. During the course of an epidemic, however, Lalaawethika was overwhelmed by a vision in a "Road to Damascus"-style revelation that swept him into sobriety and a makeover as a seer who inspired thousands.

As the Prophet, Tenskwatawa taught that the hated Americans were nothing more than white scum that had floated west from across the ocean, coalescing as a grasping crab on the land of the red men. As with Neolin, he proscribed rejecting the white mans' trade goods and vices in order to return to the old ways of purity, living on wild game and dressing in animal hides. Men must reject alcohol, kill their hunting dogs, and give up prostituting their wives and daughters.

The Prophet's teachings resonated with thousands, catapulting his brother Tecumseh into a leadership position. In 1807 they established Prophetstown near the juncture of the Tippecanoe and Wabash rivers in northern Indiana. Located in a pancake-flat area of rich farmland, Prophetstown quickly swelled to more than a thousand ecstatic residents.

Over the next few years Tecumseh traveled thousands of miles ranging from Canada to Alabama, from Pennsylvania to west of the Mississippi and elsewhere, seeking to rouse a coalition of tribes in a holy war.

Speaking to a crowd of thousands of Choctaw, Chickasaw and Creeks in Alabama, he had this to say: "Where are the Narragansett, the Mahican, the Pokanoket, and many other once powerful tribes of our people? They

Sketched on the sly by a French trader, this is the only known rendition of Tecumseh, the Shawnee diplomat and war chief. He's depicted wearing a silver peace medal of the sort passed out by both the British and Americans in negotiations. Shawnee men often wore turbans and huge silver bangles, including the kind of ear spacers worn by modern hipsters.

have vanished before the avarice and oppression of the white man, as snow before a summer sun. Shall we, without a struggle, give up our homes, our country bequeathed to us by the Great Spirit, the graves of our dead and everything that is dear and sacred to us? I know you will cry with me, *Never! Never!*"

"The words fell in avalanches from his lips," said a white observer. "His eyes burned with supernatural luster, and his old frame trembled with emotion. His voice resounded over the multitude - now sinking in low and musical whispers, now rising to the highest keys, hurling out his words like a succession of thunderbolts."

Some listened, but many older and more cautious chiefs among the bands of the Seneca, Creek, Shawnee and other tribes said, no thanks. Thus, as with Pontiac, Blue Jacket and Little Turtle before him, Tecumseh assembled a patchwork of warriors from the militant factions of various tribes that were of two minds in taking on the white man.

The tipping point for Tecumseh was the 1810 Treaty of Fort Wayne in which a handful of chieftains among the Delaware, Miami and Potawatomi sold three million acres of land in Indiana and Illinois for pennies per acre. For the first time the Indians were horrified to learn that land ownership among the whites meant its exclusive possession, barring all others from its use.

Tecumseh raged at Indiana Territorial Governor William Henry Harrison that no chieftain had the authority to speak for others or to sell any land whatsoever, land being a commons that belonged to all. He and his followers threatened to kill the chieftains who had signed the treaty. In response, Harrison ridiculed the idea that the commons were off limits to settlement.

Yet, alarmed by the growing influence of Tecumseh and the Prophet, Harrison decided to strike while the charismatic leader was hundreds of miles to the south. In the spring of 1811 he gathered a force of one thousand regulars and militia and marched from Vincennes, Indiana, building a new fort that October at Terre Haute. Negotiations with Tenskwatawa went nowhere, and on November 6, Harrison advanced his troops only two miles from Prophetstown to intimidate the Indians.

That's when Tenskwatawa made a fatal mistake. Having no sense of strategy or experience in combat, on November 7 he launched a predawn attack on Harrison's camp with six hundred disorganized and poorly-led warriors. Spotted by a sentry, the Battle of Tippecanoe was over within two hours, with about sixty deaths on both sides.

The Indians actually suffered fewer casualties, but running low on ammunition, were forced to retreat. At Prophetstown the warriors raged at Tenskwatawa, whose war magic had failed to protect them for the white mans' bullets, as promised. Tenskwatawa blamed the failure on his wife, claiming that she had corrupted his war medicine.* Standing on a boulder, he ordered a second attack, but his men refused. Thereafter, Harrison burned Prophetstown along with five thousand bushels of corn, beans and other crops. Its residents fled to the four winds.

The Prophet's medicine was broken in the wake of the battle, but not so that of Tecumseh, who rallied one thousand warriors from many tribes during the War of 1812.

An initial success was the aforementioned fall of Detroit and a victory in the first Battle of Frenchtown on the Raisin River thirty-five miles to the south. But the latter battle was marred by a massacre. A faction of warriors among the Creeks known as the Red Sticks had traveled north to fight with Tecumseh. But after the battle in early January, 1813, they fell on thirty wounded American soldiers left behind in a makeshift hospital, killing them against Tecumseh's orders. Another fifty wounded were taken to Indian villages as captives.

His greatest victory occurred on May 5, 1813 when he ambushed a brigade of eight hundred Kentuckians who were marching to the relief of Fort Meigs on the Maumee River east of Toledo. Impregnable, the fort had been constructed by Harrison, who was now a general in command of the

---

*Tenskwatawa also later blamed a party of Ho-Chunk Sioux for launching the attack against his wishes.

frontier troops. Tecumseh and his warriors fell on the arriving Kentuck-ians, killing five hundred and capturing 150. Only 150 survived to gain the shelter of the fort.

Once again, Tecumseh showed his character when British Major General Henry Procter and his cowed troops turned a blind eye to the massacre of prisoners huddled across the river in Fort Miamis. Angered at having missed the battle, a villainous chieftain of the Ojibwe began tomahawking and scalping the unarmed Kentuckians. A bloodbath ensued with a band of Potawatomi joining in and a British soldier was shot trying to intervene.

Sixteen-year-old captive Thomas Christian recalled the scene as the prisoners were attacked with "unearthly yells, killing and scalping as fast as their own crowded ranks would admit, while we, like terror-stricken sheep hemmed in by dogs, or a parcel of hogs in a butcher's pen, were piled one upon another in one corner. Those at the bottom were being smothered, while those upon the top were being drenched with blood and brains. Suddenly as a lightning flash, the yelling ceased, the uplifted war clubs descended harmlessly by the side of the now shamed warriors, and above the groans of the dying, and the prayers of the living is heard the brave Tecumseh putting a stop to the massacre, shaming his warriors for behaving like squaws."

Enraged, Tecumseh had knocked down several attackers, lambasting Col. Procter as being a coward who wore "petticoats" for not stepping in. "Never did Tecumseh shine more truly than on this occasion," said an admiring Redcoat.

Soon, however, the British were on the run back to Canada. After losing the second battle of Frenchtown they abandoned Detroit in September, 1813 and fled across the Detroit River to Fort Malden, starving, demoralized, outnumbered and short on supplies.

Tecumseh and his alliance met their end soon after at the Battle of the Thames River in southeastern Ontario on October 5, 1813 when three thousand American troops and militia under the command of Harrison attacked eight hundred British regulars and five hundred Indians under General Procter. Shot down, Tecumseh would have heard the war cry, *"Remember the Raisin!"* ringing in his ears as the Americans swept through the British line like a rock through a wet paper bag. General Procter had hoped to drive the Americans into a swamp where Tecumseh's warriors were waiting, but the soggy gunpowder of his cannon failed to fire and his men broke and ran. Tecumseh's warriors fought on valiantly, but when their leader fell the heart went out of them and they too fled.

Tecumseh's body was desecrated by the victors, who took bits of his clothing along with pieces of his flesh and skin. "I helped skin him," claimed one veteran many years later, "and brot Two pieces of his yellow hide home with me to my Mother & Sweet Harts."

As for Harrison, he was declared a national hero, winning the presidency in 1840 with the slogan, "Tippecanoe and Tyler Too." Caught in an icy rainstorm without a coat, he contracted a cold and died of pneumonia only thirty-two days after being sworn into office.

Today, there are many statues and memorials to Tecumseh throughout Canada and the United States, including at army and navy posts. Warships have been named after him, as have many towns, townships, school districts and counties. During the Civil War, a Union ironclad ship named the *Tecumseh* was sunk by a mine in the attack on Mobile Bay. A sculpture of "The Dying Tecumseh" adorned the U.S. Capitol before being transferred to the Smithsonian. His battlegrounds at Tippecanoe, Fort Meigs and the River Raisin are all historic parks worth visiting and he is on the Greatest Canadian list with his likeness depicted on a two dollar Canadian coin.

Ironically, he was also the namesake of Union General William Tecumseh Sherman, who led the scorched-earth March to the Sea in Georgia during the Civil War.

"War is cruelty," Sherman once said. "There is no use trying to reform it. The crueler it is, the sooner it will be over." In command of U.S. troops in the West after the Civil War, he advocated "the utter annihilation" of the Sioux... "even to the extermination of their men, women and children... during an assault the soldiers can not pause to distinguish between male and female or even discriminate as to age."

Inevitably, the Americans didn't exactly win the War of 1812; instead they convinced the British that fighting on was expensive and pointless, especially since the Redcoats were battling Napoleon in Europe for the fate of Britain itself. The British lost eight hundred merchant ships to American privateers during the war (privateers were government-sanctioned pirates), driving up insurance rates for shipping and hammering the British economy. And, as in the American Revolution, hundreds, if not thousands, of British sailors and soldiers had deserted in order to start new lives in the United States. The British found that trying to conquer America was a game of whack-a-mole; whenever a city or territory was captured, U.S. power simply shifted elsewhere and then back again.

Having sided with the British during the war, the Indians north of the Ohio River once again found themselves the underdogs of the Northwest Territory. Prior to the war, President Thomas Jefferson had mused that the

Most of the Shawnee declined to fight in the War of 1812 on the advice of Black Hoof - Catahecassa - a major chieftain of the Ohio members of the tribe and a rival to Tecumseh.

Although he fought in a number of battles up to and including the Northwest Indian War, after the Indians' defeat at the Battle of Fallen Timbers Catahecassa came to believe that blending in with the white culture and adopting their ways was the only way to avoid his people's destruction. He resisted removal of the Shawnee to the end of his life, but after his death in 1831, the tribe was forcibly removed to Indian Country in Kansas.

Indians might be better off if they were removed to west of the Mississippi, making way for settlers and allowing them to learn the white man's ways of farming at their own pace. His successor, James Madison, reluctantly agreed, noting, however, that the Indians were unwilling to "transition from the hunter, or even the herdsman state, to the agriculture," and would likely never be civilized.

With the pacification of the Indians and the end of the war in 1815, settlers began surging into the Northwest Territory in search of cheap land. By now the population of the United States had swollen to 7.5 million, while the Native population to the west had diminished as the result of warfare, disease and famines created by the destruction of their crops.

The Midwest was carved up with a host of treaties large and small. The Treaty of Greenville had granted northwestern Ohio to the Indians, yet the Treaty of Fort Meigs signed by seven tribes on Sept. 29, 1817, ceded an additional 4.6 million acres, making the surrender of the state complete except for a small patch occupied by a band of Shawnee and Seneca.

At the Oct. 2, 1818 Treaty of St. Mary's, the Miami and eight other tribes ceded all of central Indiana. Within a few years they would lose everything.

A Shawnee leader named Catahecassa spoke of the Indians' despair:

"We know wherever we may go, your people will follow... and we will be forced to remove again and again and finally arrive at the sea or the other side of the Great Island (at) the Pacific Ocean and then they would be compelled to jump off and perish. There would no more be any room for the poor Indian."

Book Five
The Devil's Bargain

CHAPTER 26

THE TREATY OF SAGINAW

As the nineteenth century dawned, the Michigan Territory was considered a wilderness roiling with mosquitoes, wolves, swampy terrain and bad soil.

As such, Michigan was low on the wish-list of destinations. Wolves were apparently a nuisance everywhere according to a young newspaper scribe, Darius Cook, who spent six months living as a hunter among the Indians of Allegan County and could hardly sleep for the racket at night. "Their howls and growls were terrific," he wrote. "They would often have a fight among themselves, and their clear voices would ring for miles around. When their eyes were turned towards us they would glisten by the light of the fires, and occasionally we would shoot as near as possible between them. The noise of a rifle would still them but for a moment when a louder and more terrific howling would be set up."

The bad-mouthing of the Michigan Territory by the nation's press continued into the 1820s. Surrounded by swamps, the area around Detroit gave rise to mosquito-borne malaria, one of several diseases that killed hundreds of British soldiers in late 1814. An outbreak of typhoid fever struck newly-constructed Fort Saginaw in 1823, prompting its abandonment. Spread by contamination of food or water by human feces, typhoid resulted in a high fever, headaches, abdominal pain and vomiting which could last for weeks of months, possibly including one's death.

A popular rhyme of the day warned newcomers to stay clear:

Don't go to Michigan, that land of ills;
The word means ague, fever, and chills."

Soldiers stationed in Michigan declared it was no holiday: "I have no hesitation to say that it would be to the advantage of Government to re-move every inhabitant of the Territory, pay for the improvements, and reduce them to ashes, leaving nothing but the Garrison posts," groused British General Duncan MacArthur during his station at Detroit in 1814. "From my observation, the Territory appears to be not worth defending, and merely a den for Indians and traitors."

Michigan also received a bad report from U.S. Surveyor General Edward Tiffin, whose men took a look-see around the territory in 1816, trying to determine if it was a suitable location to be shared-out by veterans of the War of 1812 as a reward for their service. Mired in a swampy area around present-day Jackson County, the surveyors reported back that Michigan was a morass of poor soil, swamps and lakes, not worth the trouble and expense of surveying. Tiffin reported back to President James Madison that only one acre out of one hundred could be farmed, and possibly not even a single acre out of one thousand.

But Michigan also had its boosters, notably the *Detroit Gazette*. Pub-lished in both French and English with subscriptions at $4 per year, this plucky broadsheet had a thirteen-year run from 1817-1830 and did much to gin up "Michigan Fever," attracting hordes of new settlers. The *Gazette* offered a surprising array of world news cribbed from newspapers on the East Coast. An issue published August 1, 1817, for instance, discusses the crime rate in Scotland, the troubles with the Spanish in Pensacola, Florida, troop actions in Portugal, the situation in Guyana, and what Lloyd's of London was doing to insure Dutch ships, among dozens of global events. Included was the following squib: "Three or four persons, convicted of kidnapping slaves, have lately been exemplarily punished in the state of Delaware. They were put in the pillory, whipped, cropped, and branded."

The front page of the *Gazette* was given over to real estate offerings, the availability of dry goods, and businesses for sale - items that would lan-guish on the back pages of any newspaper today. Land for sale at favorable rates and the paper's happy talk about Michigan was reprinted by other newspapers around the country, issuing a clarion call to settlers seeking to get their share.

The bounty of Michigan was a nut to be cracked. In 1816, construction began on a road from Detroit along an Indian trail to the small village of

The Division of Michigan

- 1795 - Treaty of Greenville
- 1807 - Treaty of Detroit
* 1817 - Treaty of Fort Meigs
- 1819 - Treaty of Saginaw
- 1820 - Treaty of Sault Ste. Marie
- 1821 - Treaty of Chicago
- 1828 - Treaty of Carey Mission
- 1833 - Treaty of Chicago
- 1836 - Treaty of Washington
- 1842 - Treaty of La Pointe

Pontiac, twenty miles to the north. A century later this became Woodward Avenue, one of the busiest highways in the Midwest. Then in 1818 the *Walk-in-the-Water* became the first steamship to reach Detroit from Buffalo, New York. Construction had also begun on the Erie Canal across New York State; with its opening in 1825 the canal and fleets of waiting steamships would release a flood of trade and settlement.

All of which had numerous settlers, traders and lumbermen eyeing the rich farm country and timber opportunities of the Saginaw River Valley lying seventy miles north of Detroit. The valley was home to some of the best white pine on earth, a highly sought-after wood for its beauty and workability. The only impediment was the settlement of Ojibwe living there, and by 1818, the whites began lobbying Washington for their removal.

Barring the way in the Saginaw River Valley were the Mississauga Ojibwe, who had established villages at the future sites of Saginaw, Flint, Frankenmuth, Pinconning, Bay City and other towns throughout the region. The Mississauga had migrated from Ontario and were distinct from their northern cousins at Sault Ste. Marie, who the French called Salteurs.

One problem with buying the Ojibwe's land, however, was that the U.S. government had failed to uphold the promises made in the Treaty of 1807. Given the expenses of the War of 1812, scant attention had been given to paying annuities and providing goods to the Ojibwe, Odawa, Potawatomi and Wyandot signatories. The promise to pay annuities "forever" hadn't lasted even ten years.

This of course made for a touchy situation, handed off to Territorial Governor, General Lewis Cass, a veteran of the War of 1812 who was the *ex officio* commissioner of Indian affairs in Michigan. In a letter to Secretary of War John C. Calhoun on September 11, 1819, Cass said he would pay the Indians what was owed to them out of his own pocket:

"I shall leave here on Monday next to meet the Indians at Saginaw, and endeavor... to procure a cession of that valuable territory. It would be hopeless to expect a favorable result to the proposed treaty, unless the annuities previously due are discharged. Under those circumstances I have felt myself embarrassed and no course has been left me but to procure the amount of the Chippewa annuity upon my private responsibility."

Cass arranged for banks in Detroit to advance him $10,000. He then employed French-Canadian trader Louis Campau to build a council house at the junction of the Shiawassee and Tittabawassee rivers. This wigwam, as it was called, was merely a roof of leafy branches lashed to some adjoining trees with the sides left open to accommodate Indian observers. A rough plank table and some hacked-together benches ran down the center for the negotiators. Word was sent out to the region's Indians to gather at the full moon in September. They did not know why they were being summoned.

Having settled in the Saginaw River Valley in the early 1700s, the Mississauga Ojibwe had lived undisturbed for more than a century prior to the arrival of General Cass. Their closest contact with the whites had been Campau, who established a trading post in 1815 on a bayou outside the present-day city of Saginaw. Twenty-seven-year-old Campau spoke an Ojibwe dialect, having been brought up with the tribe "from the time I was seven years old."

Cass was busy as a bee negotiating land-grab treaties with the Indians, and Saginaw would be his biggest score, cajoling, wheedling and tempting until the Indians gave in. He arrived on September 10, 1819 along with two ships filled with liquor, presents and a company of one hundred soldiers to protect the negotiators. There to meet him over the next two weeks of talks were 1,500-4,000 Ojibwe, Odawa, Potawatomi and Wyandot.

Called to the ramshackle wigwam, the leaders of bands throughout the region were apprised of what Cass had in mind.

"The first council was to let them know that he was sent by the great father to make a treaty with them, that he wanted to buy their lands, stating the points, and for them to go back and smoke and think about it," Campau recalled. Cass also asked the Indians to consider vacating their lands entirely for a move west beyond the Mississippi.

The Ojibwe were blindsided, thinking they'd been called to a peace council to wrap up the hostilities of the War of 1812. Astounded and dismayed, they hadn't anticipated an offer to buy their lands.

Ogemagigido, a twenty-one-year-old orator noted for his business acumen gave the Ojibwe's response:

"You do not know our wishes. Our people wonder what has brought you so far from your homes. Your young men have invited us to come and light the council fire. We are here to smoke the pipe of peace, but not to sell our lands. Our American father wants them. Our English father treats us better; he has never asked for them. Your people trespass upon our hunting grounds. You flock to our shores. Our waters grow warm; our land melts like a cake of ice; our possessions grow smaller and smaller; the warm wave of the white man rolls in upon us and melts us away. Our women reproach us. Our children want homes: shall we sell from under them the spot where they spread their blankets? We have not called you here. We smoke with you the pipe of peace."

Cass arrogantly responded that the American's had "whipped" the British and their Indian allies during the war and so their land was forfeit. But, being reasonable, the U.S. intended to purchase the Ojibwe's land, rather than simply kicking them out, and would provide reserves where they could learn the white man's ways of farming if they didn't wish to move west.

Native leaders talked among themselves for three or four days before meeting with Cass again. "After he had got the will of the principal chiefs there was much trouble to get the consent of all," Campau said. "At the second council there was great difficulty, hard words: they threatened

General Cass among the rest."

But with a company of soldiers camping on the treaty grounds and standing sentry at the talks, the Ojibwe got the hint as to what refusal would mean: removal one way or another.

Among the signatories was Neome, a principal chief of the Ojibwe and the leader of a band whose village, Mus-ca-da-wain, stood at the site of present-day Flint. Neome lobbied hard for reserves to be set aside for his four children in addition to the reserves set aside for various bands. His two girls were presented to Cass at the council table wearing calico skirts, pantalets and moccasins of smoked leather, with Neome imploring again and again on their behalf over the course of ten days: "Deny me not; grant my request that a reserve be made for my children."

"Neome was a short, thick man, a little stooped at the time of the treaty; he must have been forty-five or fifty-five years old," Campau recalled. "Neome was very ignorant, but he was very good, honest and kind."

Ignorant or not, the chief was cagey enough to provide for his children, who may have actually been those of his friend, a trader named Jacob Smith who had an Ojibwe wife in the area and a white wife in Detroit.

Neome's thirteen-year-old grandson Nau-gun-nee was on hand at the negotiations, standing by his side in the presence of Cass. More than forty years later he expressed the anxiety that Native peoples felt at the treaty signing.

"I stood so near Neome because I had by past experience learned that the white man generally takes away what he bought of the Indians, and I was anxious to see what this would lead to in this treaty," Nau-gun-nee said. "And I thought it might be possible if this land were sold to the white man that he would take away the country, or that the Indians would be driven away from the country. I did not know how the white man sold ground or land, and I had a curiosity to see. I also stood by him for I was afraid..."

Nau-gun-nee said that the Indian leaders were steadily worn down by the negotiations, and given no options:

"The treaty took a long time because the Indians were unwilling to cede their lands. I do not know how many times the Indians met with General Cass in the wigwam, (the) white man always persevering to accomplish his object. There were more than ten meetings; they were summoned by General Cass to talk about the surrender of their land the first time; then the second time for the same purpose, and the third and fourth, and the fifth and sixth, and so, ten times or more - all being for the same object."

Inevitably, the Treaty of Saginaw was signed on September 24, 1819 by 114 Indian leaders, touching a quill alongside a cross on the treaty paper with each name filled in by a secretary.

Sloppy transcription of the chiefs' names hampered the treaty's historical record. William Webber, who served as a counsel at an 1860 trial to clarify some property issues, recalled that the treaty secretaries "do not appear to have taken much pains to make the spelling of the Indian names correspond with the sound."

In exchange for six million acres in a triangular slash through the heart of Lower Michigan the signers received $3,000 cash (one-twentieth of a cent per acre) along with the promise of $1,000 annually and "whatever additional sum the Government of the United States might think they ought to receive, in such manner as would be most useful to them." They would also receive the services of a blacksmith along with tools and instruction in farming.

More than 100,000 acres were set aside as reserves for the Indians, but with no guarantee of residing thereon forever. Their residence was all contingent on the whim of the U.S. president. The reserves ranged from 640 acres to 40,000 acres, with 3,840 acres reserved for individuals and their *métis* relatives, while sixteen parcels were meant to be shared by various bands. Trader Smith, who had the ear of Neome and the Indians and had advised them against signing, was basically bribed for his support with the allotment of eleven reserves of 640 acres each.

"After the treaty was read and approved by the Indians and signed by them, which was as soon as read, General Cass ordered the money to be brought to the table; it was all in half dollars...," Campau testified at the 1860 trial.

There on the council table lay $3,000 in coins, ready to be distributed to the chiefs with hundreds of eyes looking on from the open walls of the wigwam. Campau laid claim to $1,500 of it for the repayment of debts owed him by the Indians, planning to grab his cash and skedaddle. But Smith and two other traders protested that the Indians should have it all, planning to sell them their own goods as soon as the cash was doled out. Looking on, the Indians heartily agreed. This led to cursing, shoving and fists flying as Campau leapt up from his seat and struck Smith two terrific blows to his face.

Webber said the matter was settled after the fight was broken up, with Campau receiving $1,046.50, "for many small items which seem to have been presented to the Indians - spades, shovels, scythes, rings, calico, tobacco, canoes, mats, cotton cloth and one gun..."

Feeling that Cass had betrayed him, Campau had the last laugh, albeit a bitter one. He opened ten barrels of whiskey for an anything-goes bacchanalia; this was on top of five barrels of spirits that had already been passed out by Cass to celebrate the signing.

Downing rot-gut whiskey by the dipper-full, hundreds of Indians were soon roaring drunk, weaving in the lanes and threatening violence if they didn't get more. When darkness fell, the night erupted in yells and drunken laughter as the party roared on.

At ten o'clock, Cass stepped out of his quarters in his bed clothes and ordered Campau to cut off the booze. This was denied by the petulant trader, who said in so many words, "you asked for it." Thoroughly alarmed, Cass ordered his troops to guard the storehouse and the remaining liquor. Yet soon the storehouse was under siege by newly-arrived Indians demanding whiskey. In the ensuing scuffle one of the seekers suffered a bayonet wound to his leg.

"Louis! Louis! Stop the liquor!" Cass cried. "We shall all be murdered! *Stop the liquor!*"

"General, you commenced it; you let Smith plunder me and rob me," Campau shot back before giving in, allowing the party to break up.

Later, he reflected on getting even. "I lost my money; I lost my fight; I lost my liquor; but I got good satisfaction."

Known to the Indians as "The Fox" for his wily ways, Campau is credited with the founding of Grand Rapids in 1827, establishing a post on the west side of the Grand River supplied with $5,000 in trade goods. Campau purchased seventy-two acres in what is now the heart of downtown for $90. He had this laconic comment on the dispossession of Native peoples in Michigan:

"A few white men came and there was a little trouble. A few more white men arrived and there was more trouble. Then a lot came and the Indians became bad. Finally the Indians were relieved of their possessions."

As for Cass, he and his team left before daylight the next morning, with the soldiers departing by ten o'clock. Cass had secured six million acres of some of the best farmland and white pine in Michigan for a fraction of a penny per acre. At the time, Michigan Territory land was selling at a minimum of two dollars per acre: a bonanza for the government land office in Detroit.

The following year, Cass negotiated with the Ojibwe on the south bank of the St. Marys River to build an American fort at Sault Ste. Marie. Here, Cass showed that he was no pushover. Arriving at the Ojibwe settlement at Boweting with Indian agent Henry Schoolcraft, he and his party of sixty-five received an unfriendly reception from the hundreds of Ojibwe living there, including the head chief who wore a British officer's frock coat. The chief spat out his contempt for the Americans and kicked aside the gifts that Cass had brought. Cass loathed the British and their influence over Native peoples, who still received trade goods and gifts from them. When a British flag was raised soon after his rebuff by the chief, Cass marched into the village in a huff with only his interpreter by his side and ripped it down, telling the chief that foreign flags could not be flown on U.S. soil. Cass had thirty-three soldiers with him, but they were no match for the hostile Ojibwe whose heavy investment in symbolism made such an act tantamount to fighting words. Fortunately, Schoolcraft's Ojibwe mother-in-law, Waubojeeg, reminded the Ojibwe that they'd surely be executed if they killed the governor. A council was held and the Ojibwe agreed to abide by the Treaty of Greenville for the establishment of Fort Brady. It had taken twenty-five years for the Ojibwe to buckle under.

Cass also obtained the St. Martin Islands east of St. Ignace in Lake Huron, which were noted for their rich plaster deposits. His next target was the plum Treaty of Chicago in 1821. Meeting with three thousand Potawatomi, Odawa and Ojibwe, Cass roped in nearly five million acres of southwestern Michigan in exchange for $10,000 in trade goods, $6,500 in coins and a twenty-year payout of $150,000.

Beyond his roles as a military man, governor and Indian agent, Cass was an ethnologist who made a close study of the Indians, hoping that the data he found would help to "civilize" a people he believed were driven "by impulse more than from reason." In his view, it was the age-old habits and temperament of the Indians that made them resistant to adopting the white man's religion and way of life. To this end he believed in direct observation of Native camps, villages and hunting grounds in the hope that ethnological findings in league with government action would move the Indians forward. "No rational estimate can be formed of the character of any people without viewing them at home, in their own country, engaged in their ordinary duties and occupations," he wrote. "This is particularly the case with the Indians."

Cass conducted nineteen negotiations with Native peoples during the course of his career and was so successful that Andrew Jackson appointed him Secretary of War in 1831 to implement the policy of moving the Indians west of the Mississippi. He was largely responsible for escalating Black Hawk's War in 1831-'32. Under his direction, one thousand followers of the Sauk chief Black Hawk had agreed to move west across the Mississippi where they soon ran into trouble with the hostile Ho-Chunk Sioux. Attempting to move back to the safety of Illinois, where they hoped to establish new villages and plant crops, the Sauk and their relatives among the Fox Indians were attacked by a jittery militia. When they fought back, Cass sent seven thousand troops to "chastise these Indians and ensure peace of the frontier," kicking off their extermination.

Most of what was left of the Fox and Sauk were wiped out at the Battle of

Bad Axe, Wisconsin on August 1-2, 1832. Close to five hundred starving Fox and Sauk were attacked by U.S. troops, militia, and their Menominee allies while attempting to flee back across the Mississippi River to safety. The resulting massacre and drownings killed 260, with many of those who made it across the river hunted down and killed by the Ho-Chunk Sioux.

Black Hawk's War added impetus to President Andrew Jackson's Indian Removal Order of 1830, amping up the call to remove all of the country's Indians to territory west of the Mississippi. Recognizing the effectiveness of Indian fighters mounted on horses, the war also resulted in the creation of the U.S. Cavalry.

Meanwhile, few, if any, of the Ojibwe who signed the Treaty of Saginaw were happy with the outcome and Cass predicted that, in time, they would move west despite their mistrust of U.S. intentions and fear of the hostile tribes beyond the Mississippi.

"When they are surrounded by our settlements and brought into contact with our people, they will be more disposed to migrate," he wrote. With the tools of farming, religion and Indian schools the United States would achieve "conquest by assimilation."

The Ojibwe who signed the treaty at Saginaw would have only seventeen years to enjoy their reserves before the federal government came knocking at their doors with an offer to buy them out once again in the Treaty of 1836. This, too, was a project orchestrated in part by Cass in cahoots with Indian agent Henry Schoolcraft.

CHAPTER 27

A DEMON IN THE MIDST

Demon rum earns its reputation for good reason. Whiskey, brandy and rum were the bane of Native peoples everywhere, mirroring America's crack cocaine and opioid epidemics. Emaciated, impoverished beggars, dressed in rags and ravaged by alcohol were a common sight at frontier forts and towns, heaped with scorn by contemptuous white settlers. Men, women, and even children drank heavily, with no concept of limitation at a time when many whites were hard drinkers themselves. By one estimate, the average American drank the equivalent of seven shots of rum or whiskey each day, and even toddlers might be put to bed with a taste of booze to help them sleep.

Many traders imported hundreds of gallons of liquor to lubricate the fur trade, sitting their customers down for a complimentary drink before talking terms. This had the effect of getting Native hunters and trappers drunk and then swindling them without mercy. Sometimes an inebriated Native trapper would trade all of the furs he had collected during months of working in blizzards, intense cold and deep snow for a gallon or two of spirits, returning home deathly sick with a blinding headache and nothing to show for the support of his suffering family.

Yet even the whiskey they sold was a cheat. Just as heroin dealers tend to cut their product with baking soda or powdered milk, so too did the whiskey dealers adulterate what they sold to the Indians. "Indian whiskey" or "whoop up juice" could include tobacco, red pepper, molasses, red ink and even soap added to rot-gut alcohol. A recipe in the 1840s called for mixing two gallons of poor-quality whiskey (purchased at $1.75 per barrel) with thirty gallons of water. Cayenne pepper and tobacco was then added to give the booze its punch, with barrels sold to the Indians for sixteen dollars.

Traders who had scruples against selling alcohol found themselves in a bind, with Indians trappers taking their business to those who did. John Jacob Astor, head of the American Fur Company, is said to have opposed providing alcohol to his Native customers, believing it made them less effective as trappers; yet felt he had no choice if he wished to compete with other traders. His company imported 5,000-8,000 gallons of liquor each year to their post on Mackinac Island for trade with the Indians.* Across the border in Canada, the British kept pace with similar quantities.

Indian Agent Henry Schoolcraft repeatedly blasted the American Fur Company for its trade in alcohol and in particular, its agent, Robert Stuart, who he claimed was "eloquent in defense of temperance," while pouring liquor down the throats of trappers. In his memoir Schoolcraft claimed that the depletion of animal food sources and the resulting starvation and squalor among the Indians was a direct result of alcohol being a primary trade item. Even so, Schoolcraft also used whiskey in his negotiations, supplying it as a reward across the Upper Peninsula to those who followed his dictates.

Whiskey traders typically sold liquor to Native middlemen and women in quantities of one hundred gallons. The middlemen sold it in villages where traders were too fearful of violent drunks to sell it themselves.

Working west of the Mississippi, trader W.C. Gladstone offered an insight into how alcohol was used to cheat the Indians:

*Astor would also pack along 1,500 gallons of whiskey on an 1832 expedition to establish a trading post on the Upper Missouri.

"Every Indian was given a dram of fire water by way of a starter. Speech making followed, washed down by another dram, then another drink, until every man jack of them had absorbed five drams and was ripe for business. The week's trade left us with 600 horses and our warehouses very nearly filled."

Native peoples quickly found their way of life destroyed from the inside out through the insidious effects of alcohol, which many seemed unwilling or unable to resist.

"Indian villages sank into squalor," wrote historian Peter Cozzens in *Tecumseh and the Prophet*. "Scarcely a day went by without a drunken murder or a maiming. Brother attacked brother. Inebriated Indians slaughtered their own livestock and horses in drunken fits. Neglected children fell victim to dysentery and died. Women, and sometimes children, imbibed as heavily as men. Elders lamented the loss of their young but often succumbed to drink themselves."

In Indiana, Moravian missionaries were appalled at how quickly the first go-round with alcohol plummeted their flock of fifteen Delawares into madness. "They screamed all night in the woods and acted like madmen. No one who has not seen an Indian drunk can possibly have any conception of it. It is as if they had all been changed into evil spirits... This drinking never passes without the shedding of blood."

Charles Cleland, a chronicler of the Anishinaabek, wrote that what the Indians called "the milk of the English" was considered to have magical powers of careening disassociation that touched the spirit world, becoming an essential trade item. When beaver and other fur-bearing animals became all but extinct by the 1820s, the Anishinaabek began hunting deer for their pelts, often in exchange for brandy, rum and whiskey. With the depletion of the whitetails came starvation.

Liquor was also used to grease the wheels of trade negotiations. Although the use of alcohol was officially frowned upon, prior to negotiations for the Saginaw River Valley, Lewis Cass had requested twenty barrels of whiskey, or 662 gallons, from the storekeeper of the Detroit Military District. He was given thirty-nine gallons of brandy, forty-one gallons of heavy spirits, ninety-one gallons of wine, ten gallons of whiskey and six gallons of gin. A chieftain named Kishkauko, who adamantly opposed ceding any land was kept drunk for ten days throughout the negotiations until the treaty was signed.

Cass condemned the whiskey trade among the Indians, yet had no qualms about using liquor to achieve his own ends. He used whiskey as a reward for Indians willing to sign the Treaty of Chicago in 1821, whetting their whistles with a taste and then delivering only when they placed an "X" on the treaty paper. An 1828 article in *The American Quarterly Review* claimed that nearly fourteen barrels of whiskey had been issued to the Potawatomi as part of the treaty negotiations. Cass had requested far more whiskey for the negotiations - an astonishing 932 gallons.

At his negotiations for Native land at Fond du Lac in the western Upper Peninsula in 1826, Cass made the Indians do a "begging dance" before he'd give them a taste, promising more after the treaty was signed. Commissioner of Indian Affairs Thomas McKenney, who was on the scene said the Indians agreed to everything Cass asked for "thinking of nothing but the arrival of the hour when the promised drink of whiskey is to be given, as the close of all." Many of the Indians begged for more of the white man's "milk" in speeches leading up to the signing.

By the 1820s, those seeking a license to trade in the Michigan Territory were issued the following instructions:

• They could only trade in the area where they were licensed.
• They must treat the Indians fairly and in a friendly manner.
• They were forbidden to attend Indian councils or send them any message accompanied by wampum.
• They were forbidden to bring any liquor into Indian territory or to give, sell or dispose of any liquors to the Indians. Any trader who violated it might have his goods seized by the Indians for their own use, and a trader was required to tell the Indians that they had such privilege.

Of course this boilerplate was roundly ignored, as evidenced by traders who sat in on every negotiation, hankering for their share of annuity cash and selling whiskey to anyone they could coax into drinking.

Fortunately, drinking alcohol was a situational and episodic thing for most Indians, confined to yearly contacts with traders. An Indian trapper had no access to alcohol when he was scouring the forests for furs, and those who were bamboozled once by traders offering alcohol weren't necessarily inclined to be tricked a second time. In some cases, the awarding of treaty funds or payment for furs went straight to a wife or mother, who doled out enough cash for a husband to enjoy a drunken revel without losing the whole wad.

As for scouring the land for hides or pelts leading to starvation in return for alcohol, this would have likely happened even without that incentive, given the insatiable appetite of the fur trade.

German travel writer Johann Georg Kohl, who lived among the Ojibwe to the west of Lake Superior in the early 1850s, noted that some starving Natives went "*windigo*" at the last brink of desperation, meaning cannibals in the mode of the hulking monsters of the Cree people, which only grew hungrier after devouring human flesh. Yet, as Ojibwe historian Basil Johnston has written, it was the capitalistic system that was the true *windigo*, devouring every resource with a hunger that could never be sated, always grasping for more. This was certainly true of the fur trade and the role it played in starving Native peoples and stripping them of dignity.

Opposing the whiskey epidemic was a temperance movement launched by the Indians themselves. Many Native prophets and prophetesses including Wangomend, Coocoochee, Beata, Neolin and Tenskwatawa, among others, railed against the poison of alcohol, as did numerous chieftains, missionaries, and the headmen of powerful families. These voices were listened to, often with a religious fervor that likely saved thousands from destitution and physical ruin. Then too, many Indians were simply not interested in alcohol or were wary of the bad effects they saw in others. "While much has been made of the impact of the trade in liquor among Native Americans, there is little evidence of sustained alcohol abuse among the Anishinaabe Odawa for most of the early history of North America," wrote Michael McDonnell in his history of the tribe, *Masters of Empire*. "It is likely that colonial Americans drank far more per capita than Native Americans."

CHAPTER 28

THE ROOTS OF REMOVAL

President Andrew Jackson was quite full of himself at his December 6, 1830 annual message to Congress in which he boasted of America's final solution for ridding its twenty-four states of the Indians.

Earlier that year, Congress had passed the Indian Removal Act, which Jackson had signed on May 28, fulfilling a campaign promise to remove the country's Indians to west of the Mississippi.

Now, exultant, he crowed that removal efforts were underway, adding that the Indians - who had lived on the continent for twenty thousand years or more - should be grateful for being deprived of their land and livelihoods:

"The consequences of a speedy removal will be important to the United States, to individual States, and to the Indians themselves," he said. "It puts an end to all possible danger of collision between the authorities of the General and State Governments on account of the Indians. It will place a dense and civilized population in large tracts of country now occupied by a few savage hunters... It will separate the Indians from immediate contact with settlements of whites; free them from the power of the States; enable them to pursue happiness in their own way and under their own rude institutions; will retard the progress of decay, which is lessening their numbers, and perhaps cause them gradually, under the protection of the Government and through the influence of good counsels, to cast off their savage habits and become an interesting, civilized, and Christian community..."

For Jackson, the Indians were "savages" holding up progress:

"What good man would prefer a country covered with forests and ranged by a few thousand savages to our extensive Republic, studded with cities, towns, and prosperous farms embellished with all the improvements which art can devise or industry execute, occupied by more than 12,000,000 happy people, and filled with all the blessings of liberty, civilization and religion?"

The government, he said, would evict the Indians by a "milder process" than in the past:

"The tribes which occupied the countries now constituting the Eastern States were annihilated or have melted away to make room for the whites. The waves of population and civilization are rolling to the westward, and we now propose to acquire the countries occupied by the red men of the South and West by a fair exchange, and, at the expense of the United States, to send them to land where their existence may be prolonged and perhaps made perpetual."

He added that the removal of the Indians was little different than settlers leaving Europe behind or forging west across the country:

"Doubtless it will be painful to leave the graves of their fathers; but what do they more than our ancestors (or) our children are now doing? Our children by thousands yearly leave the land of their birth to seek new homes in distant regions...

"Can it be cruel in this Government when, by events which it cannot control, the Indian is made discontented in his ancient home to purchase his lands, to give him a new and extensive territory, to pay the expense of his removal, and support him a year in his new abode? How many thousands of our own people would gladly embrace the opportunity of removing west on such conditions?"

The Indian Removal Act was bitterly debated and opposed by many, including church groups and missionaries, along with the likes of Ralph Waldo Emerson and Tennessee congressman Davy Crockett, who said his opposition to the act, "would not make me ashamed on the Day of Judgement." It squeaked through the House by a vote of 101 to 97, and then the Senate by a vote of 28 to 10.

Jackson's speech was a prelude to moving 100,000 Indians west of the Mississippi to the bleak Indian Territory of Oklahoma, Kansas and Texas. The cynical nature of the Indian Removal Act was underscored by the fact that Congress allocated only $500,000 for the massive relocation of tens of thousands, whose farms and possessions were seized as booty.

A bonus for Jackson and the South was the expansion of slavery on territory vacated by the Indians, who were initially from Georgia, Alabama, Tennessee, North Carolina and Mississippi. Jackson himself owned 161 slaves. His 1828 reelection had been a landslide victory in the Electoral College, garnering 219 votes against runner-up Henry Clay with just 49. His vow to remove the Indians and expand slavery was a one-two punch that propelled him to a second term.

Jackson was a renowned Indian fighter, and thus a hero in the eyes of many white settlers. He had served as a major general during the War of 1812 and had won the 1814 Battle of Horseshoe Bend in Alabama against Red Stick Creeks, who were so-called because they raised "the red stick of war." Infuriated by the invasion of their territory by settlers, they had attacked Fort Mims in Alabama on August 30, 1813, killing 250 and taking one hundred captives. In response, Jackson laid siege to their fortified redoubt on the Tallapoosa River and with the combination of artillery and a flanking maneuver was able to shatter the resistance of the Red Sticks, killing eight hundred of their warriors. His troops then burned nearly fifty Creek towns, including those who were neutral or friendlies. The defeated Creeks surrendered twenty million acres in central Alabama and southern Georgia.

But Jackson was hardly the only president wishing the Indians to be gone. As far back as 1776, Thomas Jefferson advocated for Indian removal, fifteen years before he was elected president. Irritated over the conflicts between settlers and the Cherokee, Jefferson wrote:

"Nothing will reduce those wretches so soon as pushing the war into the heart of their country. But I would not stop there. I would never cease pursuing them while one of them remained on this side of the Mississippi."

As President, Jefferson was intent on obtaining Indian lands, hoping to push Native peoples further west following the 1803 Louisiana Purchase of 800,000 square miles of territory west of the Mississippi. He paid Napoleon Bonaparte of France $15 million for the territory (equivalent, perhaps, to $300 million today), which had been bandied back and forth with Spain as a consequence of the wars in Europe. Not a thought was given to the hundreds of tribes that lived there.

Jefferson also wrote to Indiana Territorial Governor William Harrison in February of 1803, referring to the Miami and other tribes of the region as "this pest," and proposing that they be lured into debt to more easily acquire their lands. "We shall push our trading houses, and be glad to see the good & influential individuals among (the Miami) run in debt," he wrote, "because we observe that when these debts get beyond what the individuals can pay, they become willing to lop (them off) by a cession of lands."

This is exactly what came to pass: as the Miami lost more of their land to treaties, they also lost their hunting grounds and farming resources and had to borrow from traders to survive, a vicious circle which generated the loss of even more land.

By 1824, President James Monroe was also on the Indian removal bandwagon, albeit with a caveat, expressed to Congress: "To remove them by force even with a view to their own security and happiness would be revolting to humanity and unjustifiable."

Monroe and his Secretary of War, John C. Calhoun, proposed resettling the Indians to the little-known territory west of Lake Michigan, which at that time was referred to at the Great American Desert, where the climate and environment would be "more favorable to their habits."

But it was President Jackson who finally put Indian removal into play, including the five "Civilized Tribes" of the Cherokee, Choctaw, Chickasaw, Creek and Seminole who had adopted the clothing, farming and home styles of the whites in addition to agreeing to many egregious treaties that had gobbled 90 percent of their land one bite at a time.

The Cherokee had fought with Jackson's troops against the Red Stick Creeks in 1814 and against the Seminoles in 1818, but this earned them no credit with "Old Hickory." Over the course of more than twenty-five treaties with the British and the United States they had ceded thousands of square miles in Georgia, North Carolina, Tennessee and Alabama, but it was the 1835 Treaty of New Echota* that sealed their doom, demanding that they move west.

When thousands of Cherokee refused to move, Major General Winfield Scott scoured the countryside with seven thousand troops and state militia. The volunteers among them included gangs of thugs bent on rape, murder and the theft of Cherokee possessions and homes.

The first wave forced sixteen thousand Cherokee to journey up to one

---

* Three minor chieftains signed the treaty without the authority of the Cherokee and were assassinated in 1839 for their betrayal.

thousand miles to Oklahoma in the fall and winter of 1838-39, notable as being one of the coldest winters on record. It resulted in the deaths of four thousand along the bitter Trail of Tears.

The Miami and Shawnee, who had been so troublesome to the whites in the battle for Ohio, were also targets for removal:

By the 1800s there were two major factions of the Shawnee; those who had fought for Ohio, and those who had voluntarily moved across the Mississippi River to Missouri. In 1825 the Missouri Shawnee ceded their lands around Cape Girardeau for a reservation of more than 1.6 million acres in Kansas. In 1831, the Ohio Shawnee gave up their homeland in exchange for 100,000 acres of the Kansas reservation. They were forcibly removed from Ohio in 1832.

In time, the Shawnee eventually earned federal recognition as the Absentee-Shawnee, the Loyal Shawnee, and the Eastern Shawnee tribes. The Loyal Shawnee were so-named because they had fought for the Union Army in the Civil War,

But, having made a success of their new home in Kansas, their reservation was soon eyed as desirable by white settlers. Despite their service on the winning side of the Civil War, the Shawnee were evicted from Kansas and resettled in Oklahoma's Indian Territory.

The mighty Miami, who numbered 20,000-24,000 in 1700, were a shadow of themselves by the 1830s and heavily in debt. At treaties in 1838 and 1840, they ceded the rest of their land in Indiana for 500,000 acres* beyond the Mississippi and were given five years to relocate.

In response, many of the Miami scrambled to buy their own land in Indiana, with half of the tribe exempted from removal by the 1840s.

But not everyone was so lucky. On Oct. 6, 1846, soldiers from the U.S. Army rounded up more than three hundred Miami hold-outs and forced them to board canal boats. They were shipped like cargo down canals through Ohio to Cincinnati and from there through St. Louis and up the Missouri River to Kanza Landing, the future site of Kansas City.

A trader who witnessed their arrival said that many broke into tears and begged like children to be returned home.**

These horrors were quickly relayed to the Indians of the Great Lakes, who were virtually the last remaining tribes living east of the Mississippi.

---

* Although they were promised 500,000 acres, the Miami received only 350,000.
** Many did return to Indiana, making the harrowing walk home to disappear among their relatives.

CHAPTER 29

1836

Driven from place to place by the Iroquois and Sioux during the seventeenth century, several bands of the Odawa had migrated up the Grand River in western Michigan in the early 1700s. By the 1750s they had established eighteen villages between the Grand and Kalamazoo rivers, with outliers on the Pere Marquette and Muskegon rivers. To the south were the Potawatomi, with whom they maintained good relations.

Trapping and hunting opportunities were robust in the area until the early 1800s. Farming was good, too. As with their Potawatomi relations, the Odawa planted swidden gardens of corn, squash, beans and other crops. Other than a handful of French traders, there were few whites living in western Michigan in last half of the 1700s.

Yet paradise was slowly lost in the early 1800s, particularly with the opening of the Erie Canal in 1825, which unleashed a flood of settlers. By the 1830s settlers were pouring into the territory of the Grand River Odawa, driven by "Michigan Fever." Riverboats laden with settlers and their belongings began making their way up the Grand River and native peoples who had seldom, if ever, seen a white face before were surprised to find white hunters, surveyors and loggers leading pack trains of mules down their forest trails. Beyond their villages, the forests rang with the sound of axes as trees were leveled to provide fuel for the steamships plying Lake Michigan.

When we drive across the country today we see millions of acres of empty land with the fields of large farmers and ranchers stretching to the far horizon. We might imagine that there was plenty of room for both the Indians and for settlers back when. What we have forgotten, however, is that at the beginning of the 1800s, more than 95 percent of the world's population were farmers. The vast fields and empty spaces we witness today were once dotted with thousands of small farms, with most settlers jockeying for the richest bottomlands, hunting grounds and meadows cherished by the Indians. Over time these farms were sold off and consolidated as the Industrial Revolution prompted their owners to migrate to the cities, but by then the damage had been done to Native peoples.

By 1830 the Grand River Valley was densely populated by the Odawa who had 2,500 acres of corn and vegetables under cultivation, along with orchards of 3,000 apple trees. This cleared land was of obvious value to white settlers who wouldn't have the trouble of removing stumps if they could only seize it.

Alarmed, in June, 1834 a grand council was held at Nowaquakezick's (Noon Day's) village at present-day Grand Rapids. The council included the Odawa's northern relations from the L'arbre Croche bands of the Little Traverse area. Catholic missionary, Father Frederick Baraga, wrote that it was a solemn gathering held in a natural amphitheater along the Grand River. After smoking their pipes in silence for a time, the leaders of each band rose to speak, decrying the land-grab of the white men. At the council's conclusion, Baraga wrote that the Odawa resolved, "never to cede their lands," vowing "not to make themselves or their children unhappy."

But the Odawa's commitment to stand firm was soon in tatters. Several bitterly cold winters, years of crop failures, and a scarcity of game due to over-hunting and trapping had pushed Indian families to the brink of starvation. Odawa forests were being leveled by unfettered timber men, and their fields seized by white squatters, including some who bought Indian huts to live in while they constructed their own cabins. Added to this, a smallpox epidemic swept through the Odawa villages along the Grand River in 1835 with a staggering death toll. Moving east, smallpox killed one-third of the Indians living in the Saginaw River Valley in 1837.

The epidemic threw Odawa society into a tailspin, physically, politically and spiritually. As noted in the *People of the Three Fires* by historians James Clifton, George Cornell and James McClurken, "...the Ottawa no doubt lost many of their most influential leaders, the very leaders they needed to unite them politically and pass the traditional values on to the young. Native healers, whose power was the basis of their influence in social and political matters, were unable to cure or protect their people against the ravages of disease. Their loss of credibility and respect represented another serious challenge to fundamental Ottawa lifeways."

Many of the Odawa and Ojibwe were also heavily indebted to traders at a time when most of the fur-bearing animals in the region had been trapped out. And, since many traders had married into Indian families to grease the wheels of commerce, they often pressured their in-laws to sign bad treaties in order to recoup their losses. Traders were allowed to be on hand during annual treaty distributions and were the first to be paid for the goods they had sold to the Indians at high prices.

Trading debts provided the wedge for the 1836 Treaty of Washington, a double-cross that left the Anishinaabek suspended in a limbo of uncertainty while pressuring them to surrender 21,621 square miles and thirty-eight percent of present-day Michigan to the U.S. government.

Orchestrating the land grab was Superintendent of Indian Affairs Henry Schoolcraft, who remains reviled by many Anishinaabek to this day.

In order to resolve their debts some of the northern Odawa at L'arbre Croche had sent representatives to Washington in 1835, hoping to sell some unwanted islands in Lake Huron along with land in the Upper Peninsula that was of little use. In addition to paying off their debts, they petitioned for the services of a blacksmith, instruction in farming, and a school.

Schoolcraft saw the visit as a springboard for acquiring the bulk of the Michigan Territory. He colluded with Lewis Cass, who had moved on from the territory's governor to become the U.S. Secretary of War, the department overseeing Indian affairs. They invited a number of Odawa and Ojibwe leaders to visit Washington to negotiate a land cession.

Schoolcraft had a lock on the Ojibwe representatives to the north in that he had strong family ties within the tribe. He was married to Jane Johnston, the daughter of an Ojibwe woman named Waubojeeg and Scotch-Irish trader John Johnston whose relatives led the Sault Ste. Marie Band. He also had trading connections among the Ojibwe, and thus, influence. Other tribal leaders were coerced and cajoled into making the trip to Washington at the behest of their relatives among the traders.

"Wanting to 'appear as aloof as far as possible,' the Grand River Bands sent a delegation of young men who had no authority to make binding decisions for their bands and one trusted *ogema* who remained opposed to a treaty," noted James M. McClurken in his history of the Odawa, *Our People, Our Journey*. "However, the influence of federal treaty negotiators, fur traders, missionaries, and others who had much to gain from a large Ottawa land cession in the end convinced the delegates to negotiate a treaty."

In negotiations at the Masonic Hall outside Washington, D.C., Odawa and Ojibwe delegates were told that in return for ceding their territory they would be able to live on fourteen widely-scattered reserves forever, including the right to hunt and fish on the lands they ceded. The largest reservation intended for the Grand River Odawa was 70,000 acres along the Manistee River 120 miles to the north.

After several weeks of negotiations, in which self-interested traders participated, the Treaty of Washington was reluctantly signed by Native emissaries on March 28, 1836 and sent to the U.S. Senate for review. With their backs against the wall due to years of hardship and encroaching settlers, tribal representatives reasoned that their people would at least be able to continue their hunting and fishing lifestyle from the security of the new reserves. However, under Article Thirteen of the treaty, hunting rights would only be offered, *until the land is required for settlement*." (Italics added)

Article Eight of the treaty offered this foreboding note:

"It is agreed, that as soon as the said Indians desire it, a deputation shall be sent to the southwest of the Missouri River, there to select a suitable place for the final settlement of said Indians, which country, so selected and of reasonable extent, the United States will forever guaranty and secure to said Indians... When the Indians wish it, the United States will remove them, at their expense, (and) provide them a year's subsistence..."

The Anishinaabek clearly did not "wish" to be removed to west of the Mississippi, but felt they had no choice but to sign. In return they were promised $30,000 annually for twenty years, to be distributed to the various bands spread across Michigan. That and $5,000 per year for education along with $10,000 for farm equipment, $3,000 for health care, $3,000 for Christian missions and $2,000 for tobacco. In addition, the Indians would receive $150,000 in food and supplies such as blankets and tools. Another $30,000 was granted to various headmen and their families.

Other inducements included the addition of two blacksmiths at the reservations north of the Grand River and at the Sault, the services of a gunsmith, two farmers and their assistants, two mechanics, and the construction of a dormitory at the Michilimackinac treaty post.

It was the traders who received the lion's share off the top, however; they were awarded $300,000 to settle Indian debts, which had been usurious to begin with. Another $150,000 was awarded to the "half-blood" *métis* who were not granted reservations. Certain among the *métis* would also split $48,000. Here again the Odawa and Ojibwe were robbed in that virtually all of the *métis* were children of the traders. Thus, the traders collected once again.

Following the "touching of the pen," the Odawa and Ojibwe were given their leave, only to discover the duplicity of the U.S. Senate later that summer. In what amounted to a bait-and-switch, the Senate amended the treaty to grant the Anishinaabek only five years of residency on their reserves, after which their fate would be up to the whims of the U.S. government.

It was no secret that after their five years were up, Michigan's Odawa and Ojibwe would likely be relocated to reservations west of the Mississippi. In fact, they had already witnessed the fate of their southern kinsmen among the Odawa of Ohio, Illinois and southern Wisconsin, who were forced to relocate to reservations in Kansas, beginning in 1833. Their homelands had been nibbled away in a succession of treaties until even their smallest reservations were sacrificed.

Odawa and Ojibwe leaders were utterly shocked by the amendment of the treaty, which had been hashed out over days of council. If ever there was a raw deal, this was it, but they were under extreme pressure to sign. In July, 1836, Schoolcraft met with four thousand Odawa and Ojibwe and their leaders at the Mackinac Straits to obtain their consent to the amended treaty so that it could be ratified and put into law.

Given his blood ties and understanding of the Indian mind, Schoolcraft was well placed to manipulate the Indians into ceding their land. With Ojibwe approval all but guaranteed through his in-laws, he played upon the Odawas' fears, telling them that they would "feel ashamed at seeing their Chippewa brothers in possession of many goods, and much money and themselves entirely destitute and poor." He also told them that no treaty cash or goods would be provided until the revised treaty was signed.

Even so, the treaty might have been scuttled, or at least refined, were it not for the fact that the chieftains of the Grand River Odawa arrived too late to the gathering to give it the thumbs-down. The treaty was subsequently ratified by the Senate; yet rather than moving to their new reservations (which they called "leftovers"), many of the bands refused to budge. It made little sense to the Indians to uproot their villages in the Grand River Valley in order to build new homes and establish farms 120 miles to the north for the promise of only five years.

That, and virtually all of the fourteen reservations comprising 142,000 acres remained unsurveyed and open to white squatters for years thereafter. The Odawa's reservation along the Manistee River was quickly plundered by lumbermen who swept the region clean of its pine and then declared that their sawmill, homes and warehouses were legally theirs, despite the government's promise to the Indians. Only a handful of Odawa elected to move to the reservation, despite the creation of a blacksmith shop, a trading post, a mission, and a farm intended to teach agriculture with plowing methods. By 1841 the federal government began offering the reservation land for sale to squatters and settlers.

Nor did federal guarantees of treaty payments and provisions arrive as promised. Delivery of these and the haphazard provision of blacksmithing, schools and farming education limped on for nearly twenty years before a new treaty was signed in 1855.

The Treaty of 1836 had barely been ratified when Schoolcraft began scheming to move the Anishinaabek west of the Mississippi. In the spring of 1838, when the prairie would be lush and green, he organized a trip to

Kansas, painting a rosy picture of life on the Great Plains. The Ojibwe flatly refused to make the trip and few of the Odawa wished to go. Eventually, Schoolcraft rounded up a party of twenty-four Odawa, but there were only five headmen among them and only one had signed the treaty.

Reporting back home, some were optimistic and agreeable to selecting land, but most noted that Kansas was scorching hot in the summer and biting cold in the winter, with endless winds in all seasons. Nor were there opportunities for fishing, which provided the Odawa with much of their protein. They also believed that the hostile tribes of the Great Plains would likely make life difficult for any newcomers encroaching on their territory.

The eastern tribes had good reason to fear the Indians of the Great Plains. Consider the case of the Ponca, a small tribe from Ohio that had been driven west of the Mississippi to Nebraska in the late 1600s by the Iroquois. In 1832, frontier artist George Catlin wrote that the Ponca had become easy prey on the Great Plains, "met and killed by the Sioux on the North, by the Pawnees to the West; and by the Osages and Konzas in the South; and still more alarmed from the constant advance of the pale faces - their enemies from the East, with whiskey and smallpox, which had already destroyed four-fifths of his tribe, and soon would impoverish, and at last destroy the remainder of them."*

Add to all this, many of the soldiers and federal caretakers on the western reservations thought of the Indians as barely a step above animals, and treated them as such. An army surgeon at the Crow Creek reservation in South Dakota reported Indians being fed like livestock from a six-foot square vat constructed of cottonwood lumber and heated by a pipe from a steam-powered sawmill:

"Into this vat was thrown beef, beef heads, entrails of beeves, some beans, flour and pork. I think there was put into the vat two barrels of flour each time... This mass was then cooked by the steam from the boiler passing through the vat. When that was done, all the Indians were ordered to come there with their pails and get it... The Santees and Winnebagos were fed from this vat; some of the Indians refused to eat it, saying it made them sick."

Indian men were also denied the chance to hunt and butcher government cattle, which might have alleviated the boredom of reservation life and provided a glimmer of self-esteem and happier days.

The avoid relocation the Odawa began purchasing their own lands, but

---

* Today, survivors of the Ponca live on reservations in Nebraska and Oklahoma.

even this proved difficult. The ratification of the Treaty of Washington in 1836 enabled Michigan to gain statehood the following year in 1837, sparking a debate over whether Indians should be able to buy their own lands, since they weren't U.S. citizens. In response, some bands enlisted the help of missionaries and friendly traders to buy land in western Michigan near Holland, Lowell, the Thornapple River and Fort Village to establish their villages. Others left the United States, moving to Manitoulin Island at the northern tip of Lake Huron and other villages in Canada.

On the eastern side of the state, the Ojibwe who had signed the Treaty of Saginaw in 1819 initially had a period of prosperity, selling corn, vegetables, apples and venison to the settlers arriving in southeastern Michigan. Yet they were a small people barring an overwhelming tide of newcomers. Michigan's population went from 8,765 settlers in 1820 to nearly 170,000 by 1836, while only 3,000-some Ojibwe lived in the all the Lower Peninsula.

A cholera epidemic out of Detroit swept the Saginaw villages in 1834, killing many within a day of infection. This was followed by a crop failure in 1836 due to frigid conditions and then the smallpox epidemic of 1837 that killed at least one-third of the Native peoples in the region.

Detroit's expanding population and the allure of valuable timber put the Ojibwe in the cross hairs. Once again Schoolcraft was on the scene, negotiating two treaties in 1836, two in 1837 and a fifth in 1838.

Writing in *Diba Jimooyung: A History of the Saginaw Ojibwe Anishinabek*, editor Charmaine M. Benz notes that the treaties of the late 1830s were negotiated at a time when the Ojibwe were starving and had lost many of their leaders. "Weakened and demoralized, our ancestors allowed Schoolcraft to write a treaty that drove our once wealthy and strong tribe to the brink of extinction. In fact, the treaty was so hopelessly flawed that the United States negotiated another treaty in 1838 to keep us from losing our last remaining properties."

This was because land values had plummeted due to an economic depression and banking crisis. The government stepped in to prevent land speculators from buying Ojibwe reserves for next to nothing.

Meanwhile, the nearby Swan Creek Band to the west of the Saginaw River Valley and the Black River Band to the north were told that they would receive no annuities until the land they ceded was sold, meaning they received nothing at time when the natural resources they survived on were severely depleted. Yet they were obliged to pay the usual debts to traders; for the establishment of schools; compensation for damages incurred as far back in the War of 1812; and even for their vaccinations.

Fifty-one members of the Black River Band moved to Kansas in 1839, arriving in poor shape, suffering from disease, bad food and ragged clothing. They had to beg other tribes in Indian Territory for food to survive. Almost half of them died over the next six years.

The scattered bands struggled on as best they could, some finding a home on two hundred acres purchased by Methodist missionaries. Others purchased 520 acres west of Flint and took up farming. Still others moved to Sarnia in Canada or bought land on their former reserves near Methodist churches. Due to the reduction of annuities from the federal government, abysmal land sales and funds nibbled away by traders, the Saginaw River Valley bands came away with almost nothing to show for the sale of their last small reserves.

***

Schoolcraft was a mixed-bag in his dealings with the Indians, but certainly had a notable career, beginning as a young geologist with the 1820 expedition of Lewis Cass to the copper region of upper Minnesota and western Lake Superior. Thanks to his wife's influence, he was knowledgeable in Anishinaabemowin, the language of the Odawa and Ojibwe. He began his nineteen-year career as an Indian agent with the Sault Ste. Marie band in 1822.

In 1825, Schoolcraft and Indian agents Lewis Cass and William Clark (of Lewis & Clark fame) met with more than a thousand leaders of the Ojibwe, Sioux, Potawatomi, Sauk, Winnebago, Iowa and Fox tribes at Prairie du Chien in southwestern Wisconsin. Their goal was to mediate a peace treaty between the Ojibwe and the Dakota Sioux of Minnesota, who had been at war for centuries, causing problems with trade and white business interests.

An ancient Indian gathering-ground, Prairie du Chien was a meadow spanning eight miles at the mouth of the Wisconsin River. Cass and Schoolcraft arrived with an escort of sixty soldiers and 150 friendly Indians for protection. Greased with thousands of dollars in gifts, liquor and food for the delegates, a peace treaty was signed in the spirit of good fellowship. But the ink was barely dry on the treaty before hostilities and massacres between the Ojibwe and Sioux began again.

While exploring the Minnesota Territory in 1832, Schoolcraft discovered the source of the Mississippi at a lake he named Itasca. He was fond of inventing words, sometimes blending Arabic and Latin with Anishinaabemowin to create faux-Indian names for Michigan locales such as Leelanau, Lenawee, Oscoda, Kalkaska, Alpena and others. Lake Itasca was derived from his mash-up of *veritas*, meaning "truth" in Latin, and *caput*, which means "head."

Schoolcraft's primary mission on this trip was to vaccinate the Indians of the region for smallpox as part of the Indian Vaccination Act of 1832. Physician Douglass Houghton administered 2,070 vaccinations to the Ojibwe, Sioux and Odawa during the expedition. Tribes that were "hostile" to the United States were excluded from vaccination however, and Schoolcraft was also charged with scouting out Native strengths and resources along with the possibility of evicting the Indians to west of the Mississippi.

Vaccination in the early 1800s involved making a small incision with a knife and scrubbing the wound initially with cowpox sores and later with material scraped from smallpox sores (*vaccinia virus*) to produce antibodies. The treatment had been discovered by British physician Edward Jenner in 1796, who noticed that milkmaids who contracted cowpox were protected from smallpox. While there are a number of accounts of evil settlers and soldiers giving infected blankets to Indians as biological weapons, it's also true that some whites vaccinated many indigenous peoples. The Hudsons Bay Company, for instance, vaccinated Indians in northern Canada, if only because they were valuable trading partners.

Through the years Schoolcraft began collecting observations on Indian lifeways and wrote numerous poems, articles, books, ethnologies and reports on his explorations. His 1839 compilation of Native legends, *Algic Researches*, was avidly read by Henry Wadsworth Longfellow, contributing to his epic poem, *The Song of Hiawatha*. In 1846 Schoolcraft was commissioned by Congress to undertake a study of the nation's Indian tribes, a monumental effort which was published in six volumes.

But Schoolcraft was also a religious zealot who considered the Indians to be degenerate heathens greatly in need of the Christian faith. To him, the shamanic rituals of the Ojibwe were "little more than a midnight revel" that called upon the devil to weave their spells. "It is a mere worship of Baal," he sniffed, referring to a demon god of the Bible.

In his writings, Schoolcraft often disparaged the Indians, giving them little more credit than apes in their ability to make canoes, weave baskets or create pottery. Nor did he consider the Indians to be intellectually competent, writing that "the Indian seldom thinks, (except) when he is compelled to think, and then he is not slow to suggest plausible arguments to fortify himself in heathenish practices."

As with Lewis Cass, Schoolcraft believed the Indians were ignorant and short-sighted for preferring their own way of life, rather than the path laid out for them by the whites on the prairies of Kansas and Oklahoma. In his view, the Indians' rejection of the white man's religion and treaties was evidence that they "failed in comprehensive views, deep-reaching foresight, and powers of generalization."

Ironically, these were the same qualities that were lacking in himself.

Thus, Schoolcraft was of the mindset that the Ojibwe and Odawa would be better off if they were relocated west of the Mississippi beyond the grasp of whiskey peddlers and rapacious traders in order to gradually assimilate as Christian farmers into white society.

Yet as we have seen, the Anishinaabek wanted no part of the plan to move west and clung tenaciously, heroically, to their villages along with their way of life, hunting, trapping, foraging and maintaining small gardens, even with the pressure to move squeezing them on all sides. It wasn't until the Treaty of Detroit in 1855 that the Indians of Michigan would be free of the threat of removal, only to face new threats of a confounding nature.

CHAPTER 30

THE POTAWATOMI TRAIL OF DEATH

The sound of gunfire thundered outside a small Catholic chapel in Twin Lakes, Indiana on August 30 of 1838, where a band of Potawatomi villagers found themselves surrounded by a mob of one hundred soldiers and white settlers. The gunfire was meant to show that the militia meant business.

The village, known as Chi-Chipe-Outpe, was located in Indiana's Marshall County, just south of the Michigan border. It was home to about one hundred Potawatomi families, who agreed with their leader, Chief Menominee, that federal treaties requiring them to give up their land and move beyond the Mississippi were fraudulent. Ordered to vacate their homes and move west to the newly-created Indian Territory in Kansas, they refused to budge.

As with other Potawatomi communities, Chi-Chipe-Outpe was surrounded by corn fields and crops of beans, pumpkin, squash and sunflowers. Housing in the village ranged from wigwams paneled with slabs of elm and birch bark to a smattering of log cabins of the sort introduced by white settlers. While the Potawatomi still depended on hunting and fishing for much of their protein, by the 1830s they were also edging closer to the norms of white society, wearing manufactured clothing and immensely proud of the small, shaggy ponies they bred and raised. Many spoke pid-

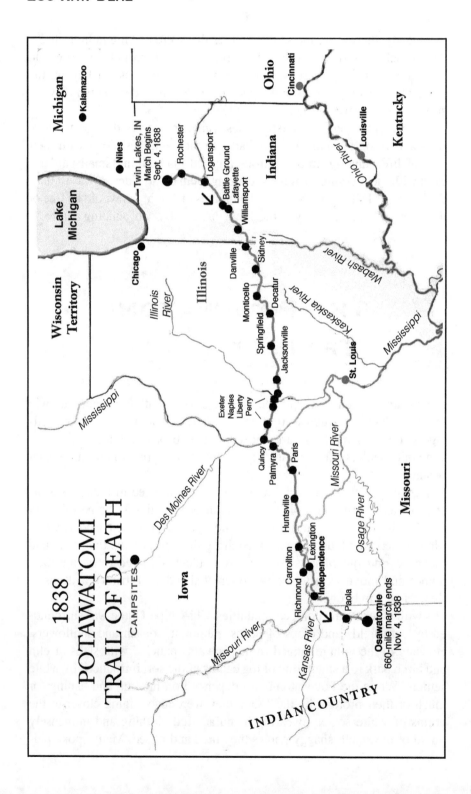

gin English and were employed by local settlers, chopping wood, plowing fields and performing other menial labor and heavy work.

Yet now, cowering in their chapel of hewn logs roofed with cedar slats, the resisters found themselves under the guns of a posse of white soldiers and settlers bent on rounding them up and burning their village.

Potawatomi author Simon Pokagon described the events of that day in a memoir written shortly before his death in 1899. The villagers had been gathered for a council in the chapel, not suspecting that they were being led into a trap:

"As our people entered the church, the door was closed behind them so that none without might suspect the fate of those within, and so we entered as lambs to the slaughter for the last time... Packed within the little church, our people were tied and handcuffed. The stoutest braves, those who had never known fear, when they thought of the cruelties and injustice that was being dealt out to them, gave up in despair and wept like children. In vain they begged and prayed not to be forced from the home of their childhood. Some were packed into wagons like sheep for market, while others were chained as criminals together and marched off double quick, not even being permitted to see friends or relatives left at home."

Chief Menominee, a religious leader who crusaded against liquor and other vices brought on by white settlement, was locked in a cage aboard a wagon along with local chieftains Black Wolf, Peepehawah and three others, bound for transport beyond the Mississippi.

Heading the roundup was General John Tipton, a veteran of the Battle of Tippecanoe in 1811. Gen. Tipton had been recruited by Indiana Governor David Wallace in the wake of violence over the pending removal of the Potawatomi and had "promptly and patriotically accepted the appointment." Riled up by threats of removal, drunken Indians had threatened whites in the area. Some had hacked at a settler's door with an axe, which resulted in the arson of a dozen Potawatomi homes in reprisal. Then too, Black Hawk's 1832 "war" in neighboring Illinois was still fresh in memory, and the white residents of the region had developed a case of the jitters, petitioning the Indiana legislature for the removal of the Potawatomi.

There were also economic factors at work: just over the border, statehood had been approved in Michigan in 1837. Within two years the new state's population nearly doubled from 90,000 in 1835 to 174,543 in 1837. Land-hungry settlers were eager to seize Potawatomi farmlands ranging from south of the Kalamazoo River in Michigan to northern Indiana, where the hard work of clearing trees and creating pastures had been done generations ago.

But Chief Menominee had good reason to oppose the move.

In 1832, Menominee and other Potawatomi leaders had been awarded small reservations in northern Indiana and southern Michigan following years of having the tribe's vast holdings nibbled away. In 1836 the government came seeking even these small holdings with a treaty offering a little over $14,000. The treaty, orchestrated by Indian Agent Col. Abel C. Pepper, stipulated that the Potawatomi would have to move west beyond the Mississippi within two years after ceding their land. Several chieftains signed the treaty, but Menominee absolutely refused. As a work-around, Pepper found three other chieftains to sign the treaty instead.

Wrapped in a rich blanket and demonstrating the gravitas of an Indian orator accustomed to speaking with passion on behalf of his people, Menominee rose at the council organized by Pepper and vowed that he and his band would never surrender their land:

"Members of the Council: The president (of the United States) does not know the truth. He, like me, has been imposed upon. He does not know that our treaty is a lie, and that I never signed it. He does not know that you made my young chiefs drunk and got their consent, and pretended to get mine. He does not know that I have refused to sell my lands and still refuse. He would not by force drive me from my home, the graves of my tribe, and my children who have gone to the Great Spirit, nor allow you to ... take me, tied like a dog if he knew the truth. My brother, the President, is just, but he listens to the word of the young chiefs who have lied; and when he knows the truth he will leave me to my own. 1 have not sold my lands. I will not sell them. I have not signed any treaty and will not sign any. I am not going to leave my lands and I don't want to hear anything more about it."

Menominee even made a visit to Washington, D.C., to speak with Secretary of War Lewis Cass, who assured him that his people would not be removed to the west. This promise was quickly forgotten. Unfortunately, Menominee and his people did not have the political connections, much less the firepower, to resist their removal two years later. General Tipton's volunteers caught the Indians by surprise, burning down their village.

Writing in 1898, historian Daniel McDonald described the scene:

"A great many of the white settlers in the neighborhood turned out to welcome the soldiers, and to render such assistance as might be necessary. The Indians were surrounded before they realized that the soldiers had been sent to remove them. They were disarmed, and preparations at once commenced for the starting of the caravan. Squads of soldiers were sent

out in every direction for the purpose of capturing the straggling bands encamped in various places in the county, and such others as might be found
hunting and fishing in the neighborhood."

The soldiers and volunteers rounded up 859 Potawatomies, of which
about 150 came from southern Michigan. The Potawatomies gathered what
possessions they could muster, and along with their ponies and wagons,
prepared to leave a homeland they had occupied for hundreds of years.

"When all was in readiness to move, the wigwams and cabins were torn
down and Menominee Village had the appearance of having been swept
by a hurricane," McDonald wrote. "Early on the morning of September 2,
1838 orders were given to move, and at once nearly one thousand men,
women and children, with broken hearts and tearful eyes, took up the line
of march to their far western home."

They would march 660 miles to Kansas on what came to be known at the
Potawatomi Trail of Death.

Coinciding with the Trail of Death was the Second Seminole War (1835-
1842) in far-off Florida. The Seminoles had also refused to relocate west
of the Mississippi and had engaged in a savage war with the United States.
In December of 1835 they slaughtered 106 soldiers under Major Francis
Dade at Bushnell, Florida, with only two surviving.

The Seminoles were made up of refugees from many tribes, including the
Timucuan, Shawnee, Calusa, Muskogee Creek, Chickasaw and Choctaw,
in addition to many escaped black slaves. Dubbed the "runaways," the
Seminoles fought three wars against the United States, yet were never
conquered. General Winfield Scott, who would later win the Mexican War
of 1847, descended on the swamps, bayous and jungles of Florida with
five thousand soldiers in a mostly futile quest to conquer the tribe. Some
1,200 federal troops would die in the attempt along with at least the same
number of white settlers, while the Seminoles would remain the only Indian tribe that was never defeated by the United States, going on to fight a
third war before retreating to the safety of the Everglades.

The Seminole War convulsed the nation's press with lurid stories and
propaganda, adding to the pressure on removing the Potawatomi.

It had been a long fall for a proud people. Once, the Potawatomi had
been a powerful tribe, ranging more than four hundred miles from the
shores of Lake Huron in southern Michigan to the prairie lands of Illinois.
During the 1600s, French explorers reported several Potawatomi villages
in the area of Green Bay, Wisconsin, coexisting with the Fox, Sauk and

Ho-Chunk.

One of the "three fires" of the Anishinaabek, the Potawatomie's roots are a bit of a mystery; historians speculate that they may have lived at the tip of Michigan's Lower Peninsula in the 1500s. Champlain claimed that they warred with the neighboring Odawa and were driven west to Wisconsin in the early 1600s, where the French encountered them on the Door Peninsula. Their name, *Potawatamink*, means "people of the place of fire," and their nation was comprised of about fifty bands spread across the Upper Midwest. Major divisions of the tribe included the prairie bands of Illinois and Wisconsin, the St. Joseph bands of southwestern Michigan and northern Indiana, and the Huron bands of southeastern Michigan. The Huron bands had migrated west following the 1807 Treaty of Detroit, settling along the Upper Grand, Thornapple and Kalamazoo rivers in Michigan.

When they arrived in southwestern Michigan the Potawatomi discovered so-called "garden beds," which had been constructed by a long-gone people. These were fashioned in low ridges about eighteen inches high in rectangular or circular patterns encompassing up to 120 acres. Possibly constructed by the Mound Builders of the Hopewell culture, their function remains a mystery, although there is speculation that they were used to trip up stampeding buffalo, which were driven to slaughter.

By 1825 there were up to four thousand Potawatomi living in southern Michigan, with perhaps two thousand spread across present-day Indiana, Illinois and Wisconsin.

Although the Potawatomi had a patrilineal society, in which inheritance and clan membership descended from the father's side of the family, women played a major role in deciding tribal matters. In her book, *Indian Nations of Wisconsin*, historian Patty Loew wrote that, "each Potawatomi village had a woman's council, or *W'okamakwe*, made up of the elder sisters of the male clan chiefs. These 'honored women' were expected to lead their clan families in paths of goodness or be impeached and stripped of any power." Major decisions for each band were approved by the woman's council before being passed on to the council of men.

Loew adds that women also played a greater role in village affairs once the demands of the fur trade sent their men far away for weeks at a time in pursuit of beaver, mink and other pelts. Gathering firewood, building and repairing their homes, tending their fields, fishing and foraging in addition to raising their children were the tasks shouldered by Potawatomi women - historically the fate of all women whose husbands were off hunting or soldiering.

Unfortunately, the political power of Potawatomi women faded with the arrival of chauvinistic French traders in the 1600s, who chose to negotiate

Although many Potawatomies converted to Christianity at the behest of missionaries, this 1837 sketch by British-born artist George Winter indicates that they also retained some of the shamanic ways of their ancestors.

only with men.

The military fortunes of the Potawatomi had waffled up and down through the years, with bands of the tribe driven from place-to-place by intermittent warfare. This was especially true during the Beaver Wars of the seventeenth century as the powerful Iroquois swept west, battling for territory that was rich in fur-bearing animals. The Beaver Wars drove the Potawatomi out of Michigan's Lower Peninsula, making it a perilous no man's land and throwing the entire region into an uproar.

Thereafter, like the Ojibwe and the Odawa, the Potawatomi ended up on the losing side in a succession of wars fought against the British and then the Americans.

The Potawatomi sided with the French during the French and Indian War, destroying a number of British forts and trading posts along the frontier. Following the defeat of the French, the tribe allied with the British in the American Revolution. This too was a dead-end. The Potawatomi went on to join the Miami and Shawnee during the Northwest Indian War of the 1790s and took part in the Battle of Fallen Timbers in 1794. Again, a defeat. Thereafter they were allies of Tecumseh in the War of 1812. Many of them were living at Prophetstown in northern Indiana when it was burned by General William Harrison and his troops following the Battle of Tippecanoe.

In short, the Potawatomie's French and British allies proved to be worthless in every conflict, and as was the case with other tribes, they were subjected to the scorched-earth tactics of the white militias and troops that came thereafter.

Following the War of 1812, the Potawatomi found themselves under the American thumb and began adapting to the white man's ways of farming, dress and shelter. As with the case with other tribes, they were eagerly sought out by missionaries in a tug-of-war between Catholics and Protestants that pitted factions against one-another in one of the religious ironies imported from Europe.

Thereafter they suffered what might be called the death of a dozen cuts as one treaty after another ravaged their homeland.

In the 1821 Treaty of Chicago, negotiated by Lewis Cass, the Potawatomi and Grand River Odawa were under extreme pressure from traders to whom they were indebted. In order to settle their debts they ceded five million acres of the southwestern quarter of Michigan, save for a few small reserves west of the St. Joseph River. As would increasingly be the case, these dwindling reserves were islands in a stream of white settlers and squatters. With their traditional resources of hunting and trapping frittered away, the tribe turned to selling produce, crops and handicrafts such as baskets to white settlers in addition to hiring themselves out as laborers.

In the Treaty of September 18, 1827, the Potawatomi lost further holdings for the construction of Michigan's Territorial Road from Detroit to Chicago. As it turned out, the road was merely a pretense for their removal, as it came nowhere near their reserves.

The following year in 1828, Cass gained another small triangular section of southwestern Michigan; once again the tribe sold its land to resolve debts with traders.

Yet another treaty ceded a strip of land one hundred feet wide and hundreds of miles long to enable the construction of a road from Michigan City in Indiana to Madison on the Ohio River.

"The wording of the treaty was a cunningly devised arrangement to swindle the Indians of an immense amount of some of the best lands belonging to them in the state," wrote historian Daniel McDonald in 1898. "The Indians had nothing to do with writing the treaty, and evidently knew little about what the result of its operation would be. They were lead to believe that a great thoroughfare between Lake Michigan and the Ohio River would be built which would enable them to travel with ease and comfort between these two important points."

In the Treaty of October 27, 1832 (ratified in 1833), the Potawatomi ceded five million acres and the last of their land south of the Grand River in Michigan, Indiana and Illinois, save for a number of small, isolated reserves, with the signers promising to move west within two years. It was following this treaty that Chief Menominee steadfastly refused to give up his land in 1836.

Faced with the threat of removal, thousands of Potawatomi fled to Canada or sought shelter among the Odawa and Ojibwe to the north. Others fled to the swamps of central Michigan or dug in their heels and refused to budge until they were forced out at gunpoint.

A lesser-known removal preceded the Trail of Death. In the fall of 1837, five hundred Potawatomies from Illinois and Niles, Michigan had been rounded up and driven west in a march that included wading waist-deep through flood waters in Missouri. It's estimated that fifty died on the march, with word of the trek's horrors quickly spreading to those who had remained home.

We know much about the 1838 Trail of Death because it was well documented in the diaries of emigration "conductor" William Polke and Catholic priest Benjamin Marie Petit, who accompanied the Potawatomies during the most harrowing leg of their removal. British-born artist George Winter also joined the expedition, sketching its people and their progress.

The 1838 march was plagued with extreme thirst and sickness. In a speech to the Indiana legislature on December 4, 1838, Governor Wallace vouched that the Potawatomi had "voluntarily prepared to emigrate," and that "Gen. Tipton and the volunteers accompanied them as far as Danville, Illinois, administering to them on the way whatever comfort and relief humanity required," neglecting to mention the bayonets, guns, beatings, bondage and terror reported by the captive Indians.

The party of 859 Potawatomies stretched for three miles along the rough roads and trails leading west, with cavalry riding ahead and behind along with a baggage train of forty wagons. In Danville, they passed into the custody of conductor Polke and federal agents.

Here, the forests of the Midwest gave way to the treeless prairies of Illinois where fresh water grew scarce or nonexistent. With bad water came disease, including malaria.

On September 5th Polke wrote that due to illness, "Fifty-one persons were found to be unable to continue the journey, the means of transportation not being at hand - they were therefore left, the most of them sick, the remainder to wait upon them."

Four days later came more illness: "Physicians came into camp today, and reported three hundred cases of sickness... A kind of medical hospital has been erected today, which is likely to facilitate the course of medical regime proposed by the physicians. A child died today."

The death of children along the march became a constant refrain in Polke's diary, ending many of his entries with a bleak note: "A child died since dark... Two deaths took place this evening... Two small children died along the road..."

At times the march struggled to make ten miles a day; at best, perhaps eighteen. Roadside graves were hastily dug and the dead were left without the ceremonies dear to the Indians.

Simon Pokagon was only eight years old at the time and was not swept up in the trek; his 1899 account was based on the memories of those who endured it: "As they were marched across the plains, under the hot, blazing sun, wolves in the distance followed in the rear, like carrion crows, to feed upon the fallen. Some of you must remember from well-authenticated reports how, on the long and weary march towards the setting sun, from fatigue and want of water, children, old men and women expiring fell; how infants untimely born, clasped in their mother's arms, together with them died and were left half buried on the plains, the prey of vultures and of wolves."

Father Petit had a similar report to his superior on September 14: " I saw my poor Christians, under a burning noonday sun, amidst clouds of dust, marching in a line, surrounded by soldiers who were hurrying their steps. Next came the baggage wagons, in which numerous invalids, children, and women, too weak to walk, were crammed. They encamped half a mile from the town, and in a short while I went among them.

"I found the camp... a scene of desolation, with sick and dying people on all sides. Nearly all the children, weakened by the heat, had fallen into a state of complete languor and depression. I baptized several who were newly born - happy Christians, who with their first step passed from earthly exile to the heavenly sojourn. "

Father Petit wrote that the death toll began well before the party reached Illinois: "We learned that the Indians on the way, with bayonets prodding their backs, had a large number of sick in their ranks - that several, crammed into baggage wagons, had already died of heat and thirst. These pieces of news were like so many swords piercing my heart."

A young man devoted to his congregation, Father Petit had been ordered to close the chapel at Menominee's village. In a letter to his family he wrote of his anguish and that of his flock: "Then my dear church was stripped of all its ornaments, and at the moment of my departure I called all my children together. I spoke to them one more time; I wept; my listeners sobbed. It was heart-rending... A few days afterward I learned that the

Indians, despite their peaceable disposition, had been surprised and taken prisoners of war."

Polke wrote of the growing desperation for water on September 14: "As we advance farther into the country of the prairies water becomes more scarce - the streams are literally dried up, and we have reason to fear that unless soon refreshed with rain, our future marches will be attended with much pain, and suffering."

The next day he wrote that the party, "arrived at an unhealthy and filthy looking stream, at which... we were forced to encamp."

On October 28th during a period of intense cold, the marchers stumbled into the 1838 Mormon War being waged in Missouri, one of three "wars" that prompted the Church of Latter Day Saints to flee first to Illinois and then west to Utah and north to Beaver Island in Lake Michigan.

"The country through which we passed today is very much excited," Polke wrote. "Nothing is heard - nothing is talked of but the Mormons and the difficulties between them and the citizens of upper Missouri. (The town of) Carrollton is nightly guarded by its citizens."

The Potawatomi were witness to a conflict that had begun in 1831 after the Mormons had migrated to northern Missouri under the leadership of their founder, Joseph Smith, who established the town of Far West. Frequent clashes between ten thousand Mormons and their neighbors prompted Missouri's territorial governor to call out the militia in September, 1838, ordering the Mormons to leave or face extermination. The resulting violence had spilled into Carroll County in the path of the Potawatomi.

"The majority of the Protestants in the country had resolved to exterminate or at least expel certain sectarians called Mormons, who refused to submit to the tax and the public charges," Petit wrote. "(One day) we heard artillery and rifle shots. We saw armed troops coming to formation from every direction, and about sixty mules - booty taken the day before from the Mormons. We passed quietly through this theater of fanatic battles, although at our arrival a message had come asking that the Indians join the troops who were attacking the Mormons. This request was wisely rejected."

And so it went for 660 miles to Indian Territory in western Missouri and Kansas, with the marchers - some who walked barefoot - afflicted by freezing rains and snow.

But this was not the end of the Potawatomie's torment. Two years later Michigan Governor William Woodbridge petitioned the federal government to round up any remaining Natives in the southern half of the state. In June of 1840 a force of two hundred infantry and one hundred cavalry marched from Detroit to Marshall under General Hugh Brady, a tough old veteran of Mad Anthony Wayne's expedition and the War of 1812.

Brady hired local settlers to rat on the Potawatomi and track them down as his troops scoured the region. Resisters were hog-tied and slung over saddles or piled into wagons for internment. One old woman was so frightened that she fled to the woods during a raid and hid there for days before being rescued, surviving on a dead pheasant that she found.

Settler David Lucas, a friend of the tribe, wrote of the Potawatomie's plight: "Soon they scattered like a flock of blackbirds. One company fled north, far into the forest. They had with them a sick squaw, which impeded their travel. They were overtaken and sought refuge in a dense swamp, which was surrounded by the cavalry, and after two or three days' siege, they were brought out of their hiding place and taken to Marshall."

By summer's end 439 Potawatomi had been interred in a prison camp near Marshall as preparations were made to march them 750 miles to a reservation in Kansas. Witnesses described funeral-like processions as long lines of the Potawatomi filed through Kalamazoo, Marshall and other towns. Grim, stone-faced men deprived of their dignity marched under the eyes of jeering soldiers. Alongside were their stricken women, some carrying babies on their backs or shepherding barefoot children. The sick and elderly were saddled on ponies or dragged along on travois made of long poles. With them went all of their possessions: pots, pans, utensils, tools, blankets and mementoes, piled atop their ponies and aboard their wagons.

They, too, endured a death march to Indian Territory, herded like animals to a reservation in Linn County, Kansas.

Accompanying them was Lucius Buell Holcomb, a white merchant who was married to a Potawatomi woman and was fluent in their language. Holcomb chronicled the fate of one party of the tribe, who were piled into steamboats at the point of bayonets on the Illinois River near the town of Peru. All of their ponies and property were left behind on the riverbank or stolen by solders. They arrived destitute in Kansas at the onset of winter.

Not all of the Potawatomi suffered removal. Some escaped the marches and fled back to Michigan or to Canada. Notably, Chief Leopold Pokagon (the father of Simon Pokagon) had convinced his band of 250 Potawatomi to use some of their treaty payments to purchase their own land. By 1838, Pokagon and his people owned 874 acres on Silver Creek near present-day Dowagiac. When General Brady's troops came calling, the chief was able to certify that he was a tax-paying, Catholic land-owner whose people had embraced the white man's language and farming techniques. They also had a legal opinion stating that Pokagon and his people had a right to remain in Michigan, signed by Judge Epaphroditus Ransom of Kalamazoo,

Stricken with guilt over the fate of the Potawatomi, the State of Indiana creat-ed a 17-foot-tall granite monument to Chief Menominee, which was unveiled at Twin Lakes on Sept. 4, 1909, with many members of the tribe attending. The chief survived the Trail of Death, but died three years later in Kansas at the age of 50. Photo courtesy of the Marshall County Library.

a friend of the Potawatomi and an associate judge on Michigan's Supreme Court. General Brady dashed off a note allowing Pokagon's band to re-main in Michigan, and headed off to search elsewhere.

The ancestors of Chief Pokagon's band carry on as the fire-bearers of the Potawatomi nation in southwestern Michigan to this day. Many other members of the Potawatomi filtered back into Michigan in the succeeding years after their removal. Michigan's only "state" reservation was created in 1845 after Chief Pamtopee purchased 120 acres near Athens in Calhoun County with annuity funds and the help of sympathetic white neighbors. A group of wandering Potawatomi from Wisconsin were also granted home-steads in the Upper Peninsula in 1913, establishing a reservation at Han-nahville near Escanaba.

CHAPTER 31

THE KING
OF BEAVER ISLAND

One day in the early winter of 1851, an Anishinaabek headman named Pay-zhick-way-we-dong and twenty of his men answered a call for help from their white friends on Beaver Island. Mormons - who called themselves Saints - had been spotted skulking in the woods around Cable's Trading Post, the home of merchant Peter McKinley at Whiskey Point on the north end of the island and he feared the worst for himself, his wife and three daughters. The last boat of the season had left for the mainland thirty miles away and there was no possible escape.

There was already bad blood between McKinley and the Mormons owing to an aborted attack on the group from his post headquarters the year before. McKinley and the few non-Mormons left on the island had a "Fort Apache" mentality toward the Saints, who they believed had beaten, robbed and even killed many farmers and fishermen who didn't submit to their will.

McKinley had also extended thousands of dollars in credit to the Indians and fishermen of the Beaver Island Archipelago and couldn't afford to leave - he was in too deep. He armed his staff of barrel-makers and clerks and stood watch all night; the next day he sent for help from Pay-zhick-way-we-dong, whose Christian name was Peaine.

Known as Cloudy Day, Pay-zhick-way-we-dong was the leader of a band of around two hundred Indians living on Minis Gitigaan - Garden Island. At 4,990 acres, it's the second largest in the Beaver Island Archipelago. In an 1840 census, Indian agent Henry Schoolcraft wrote that there were seven families on the island, including 39 men, 51 women and 109 children, headed by two chiefs and protected by seven warriors.

"Eighteen people still adhered to the traditional religion, but thirty-five were recorded as members of Christian churches," Schoolcraft noted. "The people still lived in temporary dwellings and by fishing, hunting, and making maple sugar. However, on 120 acres of cleared land, (they) raised corn, potatoes, beans, turnips and melons. Thirty hogs were owned."

Commercial fishing and cutting wood also provided income for the Indians of Garden island, but they too had no love of the Mormons.

Born in the early 1800s, Pay-zhick-way-we-dong had been orphaned as a child. As was customary in the patrilineal society of the Anishinaabek, he had been born into his father's clan, yet was sent to live with his mother's Thunder Clan in Michigan's Upper Peninsula. There he displayed qualities early on which marked him as a leader.

"They believed that he would be a leader and rid their people of a great evil that would in the future come," according to the memory of an elder of the Anishinaabek. "It was thought that with all the chiefs and headmen around the Manistique Lakes area (that) he would be trained well, and when it was time, he would return."

Pay-zhick-way-we-dong was baptized with the Christian name Pierre at the age of four by a French-speaking Catholic priest, and thereafter he became known as Peaine due to a linguistic lapse.

"The Indians do not have the *'rr'* sound in their language so to them his name (Pierre) was pronounced Peaine (Peahn)," wrote George A. Anthony in his book, *The Elders Speak*, about life on Beaver Island.

Peaine would have been in his late forties-early-fifties when Beaver Island was engulfed in the sort of drama one associates with the Wild West, including gun battles, beatings, whippings and the wrath of a drunken mob. The Mormons had landed at Beaver Island in 1847, quickly establishing a colony at St. James Harbor on the northeastern tip of the island. Just as quickly they'd thrown the whole region into an uproar that had them battling Irish settlers along with the fishermen of the Mackinac Straits and the Michigan mainland. By 1850 they had driven almost all of the locals out of town except for the McKinleys.

The family had good relations with the Indians, who often stopped by on their way to and from fishing, sometimes just sitting in the store, curious to see its operations. As one of only two trading posts on the island, Cable's was of vital interest to local Natives.

"Because of my father's honorable treatment they loved him and their affection extended to our family," recalled twelve-year-old Sarah McKinley many years later, quoted in a memoir written by island historian Helen Collar. "Our home always had a welcome place, and scarcely a day passed but some of them received its hospitality... The Indians were all given food when they came, which they ate with much relish."

Thus, when McKinley sought their help, Chief Peaine and his men offered to "drive the Mormons into the Lake, meaning to exterminate them at once." Although this was off the table, Peaine and his men stayed with the McKinleys for the next two weeks and then marched into town under a white flag to confront Mormon "King" James Strang. Peaine reminded

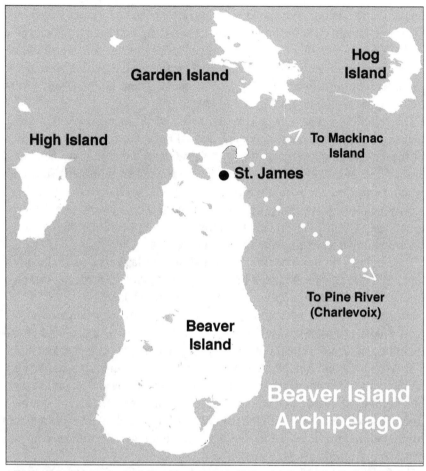

Following the arrival of the Mormons and the Irish, the Indians of Beaver Island retreated to Garden Island and High Island, with allotments granted to them in the Treaty of 1855.

Strang that the McKinleys had been island residents long before the Mormons arrived and the Indians had come to regard the trader as "more of a father than a stranger." He insinuated that the Mormons would be killed if the family was harmed, saying "If you do this I see a dark cloud hanging over you and your people."

The peace was settled for the time being, but with increasing numbers of Mormons arriving, the McKinleys fled to Ohio the following year. They returned a year later to find that their store had been burned down and five hundred cords of wood had been stolen.

Beaver Island had been a trading stop for Native peoples for thousands of years. Legend has it that it was the Beaver Clan - the *Amikwa* - who gave the island its name. French explorers continued the tradition, naming the archipelago the *Isles du Castor*, the Isles of Beaver. Called *Waguaong* by the Anishinaabek, its waters teemed with one of the richest freshwater fisheries on earth.

Following the French *voyageurs* was intrepid missionary priest, Father Baraga, who visited the island in 1832 on behalf of his sponsor, the Leopoldine Foundation of Austria. Father Baraga reported rather uncharitably that those living on the island were all "pagan Indians living in eight miserable huts."

Even so, the Beaver islands had been given to the Odawa and Ojibwe by the federal government as a reserve in the Treaty of 1836, but only for a period of five years, after which the Indians would be left to an uncertain fate. Annuity payment records show that Peaine was living on the island by 1839 with his wife, three sons and five daughters. In 1847 he was elected chief of the Beaver Island Archipelago when outgoing Chief Kinwabekisze left for the mainland.*

Almost immediately, Peaine found himself in the thick of Mormon aggression. But he also had other troubles to consider. The federal government began offering island land for sale in July, 1848 for around $1.25 per acre. Many Indian families retreated north to Garden Island and High Island to the northwest in order to continue their fishing trade and gardening unmolested.

Today, Beaver Island is a sleepy tourist destination reached by a ferry from Charlevoix on the mainland. The small town of St. James has a smattering of bars, restaurants and souvenir shops, yet most of the fifty-eight-square-mile island is heavily forested and crisscrossed by dirt lanes, with some best managed with four-wheel drive or on mountain bikes.

But in the 1840s and '50s, St. James Harbor on Beaver Island was one of the most important ports on the Great Lakes. A steamship required a staggering five hundred cords of firewood to make the trip between Buffalo, NY, and Chicago, and Beaver Island had 50,000 acres of forest along with an excellent harbor. In 1847, passing steamships were being supplied with one hundred cords of firewood per day, totaling some 20,000 cords per year. Axe men received fifty cents per cord for their efforts, with the wood selling for $1.50 per cord.

The waters around Beaver Island also teemed with lake trout, whitefish, perch, sturgeon and other fish species. Native fishermen did a brisk trade,

---

* Accounts differ on when Pay-zhick-way-we-dong was fully recognized as chief of the Garden Island Anishinaabek. Elsewhere he is said to have succeeded Kin-waw-be-kissee as chief in 1856.

sending barrels of salted fish to the mainland, while competing with French and Irish fishermen who had about one hundred cabins on the island.

It was into this scenario that future "King" James Jesse Strang arrived from Wisconsin on May 11, 1847 with four converts looking for a new home for his flock. Strang and his Saints arrived broke and in rags, according to an admiring historian/propagandist, Milo Quaife, who published *The Kingdom of Saint James* in 1930:

"So destitute of means were the Saints that they sold their blankets to pay for their steamer passage, and on reaching Big Beaver they went ashore with less than two days' supply of provisions and without a cent of money. Building themselves a shelter of hemlock boughs, they began a survey of the island, scantily clad and still more scantily fed... They camped for the night under the stars, without dinner, supper, or fire."

Strang, thirty-four, and his party had been denied lodging in town, a sign of things to come. And he was apparently so "scantily clad" that he had to stop and mend his torn trousers. But he liked what he saw, and somehow he and his party made their way home to spread the good news about Beaver Island being a likely place to create their slice of Zion.

A little background:

Born in 1805, young Joseph Smith, founder of the Latter Day Saints was reputedly a "lazy, careless and indolent person" in his youth who like many doofuses in upstate New York spent his time as a "money digger," searching for pirate treasure along the Hudson River, supposedly buried there by Captain William Kidd in 1698. Given to ecstatic visions and raised in a family of zealots, Smith was caught up in the religious fervor of America's "Great Awakening," which inspired numerous cults and spiritual movements across the country. Instead of pirate treasure, an angel named Moroni (a resurrected "Nephite historian" from 421 A.D.) led Smith to a cache of golden plates buried in a hill near his home. The plates were purportedly inscribed with ancient Judeo-Christian history and religious dogma dating back to 600 B.C.

Moroni never allowed Smith to take the plates, but he gleaned enough information from them to publish the *Book of Mormon* when he was twenty-four years old.* His new religion caught on like a barn fire and within a few years Smith and tens of thousands of followers made their way west to the Missouri Territory. Considered ignorant, impoverished blasphemers

* Curiously, Smith's story mirrors that of the Prophet Muhammad in 610 A.D., who was instructed by the Archangel Gabriel in a desert cave in Arabia, resulting in the creation of the Koran.

by many at a time when religion still inspired fighting words and blood-shed, the Mormons so alarmed the local population that Missouri's gover-nor ordered their extermination unless they departed.

Regrouping at Navoo, Illinois in 1844, Smith ordered the destruction of the printing press of a dissident group of Mormons after their newspaper, the *Navoo Expositor*, criticized his growing power and practice of po-lygamy. It was the newspaper's first and only issue. Suppression of the *Expositor* ignited a riot for which Smith and his brother Hyrum were blamed. While awaiting trial for treason in Carthage, Illinois, Smith was dragged from the jailhouse by a mob of men in blackened faces. Hyrum was shot in the face and died instantly; Smith got off three shots from a pepperbox pistol supplied by a friend, but was shot several times in return. He died in the street, only thirty-eight years old.

Then began a power struggle between Mormon high-ups Brigham Young and James Strang. Strang produced a letter, allegedly written by Smith, which passed on the leadership of the church to him. He also came up with six tiny brass plates inscribed with hieroglyphics on each side, which Strang claimed to have deciphered by viewing them through *Urim* and *Thummim*, two magical "peek stones" passed on by Smith. Add to that, Strang said that an angel had vouched for his leadership. Who could argue with an angel?

Long story short, Young led his followers to establish Salt Lake City in Utah, while Strang gathered his people at Voree, Wisconsin, southwest of Milwaukee, and from there on to Beaver Island with the promise of free land and safety from the hated gentiles. On July 8, 1850, Strang an-nounced that a divine source had given him the brass "Plates of Laban," a pre-Babylonian record of religious teachings that had once been kept in the Ark of the Covenant. The translation revealed that God Himself had commanded Strang to re-establish his kingdom on earth at Beaver Island.

Thus, Strang began building his own Zion in the Michigan wilderness.

Within a year of Strang's survey hundreds of Mormons were making their way to Beaver Island, driving out the Irish fishermen and other settlers. Some of the evicted fled to Pine River (present-day Charlevoix) on the mainland, others to Mackinac Island, from which they battled the Saints over the next decade. There was also a rough fishing camp on rainy, wind-swept Gull Island to the west where a few fishermen eked out a miserable existence. According to the 1850 census, 74 percent of the island's 483 residents were Mormons, with most non-Mormons living on the north end of the island. By 1852, the Mormons managed to drive everyone off the island who was not a Saint. Having established his own religious realm, Strang declared himself king.

Prior to the takeover, Mormon emigrants met with hostility when they landed at Whiskey Point. "They were frequently met with threats on the boat's deck, and always on the wharf," Strang wrote in his book, *Ancient and Modern Michilimackinac*. "A dozen men would generally surround a family of emigrants and order them back on the boat, telling them that they were preparing to drive off and kill all the Mormons..."

Local men also attacked Mormons building a tabernacle in town. Some took to disrupting prayer meetings until the Mormons countered by dragging them outside and beating them with sticks. For their part, Mormons were accused of attacking fishermen out on the lake, stealing their fish, killing crews and scuttling their boats, although none of this was ever proven.

Plans were hatched to attack the Mormons during the July 4 celebrations of 1850, at which time a large number of armed men gathered at Whiskey Point from Mackinac Island. Strang wrote that the conspirators planned to attend a prayer meeting with pistols and knives concealed beneath their clothing and then stage a fight, using their weapons to "disable or kill all of the leaders, before they had time to rally, arm or make a stand. This was to be followed up by a general debauching of the women, and burning of houses."

The Mormons caught wind of the plot, however, dumping some of the conspirators' gun powder into the lake and packing their whiskey with tobacco to get them uproariously drunk and stoned. They also placed a company of their own armed men on a ship in the harbor, ready for action.

On the morning of July 4, the Mormons began firing a cannon just shy of Peter McKinley's trading post where the mob was headquartered, ostensibly as a holiday salute, but actually determining the range. Later that day Mormon representatives stopped by to inform McKinley that "he would be held responsible for any attack from any quarter; and the first gun fired would be the signal for destroying his establishment and every soul in it."

Cowed, and with reinforcements failing to arrive from fishermen on the other islands, the attack was called off.

Through all of this Strang managed to establish the town of St. James, built roads across the island, launched northern Michigan's first newspaper, *The Northern Islander*, and got himself elected as a Democrat to the Michigan State Legislature. He also went to war against the whiskey trade, reeled in the lucrative fish market, and profited from supplying fuel to passing steamships. Taking a page from Joseph Smith, who had as many as forty wives, Strang also became a polygamist, marrying at least five women. He urged his inner circle to take up the polygamous path and about twenty of them obliged.

During a visit to Detroit in 1851 President Millard Fillmore was so scandalized by lurid reports of Strang's backwoods harem that he authorized a raid on the Mormon leader's palace and his band of "buccaneers." One night the following May, the *U.S.S. Michigan*, an iron-hulled warship that patrolled the Great Lakes, pulled into Paradise Bay at Beaver Island. Down its gangplank went a district attorney, leading a party of sailors armed with pistols and cutlasses to Strang's home by the light of a lantern. The D.A. claimed to have found a lavish seraglio upstairs "heavily draped with stunning calico" that was "occupied by Mormon women four in a bed." In another telling, Strang was home with only one of his wives, twenty-year-old Elvira. He and thirty-eight Mormon officials were charged with a kitchen sink of crimes including treason, robbing the mail, counterfeiting, trespass and theft among others, but the charges didn't stick.

The early 1850s were marked by gun battles, beatings, insurrection, an attempted kidnapping and other mayhem between the Mormons and their opponents. Perhaps it was only their lack of cowboy hats and horses that kept the rootin'-tootin' Wild Northwest from being as celebrated in pop culture as is the Wild West.

One other story bears repeating: the Battle of Pine River.

By 1853, Strang had established Emmet County on the mainland with plans to settle some of his flock there in order to control the entire coast of northern Lower Michigan. This did not go over well with the fishermen who'd been driven from the island and were now stuck working at a distance from their fishery. On July 13 a Mormon sheriff and thirteen Saints set out from Beaver Island to round up some residents of Pine River who had been selected for jury duty. Instead, they were ambushed by seventy armed men from the beach and bluffs of the mainland who poured a "murderous fire" into their ranks, wounding six Mormons. Fleeing, the Mormons rowed for their lives in two boats with thirty miles of open water between them and safety. Pursuing them were three boatloads of men bent on their destruction, one of which contained twenty-five rawboned, hard-living fishermen. With their boat riddled with gunfire and death being certain, the fleeing Mormons managed to hail the *Morgan*, a ship bound for Chicago, which took them on board just in time.

Strang liked to think of himself as a defender of the Indians of the island archipelago, who he felt were being cheated in the fishing trade. Initially, he wrote, the fishermen were "all Indians and Frenchmen who lived in a state of barbarism and misery, and were almost, and in some instances quite slaves to the traders. Their summers were spent in wigwams of the worst kind on the Lake shores, nearly destitute of clothing, and not infrequently reduced to subsist on fish alone for weeks. The traders so conducted their business that the fishermen were generally in debt. But if by any means one had a continual run of good success and got a little capital at command, he was induced to lay it out in whiskey..."

Strang wrote that the Indians were frequently robbed of their fish by "the worst class of men," who plundered Native fishermen without mercy.

"Numbers of them are known who boast of the amounts they have made by taking fish out of the open barrels of the Indians from night to night and placing them in their own. On a fishery where a dozen Indians were engaged, they were often plundered in this way to the amount of one hundred barrels in a season."

Native fishermen, Strang added, "did not dare resent these or greater outrages, when discovered."

Strang outlawed liquor in the islands, creating more enemies among the whiskey traders while improving conditions at the Indian villages on Garden and High islands.

He had a far different view of the events at McKinley's trading post in the winter of 1851 which began this chapter. In his telling, traders at the north end of the island began inciting the Indians against the Mormons. He claimed that Peaine and other headmen visited him under a red flag with thirty warriors painted for war, along with thirteen gentiles and two interpreters. After a long talk in which Peaine demanded that trade and timber sales be conducted through the traders alone and not the Mormons, Strang reminded the whites that it was a federal crime to incite Indians to warfare. He then coldly addressed Chief Peaine, saying, "I am no child, and I cannot understand you. Your voice is like a scolding woman. I will not hear you. March on."

Through the years, Strang's autocratic style produced enemies and defectors among his flock. He even dictated prudish dress codes for women in the mode of an *ayatollah*. Thus, in 1856, four disaffected Saints conspired to commit regicide. Thomas Bedford had been flogged for adultery after being caught in bed with another man's wife. Dr. H.D. McCulloch was a Mormon official who had been excommunicated for drunkenness and bad behavior. Alexander Wentworth and Dr. J. Atkyn were two enemies from Mackinac Island. The foursome began practicing with pistols, laying plans for an ambush.

Strang knew there was a plot against him but declined to arm himself or accept any bodyguards. Perhaps he believed that God and the angels would protect him despite the example of Joseph Smith.

On June 16, 1856, Strang was called to the dock at St. James where the *U.S.S. Michigan* lay moored. There, in front of the officers and men of the naval vessel, he was shot in the back three times by Wentworth and Bedford, then pistol-whipped as he fell with a bullet severing his spine. Captain McBlair took the murderers onboard, refusing to surrender them to the Mormon's sheriff. They were taken to Mackinac Island where they were hailed as heroes after a sham trial.

As for Strang, he lived another twenty-three days in agony, dying at his parents' home in Voree on July 9, 1856 at the age of forty-three.

King Strang had appointed no successor, nor did he have a slate of disciples who could step in to fill his shoes. Without any leadership, the Mormon colony quickly disintegrated under a wave of raids from Mackinac Island and the mainland. Soon after Strang's death a drunken mob of eighty armed fishermen, traders and off-duty soldiers from Fort Mackinac landed on the island and began rounding up Mormon farmers and their families, herding them onto steamships at Paradise Bay. A group of 490 were taken to Chicago with others dispersed to Detroit, Cleveland and Buffalo. Within days 2,600 Mormons had been driven from the island, leaving their homes and possessions to be plundered in a drunken reign that went on for weeks.

As for Chief Peaine, during the Civil War Sarah McKinley returned to Beaver Island to visit family and friends. "One afternoon... who should appear at the door but Peaine, older, bowed with years, but welcome still," she wrote. "I could scarcely believe my eyes. Peaine recognized me and remarked that the first time he saw me I was only 'so high,' illustrating with his hand my age by my size at that time. Remarking that I was now grown and married, he naively inquired, 'Have you any papooses?' 'No,' I said. 'Too bad,' replied the Chief."

Peaine had done better; he had four wives, lived to an old age, and had many descendants. During the Treaty of 1855 the lands of High Island and Garden Island were withdrawn from sale and were allotted in parcels to the Indians living on them. Their villages proved to be economically unsustainable in the twentieth century, however, and most of the island land reverted to the State of Michigan for nonpayment of property taxes. All that remains of the Indians who once lived here is the Garden Island Indian Cemetery, the site of 3,500 Native graves, including a number of low-lying "spirit houses" crafted of bark and branches, which mark the burial sites. Today, Garden Island is mostly visited by day-trippers on sailboats and deer hunters in the fall.

The Irish eviction sign on Beaver Island. By the time the Irish arrived in the 1850s, the Odawa had moved to land reserved for them on the Garden and High islands. Ironically, no sign on the island notes the eviction of the Indians.

CHAPTER • 32

THE LUCK OF THE IRISH

At the very same time that King Strang and his Saints were struggling with their version of Zion, a strange coda to the Beaver Island saga was transpiring 4,000 miles away off the northwestern coast of Ireland.

Far across the North Atlantic, the gaunt, half-starved residents of Arranmore Island endured a fate similar to that of the Potawatomi at Chi-Chipe-Outpe in Indiana. Although they were a world apart, the Irish and the Indians had a similar experience with genocide. Like the Indians, the Irish were held to be sub-human by many Europeans, "a race of utter savages," in the view of a medieval Welsh monk.* In a disparaging take on

---

* Popular German travel writer Johann Georg Kohl, who spent time with both the Ojibwe of Lake Superior and the Irish during the 1850s wrote that the living conditions of the Ojibwe rivaled or excelled that of the Irish. Like many other writers, he had a low opinion of the Irish peasants.

Darwin, some British scientists claimed that the Irish, Blacks and other persons of color were indeed descended from apes, while the English were created and blessed by God.

The story of the Irish and other brutalized Europeans sheds some light on the dog-eat-dog mentality of those who fled the troubles of the Old World, only to impose them on the Indians with a callous disregard.

With the breath of the sea creeping in a fog over the land one morning in April, 1851, 163 survivors of the Irish Potato Famine were roused by the county sheriff and his men who came from the mainland with picks and battering rams to knock down the stone walls of the homes they had lived in for generations.

Crying, cursing and wailing, with their scant possessions piled up in the dirt outside and their children running screaming through the lanes, the peasants were thrown out of their homes by the island's new owner, John Stouppe Charley. A lawyer and land speculator, Charley had purchased Arranmore and its farmsteads for £5,000 (in another account, only £200). His first move was to rid the island of its impoverished sub-tenants.

An Irish landlord exercised much the same power over his "cottars" as did a slaveholder in the American South. "Nothing satisfies him but an unlimited submissiveness," wrote travel writer Arthur Young in 1780. "Disrespect or anything tending toward sauciness he may punish with his cane or his horsewhip."

Young also fumed that some landowners even demanded sexual services of their tenants, some of who felt "honored to have their wives and daughters sent to the bed of their master."

But it was also true that a landlord who pushed too far risked the wrath of secret societies such as the Molly McGuires or the Whiteboys, who might kill a prized stallion, club hunting dogs to death, drive a herd over a cliff, or deliver a savage beating in the night. Perhaps even stretch a neck.

Sub-tenants were illiterate subsistence farmers who eked out a living on small patches of farmland, paying rent twice a year to an absentee landlord. When this hand-to-mouth system became unprofitable, as was the case during the famine, many Irish landlords decided to cut their tenants loose in order to raise cattle for the market in Britain.

Arranmore Island encompasses 8.5 square miles in County Donegal, on the northwestern rim of Ireland. It's a mostly treeless patchwork of fields divided by rock walls and browsed by sheep alongside lanes that are best suited for walking or cycling. Shell middens show that Árainn Mhór (as it is known in Gaelic) was settled at least three thousand years ago and there are still Bronze Age ruins to be found there, including a circular fortress backed by high cliffs overlooking the Atlantic.

These same cliffs were where many of the starving people of Arranmore tossed the corpses of their dead during what they called "The Great Hunger" of the famine, lacking the funds for proper burials.

Ironically, the Irish were in such straits due to their reliance on the potato - a gift from the Indians of South America.

Spaniards brought the first potatoes home from South America in 1570. For more than one hundred years the lowly potato was suspected of being poisonous, too gross to consider eating, and fit for only animals. Farmers in Burgundy were forbidden to plant potatoes under the notion that they caused leprosy, clearly evident from the "eyes," which looked like the deformed fingers of lepers. Peasants preferred moldy bread or an empty stomach to dining on "deadly" potatoes. Gradually, however, the potato was accepted by royals as an exotic menu item, but sparingly.

It was the deepening of the Little Ice Age, however, that made the potato palatable to its nay-sayers. Protected from the cold by its growth underground and highly prolific, the potato was an obvious food choice during the coldest years of the Little Ice Age from 1680-1730. The British began feeding potatoes to their poor by 1700 and the Irish quickly followed suit. This led to a population boom in Ireland with the peasants of the entire country becoming dependent on the potato as virtually their only food source. When an unstoppable blight of *Phytophthora infestans* rotted potatoes to a black mush in the fields across Europe in the mid-1800s, hundreds of thousands of starving Irish looked to their only hope of salvation, far across the ocean to where the Indians lived.

Once, Arranmore marked the end of the known world, a windswept place at the edge of a boundless sea, beyond which lay only spirits and monsters. Prior to the Bronze Age the islanders' lives were similar to those of the Indians of North America, engaging in primitive agriculture supplemented by hunting, fishing and foraging. By the 1800s, the Catholic Irish still had many pagan beliefs in line with those of America's Indians. Deeply superstitious, they believed in fairies, witches, ghosts and the wailing spirits of banshees. Some Irish laborers refused to level Indian mounds at Grand Rapids in the 1800s for fear of rousing Native spirits.

Supernatural forces could be blamed for human failings. Infanticide was practiced by claiming that one's perfect baby had been stolen by fairies and replaced with a deformed infant; the unfortunate newborn might be abandoned in the crook of a tree in the cynical hope that the "kidnapped" baby would be returned by the fairies.

The fate of Arranmore's people was sealed centuries ago with the colonization of Ireland by England. Beginning in the 1550s, the British began

"Bridget O'Donnell and Her Children," an engraving from the Illustrated London News, 1849. A landlord's hired men battered down the walls of Bridget's home as she lay starving and sick in bed. She was cast out on the rural roads with her children to an uncertain fate. Hers is believed to have been the first "human interest" story ever published in a newspaper.

subjugating the wild Irish with the goal of "civilizing" a people who lived in sod huts with their livestock, along with tons of manure piled up outside.*

The plan by Protestant England was to rid the island of Catholicism, although as events played out nearly five centuries later, nothing of the sort happened.

The British established the Ulster Plantation in which the lands of Irish Catholics in six northern counties were confiscated and colonized by more than 150,000 Protestants from the Scottish lowlands, with another 21,000 emigrating from Wales and England.

In 1641 the Irish rebelled, killing thousands of English colonists. Oliver Cromwell conquered the rebels in 1652 in a series of country-wide massacres. In lieu of taking heads as trophies of war, the British began offering bounties for Irish scalps, a practice that would soon make its way to North America. (In a subsequent rebellion in 1798, the British would punish Irish rebels by coating their heads with pitch and lighting them on fire.)

Even Arranmore suffered under the English conquest. In November, 1641, the island was invaded by Cromwell's soldiers. While the local men took to their boats, sixty-seven women and children hid in a cave on the south side of the island. Just as they were leaving, the English spotted a child outside the cave's entrance. Their captain ordered his soldiers to kill everyone hiding in what became known as the Cave of Slaughter.

*"Where there's muck there's luck" was a proverb among the Irish poor, meaning plenty of manure ensured a good crop.

As with the Indians, the Irish were considered barely human by many Europeans and fair game for slavery. Dublin was a major slave port from 871-1102 A.D., with Irish slaves sold throughout Europe, first by Viking invaders, and then the English.

The British shipped tens of thousands of Irish as convict slaves to North and South America and the West Indies starting in 1612, continuing the practice long into the 1700s. Petty thieves, rabble-rousers, political prisoners and prostitutes were frequent targets. Historian Colin Heaton notes that Irish slaves were a bargain; on the island of Montserrat, the price for a black slave was a hefty twenty to fifty pounds sterling, whereas an Irish convict could be traded for nine hundred pounds of cotton, or for tobacco or indigo at far lower cost.

Much has been written about the practice of transporting English and Irish convicts to slavery in Australia during the eighteenth century, but this was also the fate of tens of thousands of "the King's Passengers" to the Caribbean and North America. Beginning in 1615, the British began shipping criminals across the ocean to colonies in Maryland, Virginia and Georgia. The British stepped up the practice after 1718, sending more than sixty thousand convict slaves to the Americas.

At a time when the nobles of Britain owned virtually all of the common land, some of the nineteen crimes liable for transportation were as slim as "impersonating an Egyptian"; stealing roots, trees or plants; stealing fish from a pond or a river; and the grand larceny theft of anything over the value of a shilling - about one-eighth of an English pound.

Prisoners sentenced to the colonies considered it a death sentence, which in the steamy, malaria-stricken plantations of sugar cane and cotton was often the case. The Irish and other "lesser races" were fair game as slaves in the seventeenth and eighteenth centuries (and, with the Chinese, *de facto* slaves during the canal-digging and railroad building eras of the nineteenth century). In the 1886 novel, *Kidnapped* by Robert Louis Stevenson, there's a plot by an evil uncle to shanghai the rightful young heir, David Balfour, into slavery in South Carolina, from which he will never return.

The life of the Irish peasants was no less arduous, but at least they had their homes, hearths, and bellies full of potatoes until the banshees of starvation and eviction came wailing at their doors.

By the 1800s, Arranmore was under the ownership of a lord of the Irish peerage known as the Marquess Burton-Conyngham.

According to an 1845 account by Thomas Campbell Foster in the *Times of London*, Conyngham visited his island possession only once during his lifetime, and then for only a few days. As an absentee landlord, he hired a manager named John Benbow to run his estate and collect rents twice a year from his tenants.

When the famine hit, filling the fields with rotten potatoes, neither Conyngham or Benbow lifted a finger to aid their tenants, who were reduced to eating seaweed to survive. As Foster reported in the *Times*: "from one end of his large estate to the other, nothing is to be found but poverty, misery, wretched cultivation, and infinite subdivision of land."

In 1847, Quakers sent two ships from Liverpool with supplies of peas, rice, meal, biscuits and beef to aid the island's two thousand starving residents. Another ship arrived with a cargo of "Indian meal" from America, but this corn was a rotten mash by the time it arrived, infested with maggots and weevils. It was eaten nonetheless, cooked over a slow fire.

Relief efforts were too few and too late for many of those weakened by hunger and suffering from dysentery, scurvy, typhus and fever. Thirteen thousand died of starvation and disease in County Donegal under Conygngham's tenure.

It was amid this dismal scenario that John Stouppe Charley arrived, purchasing Arranmore in 1849 from the marquess.

Abandoning the centuries-old tradition of small farmsteads, Charley decided to consolidate his holdings into larger farms by reducing the island's population. This was justified by demanding rent receipts from his tenants, who had either never received one, or being illiterate, had thrown theirs away. Others had been too poor to pay up.

Charley gave his deadbeat tenants a ghastly choice: either march to the county poorhouse at the town of Glenties on the mainland or take a chance aboard a ship bound for North America. Neither was a desirable option: the Irish in America were held as virtual slaves, digging canals and serving as cannon fodder in the army. That, and transports to North America were called "coffin ships" because many of them sank in the North Atlantic, or were rife with vermin, hunger and disease. The alternative was just as bad, since the poorhouses of Ireland and England were, if anything, meant to punish and dissuade starving people who had nowhere else to turn.

A 2003 article in the *Beaver Island Beacon* describes what happened next:

"Many chose the poorhouse because they were so weak and malnourished that they did not feel they could survive an ocean crossing. But the facility at Glenties was already overcrowded – its death rate was the highest in the country because it had been built in a swamp and flooded much of the year. Even the officials admitted that it reeked of death. Its charges were given clumps of old straw as their bed, with six or seven forced to sleep in a bundle for warmth, under a single filthy rag... The braver ones forced off Arranmore went to Donegal Town, marching there on foot from Burtonport to board (Charley's) boat – but it was not there!"

Eventually, Charley sent his evicted tenants to Toronto, Canada on two ships provided by American Quakers.

Living among a large group of Irish immigrants in Toronto the Arranmore refugees heard good reports of Beaver Island from Black John Bonner, a swarthy fisherman who had persevered through the Mormon hardships at his shack on Gull Island. Add to this, a laborer named Charles O'Donnell was living in Toronto with his wife Grace and three children. While working on the local railroad, Charles was entrusted with the company's payroll, which he promptly stole, fleeing across the border to Detroit. Thereafter, he took a job on a lighthouse construction crew on Beaver Island and fell in love with the place, writing to his family and friends that the island was much like Arranmore and was filled with abandoned Mormon homes that were there for the taking. Returning to Toronto, he became an Irish Moses, leading his people to Beaver Island and the promised land of Michigan.

Today, Arranmore and Beaver are "sister" islands connected by tradition. A sign on the main street through St. James in Beaver Island commemorates the "Irish Eviction and Emigration" with these words:

"(Charley) decreed that whomever was not a full tenant had to leave Arranmore *that day*. All 163 subtenants were forced off the island and their tiny homes destroyed so that they could never return."

The people of Arranmore were hardly alone in their forced eviction; gangs of soldiers, constables and bailiffs were hired to raze the homes of peasants in many villages across Ireland. Prior to being forced to flee down the road with whatever possessions they could gather, a family's cows, pigs, sheep and food stores would be seized for back-payment of rent. An eyewitness said the mayhem was attended by "the screaming of children, the wild wailing of mothers... roofs and walls tumbling down."

The 100,000 beds of Ireland's 130 workhouses were quickly overwhelmed and filled to bursting, with many families begging at their doors for scraps of food. Across the country roadside ditches were filled with skeletal corpses, their mouths stuffed with grass.

Starvation and disease killed 1.1 million during Ireland's famine, with another two million fleeing the country for the Americas and Australia. In a ten-year period from 1845 to 1855, Ireland lost one-third of its 8.2 million population.

Of course, not everyone arriving from Ireland was as destitute as the Arranmore survivors. Some were simply plucky young men and women seeking their fortunes. Others were among the Scotch-Irish of the Ulster Plantation who soured on the old sod.

"In one of history's great migrations, nearly a quarter-million Scots-Irish left Ulster for British North America between 1717 and 1775," wrote Roxanne Dunbar-Ortiz in *An Indigenous Peoples' History of the United States*. "Although a number left for religious reasons, the majority were losers in the struggle over Britain's Irish policies, which brought economic ruin to Ireland's wool and linen industries."

Arriving poor, land-hungry and of warlike disposition, the Scotch-Irish made their way into Virginia and the Carolinas where they rained hell on the Indians, eventually forcing their way over the Appalachians. Thus, both the conquerors of Ireland and the conquered became problems for the Indians of North America over the course of two hundred years.

The experience of the Irish migration was shared by many other hardluck Europeans. This included a massive wave of Germans, with an estimated 100,000 arriving in America between 1700 and 1775, with many more hot on their heels. Many came from the Palatine lands of the southern Rhine, which were plagued by religious violence, famine and warfare. The Thirty Years War convulsed the region from 1618 to 1648 with up to eight million killed. Fearing military conscription and the ever-present threats of famine and war, the Germans had plenty of motivation to flee seven hundred miles down the Rhine and across the ocean to the relative safety of Pennsylvania.

Some 5.5 million Germans and 3.7 million from neighboring Austria-Hungary would emigrate to America between 1820-1920, with 4.4 million emigrating from Ireland. Typically, the habit of "chain migration" was what lured people in the Old Country to America. An immigrant would write positive reports of life in America to friends and family back home, who would eagerly make plans to emigrate. Yet, crossing the Atlantic aboard crowded, disease- and hunger-ridden ships was such a horrible experience that few elected to return to Europe, thus breaking ties to the Old World forever.

Finns and Swedes, Belgians, Austrians, Czechs, Danes, Swiss, Welsh, and an alphabet of nationalities fled Europe to the American Midwest in the 1800s, with freed slaves, black sharecroppers, Asians and Arabs arriving thereafter in the 1900s.

For many of these arrivals it was "every man for himself," and every woman too, and to hell with anyone who stood in the way. As noted by historian Dunbar earlier: "What the Michigan pioneer wanted was the Indian's land. What became of the Indian did not concern him."

CHAPTER 33

1855

One summer day in late May of 1858, the citizens of Grand Rapids, Michigan woke to find the first in a wave of hundreds of canoes and flatboats crowded with Indians and all of their belongings. The Odawa of the Grand River Valley were leaving.

Waiting for them was a small overcrowded steamer, the *Forest Queen*, which ferried Native families to Grand Haven on the Lake Michigan coast. From there they took another ship, the *Huron*, to the port of Pentwater sixty miles to the north. Subsequent bands of up to one hundred Odawa arrived throughout the coming year, with the last group leaving in November, 1859.

For more than twenty years the Odawa had clung to their villages along the Grand, Thornapple and Muskegon rivers following the Treaty of 1836, refusing to leave. And why should they? Nothing in the way of permanence had been promised in the reservations held out to them and even these were being seized by white squatters. The Indians had no "strong titles" to the lands set aside for them in 1836.

They had also been granted $18,000 annually in cash and goods and there was no compelling reason to abandon the villages they had lived in for generations. Payment days at Grand Rapids were festive events, drawing hundreds to camp on four islands in the river or along its banks.

Payments were made in a warehouse at a steamboat landing near present-day Market Avenue. Running down the center of the warehouse was a long table piled with coins and receipts. Checking in with agents and their interpreters, the Indians would make their mark, collect their cash and exit the back door where a crowd of traders stood waiting with irresistible goods along with the expectation of settling debts.

But the last dwindling payment of $10,000 had been doled out to 1,500 Odawa on Oct. 29, 1857, with future payments to be made to the north at Pentwater. After more than one hundred years of living in the Grand River Valley, the Odawa were heading north to an uncertain future.

In the wake of the Treaty of 1836 the Odawa, Ojibwe and Potawatomi of Michigan found themselves alone. Gone were their neighbors to the south:

the once mighty tribes of the Shawnee, Miami and Illinois had been dissipated by disease, hunger and warfare, then dispossessed of their land and pushed west of the Mississippi. Gone were the Mascouten and Wyandot, absorbed into other tribes or exiled to Oklahoma. The Fox and Sauk to the west had been hammered into oblivion, the Winnebago maintained a precarious back-and-forth existence. To the east the great Longhouse of the Iroquois was reduced to that of a matchbox. The peoples of forty tribes had been shuttled off to the treeless plains of Indian Territory in Kansas, Oklahoma and Texas. Gone too were all their lands, sold off to settlers, plowed to furrows or stripped of their timber by loggers. Cities crowded with a mongrel mix of churches and saloons along their muddy streets now rose in places that had once been Indian villages: Grand Rapids, Flint, Saginaw, Toledo, Chillicothe, Fort Wayne... Only in Michigan did the Odawa, Ojibwe and a small number of Potawatomi live on, yet with no clear title to any of the lands that had been "reserved" for them in 1836.

Yet, despite having purchased all of Michigan's land from the Indians in the treaties of 1807, 1819, 1821, 1836 and 1842 the U.S. Government had never figured out what to *do* with the Native peoples who still remained on the land. Endemic racism and cultural differences hardened by hundreds of years made assimilation into white society impossible. "Whiteness" itself was a fairly new concept created by Europeans of mixed backgrounds coming together in the face of threats from the Indians on the frontier in the 1700s; this, along with justifications of slavery by claiming superiority over blacks. In the 1840s whites were only beginning to allow admittance to the "lesser" races of the Irish, Italians and East Europeans, but there was no room in this supremacist scenario for Blacks, Asians or Indians. Even Catholics and Jews were *persona non grata* in Protestant, white America.

With their reservations guaranteed for no more than five years, some of the Odawa in the Grand River Valley had purchased their own land in the late 1830s and '40s. But since the Indians were not yet U.S. citizens, some officials believed they could not legally purchase land; at the very least their titles would likely be contested.* Thus, land purchases were made almost entirely through the help of friendly traders, white relatives or missionaries. Acreage was purchased for the creation of villages at Lowell, Holland, the Thornapple River and in the vicinity of Grand Rapids. One exception was a headman, Paquodush, who was able to purchase land in his own name at Fort Village in Ottawa County. He and other Odawa sold their land in the late 1850s when new reservations were created further north.

* The Indians were declared U.S. citizens in 1924 but did not have full rights until 1953.

Others moved north to their relatives at Grand Traverse and Little Traverse bays or to traditional Odawa homelands such as Manitoulin and Walpole islands in Canada. Many simply stayed put in their historic villages in the Grand River Valley, taking a wait-and-see attitude.

Although the Odawa of Lower Michigan continued living communally and kept on with their traditional pursuits of hunting, fishing and gathering, they also took a stab at the white man's ways of farming and husbandry, building cabins, plowing fields and joining churches. This was helpful in demonstrating that they had been "civilized" in 1854 when they appealed to the federal government to grant clear titles to their reserves.

Even the Bureau of Indian Affairs had to admit that the goals of the Treaty of 1836 had not been met: the Odawa and Ojibwe had not been resettled on the reserves set aside for them, nor had they been assimilated into white society. Into this scenario stepped a new Commissioner of Indian Affairs, George Manypenny, who succeeded Luke Lea in 1853.

In 1849, Congress had created the Department of the Interior, transferring the office of Indian Affairs from the War Department. With the transfer came a more enlightened approach toward the Indians: Manypenny was opposed to removing Native peoples to west of the Mississippi. He proposed granting private property - called allotments - to the Indians within their own reserves, serving as a buffer against whiskey traders and other bad influences while encouraging agriculture, education, religion and the pursuit of jobs in neighboring communities.

To that end, Manypenny set aside townships of thirty-six square miles each in remote areas of Michigan where the Odawa and Ojibwe could claim their own acreage on land that had not already been claimed by white settlers. Heads of households could select allotments of eighty acres and single men over the age of twenty-one could select forty acres.

There were actually two treaties signed at Detroit in 1855. One was with the Odawa and Ojibwe of western Michigan on July 31, 1855. A second treaty was signed two days later with those living in the Saginaw River Valley, along with the nearby bands of Swan Creek and Black River. As noted in the chapter on Chief Buffalo, a third treaty had been signed at La Pointe in 1854 for those living at the western end of Lake Superior, Wisconsin and Minnesota.

In all the "Ottawa and Chippewa Tribe" of the Grand River Valley, as it was legally noted, was granted 776,320 acres along Lakes Michigan and Superior, while the Saginaw, Swan Creek and Black River bands were granted 138,240 acres in Isabella County. Indian agents were supposed to compile lists of heads of households and single persons eligible for land ownership on these reserves no later than July 1, 1856. After that deadline no more applications would be accepted and eligible Indians would have five years to select their parcels on the set-aside land. After the five-year period was completed, any Indian lands that had not been selected would be available for sale to white settlers or to other Indians. After ten years of ownership, a Native owner would have the power of alienation, meaning that he could sell his land.

Yet the 1856 deadline did not provide nearly enough time to compile lists of eligible Indians, scuttling any chance for the selection of land.

Five townships were set aside for the Grand River Valley Indians in Mason, Oceana and Muskegon County with the closest towns of any size being Ludington, Muskegon and Pentwater. Six townships were set aside in Isabella County for the Saginaw River Valley people in the vicinity of Mount Pleasant. Similar arrangements were made in the Upper Peninsula, and in the Grand Traverse and Little Traverse regions of the Lower Peninsula.

The lands selected for settlement were mostly isolated, sandy patches of poor soil; hardly a good start for nascent farmers who were inexperienced with plowing and modern agriculture. White settlers who were already living in the townships set aside for the Indians had to be accommodated, meaning that only land that was not already occupied was available.

The federal government's new scheme was also calculated to break up the traditional, collective way of life that had united the Anishinaabek for centuries. An Indian farmer on eighty acres of land would find himself cut off from his people and possibly surrounded by white landowners with whom he had no sense of community. He had the temporary support of the government to get his farm up and running, but that aid wasn't intended to last forever.

Manypenny also set barriers for the new reservations to get rid of whiskey traders and other nuisances. Non-Indians were not allowed to enter reservations or use their resources without permission. Nor could a Native who was not proficient in English and deemed "competent" sell his property without permission.

Native peoples who occupied their land for ten years would be issued full-title "patents" signed by the president of the United States. Unfortunately, these patents were delayed until the 1870s, by which time Indian landowners faced a raft of complications from white squatters and speculators.

In exchange for relinquishing all claims on the homeland from which they were ejected, the Grand River Valley bands received $538,400 in goods and services, while the Saginaw River bands received $220,000.

They were also supposed to be furnished with interpreters, mechanics, farm instructors, blacksmiths, gunsmiths, cattle and farm tools. The treaty also dissolved the "Ottawa and Chippewa Tribe," representing the Grand River Valley bands, meaning that they had no legal standing whatsoever years down the road when further complications arose.

Initially, Manypenny wanted to pay the Indians off with a lump sum for debts the government owed them from the failure of past treaties. The idea was to get the feds off the hook of providing for the Indians with no end in sight. Anishinaabek leaders rejected this plan, seeking to obtain federal aid indefinitely. As a compromise, a ten-year trust fund was established, subject to renegotiation.

Both Anishinaabek and federal negotiators came away from signing the treaty with a sense of optimism that the Indians would finally have a secure home in Michigan where they belonged. But this was not to be.

On many of the townships granted to the Indians the best land had already been claimed by white settlers or timber companies. Add to that, the State of Michigan had a legal claim to "swamp and overflow" land, which included much of what had been granted to the Indians. This, and large sections of the Indian townships had been granted to the Sault Ste. Marie Ship Canal Company, with land sales used to fund construction of the canal.

In western Michigan the Grand River bands arrived to find poor, sandy soil and tracts of pine and hemlock that were useless for farming. There was a similar mess in Isabella County where Indian agent Andrew Fitch dithered for years without confirming any land allotments for the Saginaw bands. Land allotments weren't granted until 1861, but it wasn't until 1864 that five hundred full title patents were issued nine years after the treaty had been signed.

Nor did the Indians receive all of the funds due to them from the federal government until they forced the issue in a lawsuit conducted fifty years later.

At Keweenaw Bay in the Upper Peninsula, the allotment system was a scenario for starvation. The six townships granted in the Treaty of La Pointe were heavily forested, yet members of the band were expected to select eighty and forty-acre plots for farming. Native peoples of the north had enough experience with gardening to know that it was an iffy proposition at best with the fickle weather of the region; thus the idea of adopting the white man's mode of agriculture was ludicrous. As with other bands of the Ojibwe living in Ontonagon and Gogebic counties their survival depended on traveling through the seasons: to rivers when the fish were running, to nut groves in the fall, maple groves in the spring, and to warmer micro-climates such as Lake Michigamme for hunting its marshes when

Biboon, the cruel north wind and spirit of the winter swept their villages on Lake Superior. As with their relatives in Lower Michigan, the U.P. bands continued their traditional lifestyle which relied primarily on fishing and foraging.

Through all of these troubles Indians everywhere were painted with the broad brush of hysteria by the newspapers of the day in the wake of battles to the far West. In the aftermath of 1862's Dakota War in Minnesota, a kangaroo court sentenced three hundred men to death. President Lincoln commuted the sentences of all but thirty-eight who were hung at Mankato, MN, on the day after Christmas, 1862, which remains the largest single mass execution in U.S. history. This was followed up by Red Cloud's War in 1866, and then the wipe-out of Lt. Gen. George Armstrong Custer and the 7th Cavalry in 1876. Custer's defeat sent shock waves throughout the country, jeopardizing peaceful Native peoples in much the same manner as American Muslims who were persecuted after 9/11.

James McClurken, who wrote a history of the Little River Band of Ottawa Indians, noted that once again Native peoples had suffered under a treaty that failed to deliver: "In 1855, both the Ottawa and United States delegates left the negotiations hopeful, but the Treaty of Detroit would prove a lamentable failure, an embarrassment for the federal government and disastrous for the Ottawa."

CHAPTER 34

THE STRANGE TALE OF CHIEF WABASIS

A buried treasure of gold and silver, an Indian chief brutally robbed and killed, a hunt which has gone on for nearly 160 years; these are the threads which wove the tale of Chief John Wabasis, murdered in 1863.

Chief Wabasis was either a tool of the U.S. government who was punished by his people, or else a nice old man who was cruelly murdered for his money, depending on which tale of him is told.

The story of Chief Wabasis (Wahahsee) serves to underline the muddy nature of history. Through the years, heresay and what we now call urban legends were reported as fact in newspaper accounts, making the chief's story problematical. Accounts written down by amateur historians, propagandists, aspiring novelists and barely-educated reporters often seem to have more holes than a gill net, and the saga of Chief Wabasis is a good example of how daunting it is to obtain an accurate account of events set in the distant valleys of time.

Even the books of Ph.D. professors of history tend to have contradictory accounts. Was there only one British cannon trained on the American fort on Mackinac Island in 1812, or were there two? Did Pontiac arrive at the gates of Detroit with 300 warriors, or 200, or just 60? Were 200 conquistadors killed in the Battle of Mabila, or 18, or only two? Were more than 800 settlers captured during the French and Indian War, or were there more than 1,500? Did Washington own 45,000 acres or was it 53,000? History books offer differing accounts of these and other events.

Such is the case with the unfortunate Wabasis, who was likely not actually a chief, but simply the head of his family. In one telling he was killed for hoarding treaty payments all to himself after signing away Odawa land in the area around Lowell in western Michigan. In another, he was murdered by two local scoundrels for his well-known habit of carrying all of the money he owned with him at all times.

In both stories Wabasis was said to have buried a treasure in an iron kettle shortly before his death. Over the past 160 years or so, many treasure hunters have searched for the chief's pot o' silver and gold in vain.

Born around 1807 and known as White Swan, Wabasis was said to be the son of French trader Joseph Campau and a Potawatomi woman. He was adopted by Odawa chieftain Wobiwidigo of the Lowell-area band, achieving status as a headman and establishing a settlement on the western shore of the lake in Michigan's Kent County which bears his name today.

According to Rockford historian, Richard Geldhof, Wabasis inherited a great deal of land from his adopted father. A photo of him in his prime reveals a tall, solidly built man of serious mien with the look of a tough customer.

Today, the four-hundred-acre Wabasis Lake fronts a county park with a popular beach and campground. There is also a filled-in cave at the park, which is not much more than a shallow hole in the ground, but is alleged to be a possible site of the treasure.

A park handout offers the first version of Wabasis's fate, who was "well-known for his honesty, and being a well-dedicated leader.":

"On a regular basis, Wabasis would travel to Grand Rapids on Indian Payment Day where he would collect the government annuity that was due to him. This was usually less than a dollar fifty. Wabasis always car-

A photo purporting to be that of John Wabasis - Wahahsee, or White Swan - whose treasure remains hidden to this day.

ried whatever sum of money he possessed at all times. This is what may have lead to his death."

One day in the late summer of 1863, the story goes that Wabasis was attending a Green Corn festival and dance at the village of Plainfield north of Grand Rapids when he was told that there was a plan afoot to rob him. Alarmed, he left the festival early to make the fifteen-mile trek home.

Stopping by the home of a friend, Michael Smith, he asked to borrow an old iron kettle. After visiting some other Indian friends, *sans* kettle, the chief was attacked that evening on the Plainfield-Sheridan Trail. He was killed by a blow to his head with a rock, but not before hiding his kettle somewhere between the Grand River and present-day Lake Wabasis.

There's a darker version of the story, however, which claims that Wabasis earned the wrath of local Indians by keeping the proceeds of the 1836 Treaty all to himself. In this version, the chief was designated to retrieve a large payout of treaty cash by the Odawa. He returned with a far lower amount than promised, squirreling away gold and silver worth $50,000 today.

For this bit of skullduggery, legend has it that the Blackskin Odawa of the region ordered Wabasis to remain a prisoner in an area within a mile of his home or risk death. Despite his banishment, no one ever got the chief to spill the beans on the treasure's location, and twenty-five years later two ne'er-do-wells with a taste for whiskey lured him to the corn dance, killing him on his way home. The legend further states that he was buried in a sitting position with his head sticking above ground overlooking the Grand River so that he could see the flatboats of the white men coming to take the land that he had treacherously sold.

The story of Chief Wabasis has been embroidered over the decades with many fanciful twists, including the notion of his dubious burial and another tale by a romance novelist that he was burned at the stake for cheating his people. Anti-Indian stories published in the 1870s claimed that he was a habitual drunk.

But Norm Van Soest, former president of Plainfield Township's Historical Preservation Committee, noted in a video that there are gaping holes in the Wabasis legend, beginning with the fact that he was not one of the treaty signers in 1836, or in the subsequent Treaty of Detroit in 1855. Nor would he have received a large payout due to his village.

"The law was changed by the federal government so that each individual was handed their own money and the chief no longer took it," Van Soest said. "So the story that he stole the money from the rest of the Indians was not true, because he was not given it to start with."

Add to that, virtually all of the Odawa were expelled from the region following the 1855 treaty when they moved to northern reservations. Only the Odawa who had purchased their own lands were allowed to remain and the village of Plainfield no longer existed by 1863. Nor were there any payment days held in Grand Rapids after 1857.

Van Soest also disputes the claim that Wabasis was a drunk, noting that he was good friends with several respected white farmers in the area who vouched for his good character.

But he is sure that the treasure exists. "There is money buried, I'm positive of it... I contend that the gold is buried someplace between the Grand River and wherever."

Perhaps the true story of Chief Wabasis will be revealed if and when the treasure is found.

CHAPTER 35

THE THEFT
OF NATIVE LANDS

The bayonets of federal troops had been used to herd tens of thousands of Native peoples west of the Mississippi, but there were no bayonets or troops on hand to protect the reservation lands of the Indians from the predations of white settlers and timber men. Instead, when Native peoples were victimized by swindlers, squatters and outright theft they found themselves hip-deep in government bureaucracies that did little or nothing to protect their interests. Some of these bureaucracies, such as the competing interests of municipalities and the State of Michigan, were in fact actively engaged in stripping the Indians of even the small reservations they had been given.

By 1871 the United States had negotiated nearly four hundred treaties with over one hundred Indian nations over the course of ninety-three years, a land mass amounting to 815,240,410 acres. With virtually every vestige of Indian land secured in the United States, the era of signing treaties was done. After 1871, federal negotiations with Native peoples would be conducted through congressional legislation.

But the fallout from the broken promises of the treaties of the past was far from over. By 1880 the United States had paid $275 million for the public domain of the Indians, with another $46 million paid to survey ceded lands. Yet ceded lands had invariably been purchased for far less than their value - sometimes, as Lewis Cass and William Hull had noted, on the basis of a wild guess, rather than as the result of a carefully considered survey. This, and promises of treaty cash, food, cattle, blankets, clothing, tools, land allotments and services such as blacksmiths, farm instruction, gunsmiths and education often fell far short of what had been promised, if and when they were delivered at all. Only the Indians lost out on these one-sided treaties, surrendering their ancestral homelands to what was essentially theft by legal means and broken promises.

By 1859 the Grand River bands of the Odawa of western Michigan had established two villages at obscure locations in Oceana and Mason counties. One was near the village of Eldridge, about twenty miles inland. In the 1800s Eldridge was a small farm community with a general store and a church, but today it's not even a ghost town - just a crossroads with no stores or gas station.

A smaller group of Odawa had made their way further north to present-day Ludington. Traveling in three flatboats the Odawa journeyed twelve miles up the Pere Marquette River to present-day Custer and the village of a chieftain named Nawgawnequong in northern Mason County. Nawgawnequong's people were farming one hundred acres of cleared land, and along with the newcomers they established a new village called Indian Town. Their homes were log cabins with a few frame houses, rather than bark wigwams, but these were congregated in ways that resembled their traditional villages.

Thereafter, the Odawa continued their traditions of living communally, hunting, fishing, foraging, maple sugaring and tending small gardens. The newcomers relied on one-another to build new homes, stave off hunger, and get by with few of the tools promised by the government. Historian McClurken notes that by 1865 there were twenty Grand River bands living in the new reservations to the north.

Elsewhere, reservations had been established in Michigan's Upper Peninsula at Bay Mills, Sault Ste. Marie, Hannahville, Keweenaw Bay and L'Anse. Reservations in the Lower Peninsula were at Mt. Pleasant, in the Little Traverse area north of Petoskey, and in Leelanau County north of Traverse City. All of these were subject to outrageous land and timber rip-offs that federal Indian agents seemed either powerless to stop, or who colluded in the thefts.

Even at their remote locations the Anishinaabek were easy pickings for squatters and timber companies, particularly with the flood of new settlers after the Civil War of 1861-'65. Veterans of the Union Army poured into Michigan with their families seeking new homes. The western half of Lower Michigan remains primarily Republican to this day, that being the party of the dyed-in-the-wool Yankee veterans who settled the area.

Despite the supposed protection afforded them by setting aside townships for reservations, Native peoples were plundered in a variety of ways.

For starters, timber companies laid claim to pine forests in Mason, Oceana and Isabella counties even before the Anishinaabek arrived at their reservations. Elsewhere, loggers were busy clear-cutting timber on Indian land throughout the state.

The Indians were expected to claim their acreage for allotments within five years, but federal agents were either so overworked or incompetent that this period often came and went without any allotments being made, opening the door for settlers to stake their own claims. Adding to this was the fact that no provision had been made for children who reached the age of twenty-one. This was a glaring omission in the Treaty of 1855 that created continuing problems, robbing new generations of land ownership.

Due to years of delays in determining who was eligible for land, the delay of allotments, and what to do about those coming of age, a new Indian Homestead Act was enacted in June of 1872 in the hope of cleaning up the mess. This was another rush job, giving eligible Indians just six months to select 80 or 160 acres of reservation land, after which the unclaimed land would be put on the market. Homesteaders would have ten years to build homes and improve their land in order to receive titles in the form of patents signed by the President of the United States.

But Indians seeking land were set up to fail. They were required to travel to land offices in Traverse City or Ionia, Michigan to review available lands in tract books. Once there, however, many applications were denied, with seekers told that others had already staked claims. Many would-be homesteaders returned home empty-handed.

Indian agents had the power to classify landowners as "competent" to make their own decisions regarding the sale (alienation) of their land and timber, or "incompetent," meaning unable to speak English and obviously in need of help. Unfortunately, many Indian landowners were declared competent by unscrupulous agents long before they had a chance to understand the risks of this supposed freedom, paving the way for the loss of their land through many devious schemes.

Most Indian landowners had no chance to make a go of it as farmers, despite the insistence of federal agents that they perform miracles. Annuities granted to them were supposed to pay for farm tools, seeds, oxen and other necessities, but after dividing annuity cash with thousands of Indians the average payout for individuals was $1.70 or less; not nearly enough needed to establish a working farm.

Nor did most Native peoples receive the services of blacksmiths that they had been promised, which were needed to produce farm tools, axes, saws and shovels. Some of the smiths sold government materials and metal to white settlers; others double-dipped by working for settlers while ignoring requests from Indians for whom they had been paid to help. Some were simply incompetent or weren't provided with the metal they needed to do their work.

Similarly, government farm instructors sometimes farmed Indian-owned land themselves and sold the produce in town, rather than teaching their charges how to plow and plant their fields.

Since bad soil and heavy pine cover made agriculture difficult or impossible, the Anishinaabek relied on hunting, fishing and gathering to get by. They earned cash by working in Michigan's lumber camps in the winter and at sawmills during the summer. Since many timber operations were located near Indian communities this symbiotic relationship benefited the timber barons as well as the Anishinaabek; albeit often with the loss of Indian lands. This was at a time in the late 1800s when white farmers throughout Michigan headed north for the winter lumbering season, working alongside Native woodcutters. (As an aside, my own great-great-grandfathers were employed in the timber camps each winter after they'd completed the fall harvest.)

As the fruit industry took root in Lower Michigan in the late 1800s, Native peoples began working as migrant laborers, establishing temporary villages near the orchards. They engaged in planting and pruning trees and picking fruit through the summer and fall before returning to their reservation villages.

One problem with this scenario was that Native peoples who were off lumbering, hunting, foraging for berries, visiting relatives, or working in orchards often left their allotted lands vacant for weeks or months at a time. Since allotted lands were often useless for horse-and-plow agriculture, Native peoples might visit them infrequently to strip hemlock trees of their bark to be sold for tanning, or use their land for hunting, maple sugaring, and perhaps to grow a few potatoes and corn. This made it easy for settlers to allege that the land had been abandoned, claiming it as their own. Nor did the Indians have the financial resources to defend themselves against fraud when titles to their land were challenged.

In 1877 Special Agent Edwin Brooks, a clerk from Michigan's General Land Office was dispatched to investigate the many allegations of fraud. He reported forty cases of "robbery & cruelty in the extreme" while investigating as many as sixty-four cases of fraud per month.

The Indians were not without friends in the white community. Time and again, white missionaries, educators, neighbors and trustworthy state and federal agents strongly advised them not to sell their land or timber. Yet often, Native peoples were so impoverished or bound by circumstances that they were easily coerced or defrauded.

Widows were easy targets. In one case, a Little Traverse area woman named Najiwekwa was swindled of her land without even knowing that a claim had been made in Traverse City, seventy-five miles to the south. Known by her Christian name as Lucy Penaseway, she was the widowed mother of four who had nonetheless managed to homestead her property, building a house and improving her land with an orchard and garden. Like many Native women, she earned a little cash in the summer by picking blueberries and selling them door-to-door. It was the only avenue she had for making improvements to her homestead and supporting her children.

Yet while she and her children were away picking berries in the summer of 1878, a white speculator named William Thompson bribed a land office clerk in Traverse City to advertise her property as being abandoned and then broke into her home.

"Upon returning, the Indian family found their furniture broken and strewn outside, the vegetable garden ploughed, and every fruit tree uprooted," wrote historian Bruce A. Rubenstein in *The Old Northwest*. "All proof of improvement and residence was destroyed."

Agent Brooks, who fought on her behalf, noted that Mrs. Penaseway was too poor to afford traveling seventy-five miles to Traverse City where hearings were conducted on contested land claims. His investigation found that Mrs. Penaseway "had been treated as bad as the most heartless treatment of the ex slaves of the South through scheming and rascality done at the Land Office."

Mrs. Penaseway gained her property back five years later, but by that time Thompson had stripped her property of its valuable timber, leaving her an eroded wasteland of pine stumps.

Other methods of stealing from the Indians were just as diabolical. Indians who were starving in the winter were given five dollars for food by swindlers pretending to represent charities, with the provision that they sign receipts that were actually the deeds to their property. A common practice was to offer a Native landowner a cordial drink, getting him progressively drunk, then offering to purchase his land for a pittance or provide a small loan secured by his deed. Elsewhere, unscrupulous store owners made a practice of offering their customers mortgages and then foreclosing on their property for nonpayment, demanding their money in the depths of winter when they knew the landowner would be without funds. Another scheme was to give an Indian landowner a small loan to improve his property and then demand payment soon thereafter unless a deed was signed over. Threatened with the possibility of lawsuits and prison over mortgage payments and bad loans, frightened Indians quickly caved to these demands.

"In 1878 the prosecuting attorney of Mason County reported that local loan sharks were merciless with Indians who fell into their power," Rubenstein wrote. "One man acquired nearly an entire township in Mason County (thirty-six square miles) through foreclosure of twenty-dollar loans to the Indians."

One of the more bizarre schemes involved selling cheap sewing machines, parlor organs and other status symbols of the dominant white culture on time payments with mortgages secured as collateral. When Indians failed to make a payment, both their goods and land were seized as repayment.

There were even cases where speculators bribed Natives to pose as other Indian landowners, signing away their titles in swindles that were difficult to contest.

Illegal taxes and the nonpayment of taxes were also employed to steal Native lands. In the Little Traverse area in the 1870s, for instance, Indians were assessed $32.85 for eighty acres of unimproved land at twice the rate of white settlers. An Emmet County official said that taxes on Native landowners would keep rising until the county had "relieved itself of the presence of Indians."

Further north, historian Bradley J. Gills of Grand Valley State University notes that "The Bay Mills reservation was almost entirely lost due to illegal taxes imposed by local authorities. These taxes went unpaid for years and were then used as the basis to acquire the Anishnabeg's lands."

Most Indians did not know that after they had been granted patents (clear titles) to their land, they were required to pay property taxes. Sometimes they got bad advice from white friends or even BIA agents who were clueless about tax obligations themselves. But land sharks surely knew the law and were quick to pay the back taxes owed as a way to divest Indians of their property and homes. As some schemers at Bay Mills and Sault Ste. Marie admitted to Special Agent Brooks, "if they could not relieve themselves of the presence of Indians in any other manner they would 'tax them out of the country.'"

Fraud cases were almost impossible to contest. Indian landowners had to respond to newspaper want ads claiming their land had been abandoned, and were thus often unaware that a claim had been made. Land office hearings were often a mockery of justice, with witnesses bribed to contest Indian claims or agents adopting paternalistic attitudes of "you asked for it" regarding tax grievances or loan shark swindles. Defrauded land owners also had to bear the costs of an interpreter and an attorney along with the transportation and lodging of three witnesses on their behalf. These costs totaling more than $50, along with the long journey to a hearing, were insurmountable for most Indians, who bore the added expense of having to pay the cost of a hearing in the unlikely event that they won their case.

The theft of Indian land only got worse during the notoriously corrupt administration of President U.S. Grant from 1869-1877, whose patronage system appointed officials who had little or no interest in Native peoples beyond seeking ways to get their hands on government cash or the proceeds from the sale of timber or land.

One of the biggest land frauds in Michigan history was perpetrated by Indian Agent George I. Betts, a Methodist preacher with a demonic streak who engaged in multiple swindles. Upon gaining office in 1871, Betts became a partner in five real estate firms and timber interests in the Saginaw area and began preying on the Anishinaabek, seeking their land and timber in Isabella County. For starters, Betts told the Indians that they could apply for their land allotments, but only through his deputies, Alexander and Peter Andre, who happened to be his business partners. No allotments would be allowed, however, unless the Anishinaabek permitted the Andres to choose the land for them and purchase the timber on it. When this didn't work out, Betts paid his half-blood interpreter five dollars per deed to ferret out land purchases in Isabella County. This enabled Betts and his partners to buy up hundreds of deeds for $25 each from desperate Indians who were often elderly, illiterate or widowed.

When these practices were protested by Native leaders, Betts threatened them with harm and had them replaced with a council of yes-men. "Soon Washington officials received a letter praising Betts as the best agent Michigan Indians ever had and declaring that all accusations made against him were false," wrote historian Rubenstein. This bogus letter was translated by Betts' interpreter and transcribed and witnessed by the Andres.

In Isabella County, Betts issued 1,711 patents to Native landowners that he declared "competent," clearing the way for the sale of 75,000 acres of prime Indian woodlands. Seeking ready cash, many gullible Indians sold their timber (against the wishes of other state and federal agents) to "timber sharks" who used various subterfuges to gain their land as well as their lumber.

Betts was suspended in 1876 and prosecuted for his crimes. He was replaced by George Lee who, along with Special Agent Brooks, did his best to help the Indians despite rampant fraud in the Indian Bureau. But by then the damage had been done. The Odawa who had been defrauded were given permission to select new land, but the best properties had been taken.

Despite endemic fraud, tax seizures and the theft of lands allotted to them, Native peoples managed a workaround by seeking wage-paying jobs, migrant work in orchards, seasonal work in the timber industry, commercial fishing, as stevedores in Michigan's port cities, and as support for miners in the Upper Peninsula. They also continued to rely on hunting, fishing and foraging. In western Lower Michigan, the displaced Odawa of the Grand River Bands began gravitating to the marshes and tributaries of the Manistee River, hunting, trapping and fishing on land that was of no interest to white settlers; in time they would coalesce as the Little River Band. Native peoples also established villages on the margins of white communities, such as Indian Town in Manistee and outside the small towns of Fountain,

Brethren, Harbor Springs, Omena, Marquette and Mount Pleasant. These Native villages were often established on the few remaining parcels of land that had kept pace with taxes.

"Indeed, in many areas land theft had little real impact on the Anishnabeg's material well-being, as very few individuals made homes on their allotments in the first place," noted historian Gills. "... in the end the availability of lumbering wages coupled with the maintenance of traditional subsistence methods created a relatively prosperous niche that the Anishinaabeg took full advantage of."

This far from rosy, but tenable, scenario evaporated with the dawning of 1900. By the early twentieth century, virtually all of Michigan's forests had been leveled to the ground, leaving millions of acres of stumps and erosion. Awakened to the need for conservation, the State began requiring a ten dollar license to hunt and fish, which most Indians could not afford, adding another barrier to their survival. The license requirement was enforced by game wardens, who could search Native homes without warrants.

Conservation measures had ramifications for the Bay Mills bands, who relied on the blueberry harvest for income. In 1908 they picked two thousand crates of blueberries for sale at two dollars per crate. But after the State and National Forest purchased the nearby blueberry plains, Native peoples were denied their age-old practice of burning the plains to regenerate the plants. In 1930, Chippewa County began paying families of the Bay Mills bands ten dollars per month to keep them from starving to death.

Rather than establishing the Anishinaabek as prosperous farmers owning hundreds of thousands of productive acres the Treaty of 1855 and the Homestead Act of 1872 had been abject failures. The awarding of poor land along with insufficient resources and protections against fraud had stripped Native peoples of ninety percent of the reservation lands set aside for them.

Thirty years after the signing of the Treaty of 1855, former Commissioner of Indian Affairs George Manypenny wrote that his land allotment plan had been a disaster. "Had I known then, as I now know, what would result from these treaties I would be compelled to admit that I had committed a high crime."

Rather than turning the Indians into prosperous farmers, the allotment system had the effect of making a checkerboard of reservations, honeycombing Native peoples alongside white settlers and disrupting their communal way of living.

Despite the crushing failure of the land allotment scheme in Michigan, the U.S. Congress pushed it nationwide in 1887 with the Dawes Act (also known as the Allotment Act) under the administration of President Grover Cleveland. As in Michigan, the federal government privatized Indian land in an attempt to break up tribal identities by dividing reservations into allotments of 10-160 acres for farmland or 320 -640 acres for grazing. The hoped-for outcome was that this would lift the Indians out of poverty by assimilating them into taxpaying farmers and ranchers. Natives who registered for land and agreed to allotments were granted U.S. citizenship.

But this was in essence a bald-faced land-grab because any "surplus" reservation lands that were not selected were offered for sale to white settlers, boosting the coffers of the U.S. Treasury. Tens of thousands of German, East European and Russian immigrants poured into the Great Plains and Indian Territory as part of an overseas marketing campaign launched by railroad companies seeking farm customers for their new train routes. The peasant immigrants were soon to be as disappointed as the Indians with the mostly futile task of trying to wrest crops from the dry, brick-hard sod of the Great Plains.

In his book, *Indians*, historian William Brandon wrote that more than one hundred reservations were allotted on the Great Plains, the Pacific coast and amid the Great Lakes region. "Of the approximately 150 million acres owned by the Indians in 1880, most of it guaranteed by treaties... over 90 million acres - an area more than twice the size of Oklahoma - were abstracted from the Indians' pocket."

Over the course of many treaties from the 1700s onward, roughly 25,000 square miles had been reserved for the Indians of the Great Lakes, along with almost 700 square miles for their *métis* relatives. Yet under the new rules of the Allotment Act, much of this land was declared "surplus" and sold to white settlers. This legal theft of reservation lands - which had been guaranteed by treaties - remains a contention for a number of tribes to this day.

As in Michigan, the Indians of the West were set up to fail, with poor land offered for farm allotments, along with a lack of tools and support. By then many Native children had also been forcibly removed to Indian boarding schools and had no experience farming when they returned home. Then too, the division of inherited land left a deceased farmer's children with not enough acreage to sustain working farms.

As soon as they were legally able to sell their land, many Indians in the western reserves found themselves swindled or given far less than its value. Having little experience with cash, those who sold their land soon found themselves with empty pockets to boot.

Going along with this, a series of congressional acts in the late 1800s criminalized the expression of Native culture, language and religion, attempting to bleed the red people white.

Rather than establishing Native peoples as successful farmers, the Dawes Act stripped them of ninety million acres and had the effect of fragmenting Indian communities, gutting tribal hierarchies of chieftains, and destroying their collective way of life.

It wasn't until enduring the horrors of the Great Depression that Native peoples began to claw back something of their culture and traditions under an Indian "New Deal" offered by the administration of Franklin D. Roosevelt. The Indian Reorganization Act (IRA) of 1934 allowed Native bands to petition the government for legally-empowered tribal recognition, creating the organizations which exist today in reservations across the country.

The IRA re-established tribal governments, allowed tribes to conduct their own business, and decriminalized the expression of Native culture and religion, among other reforms. It required federally-recognized tribes to draft their own constitutions and elect tribal councils headed by a chairperson. The IRA also ended the land allotment system and the federal government began purchasing land to be held in trust for the new tribal organizations.

Only persons who could prove that they had one-quarter percentage of Indian blood could be considered members of a tribe, a "blood quantum" fix that has bedeviled Native communities ever since over the division of government annuities and today, casino cash.

As with past attempts at reforms, some of the IRA's provisions were underfunded and failed to materialize. Additionally, its one-size-fits-all provisions didn't always suit the particular needs of hundreds of tribes. Nor did Indian leaders relish the fact that tribal self-governance would be subject to federal approval and would do away with the traditional roles of chieftains. Also, by the 1930s a substantial number of Indians had managed to make a success of land ownership or had moved to the cities to find employment. How would they fit in? Those who remained on the reservations had no reason to believe that the U.S. Government would come through with its promises, yet many bands across the country quickly began petitioning for tribal recognition. Some of them have yet to be accepted.

CHAPTER 36

THE BURNOUT

The women, children and elderly of Indianville had just finished break-fast when they heard the clatter of horses and buggies outside their homes on a rainy Monday morning, Oct. 15, 1900.

Indianville was set in Cheboiganing, a reserve that was the home of nine-teen families of Odawa and Ojibwe Indians on Burt Lake, some twenty miles south of Cheboygan, Michigan. The thousand-acre peninsula jutting into the northwest side of the lake had been their home for 180 years, hav-ing been settled around 1720.

But on that Monday morning, it was their home no longer. Outside was timber speculator John McGinn, who had paid the back-taxes on land that the Indians thought had been granted to them forever with no strings at-tached. Backing him up was county sheriff Fred R. Ming and his depu-ties. Ordering the village residents out of their homes, they began empty-ing their log cabins of possessions, piling them up alongside the dirt road which served the village. Then, after dousing the floor of each cabin with kerosene, the lawmen sent the entire village up on flames.

The villagers looking on in the chill rain could only scream, cry or gaze in horror as fifteen buildings of highly-combustible pine burned to the ground in a roaring inferno. Most of the village men worked in the region's timber industry and were more than twenty miles away in Cheboygan col-lecting their pay when the attack on Indianville took place. Yet the smoke from the fire could be seen for many miles around, and surely they would have seen their doom written on the southern horizon.

All that was left of Indianville was a small Catholic church, St. Mary's, established by Father Frederic Baraga in the late 1830s.

With no shelter and no defense against the armed lawmen, most of the res-idents of Indianville moved a short way inland with relatives who owned land to the north along nearby Indian Road. A few headed west to relatives living at Cross Village on Lake Michigan, thirty-five miles away.

Today, there's no trace of what came to be known as the "Burnout" on Burt Lake, save for a small cemetery at the site of the long-gone church.

Located on a two-mile-long peninsula called Indian Point, their village was strung out along Chickagami Trail, across from which lay their fields of corn and other crops. Along with the fish taken from Burt Lake and work in the region's lumber operations, the people of the Cheboiganing reserve eked out a humble, but reliable living.

As with other Native bands whose land was rich in minerals, timber and fertile soil, the people of Indianville were targeted because their band owned a valuable stand of old-growth oak trees. Nearby Cheboygan had exploded into a lumber boomtown by the 1860s and lumber barons and their crews were decimating forests on a ninety-mile stretch along the Lake Huron coast from Alpena to the Straits. By 1894 a train route known as the Turtle Line had been established through the cut-over forest from Cheboygan, transporting the green gold of the north to Bay City, 173 miles to the south.

But with the timber rapidly dwindling, speculators were on the lookout for the remaining stands, and that led them to Indian Point.

As it happened, the Indians of Cheboiganing were delinquent in paying their property taxes and had long lived under the assumption that they didn't owe any. This made them a prime target for John McGinn of Cheboygan, who had been eyeing Indian Point for several years. An influential businessman with strong political connections in the region, McGinn used legal loopholes in the state's tax code to acquire several large parcels of Indian Point in 1895, making him the new owner of Indianville.

But the residents of Indianville had their own justification for refusing to budge. Historically known as the Cheboiganing Band, they had been granted a one-thousand-acre reserve as part of the 1836 Treaty of Washington.

As with other Native reserves, the treaty stipulated that the land would be held in common by the band for a period of five years, "and no longer; unless the United States shall grant them permission to remain on said lands for a longer period."

In the face of this threat those living at Indianville had pitched in to purchase much of Indian Point in 1846-'47. Under the advice of federal Indian agents, they had deeded the property to the governor of Michigan to be held in a tax-exempt trust.

"The reason behind this move was simple enough," wrote Cheboygan historian Matthew J. Friday in a 2007 article in the *Michigan Historical Review*. "By holding the land together, the Burt Lake Indians remained a community, a united group, and not individual landowners like the United States government wanted them to become. In this way they were able to preserve their tribal identity and dodge the white man's demands for individualism."

The Treaty of 1855 further complicated the issue of land ownership. As noted earlier, this treaty was meant to phase out Indian dependence on the federal government by granting them allotments in order to become private landowners. Under the new treaty Indian families were expected to choose private parcels for themselves within five years. By 1870, the government had awarded patents for land selected by some, but not all, of those living on Indian Point. Some still preferred to live on the land held in trust by Michigan's governor.

By this time, however, the reservation at Indian Point had lapsed, including the land held in trust.

Initially, the people of Indian Point paid their taxes on the advice of school teacher and Burt Lake Township Supervisor Lorin P. Biggs. However, when Biggs left the scene, a new teacher by the name of Cross mistakenly told the locals that they were still living on a reservation and didn't need to pay taxes.

Thus, by the early 1890s the unpaid taxes piled up and the land reverted to state ownership, where it soon became a target for lumberman McGinn. After McGinn acquired legal ownership of Indianville he purchased other tracts in the area.

McGinn informed the Anishinaabek households that they could reclaim their land by reimbursing him for the back taxes. The Indians declined, holding to the belief that their land was still held in trust and that federal treaties could not be superseded by local governments. In time, the U.S. Supreme Court would agree with them to some extent, but that was many years down the road.

McGinn then offered one-acre leases for those wishing to retain their homes, but this too was ignored. Even if they had wished to comply with McGinn's demands, the low wages granted to Native workers in the lumber and millwright trades were not enough to pay for what by then amounted to a substantial tax bill, not to mention the outrage of leasing homes they had lived in for generations.

In October of 1899, McGinn received a Writ of Assistance from the local Circuit Court, which authorized him to evict the residents of Indianville. This, too, was ignored, according to accounts in the *Cheboygan Democrat* newspaper. In response, McGinn gave the residents of Indianville a year to move on, but only two families did so, including that of Chief Joseph Parkey.

McGinn wasn't alone in wanting the residents of Indianville to move. He had an ally in Samuel H. Price, who owned a hotel at the tip of Indian Point. Although tourists who traveled by the Turtle Line to Price's hotel enjoyed purchasing native crafts at Indianville, the hotelier had a low opinion of Indians and was eager to see them removed. In time, Indian Point was renamed Colonial Point in an apparent attempt to whitewash history.

Three years after the Burnout state investigators agreed that McGinn had fraudulently acquired the Indians' land, but by then the damage had been done. Yet, rather than reinstating their property, the State offered the Burt Lake Band a new parcel of swampland that was unsuitable for farming. Instead, a new village was established on Indian Road, including the construction of a new St. Mary's Catholic Church.

The Indianville Burnout is known to us today thanks to newspaper accounts from the period. Vacant from memory are similar scenes of the destruction of hundreds, if not thousands of Indian communities in a wave of ethnic cleansing and genocide that flooded North America over the past five centuries.

Nearly 125 years after the Burnout, the Burt Lake Band of Ottawa and Chippewa Indians has still not been granted federal recognition as a tribal entity with the Bureau of Indian Affairs, a move that would allow them to prosper via the gaming industry, among other benefits.

The band has been seeking federal recognition since the 1930s, yet has been repeatedly denied by the BIA, despite overwhelming evidence of their governing body, communal activities, and their official recognition in the federal treaties of 1836 and 1855.

Part of the problem is that after more than twenty years of dithering by the BIA, some members of the Burt Lake Band joined the Little Traverse Band, headquartered in Harbor Springs, in order to obtain long-denied health and education benefits. This only served to give the BIA more justification for denying the band federal recognition - a problem that the agency itself created. Add to that, recognition of the Burt Lake Band (among other bands) has been denied under an arcane rationale that they are a "landless" tribe, which again, was the outcome of federal machinations, stripping Natives of their land in the first place.

Today, the peninsula on which the Odawa and Ojibwe lived for centuries is now strung with the million dollar homes of those who came long after McGinn and his lumber operation vanished. For what it's worth, McGinn never managed to harvest the red oaks of the peninsula.

In 1985, the peninsula was threatened with a sawmill operation that planned to cut down the old-growth trees and ship them off to Germany in order to create laminate flooring. Peninsula residents joined forces with the Little Traverse Conservancy, the Michigan Chapter of the Nature Conservancy, the University of Michigan and the state Natural Resources Trust Fund and bought the land. The three hundred acre forest is now known as the Cheboiganing Nature Preserve.

CHAPTER 37

UPRISING

Heading north to Traverse City from Detroit in 1978, my then-wife and I drove up the Leelanau Peninsula on a fall color tour that was notable mostly for its smothering blanket of iron-gray clouds that muted the colors of the changing leaves to a dim mush. Twenty-three miles north of Traverse City we passed through Peshawbestown, a village that was home to the Grand Traverse Band of Ottawa and Chippewa Indians. There were no stores or gas station along the half-mile strip that constituted the village; instead there were decrepit shacks, rusted mobile homes, and camping trailers blackened by sooty rain that looked barely livable. Broken windows were patched with cardboard, and newspaper served as insulation against the biting cold of winter. Some of the homes were in ruins, sheathed in tar paper, shingles blown away, rotted to skeletal timbers, sitting alongside wrecked vehicles tangled in weeds. Some had no electricity or running water. What some of the locals called "Shabbytown" looked even more pitiful than the ghettos of Detroit that I knew while living in the inner city during my college years. We drove on, startled by the shift from touristy Traverse City to an abject poverty that we, as a privileged white couple, had no clue as to its existence.

The Grand Traverse Band had been robbed many years in the past. Six townships had been set aside for allotments in 1855 encompassing 87,000 acres, including virtually all of Leelanau County and a portion of Antrim County, but seventeen years passed before President Grant signed patents for their holdings in 1872. The set-aside land was quickly plundered through fraud, squatters, or sold by desperate, impoverished Indians themselves. The perpetrators included two members of the band who swindled or cajoled the elderly, disabled and widowed out of their land holdings on behalf of speculators from Chicago. By 1892 the band had less than seven hundred acres to its name, mostly around Peshawbestown. More than 86,000 acres... *gone*.

Poverty had stalked the Anishinaabek from the get-go under the economic system of capitalism. With the loss of their lands, Native peoples throughout the Upper Great Lakes formed villages on the few small acres that remained, but these were plagued by joblessness and despair. The average annual income for a family living on the Isabella County reservation in 1937 was just $198.57 with 127 families living in seventy-one houses that had only two or three rooms each, making privacy and sanitation impossible. Some families had to carry water from springs, owing to a lack of wells, or else wells that were polluted. In later years elders reported that they were so poor they barely noticed the Great Depression; it was just another time of want and hunger like any other, with women weaving baskets or creating buckskin clothing to sell as souvenirs for a little cash. By 1975 the median income of those living on the Isabella reservation was just $5,000 per year, compared to $16,000 for non-Indian county residents. These same conditions, or worse, could be applied with a broad brush to Native peoples living on reservations throughout the country.

Today, however, subsistence-level poverty has been eradicated by the economic miracle of the gaming industry: Isabella County's Soaring Eagle Casino and its 512-room hotel and concert hall now supports more than four thousand employees, pumping hundreds of millions into the local economy. Hourly pay for casino staff is equal or better than wages at non-Indian businesses in nearby Mount Pleasant. In 2022, for instance, a bartender at the casino could earn up to $27 per hour, not counting tips.

And in Leelanau County, over the past three decades Peshawbestown has become a major destination, thanks to the establishment of the Leelanau Sands Casino, which was one of the first Indian gaming operations in the state. There's a sprawling gas station and mini-mart there now, and the homes are modest, but a vast improvement over what came before. A huge recreational facility and gym is large enough to accommodate flights of indoor drones, while alongside West Grand Traverse Bay sits the Eyaawing Museum and Cultural Center, offering information on Native history and culture. Language classes in Anishinaabemowin are available and an annual powwow featuring jingle dances and traditional clothing draws thousands of spectators and participants.

This same scenario - a phoenix rising from ashes - has been repeated at Anishinaabek reservations throughout Michigan, Wisconsin and Minnesota, and of course, at reservations across the country. Yet, in the Upper Great Lakes, this uprising in prosperity and Native pride only came about after more than two hundred years of painful struggle, false starts, dead ends and renegotiations with federal and state governments.

A generation of Native writers and scholars have taken a deep dive into the horrors of Indian boarding schools and the attempt to strip away the language, religion, culture, clothing and even hair styles of the Anishinaabek and other tribes. That story, encompassing the last one hundred years or so is best told by them and there are a number of excellent tribal histories, some commissioned by the tribes themselves, that offer the full story of this titanic struggle.

In the twentieth century tribal leaders began organizing and lobbying the government for the redress of past wrongs. Often, this was accompanied by lawsuits, such as a battle over fishing rights in the 1980s. Unfortunately, many tribal attempts to claw back their treaty rights were hampered by government claims that denied their very existence as legal entities, a fight that continues to this day for some dispossessed Native peoples.

In 1923, Odawa activist Sampson Robinson of Mason County established the Michigan Indian Organization to unite the historic bands of the Odawa. This got the snowball rolling, with the establishment of the Michigan Indian Defense Association by the Grand Traverse and Little Traverse Bay bands in 1934. This in turn led to the formation of the Northern Michigan Ottawa Association in 1947, which represented the political interests of thousands of Odawa and Ojibwe. As tribal political power increased, so did membership. In 1966 the InterTribal Michigan Indian Council was founded, today representing eleven federally-recognized tribes in Michigan. In more recent years the United Tribes of Michigan have advanced Native causes under the leadership of Frank Ettawageshik, the former Tribal Chairman of the Little Traverse Bay Bands of Odawa Indians. An artist and story-teller, Ettawageshik has reaped numerous honors for his work with many organizations and initiatives.

These organizations have ardently pursued Native interests such as education, fishing and hunting rights, and recouping land lost to fraud. But for many bands it was a long, slow crawl just gaining federal recognition.

Some had an easier path than others. Under the Indian Reorganization Act, Native bands had to adopt a constitution and elect a tribal council in order to gain federal recognition.

First out of the gate in gaining federal recognition in 1937 were:
• The Saginaw Chippewa Indian Tribe
• The Bay Mills Indian Community representing five of the six original Sault Ste. Marie bands.
• The Hannahville Potawatomi Community.
• The Keweenaw Bay Indian Community.

Thereafter, many tribal entities lobbied for decades to have their federal status acknowledged:

• The 44,000-member Sault Ste. Marie Tribe of Chippewa Indians gained federal status in 1972.
• The Lac Vieux Desert Band of Lake Superior Chippewa Indians was

recognized in 1988.

• The Grand Traverse Band of Ottawa and Chippewa Indians gained federal recognition in 1980, but it wasn't until February, 1998 that they adopted a tribal constitution and the bylaws and charter that would oversee the 450 acres they had acquired as trust lands and through purchase.

• The Little Traverse Bay Bands of Odawa Indians in Harbor Springs earned federal recognition in 1994. Today, they have more than four thousand members living in and around Cross Village, Harbor Springs, Petoskey and Charlevoix, resurrecting the historic domain of Waganawkezee.

• The Little River Band of Ottawa Indians also gained federal recognition in 1994. Since their federal recognition, the tribe's casino operation has done immeasurable good in transforming the moribund salt-mining town of Manistee into a vibrant tourist destination on Lake Michigan.

• In southwestern Michigan and northeastern Indiana, the Pokagon Band of Potawatomi Indians had its status reaffirmed in 1994.

• The Huron Potawatomi Nation had its federal status acknowledged in 1995.

• The Match-e-be-nash-she-wish Band of Potawatomi Indians of Gun Lake was recognized in 1999.

For the Odawa, at least, federal recognition has meant closing the chapter on an odyssey of more than 350 years. That included being driven west by the Iroquois in the 1650s before resettling back in Michigan in the 1700s and resolving their issues with the government of the United States thereafter.

In recent decades, tribal attorneys across the country have launched a blizzard of lawsuits seeking to recover jurisdiction over reservation lands taken by fraud or government malfeasance; to be compensated for theft of the same; and to uphold treaty rights relating to hunting, fishing, the environment and other matters. These have been met with varying degrees of success.

In Michigan's Leelanau County, for instance, the Grand Traverse Band of Ottawa and Chippewa Indians has spent more than twenty years seeking compensation for the 87,000 acres spirited away by land speculators and settlers. The band is seeking compensation for what the land was worth at the time it was taken, along with interest, which of course, could be considerable. The rationale for the proposed suit is that under the Takings Clause in the Fifth Amendment of the Constitution, "private property (shall not) be taken for public use, without just compensation."

Yet even before the band can file suit in the U.S. Court of Claims, it must

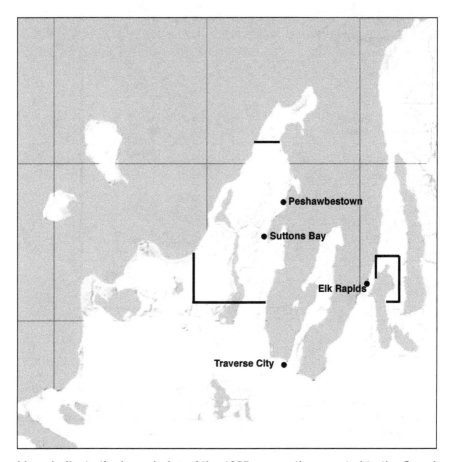

Lines indicate the boundaries of the 1855 reservation granted to the Grand Traverse Band of Ottawa and Chippewa indians totalling 87,000 acres in Leelanau and Antrim counties. As of 2024, the band has tried without success to be reimbursed for lands taken by white settlement and fraudulent means.

get the go-ahead through an act of Congress, either the U.S. House or Senate, and thus far, no bill has been forthcoming despite the support of Leelanau County and several of its townships.

Further north, in the mid-1990s the Little Traverse Bay Bands of Odawa Indians began seeking affirmation of its reservation created by the Treaty of 1855. The band's intent was not to reclaim property taken by white settlers and speculators, but to "fully exercise its sovereignty and protect its citizens, natural resources, environment and ancestral remains, along with its cultural identity and the history of its members." Add to that, recognizing the historic reservation boundaries would resolve "conflicts between

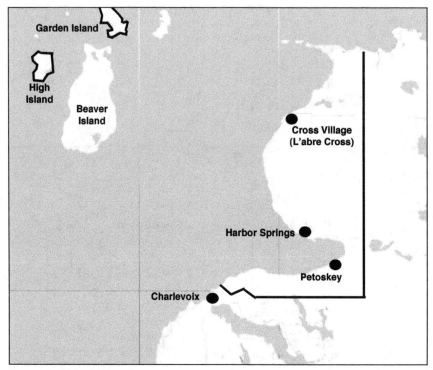

Boundaries of the 1855 reservation set aside for the Little Traverse Bay Bands of Odawa Indians, including Garden and High Islands. In 2022 the U.S. Supreme Court denied the band a review of its case seeking affirmation of reservation lands taken under the allotment system.

the Tribe, State and local governments," according to a 2022 statement by Tribal Chairperson Regina Gasco-Bentley.

"The Federal Court affirming the reservation would have put the whole world on notice that the entire area reserved for us in the 1855 Treaty is our permanent reservation home," she wrote.

The suit was filed in Michigan's Western District Federal Court in 2015, which arrived at a summary judgment that the 1855 Treaty never actually created a reservation, but simply set aside land for allotments to members of the band. The tribe filed an appeal in 2019, but this too was denied by the U.S. Court of Appeals. The matter then went all the way to the U.S. Supreme Court, which declined to review the decision, "without even an opportunity to present our testimony at trial."

The upshot is that the Little Traverse Bands spent $8.5 million on trial research and preparation along with $670,400 on appeals without receiving what was promised in 1855.

By itself, federal recognition did little to improve the fortunes of the new tribal units. It was the spread of humble bingo parlors that sparked the economic engine that raised the living standard for Native peoples.

Ecstatic shouts of *"bingo!"* and the cash the parlors brought in led to the first crude casinos and then full-blown gaming operations across the country. The National Indian Gaming Commission reported that Native casinos reaped $39 billion in revenues in 2022, despite being strapped with the challenge of the Covid 19 pandemic.

The establishment of Indian casinos followed a curious and unexpected path.

In 1972, Russell and Helen Bryan were sitting in their new Skyline trailer on the Ojibwe reservation at Leech Lake, Minnesota when they spotted a white man outside who was taking measurements of their home. He turned out to be the Itasca County tax assessor, and soon the Bryans received their very first property tax bill of $29.85.

A member of the Leech Lake Band of Ojibwe, Helen had been born on her grandfather's land near Squaw Lake in northern Minnesota. In 1957 she married Russell Bryan of the White Earth Band of Ojibwe and raised five children together. After a fire destroyed their home they were able to purchase their two-bedroom trailer in 1971, thanks to a down payment that was the result of a cash settlement when Helen's brother died in a car crash. Their new home sat on reservation property that had been held in trust by the federal government for more than one hundred years.

Now they had a home to replace one that had burned down, but they also had a tax bill, which they had never received before. The first bill of $29.85 for two months in 1971 was followed by another assessment of $118.10 for 1972. Soon enough their assessment rose to $147.95, and as the parents of five children with few resources and a mortgage of $92 per month the Bryans were devastated.

"I was desperate," Helen was quoted in the *Minnesota Law Review.* "I couldn't figure out how we would pay the taxes, and that would be every year, you know." The Bryans were told they had to pay the bill within a month's time, and they were well aware that nonpayment could mean foreclosure of their new home.

Helen took her plight to the newly-established Leech Lake Reservation Legal Services Project, which took the matter to court with the help of an ever-changing, idealistic *pro bono* team of attorneys and law students. They lost in district court and then lost their appeal in an unanimous decision by the Minnesota Supreme Court, but the Bryans and their legal team didn't give up. Represented by law professor and legal aid advocate Bernie Becker, they took their case all the way to the U.S. Supreme Court which began hearing oral arguments in *Bryan v. Itasca County* in April, 1976.

Becker was a bear of a man - grossly overweight, he spoke in a gravelly voice rimmed with thunder, owing to his habit of chain-smoking cigars. But he could spin a good yarn as a skillful raconteur, and along with his *pro bono* work in legal aid was said to have "a heart of gold."

His challenge at the U.S. Supreme Court was getting the judges up to speed on a century of law related to Native peoples, as well as the living conditions and customs of the Indians. After overcoming a good deal of skepticism, Becker managed to sway the court and the Bryans won a sweeping, unanimous decision authored by Justice William J. Brennan, Jr. The court ruled that not only did states *not* have the authority to tax Indians on their reservations, but they also had *no authority* to regulate Indian activities on their reservations.

This completely unexpected and transcendent ruling encouraged the Seminole Tribe of Florida to open a high-stakes bingo parlor on their reservation land near Fort Lauderdale. They were raided and shut down by the Broward County Sheriff on the same day that the parlor opened, but backed by the Supreme Court decision, the Seminoles ultimately prevailed, spreading the news of their operation to tribal organizations across the country.

In 1980, the miserable, dirt-poor Cabazon Band of Mission Indians outside Indio, California opened a bingo parlor and poker hall, resulting in arrests and the seizure of cash and equipment by local law enforcement. In the resulting 1986 case the U.S. Supreme Court again ruled in favor of tribal sovereignty, opening the floodgates for Indian casino operations across the country. This was followed up by the Indian Gaming Regulatory Act, signed by President Ronald Reagan in 1988, which enacted tribal sovereignty over casinos, provided they were regulated by the federal government and entered into contracts with their home states.

Curious, members of the Tribal Council of the Saginaw Chippewa Indian Tribe visited the bingo hall operated by the Seminoles in Florida and were inspired to trying gaming in Mt. Pleasant. The tribe began offering bingo at their reservation's gym in April, 1981 and were quickly surprised by the arrival of bingo players from hundreds of miles around, eager to win the big jackpots being offered. This led to offering blackjack games in a former pallet storage building in 1987, and then the inclusion of slot machines in 1990.

By then bingo parlors had spread to Native reservations across the state, bringing in astounding revenues that only hinted at what was possible. In

1993, seven federally-recognized tribes met at Hannahville, Michigan to sign the first gaming compact with the State of Michigan. This was a sweet deal for the state, reaping 8 percent of casino revenues. Local municipalities, such as the City of Mount Pleasant, would receive a 2 percent taste of gaming revenues.

From there, the genie was out of the bottle, raining cash on impoverished Indian tribes across the nation. But, as with cautionary tales of genies, this also gave rise to widespread dissension as to who would qualify as a tribal member in order share casino payouts. This "blood quantum" issue remains a heated controversy to this day.

Even so, the influx of cash from the gaming industry has helped Native peoples to bolster their health and education services and begin the long path to reclaiming their cultural heritage in a way that was unimaginable only a generation ago.

Writing in the *Minnesota Law Review*, Kevin K. Washburn said that the *Bryan v. Itasca County* case "was the bedrock upon which the Indian gaming industry began... *Bryan* may be the most important victory for American Indian tribes in the U.S. Supreme Court in the latter half of the twentieth century. Indian gaming is simply the most successful economic venture ever to occur consistently across a wide range of American Indian reservations."

Thirty-five years after seeking legal help for her tax bill, Helen (now Johnson) was retired and celebrated as a hero by the tribe. Her old trailer that had sparked so much controversy was long gone, replaced by a four-bedroom home, financed by the tribe through its gaming revenues.

Today, Native gaming establishments face a challenge from online sports gambling, which threatens the economic gains they've made over the past generation. As is the case with indigenous peoples around the world, the Indians continue to face the problems of domestic violence, poor education, substance abuse and poverty, the legacies of cultures that were shattered by colonialism and greed. The disastrous trials Native peoples have endured for more than five hundred years have not yet been laid to rest, yet even so, the scales of justice and retribution have begun tipping in their favor.

###

MY THANKS

Although I spent more than thirty years slaving in the vineyards of journalism, I'm at best a journeyman historian and as such have peered over the shoulders of giants in writing this book - true historians who spent their lives digging through thousands of documents to bring the past to life. To all who fill the bibliography of this book I am indebted, in particular to Charles E. Cleland, Edmund Jefferson Danziger, William Warren, Charmaine M. Benz, Eric J. Dolin, James M. McClurken, Michael McDonnell, Charles C. Mann, Helen Tanner, Jon Parmenter, James Clifton, George Cornell, Peter Cozzens, Alan Axelrod, Roxanne Dunbar-Ortiz, Brian Fagan, Kevin Siepel, Marvin T. Smith, Willis F. Dunbar and Ronald N. Satz, to name a few.

Thanks also to MSU Archeologist Mike Hambacher; Cahokia Mounds Superintendent Lori Belknap; John Petoskey, legal council for the Grand Traverse Band; Potawatomi source John N. Low, associate professor, Ohio State University; my good friend and accountant George Foster for number-crunching; with George and Bill Danly serving as first readers. Sandy Franklin for her wise advice in guiding the manuscript, and my wife and stalwart supporter, Jeannette Wildman for her patience and encouragement.

Whenever possible I make it a point to visit all of the places I've ever written about, be it in a novel or this work of nonfiction, so many thanks to the archeological parks of Cahokia, IL; Moundville, AL; Poverty Point, LA; Cedar Key, FL; Crystal River, FL; the Red Pipestone Quarry, MN; the Huron/Wendake Village of Quebec; the Crawford Lake Iroquoian Village, Ontario; Plaza Major in Mexico City, the L'anse Aux Meadows National Historic Site in Newfoundland and the Mandan villages of Fort Lincoln and Knife River, ND. Also these historic sites: Fort Meigs, OH; Prophetstown, IN; Fort Michilimackinac and Mackinac Island, MI; the Raisin River Battleground, MI; the Fallen Timbers Battleground, OH; Beaver Island and Isle Royale, MI, among others.

Museum exhibits of inestimable value included those at Fort Pitt, Pittsburgh, PA; the Madeline Island Museum; the Smithsonian Museums of the American Indian and Natural History; Buffalo Bill Center of the West, Cody, WY; the Museo Nacional de Antropología in Mexico City, and especially the Museum of Ojibwa Culture, St. Ignace, MI.

Also invaluable were the back issues of *Michigan History*, the National Archives, *The Michigan Historical Review* and the Michigan Pioneer and Historical Collection. Thanks also to the Clarke Historical Library of Central Michigan University and to the Traverse City Area District Library, where I spent many hours working on this book at a quiet table on the second floor.

NOTES

CHAPTER 1 THE WISCONSIN DEATH MARCH

"It was as if the snow... Minnesota Public Radio - Dan Gunderson, July 28, 2016.

...many made trips from 220-460 miles home... Monument, "The Ojibwe's Sandy Lake Journey, Sandy Lake, MN/

America's infamous reservations.. John Toland, *Adolph Hitler: The Definitive Biography.*

Madeline Island/Shaguamikon... Kohl, *Kitchi Gami*, p. 2

By 1850, there were an estimated nine thousand Ojibwe... Warren, *History of the Ojibway People*, p. 21.

At the western end of Michigan's Upper Peninsula.. population statistics, Clarke Historical Library, CMU

Foundry owner and New York Congressman Gouverneur Kemble... "An Economic History of Indian Treaties in the Great Lakes Region" by Robert H. Keller, American Indian Journal, Feb. 1978, pp. 2-20.

Thus in 1842, forty-one chieftains... 1842 Treaty of LaPointe.

Madeline Island is the largest... Warren, *History of the Ojibway People*, p.p. 53 & 69. Also, Cleland, *Rites of Conquest*, p. 94.

Here, over three days... 'Lake Superior Ojibway losses highest with treaty," by Graham Jaehnig, *Daily Mining Gazette* of Houghton, May 26, 2018.

In his opening remarks Stuart... Spatz, *Chippewa Treaty Rights,* Appendix 3C.

The proposed cession of 12 million acres... Treaty of La Pointe. The Keweenaw Bay Indian Community 7/10/20 letter to Wisconsin DNR Division of External Services.

Robert Stuart and the Oregon Trail... Dolin, *Fur, Fortune, and Empire*, pp. 198-204.

Gathered in the council room... Satz, *Chippewa Treaty Rights*, p. 38.

The silence continued as Stuart fidgeted... Satz, *Chippewa Treaty Rights*, pp. 41-42

Here though, as in many other treaty negotiations... Cleland, *Rites of Conquest*, p. 206.

In return for ceding... Article IV, 1842 Treaty of La Pointe.

Most of the $75,000 debt-repayment... 'Lake Superior Ojibway losses highest with treaty," by Graham Jaehnig, *Daily Mining Gazette* of Houghton, May 26, 2018.

These sentiments were echoed... Letter from Alfred Brunson to Sec. of War J.C. Spenser, Jan 8, 1843. "Letters Received, La Pointe Agency," Washington National Archives and Records Service.

... four cents per acre... Schenck, *William W. Warren, The Life, Letters, and Time of an Ojibwe Leader*, p. 22.

Speaking up on behalf of the Ojibwe... Letter to Commissioner of Indian Affairs T. Hartley Crawford, March 29, 1844. National Archives.

Agent Stuart may have believed... Letter to Rev. David Greene of the American board of Commissioners for Foreign Missions, Boston, 1843,

Unlike the Southern Peninsula of Michigan... Daniel H. Johnson, Census of 1850, report: 1858, p. 2.

Nonetheless, Gov. Ramsey lobbied to have the Ojibwe removed... "Sandy Lake Tragedy," *Dictionary of Wisconsin History,* Wisconsin Historical Society.

The rationale for removal... Satz, *Chippewa Treaty Rights*, pp. 53-54.

Adding pressure... Schenck, *William W. Warren – The Life, Letters, and Times*, p. 82.

Deliberating over all of this was Zachary Taylor... "Zachary Taylor, Soldier in the White House" by Holman Hamilton.

As might be imagined, Taylor's decision... "Wisconsin Death March: Explaining the Extremes in Old Northwest Indian Removal" by James A. Clifton. Wisconsin Academy of Sciences, Arts and Letters, p. 18.

The soldiers of the Ojibwe... Warren, *History of the Ojibway People*, pp. 107-108, p. 180.

For the Ojibwe of 1849... "Petition of the Head Chiefs of the Chippewa Tribe of Indians on Lake Superior," Feb. 7, 1849.

Commissioner Stuart had concerns... Robert Stuart letter to T. Harley Crawford. Wisconsin Academy of Arts, Sciences and Letters.

Ojibwe leaders launched a public relations campaign... "Dream Catchers," by Allen Asian Heart, 2007

Stymied, the conspirators came up with a ruse... Satz, *Chippewa Treaty Rights*, p. 57

Gov. Ramsey outlined his plan... "The Sandy Lake Tragedy in Three Minutes," Colin Mustfil, YouTube, April, 2012

Native peoples rarely made a move... Clifton, "Wisconsin Death March:h," Vol. 5, pp 1-40

Lewis Cass: "The Government of Indians..." "Removal of the Indians: Documents and Proceedings." North American Review, Jan. 1830.

With few provisions... "Dream Catchers" by Allen Asian Heart. Also, Dictionary of Wisconsin History.

A number of Michigan bands flatly refused to make the trip... Clifton, *Wisconsin Death March*

What transpired was a repeat... Satz, *Chippewa Treaty Rights*, p. 53

Typically, a family arriving... Danziger, *The Chippewas of Lake Superior,* p. 80.

But, as noted by the *Herald's* reporter... Ross, *La Pointe*, p. 106.

Ramsey and Watrous knew that Congress ... Wildenthal, Bryan H. (2003). Native American Sovereignty on Trial: A Handbook with Cases, Laws, and Documents, pp. 172-73.

Speaking before the Minnesota Territorial Legislature... Schenck, pp. 103-104

Switched-out flour... Schenck, p. 108.

The Ojibwe also protested... Ibid., p. 14

Months later, Methodist Episcopal missionary John Pitezel... Pitizel, *Lights and Shadows of Missionary Life,* pp. 300-301.

If Ramsey and Watrous had any remorse... Satz, *Chippewa Treaty Rights*, p.58.

CHAPTER 2 - THE WORLD IN 1850

Sources:

Mercer, Derrik, ed., *Millennium Year by Year*;

Marr, *A History of the World*

Sullivan & Eberly, *Michigan Every Day*

CHIEF GREAT BUFFALO – CHAPTER 3

Many Indians had no idea... "Indian Treaty of Saginaw," Michigan Pioneer and Historical Collections, by William L. Webber, XXVI, pp. 517-534.

The stakes were high... Armstrong, *Early Life Among the Indians*, p. 294.

Buffalo began his trip in the spring of 1852... "The Indian Chief and the President" by Nicolas Brulliard - National Parks Conservation Association - www.npca.org (Spring, 2018)

Zachary Taylor's untimely death... Soon thereafter, President Fillmore received an anonymous letter claiming that Taylor had been poisoned by a Jesuit priest. Other conspiracy theories held that Taylor had been poisoned by Catholics or pro-slavery Southerners, including by Jefferson Davis (!). Taylor's body was exhumed in 1991, with a test for arsenic conducted by the national Oak Ridge National Laboratory, which found no significant traces of the poison. It was later argued that the test was flawed; the controversy continues to this day.

The petition argued that the Ojibwe... Petition to President Millard Fillmore, June 4, 1852.

Reaching Washington... Armstrong, *Early Life Among the Indians*, pp. 296-297. Accounts differ as to where Buffalo and his party met the New York legislator who secured their meeting with President Fillmore; some claim at a restaurant, others at a hotel or a public gathering.

Blessed with broad avenues... Snow, *When Britain Burned the White House*, p. 122

..."the noblest cities..." Ibid. p. 104.

President Fillmore had acted... "Letters received," Chippewa Agency, 1852.

Once again, Chief Buffalo... Armstrong, p. 301.

Under the terms of the treaty... Madeline Island Historical Museum exhibit.

Buffalo had joined the Catholic faith... Ibid.

It wasn't a happy ending for everyone... Satz, *Chippewa Treaty Rights*, p. 69.

On the darker side... Danziger, *The Chippewas of Lake Superior.* pp. 89-90.

As for Chief Great Buffalo - Kechewaishke Pezheke - he died September 7, 1855... Non-natives are requested not to enter the Indian Cemetery on Madeline Island, so I was not able to personally confirm this, but at last writing it was claimed that Buffalo was buried under a simple grave marker, which has since become marred and obscure.

CHAPTER 4 - WILLIAM WARREN
AND THE THREE FIRES OF THE ANISHINAABEK

Biographical details... Warren, *History of the Ojibway People;*

-- Also, *William W. Warren - The Life, Letters, and Times of an Ojibwe Leader* by Theresa M. Schenck.

Mide-wi-win shamans of the Ojibwe (literally, "the good-hearted ones")... Johnston, *Ojibway Ceremonies*, p. 95. Shamans generally had specialties; some were purely medicine men, others "jugglers of spirits" who communicated with the spirit world and the dead. There were also medicine women versed in herbal healing.

Primitive peoples around the world... Horwitz, *A Voyage Long and Strange*, p. 33. Also: "Clans and Tribes," https://www.cliffdwellingsmuseum.com.

In the patrilineal society... Warren, p. 17. Not every tribe was patrilineal; the Iroquois were famously matrilineal, passing inheritance down the mother's side of the family.

...the Third Stopping Place... Benz, *Diba Jimooyung: Telling Our Story*, pp. 4-5. This alleged division may actually have been an alliance between three Algonquin peoples who in effect bumped elbows while heading west.

Yet this division... Cleland, *Rites of Conquest*, p. 93.

In 1641 Jesuit Fathers... 'The Journey of Raymbault and Jogues to the Sault, by Father Jerome Lalemant, 1641," Northern Illinois University Digital Library

CHAPTER 5 – OSHKOSH

Biographical details... "The Trial of Chief Oshkosh," Wisconsin Historical Society, wisconsinhistory. org.

-- Also, *Like a Deer Chased by Dogs: The Life of Chief Oshkosh*, Cross, Scott, Oshkosh Public Museum (2002)

CHAPTER 6 – THE FIRST PEOPLE

Ten thousand years ago... Halsey, Retrieving Michigan's Buried Past, p. 41.

No human remains... Ibid., p. 54.

... providing Native peoples with tons of nuts and acorns... Cleland, *Rites of Empire*, p. 17

At its lowest ebb... "After the Thaw - The Development of Lake Michigan" by Todd A. Thompson, Indiana Geological and Water Survey, Indiana University)

Even today, the north end of Lake Michigan... "An Overview of Beaver Island's History", beaverisland.net)

They are hunter-gatherers, moving every three-to-six days.. Starbuck, *The archeology of New Hampshire: exploring 10,000 years in the Granite State.*

Of course, it's one thing to wander the environs... Fagan, *The First North Americans*, pp. 27-27.

Thus, by the passing of the megafauna... "The Paleo-Indians: Michigan's First People" by Michael J. Shott and Henry T. Wright, in *Retrieving Michigan's Buried Past*, Halsey.

It's estimated that 15 percent of Paleoindians died at the hands of other men... "How common was violence in the distant past?" by Max Roser, ourworldindata.com

The paths funneled caribou along a 25-foot wide channel... John O'Shea, "Proceedings of the National Academy of Sciences" magazine, April 28, 2014.

Lightweight, water-proof caribou hides... Michael Engelhard, "Alaska Native Clothing," *Alaska*

Magazine, Sept. 2020.

Maize, the ancestor of modern corn... Fagan, p. 95.

Female agriculturalists also raised sunflower... Smith, *Coosa,* p. 10

... an area the size of France: Drury, *Blood and Treasure,* p. 22. This is admittedly a mind-boggling assertion and possibly open to dispute, but is included here to demonstrate that Native peoples were quite serious about expanding and maintaining their hunting and agricultural grounds.

 When the first expeditions... Dunbar-Ortiz, *An Indigenous Peoples' History of the United States,* pp. 45-47.

CHAPTER 7 - THE COPPER AGE

 Sometime around 200 B.C.... "The Ancients of Beaver Island" by M.T. Bussey, "The Journal of Beaver Island History," Vol. 3, 1988.

 The copper was extracted... NPS Natural History Handbook: Isle Royale

 Mining engineers who visited Isle Royale... The Mound-Builders and Platycnemism in Michigan," by Henry Gillman reprinted from a Report to the Smithsonian, 1873.)

 Copper melts at 2,000 degrees... "Metal Alloys Explained," by Terence Bell in "The Balance," 9/2/2018) Worth noting, gold melts at a slightly lower temperature of 1,948 degrees F. Possibly this made it slightly easier for MesoAmerican artisans to work with, albeit with a great deal of huffing and puffing to fire up their coals for smelting.

 ... copper artifacts have been found... Bussey, *The Ancients of Beaver Island.*

 But starting with the Adena culture... Hudson, *The Southeastern Indians,* p. 75. Adena era homes were built with four or five posts driven into the ground to support their roofs.

 The Adena... liked to get high, Mann, *1491,* p. 292.

 The mounds indicate the beginning of a caste system... Exhibit, Crystal River Archeological State Park, Crystal River, FL.

 Burial mounds... "The Early Woodland: Ceramics, Domesticated Plants, and Burial Mounds Foretell the Shape of the Future," by Elizabeth B. Garland and Scott G. Beld, Halsey, *Retrieving Michigan's Buried Past.*

 In Grand Rapids, Michigan, for instance... "Excavating the Hopewell Burial Mounds at Grand Rapids," by Robert Smith, *Research News,* February, 1966.

 The Hopewell people traded... Ballantine, *The Native Americans,* pp. 82-83.

 Obsidian from Montana... "Obsidian Cluff: Humanity's Tool Shed for the Last 11,550 Years" by Jim Robbins, New York Times, March 20, 2003.

 In his report to the Smithsonian... "The Mound-Builders and Platycnemism in Michigan," Gillman.

 Mound builders as slaves... Ibid.

 That said, there is evidence... NPS Natural History Handbook: Isle Royale.

 Mining for red pipestone... Exhibit, Pipestone National Monument, Minnesota.

 Tribes, chiefdoms and states... Hudson, *The Southeastern Indians,* p. 96.

 If we were to stop by a typical Mississippian-era community... Smith, *Coosa,* pp. 17-18

 ...life was good for the chief... exhibit, Moundville Archeological Park, Moundville, Alabama.

 The greatest chiefdom of all, possibly attaining the level of a state ..." Mann, *1491,* pp. 295-298.

 -- Also, Hudson, *The Southeastern Indians,* p. 96.

 -- Also: Illinois State Museum, www.museum.state.il.us/RiverWeb/landings/Ambot/prehistory/mississippian/society/

 ... 38,000 living in the region around the city... Hudson, p. 77.

 The extent of Cahokia, stockade, plaza, pyramid details: see Iseminger, *Cahokia Mounds: America's First City.* Also, Pauketat, *Cahokia: Ancient America's Great City on the Mississippi.*

 At Poverty Point... Fagan, *The First North Americans,* pp. 138-139 and 228-230.

 Also - exhibits, Poverty Point National Monument. Although farmers and developers leveled mounds at numerous sites across the eastern U.S., the archeological parks at Poverty Point, Moundville and Cahokia still capture the ethos of the past to a remarkable degree and are well worth visiting.

 Moundville details: Moundville Archeological Park, Moundville, AL.

 No one knows why Cahokia was abandoned ... Iseminger, pp. 148-155.

-- **Also,** "Plaza in ancient city of Cahokia near today's St. Louis was likely inundated year-round, " National Science Foundation, Aug. 11, 2022.

Earthquake damage to Monk's Mound; deforestation, over-hunting...... Mann, p. 298-304

Social disorder..."Ancient bones, teeth, tell story of strife at Cahokia" by Diana Yates, Life Sciences Editor, news.illinois.edu., Aug. 4, 2016.

The field of archeology was upended in 2016... "Fresh Look at Burials, Mass Graves, Tells a New Story of Cahokia" by Diana Yates, University of Illinois Urbana-Champaign News Bureau, Aug. 4, 2016.

... 20,000 shell beads, 800 arrows, mica... Iseminger, p. 73.

Mound 72... Young and Fowler, "The Excavation of Mound 72," *Cahokia: The Great Native American Metropolis*. pp. 123–153.

-- Also: "Metropolitan Life on the Mississippi" by Nathan Seppa, The Washington Post, March 12, 1997.

Possibly, those who abandoned the city resurfaced as... Iseminger, p. 156.

... a famous buffalo robe painted by the Quapaw... Pauketat, *Cahokia: Ancient America's Great City on the Mississippi*, p. 158.

"The odd thing about Cahokia is that... Pauketat, p.159.

CHAPTER 8 - THE NEW FOUND LAND

... perhaps this is how they also discovered Greenland. Apparently, the Vikings were also savvy marketers in addition to mariners and raiders. Dubbing Greenland and Vinland as such was a ploy to lure immigrants to iffy lands with pleasant names.

Knarr, description... Viking Ship Museum, Roskilde, Denmark. Located west of Copenhagen, the museum offers both ancient ships excavated from bogs as well as modern recreations.

Viking accounts... Kellogg, *The Sagas of Icelanders*.

It's possible that L'anse aux Meadows... Hensen, *The Year 1000*, p. 44.

Timbering between Greenland... Kellogg, Introduction: *The Sagas of Icelanders*.

... abandoned their farms... Winroth, *The Age of the Vikings*, p. 68.

Primogeniture... Exhibit, L'anse aux Meadows National Historic Site, Newfoundland, Canada.

Primogeniture filled the armies and navies... Toll, *Six Frigates*, p. 218.

-- Also, "Arguments in favour," https://en.wikipedia.org/wiki/Primogeniture

CHAPTER 9 THE NEWCOMERS - IN BRIEF

"By the signs they made..." Fuson, *The log of Christopher Columbus*, Oct. 14, 1492.

"On the very same day that he landed ..." Ibid.

"I hope to God..." Ibid, Dec. 26, 1492. It's hard to imagine that Christian Europe was still holding a torch for the Crusades, which had consumed hundreds of thousands of lives and staggering amounts of treasure for more than two hundred years since 1095 A.D., but the quest to retake the Holy Land and power struggles betweeen Muslims and Christians carried on in other guises, including the fall of Constantinople in 1453.

Cortes in Mexico... Siepel, *Conquistador Voices*, Vol. I pp. 143-299.

Cortes was "Patient Zero" in the deaths... exhibits, Museo Nacional de Antropología, Mexico City.

As luck would have it - smallpox... Ibid, pp. 268.

"an orgy of slaughter"... Ibid. p. 298.

Narvaez was noted for his cruelty... Josephy, *500 Nations*, pp.157-158. Florida's panhandle offers a number of sites comemmorating the Narvaez expedition, particularly around St. Marks, south of Tallahassee.

It wasn't just disease that devastated... Dunbar-Ortiz, *An Indigenous Peoples' History,* pp. 39-41

The refugees of these, and many other ruined chiefdoms... Josephy, p. 141.

In the 1560s, some of Soto's veterans... Smith, *Coosa*, pp 42-43. Several expeditions searched for fabulous Coosa, all disappointed.

Kingdom of Saguenay... Axelrod, *Savage Empire...* p. 32.

CHAPTER 10 – THE LOST CENTURY

The elites of Coosa had marched out to meet the men from Spain... Smith, *Coosa,* p. 35-37. Details on the palanquin of Coosa's chieftain and his welcoming parade are also drawn from conquistador accounts.

The 1500s have been called the "Lost Century"... Beaufort History Museum, SC.

Other than archeological discoveries... Hudson, *The Southeastern Indians,* p. 94.

De Soto's fleet landed at Tampa, Florida... Siepel, *Conquistador Voices,* Vol. II, p. 271. De Soto didn't find the Tumucuans of the Tampa area much to his liking and left shortly after landing. His army marched north to Florida's panhandle where they endured heavy attacks from the warriors of Apalachee, who had been schooled by the prior expedition of Panfilo Narvaez.

Coosa: "The country, thickly settled... Smith, *Coosa,* p. 37.

Smallpox among the Aztecs... Siepel, *Conquistador Voices,* pp. 268-269.

Spanish legend - Antillia... Downes, *The Wolf and The Willow,* p.150.

Cultural misunderstandings abounded... Hudson, p. 102.

De Soto's expedition was attacked repeatedly.. Josephy, *500 Nations,* p. 142. The survivors who fled down the Mississippi in rag-tag rafts and boats were virtually defenseless, having melted their weapons down to make the nails for their vessels. They cowered behind whatever barricades they could muster under a rain of arrows.

At a major battle in Mavila... Ibid, p.150-151.

Coosa was utterly destroyed... Smith, p. 42-43.

The refugees of these, and many other ruined chiefdoms... Treuer, *Atlas of Indian Nations,* p. 62, 86 and 162.

... the sudden disappearance of what is called the Fort Ancient culture... Peregrine, Peter Neal; Ember, Melvin, eds., *Encyclopedia of Prehistory: Volume 6: North America,* pp. 175–184. As with a number of other chiefdoms during their heyday, the Fort Shawnee used crossbeam timbers to reinforce their palisades, covering the whole with a plaster of mud and straw.

-- Also: exhibits; Fort Ancient Earthworks & Nature Preserve, Lebanon, Ohio.

CHAPTER 11 – A PLAGUE OF PATHOGENS

"Infinite thousands"... Mann, *1491.* pp. 99-100, 105-106, 108.

Native peoples who contracted measles... Tierney, *Darkness in Eldorado,* p. 66.

Dobyn's research... ibid, pp. 106-108.

"...a great plague broke out... Siepel, Conquistador Voices, Vol. 1, pp. 268-269. A small baptismal pool in Mexico City was later notorious for killing thousands of Indians infected by cholera while being bapitized by unsuspecting clergymen.

Similiarly, there were tens of thousands of the Timucuan people... exhibit, Tomoka State Park, Ormand Beach, Florida.

New England had up to 90 percent... Mann, 1491, p. 62.

"An unidentified epidemic or epidemics caused the Winnebago in Wisconsin... " Tanner, *Atlas of Great Lakes Indian History,* p. 169.

Smallpox also utterly destroyed the Mandan... Fenn, *Encounters at the Heart of the World,* p. XIV. For an interesting and informative road trip, stop by the Mandan historical villages at Knife River and Fort Lincoln the next time you're in North Dakota. Both offer recreations of Mandan earth lodges.

Norway rats... Ibid, pp. 290-292.

Tanner noted that historians have tended to attribute smallpox, Tanner, p. 160.

La Salle expected... Parkman, *France and England in North America, Vol, 1,* p. 765.

Zoonotic diseases... Zoonotic Diseases, *One Health,* Centers for Disease Control and Prevention.

... few animals... could be domesticated... Diamond, *Guns, Germs and Steel.*

Measles, for instance... Kenny, *The Plague Cycle,* p. 21

By 1000 BCE, Thebes... Harper, *Plagues Upon the Earth,* p. 164.

Among the Iroquois, the "false face" ceremony... False Face Society, *The Canadian Encyclopedia,* www.thecanadianencyclopedia.ca.

... the unintended effect of Christianizing... McNeil, *Plagues and Peoples,* p. 2.

CHAPTER 12 - MARRIED TO THE ANIMALS

Much of the material from this and the following chapter has been gleaned from the works of Charles Cleland (*Rites of Conquest*), W. Vernon Kinietz (*The Indians of the Western Great Lakes*), Johann Kohl (*Kitchi-Gami*), Frances Densmore (*Chippewa Customs*), William Warren (*History of the Ojibway People*) and Basil Johnston (*Ojibwe Ceremonies*). Readers interested in a deeper dive into Anishinaabek customs will want to check these out.

Also called totems or *dodems*... Cleland, *Rites of Conquest*, pp. 50-51.

Worse than a death sentence... Kohl, *Kitchi-Gami*, pp. 356-357. Widely traveled and a bestselling writer in the early 1800s, Johann Kohl compared the Ojibwe favorably to the Irish, who he considered the lowest of the low among all of the peoples he had encountered.

The Anishinaabek believed... Ingold, *What is an Animal?* Introduction.

Guardian spirits.... Kinietz, *The Indians of the Western Great Lakes 1615-1760,* p. 326.

The Ojibwe tended to establish their villages on islands... Cleland, pp. 23-24.

Champlain told of Hurons howling like wolves... Kinietz, p. 21. Elsewhere among many tribes, warriors dancing in the guise of wolves, buffalo and other animals were common in the hope of a propitious hunting season.

An explorer named Lahontan.. Ibid., p. 238.

CHAPTER 13 - FIRST CONTACT

Initially the Anishinaabek could not believe... Dolin, *Fur, Fortune, and Empire*, pp. 28-29.

The Little Ice Age... Fagan, *The Little Ice Age*, p. 113.

Life of Brûlé... "Etienne Brûlé, The First Franco-Ontarian," *Encyclopedia of French Cultural Heritage in North America.*

Then in an account worthy of a chivalric romance novel... Axelrod, *Savage Empire*, pp. 39-40.

Jean Nicolet... . Stiebe, *Mystery People of the Cove: A History of the Lake Superior Ouinipegou.*

-- Also, *The Journey of Jean Nicolet, 1634,* by Father Vimont, 1647.

The most common way of taking a beaver... Henry, Armour, ed., *Attack at Michilimackinac*, p. 82. Anyone who's ever chased a beaver in a canoe knows that these creatures are impossible to catch in open water; with a slap of their tail as warning to others, they disappear underwater in a twinkling.

Getting bitten by a beaver... Dolin, pp. 13-14.

A dirty and dangerous business... Axelrod, p. 19.

CHAPTER 14 - EMPIRE OF THE IROQUOIS

Dawn rose on July 4 of 1648... Parmenter, *The Edge of the Woods*, p. 72.

Fortified towns... Kinietz, *The Indians of the Western Great Lakes 1615-1760,* p. 39. Longhouses in one form or another were common to Indians across what is now the eastern United States and Canada. One can find recreations of Iroquois and Huron villages in southern Ontario and outside the city of Quebec.

Between 1300 and 1600... Parmenter, introduction.

Arising from the agricultural communities... Dunbar-Ortiz, An Indigenous People's History of the United States, p. 17.

Disparaging of the Wendats... Trigger, *Children of Aataentsic: A History of the Huron People to 1660,* p. 27.

Killer people... Chacon and Mendoza, *North American Indigenous Warfare and Ritual Violence*, p. 149.

For their part, Iroquois was not a name... Kubiak, *Great Lakes Indians*, p. 153.

The Deganawidah Epic... Mann, *1491*, pp. 380-381; Parmenter, introduction.

Snakes in his hair... "What Was Life Really Like in America Before Columbus?" 1491 Chronicle - Medieval History Documentaries.

Government of the Iroquois... Ibid, pp. 381-385. Being the most militaristic and powerful of the Iroquis tribes, it's likely that the Mohawks had more clout than other members of the Longhouse.

Their culture was rife with revenge... Chacon and Mendoza, pp. 151-152. Revenge and blood feuds lasting generations were also motivating factors for many other tribes.

... similar to the Waorani... "Warfare and Social Institutions: Some Ethnographic Examples," S. Beckerman, 50th International Congress of Americanists, Warsaw, 2000.

It wasn't all revenge and mayhem for the Iroquois, however... Josephy, *500 Nations*, p. 47.

Often, raids by the Hurons and Iroquois... Trigger, *The Huron Farmers of the North*, p.45

Over the course of decades... Ibid, p. 24.

They also had an axe to grind... Brandon, *Indians*, p. 187.

Initially more numerous than the Iroquois... Trigger, p. 52

The Hurons had a fabulous cult... Brandon, p. 152. Many other tribes had their version of the Feast of the Dead, including the Odawa. Today the tradition lives on as the "Ghost Supper."

They had plenty of bones to bury... Kinietz, p. 3.

Smallpox swept through the Five Nations... Chacon and Mendoza, p. 152.

Population of 12,000 each... Tanner, *Atlas of Great Lakes Indian History,* p. 29.

... torture as a way of humbling captives.... Chacon and Mendoza, p. 153.

... hideous tortures... Trigger, pp. 49-51.

Iroquoian warriors were not known to rape... Drimmer, *Captured by the Indians,* pp 12-13.

A typical execution... Axelrod, *Savage Empire*, p. 5

Also during this same period the Dutch... Ibid, p. 111-112

Flogging... Toll, *Six Frigates*, p. 227.

1,600 white settlers were captured on the frontier... Drimmer, p. 11

Father Brebeuf died bravely... Flaherty, *Realm of the Iroquois*, Time-Life Books, p. 91.

The surviving Hurons scattered to the winds... Ibid., p. 92.

Over the next few decades between 1,600 and 2,800 Hurons... Parmenter, p. 80.

CHAPTER 15 - THE GREAT DIASPORA

These raids were sporadic... Tanner, *Atlas of Great Lakes Indian History***,** p. 29. The five tribes of the Iroquois rarely fought as one; typically it was one or two united tribes on the warpath. During the American Revolution it was primarily the Mohawks who warred on behalf of the British, with other members of the confederation sitting it out for the most part.

"destroy them utterly"... Parmenter, *The Edge of the Woods*, p. 74.

Iroquois tomahawks... Brandon, *Indians*, pp. 152-153.

Chief Blackbird... *History of the Ottawa and Chippewa Indians of Michigan*. One can visit the home of Chief Blackbird in Harbor Springs, MI, where it carries on as a museum.

"in the main they fled to the west..." Cleland, *Rites of Conquest*, p. 94.

Migration to Madeline Island... Tanner, *Atlas of Great Lakes Indian History,* p. 31

The Great Trail ... Ayres, *The Great Trail of New England.*

... members of the "Fire Nation"... Deale, *History of the Potawatomies Before 1722,* p. 305.

In 1653, the Eries... Brandon, p. 189.

The Westos, Indian slavers... Calloway, *The Indian World of George Washington*, p. 27.

Michigan was hollowed out... Cleland, p. 93.

Green Bay drew an estimated 10,000 refugees... Conlan, *People of the Lakes*, pp. 136-137.

Almost comically, in 1655... Kellogg, *The French Regime in Wisconsin and the Northwest,* p. 98.

The Iroquois were also hammered by the French... Brandon, p 191.

By 1742 they had established Waganawkezee... Colonial Michilimackinac History, Mackinacparks. com.

All was not lost for the Iroquois... Calloway, p. 34.

In 1695, Iroquoian diplomats... Parmenter, p. 270

That same year the Iroquois also met with the British... Calloway, p. 30. Of note, after a fractious start with the English the Iroquois and their allies had negotiated a "Covenant Chain" of peace with the colonists of Virginia in 1677.

CHAPTER 16 – THE SAUK AND THE FOX

Saginaw is variously thought to mean... https://www.britannica.com

"The invaders entered the country of the doomed tribes... Teelander, *Flint Michigan History and Early North American Indians.*

When the Odawa fled the invasion... Kinietz, *The Indians of the Western Great Lakes 1615-1760*, p. 245

Cadillac then sent out a blanket invitation... Tanner, *Atlas of Great Lakes Indian History*, p. 39.

Thus a war of extermination began... McDonnell, *Masters of Empire*, pp. 83-85; Dunbar, *Michigan, A History of the Wolverine State*, pp. 82-85;

English explorer Jonathan Carver... Kubiak, *Great Lakes Indians*, p. 129.

CHAPTER 17 - THE FIRST WORLD WAR

Michigan's Odawa and Ojibwe warriors... McDonnell, *Masters of Empire,* p. 3-4

Satisfied with the destruction of the post... Treuer, David, *The Heartbeat of Wounded Knee*, p. 50.

By one account, Jumonville was on his knees and pleading... Calloway, *The Indian World of George Washington*, pp. 89-90.

.... a chieftain named Shingas... Faragher, *Daniel Boone: The Life and Legend of an American Pioneer*, p. 37

Braddock's defeat... Kopperman, *Edward Braddock*

As for Braddock.. "The Braddock Campaign," National Park Service notes, April, 2019.

Most tribes living in Ohio, Pennsylvania and Kentucky had attempted to remain cautiously neutral... Calloway, pp. 157 & 161.

Mary Draper... Thom, *Follow the River.*

An outbreak of smallpox... Journal of Occurrences in Canada by Pierre Pouchot, Oct. 1757-1758.

CHAPTER 18 - PONTIAC'S WAR

Simply put the Indians were not happy... McDonnell, *Masters of Empire* pp. 210 & 238.

His wrath extended to genocide and germ warfare... Dunbar-Ortiz, An Indigenous Peoples' History of the United States, p. 68.

Swiss mercenary... Drury, *Blood and Treasure*, p. 99.

"We are not your slaves!" Conlan, *People of the Lakes*, Time-Life Books, p. 153.

At the Mackinac Straits, some 2,500-3,000 Odawa and Ojibwe... McDonnell, p. 206-207

"Englishman, we are informed... from the memoirs of British trader Alexander Henry.

The son of a minor Odawa chieftain... Woodhead, *The Mighty Chieftains*, p. 21.

Described as being "proud, vindictive, warlike... Peckham, *Pontiac and the Indian Uprising*, p. 4.

Neolin's teachings... Cozzens, *Tecumseh and the Prophet*, p. 14.

At a council of 400 chieftains... Woodhead, p. 23.

Pontiac was nervous but optimistic... Ibid. p. 24.

... headquarters of the American Fur Company... Dunbar, *Michigan, A History of the Wolverine State*, pp. 230-231.

"Thrilled at the sight of scores of Indians... Henry & Armour, *Attack at Michilimackinac 1763*, pp 49-51.

"Shortly after my arrival at Michilimackinac... Ibid, pp. 46-47, 68-69

500 lb. bear... ibid, p. 90-91

As for Pontiac... Woodhead, p. 28

Another blow came that fall... Ibid., pp. 32-34

In its aftermath... Cleland, *Rites of Conquest*, p. 144

... estimated annually at £214,340 (totaling more than $47 million today... "Pounds Sterling to Dollars: Historical Conversion of Currency" by Eric Nye, Department of English, University of Wyoming, uwyo.edu.

British Prime Minister George Grenville... Roberts, *The Last King of America*, p. 106.

The quintessential tough guy... Cleland 137.

CHAPTER 19 - THE FLOODGATES OPEN

Hastily written... Roberts, *The Last King of America*, pp. 105-107, 124.
Among his other projects... Hogeland, *Autumn of the Black Snake*, p. 58.
Mississippi Land Company... Abbot and Twohig, *The Papers of George Washington: Colonial Series Vol 7*, p. 249.
... a deeply obscure hint... Elllis, *American Sphinx: The Character of Thomas Jefferson*.
Washington, who was bitterly disappointed.. Abbot and Twohig, p. 28
As with many other speculators... Hogeland, p. 60
Gazing from the bastion of Fort Stanwix... "Sir William Johnson and the Treaty of Fort Stanwix, 1768," by Peter Marshall, *Journal of American Studies* (1967) pp 149-179.
It was plum pudding... Merrill, *Into the American Woods: Negotiations on the Pennsylvania Frontier*.
The Iroquois claimed... Hogeland, p. 6, 46, 63. Aside from considering themselves the "elder brothers" of the tribes to the west, the Iroquois ironically felt that they had sponsored the resettlement of many Native peoples they had displaced.
Sir William Johnson died of a stroke... O'Toole, *White Savage: William Johnson and the Invention of America*, pp. 19-20, 25.

CHAPTER 20 - A LAND BEYOND THE LAW

... raiders would amplify terror... Silver, *Our Savage Neighbors*, p. 42.
These same macabre tactics... Calloway, The Indian World of George Washington, p. 145.
Europeans assumed that the "rules of war"... ibid. p. 34. Historially, the "rules of war" against killing non-combatants have been ignored by every nation in virtually every conflict to this day; U.S. firebombing of Japanese cities and the Russian missile attacks on Ukrainian civilians being but two examples.
Huddled into forts or barricaded within their own homes... ibid, pp. 69-71.
Despite their fears... Brandon, *Indians*, pp 207.
... a plague of market hunters... Drury, *Blood and Treasure*, pp, 32-33.
Yet who could resist these easy riches? Calloway, p. 42.
***Kantake* and John Findley...** Faragher, *Daniel Boone: The Life and Legend of an American Pioneer*, p. 68-70.
It was through this gap... Ibid, p. 68.
A far grimmer source... Cozzens, *Tecumseh and the Prophet*, p. 81.
... a bounty for Irish heads... Dunbar-Ortiz, *An Indigenous Peoples' History of the United States*, p. 38.
Boone's many adventures... Faragher, pp 154-166.
Murder at Bakers Tavern... Drury and Calvin, 173.
Eager to field a proxy army... Ibid., p. 232
Weary of warfare... Ibid, p. 248.
Notable victims... Foster, *The Ohio Frontier*, p. 64
Following the American Revolution... Felch, *Michigan Indians of the Historic Period*, pp. 274-297.
Treaty of Fort McIntosh... ohiohistorycentral.org.
But the six tribes of the once-mighty Iroquois inexorably lost all of their land... Exhibits Smithsonian Museum of the American Indian.

CHAPTER 21 – THE NORTHWEST TERRITORY

"An Ordinance for the Government of the Territory of the United States North West of the River Ohio," Library of Congress, Collections Division.
Taken prisoner, an elderly chief named Moluntha... Hogeland, *Autumn of the Black Snake*, p. 103.

CHAPTER 22 - BATTLE OF 1,000 SLAIN

Custer's Last Stand... Miller, *Custer's Fall: The Native American Side of the Story.*

The Miami are thought to be... Costa, *Miami-Illinois Tribe Names*, pp. 30-53.

Origins of the Shawnee... Treuer, *Atlas of Indian Nations*, p. 162.

Little Turtle and Blue Jacket... Cozzens, Tecumseh and the Prophet, p. 103.

St. Clair had busied himself pursuing the country's policy... Hogeland, pp. 107-108.

The deal was brokered by Mohawk war chief Joseph Brant... Brandon, *Indians*, pp 208-209.

"Your warriors will be slaughtered..." Dunbar-Ortiz, *An Indigenous Peoples' History of the United States*, p. 82.

Harmar retreated... Flaherty, *The Mighty Chieftains*, p. 57.

Within sight of Marietta was Fort Harmar... Hogeland, p. 109.

The entire Continental Army was disbanded... Ibid, p. 95.

St. Clair was flippant... Ibid, p. 114.

... fears of a standing army, Toll, p. 42

... the militias of early America were better known for drinking than fighting... Hogeland, p. 128.

... the battle & retreat... Hogeland and Ohio History Central, www.ohiohistorycentral.org

...the United States spent $5 million fighting Indians from 1790-'96... Taylor, *Divided Ground*, p. 238

Washington on the Indians... Fitzpatrick, *The Writings of George Washington, Vol. 27,* pp. 136, 140.

Constitution gave Congress authority over Indian affairs... Calloway, *A Victory with no Name*, p 25.

... The only beneficial result of the disaster... Hogeland, p.p. 160-164.

CHAPTER 23 — THE BLACK SNAKE COMETH

Both emissaries were murdered... Hogeland, *Autumn of the Black Snake*, p. 230.

a "lamentable proof of Indian barbarity"... Calloway, *The Indian World of George Washington*, P. 412.

... brimming with a sort of United Nations of tribes... Calloway, p. 416.

Working through British, Mahican and Iroquois intermediaries... Flaherty, *The Mighty Chieftains*, p. 58.

A peace delegation of fifteen Native men and three women from several tribes... Calloway, pp. 414-415.

...he prided calling himself Conotocarious, an Iroquois word meaning "Town Destroyer"... Calloway, p. 7.

Mad Anthony Wayne, biographical details: Stockwell, *Unlikely General: "Mad" Anthony Wayne and the Battle for America.*

... bayonet attack at Paoli's Tavern... Cornwell, *Redcoat*, pp. 1-4.

But then Wayne drew even closer, establishing Fort Defiance... fortdefiance.joshuacataloano.org.

Little Turtle was not as sanguine... https://aacimotaatiiyankwi.org/2020/01/20/biography-of-little-turtle/

One doubter was Little Turtle... Cozzens, *Tecumseh and the Prophet*, p. 114.

Battle of Fallen Timbers... Exhibits, Fallen Timbers State Memorial, Maumee, Ohio.

British treachery... Sugden, *Tecumseh, A Life*, p. 90.

Treaty of Greenville, National Archives

CHAPTER 24 - 1807 & 1812

Treaty with the Ottawa, Nov. 17, 1807, Potawatomi Web & Waysabek.com

Sealing the deal in 1807... Dunbar, *Michigan: A History of the Wolverine State,* pp. 195-196.

...the bloodless surrender of Mackinac Island... Dunigan, *A Picturesque Situation,* pp. 101-102

British Major General Isaac Brock laid siege to Detroit... Hickey, *The War of 1812 - A Forgotten Conflict,* p. 84.

Psychological warfare... Flaherty, *The Mighty Chieftains*, p. 67.

Attack at Fort Dearborn... Hickey, p. 84.

An appalled British officer... "This Week in History" by Cody K. Carlson, Deseret News, April 8,

2015.

Gen. Brock played on well-known fears... Tupper, *The Life and Correspondence of Major-General Sir Isaac Brock*, p. 246.

"My God!"... Hickey, p. 84.

Brock had crossed the river... Tupper, p. 248.

One of the ironies of the fall of Detroit... Toll, *Six Frigates*, p. 359.

Even then, fears of a standing army and navy persisted... Toll, p. 331.

CHAPTER 25 - THE SKY PANTHER, TECUMSEH

Prior to his birth, Tecumseh's family had lived among the Creeks... Cozzens, *Tecumseh and the Prophet*, p. 11.

... "when prisoners fell into his hands... Ibid, p. 70 and 78.

...The Shawnee culture encouraged men to delay sexual liaisons, Ibid, p. 71.

... Tecumseh's celebacy & romances, Ibid, pp. 70 and 78-79.

The Prophet's teachings resonated with thousands... Ibid. pp. 13-14.

Over the next few years Tecumseh traveled thousands of miles... Hickey, *The War of 1812 - A Forgotten Conflict*, p. 146-147.

Speaking to a crowd of thousands.... Flaherty, *The Mighty Chieftains*, p. 64.

The tipping point... Cleland, *Rites of Empire*, p. 166.

Alarmed by the growing influence... Flaherty, p. 66.

Sixteen-year-old captive Thomas Christian... Combs, *Col. Wm. Dudley's Defeat Opposite Fort Meigs, May 5th, 1813: Official Report from Captain Leslie Combs to General Green Clay* (1869) pp. 7-8.

Tecumseh and his alliance met their end... Hickey, p. 139.

General William Tecumseh Sherman... Dunbar-Ortiz, *An Indigenous Peoples' History of the United States*, pp. 9-10.

The British lost eight hundred merchant ships to American privateers... Toll, *Six Frigates*, p. 439.

Treaty of the Maumee Rapids - Ohio History Central

Miami Treaty of St. Mary's, Digital Collections, Indiana State Library

A Shawnee leader named Catahecassa... Shawnee Nation Case Study, National Museum of the American Indian.

CHAPTER 26 - THE TREATY OF SAGINAW

Wolves were apparently a nuisance... Cook, *Six Months Among the Indians, Wolves and Other Wild Animals*, p. 36.

"Don't go to Michigan... "Fort Saginaw" by B. Frank Emery, Michigan History magazine, July-Sept. 1946, pp 476-503

Soldiers stationed in Michigan declared it was no holiday... Bald, *Michigan in Four Centuries*, p. 144

... a bad report, Ibid... p. 157

The bounty of Michigan... https://detroithistorical.org/learn/timeline-detroit/early-american-detroit-1787-1820

Barring the way in the Saginaw River Valley were the Missauga Ojibwe... Benz, *Diba Jimooyung: Telling Our Story*, p. 7.

Ogemagigido, a 21-year-old orator... Benz... p. 41.

Among the signatories was Neome... "Indian Treaty of Saginaw," by William L. Webber, Michigan Pioneer and Historical Collections, XXVI, (1924) pp. 517-534.

... After the treaty was read... Webber.

Downing rotgut whiskey by the dipper-full... Teelander, Alan, "Flint Michigan History and Early North American Indians," Imagesofmichigan.com

Known to the Indians as "The Fox"... A Story of Grand Rapids, Z.Z. Lydens, ed., Kregel Publications (1966), p. 2.

The following year, Cass... Tanner, *Atlas of Great Lakes Indian History*, p. 159. Dunbar, *Michigan, a*

History of the Wolverine State, p. 243-245.
Treaty of Chicago... Michiganology.org.
Cass was an ethnologist... Kohl, *Kitchi-Gami*, p. XXIX.
"When they are surrounded..." Benz, pp. 42-43.
Cass and Black Hawk's War... Lewis, *The Black Hawk War of 1832*.

CHAPTER 27 - A DEMON IN THE MIDST

Even the whiskey they sold was a cheat... Fitzpatrick, *The King Strang Story,* p. 47. Also, "The Whiskey Trade," www.cbc.ca.
Indian Agent Henry Schoolcraft repeatedly blasted... "Hypocrisy on the Great Lakes Frontier: The Use of Whiskey by the Michigan Department of Indian Affairs" by Bernard C. Peters, Michigan Historical Review, Vol. 18, no. 2, (Fall 1992) pp. 1-13.
Indian villages sank into squalor... Cozzens, *Tecumseh and the Prophet*, p. 135.
Cass had requested twenty barrels of whiskey... Peters, Michigan Historical Review, pp. 5-6.
By the 1820s, those seeking a license to trade... Etten, *A Citizen's History of Grand Rapids*, p. 11.
... many Indians were simply not interested... McDonnel, *Masters of Empire*, pp. 319-320.

CHAPTER 28 - THE ROOTS OF REMOVAL

President Andrew Jackson's Message to Congress "On Indian Removal"; 12/6/1830; Presidential Messages, 1789 - 1875; Records of the U.S. Senate, Record Group 46; National Archives Building, Washington, DC.
As far back as 1776, Thomas Jefferson... "Thomas Jefferson: Architect of Indian Removal Policy" by Alysa Landry, Indian Country Today, Sept. 13, 2018.
By 1824, President James Monroe... 1824 inaugural message of James Monroe.
   Monroe and his Secretary of War... Dunbar, *Michigan: A History of the Wolverine State,* p. P. 40-41.
Jefferson's letter to Harrison... "Treaty of 1838" by Diane Hunter, April 2, 2021, Tribal Historic Preservation Officer, Miami Tribe of Oklahoma.
   Removal of 100,000 Indians/fate of the five "Civilized Tribes"... "What Happened on the Trail of Tears?" National Park Service, www.nps.gov
   ... 1835 Treaty of New Echota* that sealed their doom... "Trail of Tears," Cherokeehistorical.org.
   By the 1800s there were two major factions of the Shawnee... Shawnee Tribe v. U.S., March 30, 2004, U.S. District Court, Kansas.
   The mighty Miami, who numbered 20,000-24,000 in 1700... "Miami Nation: Forced way Once, Forced Away Again," by Jim North, Gaylord News, University of Oklahoma, July 21, 2020.

CHAPTER 29 - 1836

By 1830 the Grand River Valley... Tanner, *Atlas of Great Lakes Indian History,* p. 133.
Alarmed... Letter, Father Frederick Baraga to Most Reverend Directions, Leopoldine Foundation, June 1834. Baraga Archives, Marquette.
The epidemic... Clifton, Cornell and McClurken, *People of the Three Fires*, pp. 27-28.
Orchestrating this land grab ... Cleland, *Rites of Conquest*, pp. 225-226.
Wanting to appear as aloof as possible... McClurken, *Our People, Our Journey*, po. 31-32.
The tribes were also promised... Treaty of Washington 1836, Articles 4-11.
Treaty details, deceptions... Little Traverse Bay Band of Odawa Indians v. Gretchen Whitmer, opinion, U.S. District Judge Paul. L. Maloney, Michigan Southern Division, 8/15/2019.
It was no secret that after their five years were up... Clifton, Cornell and McClurken, pp. 24-25.
Odawa and Ojibwe leaders were utterly shocked by the amendment of the treaty... Cleland, p. 228.
Given his blood ties... Ibid, p. 227.
The Grand River Odawa were granted... Clifton, Cornell and McClurken, pp. 36-37.

On the eastern side of the state... Benz, *Diba Jimooyoung: Telling Our Stories*, pp. 43-48.

The Treaty of 1836 had barely been ratified... "Henry Schoolcraft," Encyclopedia of Detroit. Detroit Historical Society. April 21, 2022.

The eastern tribes had good reason to fear the Indians of the Great Plains... Eisler, *The Red Man's Bones*, p. 108.

Add to all this, many of the soldiers and federal caretakers on the western reservations... Brandon, *Indians*, p. 386.

Schoolcraft was a mixed-bag... "Henry Schoolcraft," Encyclopedia of Detroit.

-- Also, Mason, *Schoolcraft: Literary Voyager or Muzziegun*.

-- Also, Bremer, *Indian Agent & Wilderness Scholar: The Life of Henry Rowe Schoolcraft*. Clarke Historical Library, Central Michigan University.

Vaccination expedition: "An Insidious Expedition" by Jeremy W. Kilar, *Michigan History Magazine*, July/August, 2023.

Schoolcraft was also a religious zealot... Kohl, *Kitchi-Gami*, p. XXXI.

CHAPTER 30 - THE POTAWATOMI TRAIL OF DEATH

The sound of gunfire... Swindell, *The Story of Marshall County*, p. 19.

The village, known as Chi-Chipe-Outpe... "Recollections of the Village" by Rev. Warren Taylor, Culver-Union Public Library collection.

Heading the roundup was General John Tipton... Massie, *Potawatomi Tears & Petticoat Pioneers*, p. 27

There were also economic factors... "Michigan Fever," project.geo.msu.edu.

Menominee even made a visit to Washington, D.C... / **refusal to sign treaty...** Exhibits, Smithsonian Museum of the American Indian.

"A great many of the white settlers in the neighborhood turned out" ... McDonald, *Removal of the Pottawattomie Indians*, p. 17.

...by 1500 the Potawatomi had split... Loew, *Indian Nations of Wisconsin* p. 99

One of the "three fires" of the Anishinaabek... Kubiak, *Great Lakes Indians*, p. 115

Their name is taken from the Anishinaabemowin word, Potawatamink... Kinietz, *Indians of the Western Great Lakes 1615-1760*, p. 308.

Garden beds... Dunbar, *Michigan: A History of the Wolverine State*, p. 28.

Potawatomi population... Cleland, *Rites of Conquest*, p. 221.

Potawatomi customs... Loew, pp. 15-16 and p. 106.

In 1615, Samuel de Champlain... Kinietz, pp. 308-309.

In the 1821 Treaty of Chicago... Cleland, p. 220.

The wording of the treaty... McDonald, *Removal of the Pottawattomie Indians*.

But this was not the only exodus marked by death... Massie, p. 27.

Thirst & disease... Journal of the Emigrating Party of Pottawattomie Indians, 1838," Indiana Magazine of History, 1928, p. 317-18

Father Petit's observations... "The Trail of Death: Letters of Benjamin Marie Petit", University of Illinois Library at Urbana Champaign, p. 128, pp. 51-52.

Settler David Lucas... Massie, p. 29.

Accompanying them... Journal of Lucius Buell Holcomb, Kingman Museum, Battle Creek, MI.

Many other members of the Potawatomi filtered back into Michigan in the succeeding years... Tanner, *Atlas of Great Lakes Indian History*, p. 166.

CHAPTER 31 - THE KING OF BEAVER ISLAND

Chief Peaine... Anthony, *The Elders Speak*.

The McKinleys... "Chief Peaine and the Mormons" by Sarah McKinley and Helen Collar, The Journal of Beaver Island History, Vol. 3, pp. 19-28.

Following the French *voyageurs*... Collar, Helen, "The Pre-Mormon Settlement on Beaver Island, 1837-1852. The Journal of Beaver Island History, Vol. 2, p. 9.

In an 1840 census... Garrad, Charles, "Some Notes on the Ojibwa of the Beaver Islands." The Journal of Beaver Island History, Vol. 3, p. 9

Island land was put up for sale... Collar, Helen, "Irish Migration to Beaver Island." The Journal of Beaver Island History, Vol. 1, p. 27.

A steamship required 500 cords... Fitzpatrick, *The King Strang Story*, p. 55.

Strang's arrival on Beaver Island... Ibid, pp. 51-52.

Young Joseph Smith... Ibid, p. xxii.

Landing at Whiskey Point... Strang, *Ancient and Modern Michilimackinac,* p. 24

In 1851 President Millard Fillmore... "The Kingdom of St. James and 19th Century Utopianism" by Robert P. Weeks, The Journal of Beaver Island History, Vol. 1, pp. 23-24.

The Battle of Pine River... Fitzpatrick, pp. 105-107.

Strang like to think of himself... Strang, pp. 17-18.

Strang had appointed no successor... Weeks, pp. 22-23.

As for Chief Peaine... McKinley and Collar, "Chief Peaine and the Mormons," pp. 29-30.

CHAPTER 32 — THE LUCK OF THE IRISH

In a disparaging take on Darwin... Dunbar-Ortiz, *An Indigenous Peoples' History of the United States*, p. 39.

...**"a race of utter savages"...** Kelly, *The Graves Are Walking*, p. 16

"(Charley) decreed that whomever was not a full tenant ... "Irish Eviction and Emigration" plaque, St. James, Beaver Island, MI.

An Irish landlord exercised much the same power over his "cottar" peasants as did a slaveholder in the American South... Kelly, p. 20

But it was also true that a landlord who pushed too far... Ibid, p. 13.

Spaniards brought the first potatoes home from South America... Fagan, *The Little Ice Age*, pp. 111-112.

... stolen by fairies... a short story by Sheridan Le Fanu, "The Child that Went with the Fairies," illustrates this peasant belief.

The British established the Ulster Plantation... Dunbar-Ortiz, *An Indigenous Peoples' History of the United States*, pp. 52-53.

-- Also, the chapters on Cromwell and the Cromwellian Settlement in MacManus, *The Story of the Irish Race*.

In 1641 the Irish rebelled, killing thousands of English colonists... MacManus, pp. 408-411.

Dublin served as the largest slave market... Lacy and Danziger, *The Year 1000*, p. 46.

Irish Slaves... Heaton, Colin, "The Truth About the Irish," Forgotten History Channel, YouTube.

According to an 1841 account... "Sketches in Erris and Tyrawly" by Otway Canon Caesar (1841)

... transporting English and Irish convicts... "Convict Servants in the American Colonies," Brian Naylor, National Public Radio, July 24, 2004.

The 19 crimes... https://19crimes.com/pages/the-19-crimes

According to an 1845 account.... "Friends in a Time of Famine" by Lorna Siggins, The Irish Times, Oct. 3, 2013.

Many chose the poorhouse... "The Way it Was: The Arranmore Connection," Beaver Island Beacon, 2003

Charley sent his exiled tenants... 2003 letter from Anne Walsh, re: Conyngham Estate Records, National Library in Dublin.

Living among a large group of Irish immigrants in Toronto... Collar, Helen, "Irish Migration to Beaver Island," The Journal of Beaver Island History, Vol. 1 (1976), pp. 39-40.

The people of Arranmore were not alone in their forced eviction... Kelly, pp. 80-81.

Starvation and disease killed 1.1 million... Ibid., p. 2.

These included a massive wave of Germans... Silver, *Our Savage Neighbors*, pp. 5-6

CHAPTER 33 — 1855

One summer day in late May of 1858... McClurken, *Our People, Our Journey,* p. 56.

For 20 years many of the Odawa... Etten, *A Citizen's History of Grand Rapids*, p. 67
"Whiteness" itself... Silver, *Our Savage Neighbors*, pp. 303-304.
...some of the Odawa began purchasing their own land... McClurken, pp. 39-39.
"The new Indian policy... Cleland, *Rites of Conquest*, p. 234.
Manypenny set aside townships... Treaty of Detroit, 1855.
There were actually two Treaties of 1855... Felch, *Michigan Indians of the Historic Period*, pp. 54-57.
Five townships were set aside... Treaty of Detroit, 1855.
There was a similar mess in Isabella County... Benz, *Diba Jimooyung: Telling Our Story*, p. 60.
At Keweenaw Bay... Cleland, p. 240
"In 1855, both the Ottawa and United States delegates left the negotiations hopeful... McClurken, p. 51.

CHAPTER 34 - THE STRANGE TALE OF CHIEF WABASIS

The Wabasis story... park handout, Wabasis Lake County Park, Kent County, MI.
There's a darker version... Grand Rapids Press, 10/3/11, "Wabasis Lake Park holds story of murder, treachery, treasure."
-- Also, "Wabasis Gold," https://www.treasurenet.com/threads/wabasis-gold.97819/
Born around 1807 and known as White Swan... County Park handout.
But in an oral history video... "Legend of Chief Wabasis and the Hidden Gold," Plainfield Township Historical Advisory Committee Oral Histories, www.plainfieldmi.org.

CHAPTER 35 - THE THEFT OF NATIVE LANDS

By 1871 the United States had negotiated nearly four hundred treaties ... From Michiganology - Michigan History Center staff.
By 1880 the United States had paid... Dunbar, *Michigan - A History of the Wolverine State*, p. 149.
By 1859 the Grand River bands of the Odawa... McClurken, *Our People, Our Journey*, p. 57.
Indians seeking land... Ibid, p. 82.
Nor could Indian landowners... "The Anishinaabeg and Federal Indian Policy" by Bradley J. Gills, Michigan Historical Review, p. 61. Turtletalkfiles.wordpress.com.
This was at a time... when white farmers throughout Michigan headed north for the winter lumbering season... "When Men Were Men and Michigan Had Trees," by Robert Downes, Detroit Free Press Magazine, 9/23/90.
Thus they often lived in villages... McClurken, pp. 87-88.
... 64 cases of fraud per month... "Justice Denied: Indian Land Frauds in Michigan, 1855-1900," by Bruce A. Rubenstein, The Old Northwest (1976), p. 133
Widows were easy targets... Ibid, p. 134.
Indians who were starving... Ibid, p. 13.
An Emmet County official... Cleland, *Rites of Conquest*, p. 254.
Fraud cases were almost impossible to contest... Rubenstein, p. 135.
... corrupt Indian agents... Gills, "The Anishinaabeg and Federal Indian Policy."
One of the biggest land frauds... Rubenstein, pp. 135-136
Conservation measures had ramifications... Cleland... p. 268
Thirty years after signing the Treaty of 1855... Priest, *Uncle Sam's Stepchildren*, p. 178
Tens of thousands of German, East European and Russian immigrants... Frazier, *The Great Plains*, pp. 70-71.
As in Michigan the Indians of the West were set up to fail... "The Dawes Act," National Park Service, https://www.nps.gov/articles/000/dawes-act.htm
"Of the approximately 150 million acres owned by the Indians in 1880... Brandon, *Indians*, p. 388.
Over the course of many treaties... roughly 25,000 square miles, Tanner, *Atlas of Great Lakes Indian History*, p. 162.
The Indian New Deal... https://coloradoencyclopedia.org/article/indian-reorganization-act-indian-new-deal .

CHAPTER 36 - THE BURNOUT

The women, children and elderly of Indianville had just finished breakfast..."Burnout" by Patrick Sullivan, Northern Express Weekly, March 23, 2015.

-- "The Burt Lake Burn-out" by Eric Hemenway, Michigan History Magazine, January/February 2016.

... the Burt Lake Indians remained a community, a united group... "Legality: Michigan's Burt Lake Indians and the Burning of Indianville," Matthew J. Friday, Michigan Historical Review, Spring 2007, pp. 87-97

McGinn informed the Anishinaabek households... Ibid.

Three years after... "Indian/Colonial Point's Shameful Past" by Mike Norton, Traverse City Record-Eagle, Aug. 20, 2000.

Part of the problem that after more than 20 years of dithering by the BIA... Ibid.

-- Also, Congress' Findings on 'The Burt Lake Band of Ottawa and Chippewa Indians Reaffirmation Act', March 19, 2007

CHAPTER 37 - UPRISING

The Grand Traverse bands had been robbed many years in the past.... Cleland, *Rites of Conquest,* pp. 255-256.

Also, *Stolen: Grand Traverse Band Seeks its Day in Court for Theft of Reservation Lands* by Patti Brandt Burgess and Sierra Clark, Traverse City Record-Eagle, 12/21/220.

The perpetrators included two members of the band who swindled or cajoled... *Stolen*, Burgess & Clark.

Poverty had stalked... Benz, *Diba Jimooyung: A History of the Saginaw Ojibwe Aniishinabek*, pp. 103-105, 124.

In Michigan's Leelanau County, for instance... Brant Burgess and Sierra Clark, *Stolen.*

Further north, in the mid-1990s the Little Traverse Bay Bands... Regina Gasco-Bentley, "Tribal Chairperson's Statement Regarding Reservation Litigation," March 8, 2023.

... casino reaped $39 billion... "Indian Gaming Revenues" by Acee Agoyo, Indianz.com.

In 1972... "The Legacy of Bryan V. Itasca County" by Kevin K. Washburn, Minnesota Law Review

Becker was a bear of a man... Washburn, p. 938

Bryan V. Istasca County... Anishinabe Legal Services, "ALS Celebrates 50th Anniversary!" alslegal. org

Helen Johnson's role... "June 14 Marks Anniversary of Bryan v. Istasca Decision," Leech Lake News, June 14, 2018.

BIBLIOGRAPHY

Abbot, W.W., and Dorothy Twohig, ed., *The Papers of George Washington:*
Colonial Series Vol 7, University of Virginia Press (1990)
Anthony, George A., *The Elders Speak: Reflections on Native American Life Centering on Beaver Island, Michigan, in the Nineteenth and Twentieth Centuries,* Beaver Island
Historical Society (2009)
Armstrong, Benjamin, *Early Life Among the Indians* (1892)
Axelrod, Alan, *A Savage Empire*, St. Martin's Press (2011)
Ayres, Harral, *The Great Trail of New England*, Boston, MA: Meader
Publishing Co. (1940)
Bald, Clever, *Michigan in Four Centuries*, Harper (1954)
Ballantine, Betty and Ian, ed., *The Native Americans*,
Turner Publishing, Inc. (1993)
Beckerman, S., *Warfare and Social Institutions: Some Ethnographic Examples*,
50th International Congress of Americanists, Warsaw (2000)
Benz, Charmaine M., ed., *Diba Jimooyung: Telling Our Story*,

Saginaw-Chippewa Indian Tribe of Michigan (2005)

Blaisdell, Bob, ed., *Great Speeches by Native Americans*, Dover Publications (2000)

Brandon, William, *Indians*, American Heritage Press (1985)

Bremer, Richard, *Indian Agent & Wilderness Scholar: The Life of Henry Rowe Schoolcraft*, Clarke Historical Library, Central Michigan U., (1987)

Bussey, M.T., *The Journal of Beaver Island History*, Vol. 3 (1988)

Calloway, Colin G. *The Indian World of George Washington*, Oxford University Press (2018)

Campbell, T.J., *Pioneer Priests of North America, 1642-1710*, Fordham University Press (1910)

Catton, Bruce, *Michigan, A History*, W.W. Norton & Co. (1984)

Chacon, Richard, and Ruben Mendoza, ed., *North American Indigenous Warfare and Ritual Violence*, University of Arizona Press (2007)

Cleland, Charles E., *Rites of Conquest*, University of Michigan Press (1992)

Clifton, James, George Cornell, James McClurken, *People of the Three Fires*, The Michigan Indian Press, (1986)

---- *Wisconsin Death March: Explaining the Extremes in Old Northwest Indian Removal*, Wisconsin Academy of Sciences, Arts and Leters (1987)

Colloway, Colin G., *Victory With No Name*, Oxford University Press (2016)

Combs, Leslie, *Col. Wm. Dudley's Defeat Opposite Fort Meigs, May 5th, 1813: Official Report from Captain Leslie Combs to General Green Clay* (1869)

Conlan, Roberta, ed., *People of the Lakes*, Time-Life Books (1994)

Cook, Darius Burgess, *Six Months Among the Indians, Wolves and Other Wild Animals* (1889)

Cornwell, Bernard, *Redcoat*, Harper (2003)

Costa, David J., *Miami-Illinois Tribe Names*, University of Manitoba (2000)

Cozzens, Peter, *Tecumseh and the Prophet*, Knoff (2020)

Danziger, Edmund Jefferson, Jr., *The Chippewas of Lake Superior*, Jr. University of Oklahoma Press (1990)

Deale, Valentine, *History of the Potawatomies Before 1722*, Ethnohistory, 1958)

Densmore, Frances, *Chippewa Customs*, Minnesota Historical Society Press (1979)

Detroit Historical Society, *Encyclopedia of Detroit* (2023)

Dicky, J.D., *Empire of Mud*, Lyons Press (2014)

Dolin, Eric Jay, *Fur, Fortune, and Empire*, Norton (2010)

Downes, Robert, *The Wolf and The Willow,* The Wandering Press (2021)

Drimmer, Frederick, *Captured by the Indians*, Dover (1961)

Drury, Bob, and Tom Clavin, *Blood and Treasure*, St. Martin's Griffin (2021)

Dunbar-Ortiz, Roxanne, *An Indigenous Peoples' History of the United States*, Beacon Press, (2014)

Dunbar, Willis F., *Michigan A History of the Wolverine State*, William B. Eerdsmans Publishing Co. (1965)

Dunnigan, Brian Leigh, *A Picturesque Situation*, Wayne State University Press (2008)

Eckert, Allan W., *That Dark and Bloody Ground*, Bantam Books (1995)

Eisler, Benita, *The Red Man's Bones*, W.W. Norton & Co. (2013)

Etten, William, ed., *A Citizen's History of Grand Rapids,* A.P. Johnson Company (1926)

Fagan, Brian, *The First North Americans*, Beacon Press (2012)

----*The Little Ice Age*, Basic Books (2000)

Faragher, John Mack, *Daniel Boone: The Life and Legend of an American Pioneer*, Holt (1992)

Felch, Alpheus, *Michigan Indians of the Historic Period*, Michigan Pioneer and Historical Collections (1894)

Fenn, Elizabeth, A., *Encounters at the Heart of the World*, Hill & Wang (2014)

Fitzpatrick, Doyle, C., *The King Strang Story*, National Heritage (1970)

Fitzpatrick, John C., ed., *The Writings of George Washington*, Vol. 27., Government Printing Office (1938)

Flaherty, Thomas H., ed., *Realm of the Iroquois*, Time- Life Books (1993)

Fuller, George, N., *Historic Michigan, Vol. 1*, ed., National Historical Ass. Inc. (1924)
Fuson, Robert H., *The Log of Christopher Columbus*, Intl. Marine Pub. Co. (1991)
Gillman, Henry, *The Mound Builders and Platycnemism in Michigan*,
      Report to the Smithsonian, 1873
Glazier, Jack, and Arthur Helweg, *Ethnicity in Michigan*, Michigan State
      University Press (2001)
Goetzmann, William and Glyndwr Williams, *The Atlas of North American Exploration*,
University of Oklahoma Press (1992)
Halsey, John R., *ed., Retrieving Michigan's Buried Past*, Cranbrook Institute (1999)
Hansen, Valerie, *The Year 1000*, Scribner (2020)
Harper, Kyle, Plagues Upon the Earth, Princeton University Press (2021)
Henry, Alexander, David Armour, ed., *Attack at Michilimackinac 1763*,
      Mackinac Island State Park Commission (1971)
Hickey, Donald R., *The War of 1812 A Forgotten Conflict*, University of
      Illinois Press (1989)
Hogeland, William, *Autumn of the Black Snake*, Farrar, Straus and Giroux (2017)
Horwitz, Tony, *A Voyage Long and Strange*, Henry Holt & Co. (2008)
Hudson, Charles, *The Southeastern Indians*, University of Tennessee
      Press (1976)
Ingold, Tim, *What is an Animal?* Psychology Press (1994)
Iseminger, William, *Cahokia Mounds: America's First City*. The History Press (2010)
Johnson, Donald, S., *La Salle*, Cooper Square Press (2002)
Johnston, Basil, *Ojibway Ceremonies*, University of Nebraska Press (1982)
Josephy, Alvin M.Jr., *500 Nations*, Alfred A. Knopf (1984)
Kellogg, Louise P., *The French Regime in Wisconsin and the Northwest*, State
      Historical Society of Wisconsin (1925)
Kenny, Charles, The Plague Cycle, Scribner (2021)
Kinietz, W. Vernon, ed., *The Indians of the Western Great Lakes 1615-1760*, Ann Arbor Paperbacks
(1965)
Kohl, Johann Georg, *Kitchi Gami*, Minnesota Society Press (1985)
Kopperman, Paul, *Edward Braddock*, Oxford University Press (2004)
Lewis, James, *The Black Hawk War of 1832*, Northern Illinois University Press (2009)
Loew, Patty, *Indian Nations of Wisconsin*, Wisconsin Historical
      Society Press (2001)
Lydens, ZZ, ed., *A Story of Grand Rapids*, Kregel Publications (1966)
MacManus, Seumas, *The Story of the Irish Race*, Deven-Adair Co. (1944)
Mann, Charles C., *1491*, Vintage Press (2006)
----- *1493*, Alfred Knopf (2011)
Marr, Andrew, *A History of the World*, Macmillan (2012)
Mason, Philip, ed., *Schoolcraft: Literary Voyager or Muzziegun*, East Lansing:
      Michigan State University (1962)
Massie, Larry B., *Potawatomi Tears & Petticoat Pioneers*, The Priscilla Press (1992)
Mason, Philip, ed., *Schoolcraft: Literary Voyager or Muzziegun*, Michigan State University Press,
(1962)
McCullough, David, *1776,* Simon and Schuster (2006)
McDonald, Daniel, *Removal of the Pottawattomie Indians* (1898)
McDonnell, Michael A., *Masters of Empire*, Hill & Wang (2015)
McClurken, James M., *Our People, Our Journey*, Michigan State University
Press (2009)
McMurtry, Larry, *Custer*, Simon and Schuster (2012)
McNeil, William H. Plagues and People, Doubleday (1976)
Mercer, Derrik, ed., *Millennium Year by Year*, Dorling Kindersley (200)
Merrill, James, H., *Into the American Woods: Negotiations on the Pennsylvania Frontier*,
      W.W. Norton & Co. (2000).
Molzahn, Arlene, *La Salle: Explorer of the Mississippi*, Enslow Publishers (2004)
O'Toole, Fintan, *White Savage: William Johnson and the Invention of America*. Farrar, Straus and Gir-

oux (2005)

Parkman, *France and England in North America, Vol, 1, New York Library of America* (1865)

Parmenter, Jon, *The Edge of the Woods*, Michigan State University Press (2010)

Pauketat, Timothy R. *Cahokia: Ancient America's Great City on the Mississippi*, Viking (2009)

Peckham, Howard, *Pontiac and the Indian Uprising*, University of Princeton Press (1948)

Pitezel, Lights and Shadows of Missionary Life (1859)

Pouchot, Pierre, *Journal of Occurrences in Canada*, Oct. 1757-1758.

Roberts, Andrew, *The Last King of America*, Viking (2021)

Ross, Hamilton Nelson, *La Pointe*, Wisconsin Historical Press (1960)

Satz, Ronald, Chippewa Treaty Rights, Wisconsin Academy of Science (1996)

Schenck, Theresa M. *William W. Warren - The Life, Letters, and Times,* University of Nebraska Press (2007)

Siepel, Kevin, H., *Conquistador Voices*, Spruce Tree Press (2015)

Silver, Peter, *Our Savage Neighbors*, Norton, (2008)

Smith, Marvin T., *Coosa*, University Press of Florida (2000)

----- *Archeology of Aboriginal Cultural Change in the Interior Southeast: Depopulation During the Early Historic Period*, University Press of Florida (1987)

Snow, Peter, *When Britain Burned the White House*, Thorndike Press (2015)

Steibe, Ronald, *Mystery People of the Cove: A History of the Lake Superior Ouinipegou*, Lake Superior Press (1999).

Stockwell, Mary, *Unlikely General: "Mad" Anthony Wayne and the Battle for America*, Yale University Press (2018)

Sugden, John, *Tecumseh, A Life*, Holt (1999)

Sullivan, Patrick and Eberly, Carole, *Michigan Every Day*, Eberly Press (2009)

Swindell, Minnie Harris, *The Story of Marshall County* (1923)

Tanner, Helen, *Atlas of Great Lakes Indian History*, University of Oklahoma Press (1986)

Taylor, Alan, *Divided Ground*, Vintage (2007)

Taylor, Rev. Warren, *Recollections of the Village*, Culver-Union Public Library collection

Teelander , Alan, *Flint Michigan History and Early North American Indians* (2009)

Thom, James Alexander, *Follow the River*, Ballantine Books (1986)

Tierney, Patrick, *Darkness in Eldorado*,W.W. Norton & Co. (2002)

Toll, Ian W., *Six Frigates*, W.W. Norton & Co. (2006)

Treuer, Anton, *Atlas of Indian Nations*, National Geographic (2013)

Treuer, David, *The Heartbeat of Wounded Knee*, Riverhead Books (2019)

Trigger, Bruce G., *Children of Aataentsic: A History of the Huron People to 1660*, McGill-Queen's University Press (1976)

--- *The Huron Farmers of the North*, Holt, Rinehart & Winston (1969)

Various, *The Sagas of the Icelanders*, Penguin Books (2000)

Warren, William, *History of the Ojibway People*, Minnesota Historical Society Press (1885)

Webber, William, L., *Michigan Pioneer and Historical Collections* (1895)

Winroth, Anders, *The Age of the Vikings*, Princeton University Press (2014)

Woodhead, Henry, ed., *The Mighty Chieftains*, TimeLife Books (1993)

Young, Biloine Whiting and Fowler, Melvin. J, *Cahokia: The Great Native American Metropolis, Uni-*

INDEX

ABOUT THE AUTHOR

Robert Downes is the author of eight books, including two novels of the prehistoric Anishinaabek: *The Wolf and The Willow* and *Windigo Moon*. He and his wife Jeannette live in Traverse City, Michigan.

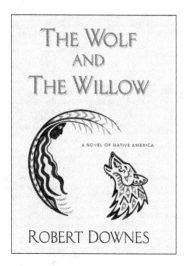 

Enjoy these two historical novels of the Anishinaabek,
with a story that begins in 1528 and carries on to 1619
- details at www.robertdownes.com -